EU SOFT LAW IN THE MEMBER STATES

This volume analyses, for the first time in European studies, the impact that non-legally binding material (otherwise known as soft law) has on national courts and administration.

The study is founded on empirical work undertaken by the European Network of Soft Law Research (SoLaR), across 10 EU Member States, on competition policy, financial regulation, environmental protection and social policy. The book demonstrates that soft law is taken into consideration at the national level and it clarifies the extent to which soft law can have legal and practical effects for individuals and national authorities.

The national case studies highlight the points of convergence or divergence in the way in which judges and administrators approach soft law, while reflecting on the reasons for and consequences of various national practices. A series of horizontal studies connect this research to the rich literature on new modes of governance, by revisiting traditional theories on soft law, and by reflecting on the potential of such instruments to undermine or to foster rule of law values.

Volume 8 in the series EU Law in the Member States

EU Law in the Member States

Located at the cross-section between EU law, comparative law and socio-legal studies, *EU Law in the Member States* explores the interaction of EU law and national legal systems by analysing comparative evidence of the impact landmark EU measures – from CJEU decisions and secondary legislation to soft-law – have had across different Member States. The nature and operation of EU law has traditionally been analysed in a highly 'centralised' way, through the lenses of Brussels and Luxembourg, and in terms of the Treaty and its interpretation by the Court of Justice. Beneath this orthodoxy, however, lies the complex world of the genuine life of EU law in the Member States. Judicial and administrative practices across the Union's 28 Member States considerably qualify and sometimes even challenge the long-standing assumption that doctrines such as the direct effect and supremacy of EU law ensure a uniform and effective application of its provisions.

Each volume brings together leading academics, national experts and practitioners in order to draw conclusions both for EU law generally and the specific area in question on the basis of Member State reports and broader horizontal papers, and will be of interest to generalist EU lawyers and specialists in each field across the Member States. Academic audiences will benefit from the tight integration of national case studies and doctrinal analysis, whilst practitioners and policy makers will find systematically presented comparative evidence and commentary.

Volume 1: *Viking, Laval* and Beyond
Edited by Mark Freedland and Jeremias Prassl

Volume 2: Central European Judges under the European Influence: The Transformative Power of the EU Revisited
Edited by Michal Bobek

Volume 3: Air Passenger Rights, Ten Years On
Edited by Jeremias Prassl and Michal Bobek

Volume 4: The Eurosceptic Challenge
Edited by Clara Rauchegger and Anna Wallerman

Volume 5: The Impact of European Institutions on the Rule of Law and Democracy: Slovenia and Beyond
Matej Avbelj and Jernej Letnar Cernic

Volume 6: The Effectiveness of the Köbler Liability in National Courts
Zsófia Varga

Volume 7: The EU Charter on Fundamental Rights in the Member States
Edited by Michal Bobek and Jeremias Prassl

EU Soft Law in the Member States

Theoretical Findings and Empirical Evidence

Edited by
Mariolina Eliantonio
Emilia Korkea-aho
and
Oana Ştefan

•HART•
OXFORD • LONDON • NEW YORK • NEW DELHI • SYDNEY

HART PUBLISHING

Bloomsbury Publishing Plc

Kemp House, Chawley Park, Cumnor Hill, Oxford, OX2 9PH, UK

1385 Broadway, New York, NY 10018, USA

29 Earlsfort Terrace, Dublin 2, Ireland

HART PUBLISHING, the Hart/Stag logo, BLOOMSBURY and the Diana logo are trademarks of Bloomsbury Publishing Plc

First published in Great Britain 2021

A catalogue record for this book is available from the British Library.

Library of Congress Cataloging-in-Publication data

Names: Eliantonio, Mariolina, 1978- editor. | Korkea-aho, Emilia, editor. | Ştefan, Oana, editor.

Title: EU soft law in the member states : theoretical findings and empirical evidence / edited by Mariolina Eliantonio, Emilia Korkea-aho and Oana Ştefan.

Description: Oxford, UK ; New York, NY : Hart Publishing, an imprint of Bloomsbury Publishing, 2021. | Series: EU law in the member states ; volume 8 | Includes bibliographical references and index.

Identifiers: LCCN 2020051779 (print) | LCCN 2020051780 (ebook) | ISBN 9781509932030 (hardback) | ISBN 9781509946655 (paperback) | ISBN 9781509932054 (pdf) | ISBN 9781509932047 (Epub)

Subjects: LCSH: Soft law—European Union countries.

Classification: LCC KJE964 .E975 2021 (print) | LCC KJE964 (ebook) | DDC 341.7094—dc23

LC record available at https://lccn.loc.gov/2020051779

LC ebook record available at https://lccn.loc.gov/2020051780

ISBN: HB: 978-1-50993-203-0
ePDF: 978-1-50993-205-4
ePub: 978-1-50993-204-7

Typeset by Compuscript Ltd, Shannon

To find out more about our authors and books visit www.hartpublishing.co.uk. Here you will find extracts, author information, details of forthcoming events and the option to sign up for our newsletters.

Acknowledgements

THIS BOOK IS the result of three years of friendship and work. We are grateful to the European Commission for funding our European Network for Soft Law Research – SoLaR. Working on this project has helped us create ever stronger links within the EU soft law community and expand it to include new voices. To all our interviewees and collaborators, policymakers, administrators, judges, researchers, and students: this book was written for you and with you. It has been a privilege to learn from your expertise on soft law.

Mariolina Eliantonio would like to thank Emilia and Oana for the academic inspiration they have been in these three years, for their readiness to help and advance the discussion on EU soft law with such tireless enthusiasm, and for all the non-academic chats in these years. She also is grateful to Paul and Alma for being such great companions during the editing months of this volume.

Emilia Korkea-aho thanks her two SoLaR co-mothers for being, among many other things, such good friends and colleagues. She is grateful to Panu for doing a brilliant job as the SoLaR research assistant on top of his own professorial tasks.

Oana Ştefan is thankful to her co-editors for their patience and friendship as she tried to multitask between editorial duties and a new-born. Constantin, Théodore, and Antoine have to be commended for wonderfully cohabitating with SoLaR work during the first London lockdown.

24 November 2020
Brussels-Helsinki-London

Contents

List of Contributors

Jacopo Alberti is Associate Professor of EU Law at the University of Ferrara.

Luis Arroyo Jiménez is Professor of Administrative Law and holder of the Jean Monnet Chair on European Administrative Law at the University of Castilla-La Mancha.

Matej Avbelj is Professor of European Law at the New University in Ljubljana.

Barbara Beijen is Assistant Professor of Administrative Law at Radboud University, Nijmegen.

Mary Dobbs is a Lecturer in the Department of Law in Maynooth University, Ireland.

Mariolina Eliantonio is Professor of European and Comparative Administrative Law and Procedure at Maastricht University.

Giulia Gentile is a Lecturer in Comparative and European Law at Maastricht University.

Miriam Hartlapp is Professor for Comparative Politics: Germany and France, at the Freie Universität Berlin.

Katri Havu is Assistant Professor of Private Law at the Faculty of Law, University of Helsinki.

Andreas Hofmann is a researcher at the Otto Suhr Institute of Political Science, Freie Universität Berlin.

Niilo Jääskinen is a judge at the Court of Justice of the European Union.

Anastasia Karatzia is a Lecturer in Law at the School of Law, University of Essex.

Matthias Knauff is Professor of Public Law at the University of Jena (Germany) and judge at the Higher Regional Court of Thuringia.

Emilia Korkea-aho is Associate Professor of European Law and Legislative Studies at the University of Eastern Finland Law School, and Academy of Finland Research Fellow.

Petra Lea Láncos is Associate Professor at Pázmány Péter Catholic University, Faculty of Law in Budapest.

Päivi Leino-Sandberg is Professor of Transnational European Law at the University of Helsinki.

Imelda Maher is Dean of Law and Full Professor of European Law at University College Dublin.

Ulrika Mörth is Professor of Political Science at Stockholm University.

José María Rodríguez de Santiago is Professor of Administrative Law at the Universidad Autónoma de Madrid.

Nathalie Rubio is Professor of European Law at Aix-Marseille University.

Francis Snyder is C.V. Starr Professor of Law, EU Jean Monnet Professor *ad personam*, and Director, Centre for Research on Transnational Law at Peking University School of Transnational Law, Peking University Shenzhen Graduate School, Emeritus Professor Aix-Marseille University, and Visiting Professor at the College of Europe, Bruges.

Oana Ştefan is Reader in Law at The Dickson Poon School of Law, King's College London.

Liisa Tarkkila is a PhD student at the University of Helsinki, and a Legal Counsel in a global stock-listed company.

Katarina Vatovec is Assistant Professor of EU Law at the European Faculty of Law and at the Faculty of Government and European Studies, New University in Ljubljana.

Napoleon Xanthoulis is a Senior Lecturer in Law at the University of Portsmouth.

1

Introduction

MARIOLINA ELIANTONIO, EMILIA KORKEA-AHO AND OANA ŞTEFAN

FOUR YEARS AGO, our opening sentence for a Jean Monnet Network grant application read as follows: 'Boosted by the 2001 Commission White Paper on Governance and the 2010 Lisbon Strategy, "soft law" is present in nearly every EU policy.' Little did we know that, as our winning project, the European Network of Soft Law Research (SoLaR),[1] was entering in the final drafting stages in the early spring of 2020, the EU were to resort again to soft law in order to tackle an unprecedented health crisis. In the span of four months, a record-breaking 238 soft law instruments[2] set exceptional rules to deal with or counteract the effects of the COVID-19 pandemic in most of the areas of EU law, from antitrust and State aid to the digital single market, from immigration to transport, from economic and monetary affairs to human rights.

Usually defined as rules of conduct having no legally binding force but producing legal and practical effects,[3] EU soft law is enshrined in Article 288(5) of the Treaty on the Functioning of the European Union (TFEU). This provision makes direct reference only to recommendations and opinions, whereas the real list of instruments issued in practice is copious: frameworks, communications, guidelines, letters, codes, notices etc. Such a vast variety of instruments, as well as their sheer volume, might be questionable from the point of view of transparency. Take, for instance, the regulation of contact tracing apps, which have become, overnight, crucial for initiatives to contain the virus in the post lockdown EU. Mid-April 2020, no fewer than four soft law instruments were issued

[1] The project on which this book is based was co-financed by the European Commission through grant 575097-EPP-1-2016-1-FI-EPPJMO-NETWORK.

[2] Compiled from https://eur-lex.europa.eu/content/news/Covid19.html as of 20 June 2020. This represents 62 per cent of the output published, with 21 per cent hard law and 17 per cent other various proposals, drafts, and corrigenda. See also O Ştefan, 'The Future of EU Soft Law' (2020) *Journal of International and Comparative Law*, forthcoming.

[3] F Snyder, 'The Effectiveness of European Community Law: Institutions, Processes, Tools and Techniques' (1993) 56 *Modern Law Review* 19.

on the topic by the European Commission,[4] the European Data Protection Board[5] and the eHealth network,[6] often overlapping and creating confusing duplications. Such a wealth of instruments is explained by the fact that EU soft law is cheap, fast, flexible and easy to issue. It is thus particularly adapted to rapid evolutions and changes in policies and is well suited to deal with emergencies such as the pandemic. To give another example, the Commission issued and updated twice, in less than two months, a Temporary Framework[7] setting the parameters for the Member States to grant legal State aid to their economies in the context of the COVID-19 outbreak. Such swiftness raises important issues of legitimacy, as the procedures for the adoption of soft law tend to circumvent more lengthy and costly decision-making ways, which in turn might enhance the discretion of some of the EU institutions and bodies to the detriment of parliamentary and/or Member State competences.[8] In this context, the hope is that the European Court of Justice (ECJ) would step in, relying on its role of guardian of the Treaties, and scrutinise soft law instruments. Yet, in a judgment which only reaffirms a long line of case law, the Court has denied the justiciability of such instruments on the grounds that they lack legally binding force.[9]

Moreover, absent legally binding force, the legal and practical effects that soft law can produce are blurred. Legal effects generally consist of the capacity of EU legal instruments to change the rights and obligations of actors.[10] For instance, as established by case law, soft law binds the discretion of its authors,[11] EU institutions or bodies. This is a specific application of the general principles of law, as legitimate expectations or legal certainty dictate that the author adheres to what they have publicly committed to undertake. However, in the multi-level governance system of the EU, national authorities and courts are not

[4] Commission Recommendation (EU) 2020/518 of 8 April 2020 on a common Union toolbox for the use of technology and data to combat and exit from the COVID-19 crisis, in particular concerning mobile applications and the use of anonymised mobility data [2020] OJ L114/7; European Commission, 'Communication from the Commission of 16 April 2020, Guidance on Apps supporting the fight against COVID 19 pandemic in relation to data protection' [2020] OJ C124I/1.

[5] European Data Protection Board, 'Guidelines 04/2020 on the use of location data and contact tracing tools in the context of the COVID-19 outbreak' (21 April 2020).

[6] eHealth Network, 'Mobile applications to support contact tracing in the EU's fight against COVID-19. Common EU Toolbox for Member States' (15 April 2020).

[7] European Commission, 'Communication from the Commission Temporary Framework for State aid measures to support the economy in the current COVID-19 outbreak' [2020] OJ C91I/1, 20 March.

[8] Résolution du Parlement européen du 8 mai 1969, sur les actes de la collectivité des États membres de la Communauté ainsi que les actes du Conseil non prévus par les traités adoptée à la suite du rapport fait au nom de la Commission juridique par M. Burger [1969] OJ C63/18; European Parliament, 'Resolution of 4 September 2007 on institutional and legal implications of the use of "soft law" instruments 2007/2028(INI)' [2008] OJ C187E/75, at 1.

[9] Case C-16/16 P *Kingdom of Belgium v Commission* [2018] EU:C:2018:79.

[10] T Hartley, *The Foundations of European Community Law*, 7th edn (Oxford, Oxford University Press, 2010) 354.

[11] Joined Cases C-189/02 P, C-202/02 P, C-205–208/02 P and C-213/02 P *Dansk Rørindustri A/S and Others v Commission* [2005] EU:C:2005:408.

asked to follow EU soft law instruments, but are, at most, advised to take them into consideration.[12] Soft law could also produce practical effects. These are transformations that soft law may generate in the behaviour and practices of individuals, national authorities, and the institutions of the EU. Soft law can thus be influential and lead to policy change.

It is still very early to see what effects COVID-19 EU soft law instruments will have at the national level, but some confusions and contradictions are easy to predict.[13] With national authorities not bound to respect EU guidance, it might not come as a surprise to still find a patchwork of uncoordinated national reactions across Europe, inconsistency which has been heavily criticised since the beginning of the pandemic.[14] With soft law issued on a treadmill in Brussels, lacking the involvement of the European Parliament and often omitting even usual public consultations, legitimacy is, once again, at a loss. Such concerns are not specific to COVID-19 soft law, but they reflect wider and deep-rooted concerns regarding soft law in the EU. The arguments relating to the uncertainty of legal effects of soft law or its legitimacy drawbacks have been well rehearsed by the literature dealing with the EU level of governance,[15] but there has been relatively little analysis of the way in which EU soft law is received in Member States.[16] This lack of attention is problematic for many reasons. First, the uncertainty surrounding EU soft law in national settings can endanger the principles of legal certainty, transparency and legality. Second, ambiguity may negatively affect the effective and uniform implementation and enforcement of EU law, if national administrations and judges, who are key actors interpreting soft law instruments nationally, are unsure whether and how to apply soft law documents. Third, soft law may also have positive effects, but its potential to contribute to legitimizing European governance remains unexplored and underexploited.

[12] Case C-322/88 *Salvatore Grimaldi v Fonds des maladies professionnelles* [1989] EU:C:1989:646 and Case C-226/11 *Expedia Inc. v Autorité de la concurrence and Others* [2012] EU:C:2012:795. See also E Korkea-aho, 'National Courts and European Soft Law: Is *Grimaldi* Still Good Law?' (2018) 37 *Yearbook of European Law* 470; O Ştefan, 'Helping Loose Ends Meet? The Judicial Acknowledgement of Soft Law as a Tool of Multi-level Governance' (2014) 21 *Maastricht Journal of European and Comparative Law* 359.

[13] See also a forthcoming special issue of *European Journal of Risk Regulation* on the use of soft law guidance in dealing with COVID-19 in a comparative perspective.

[14] A Alemanno, 'The European Response to COVID-19: From Regulatory Emulation to Regulatory Coordination?' (2020) 11 *European Journal of Risk Regulation* 307.

[15] O Ştefan et al, 'EU Soft Law in the EU Legal Order: A Literature Review' (2019) SoLaR Working Paper, https://ssrn.com/abstract=3346629.

[16] C van Dam, 'Guidance Documents of the European Commission in the Dutch Legal Order' (PhD thesis, 2020, https://openaccess.leidenuniv.nl/handle/1887/86926); Z Georgieva, 'Soft Law in EU Competition Law and its Reception in Member States' Courts: An Empirical Study on National Judicial Attitudes to Atypical Legal Instruments in EU Competition Law' (PhD thesis, 2017, https://research.tilburguniversity.edu/en/publications/soft-law-in-eu-competition-law-and-its-reception-in-member-states); E Korkea-aho, 'EU Soft Law in Domestic Legal Systems: Flexibility and Diversity Guaranteed?' (2009) 16 *Maastricht Journal of European and Comparative Law* 271.

In this context, the current volume presents the results of an empirical project asking the question whether, and how, soft law is used by national administrations when implementing EU policies, and by national courts when ruling in cases falling within the scope of application of EU law. The hope is that the lessons learned from studying non-emergency soft law would reveal important findings that will help shape the field for the future, which would be useful not only in the event of a crisis, but also for usual policy-making.

The project, co-financed by the European Commission under its Jean Monnet programme, unfolded over three and a half years, and gathered an interdisciplinary team of academics led by six universities.[17] The research relied on socio-legal methods, combining doctrinal analysis of national cases and administrative decisions with expert interviews with judges and civil servants. Geographically, the project covered the following jurisdictions: Cyprus, Finland, France, Germany, Hungary, Italy, the Netherlands, Slovenia, Spain and the UK.[18] Materially, four policy areas were considered: environmental law, social policy, competition and State aid law, and financial regulation. Given the breadth of research, there have been at times variations in the methodology according to the specificities of each jurisdiction and field. The case law and the administrative decisions were compiled mostly from publicly available databases in the relevant jurisdictions, with a particular focus on higher courts. In certain jurisdictions, interviews were more difficult to obtain than in others, for reasons relating to the particular historical context (ie, covering the Brexit years in the UK) or to the specificities of legal research (such as in France and Italy, where the technique of interviewing is unusual for legal research).[19] Within the policy areas, the research teams considered a selected pool of instruments, as detailed in Annex I. Particularly insightful findings regarding other instruments have been recorded and occasionally discussed in the chapters of this book.

The book is divided into three parts. Part I, entitled 'Normative Assumptions', introduces and contextualises the main themes of the collection with respect to past and present theoretical debates in research on soft law. In Chapter 2, Imelda Maher conceptually situates the book among the vast body of literature discussing the 'woolly' relationship between governance, soft law and networks. Using competition law as a case study, she concludes that, in the EU, laws are often hybrid, and that soft law and networks are both tools of governance that can shape and reshape legal norms and the exercise of public power at the EU and

[17] The University of Helsinki, Maastricht University, King's College London, Université d'Aix-Marseille, the Kranj Graduate School of Government and European Studies, Slovenia, and Freie Universität Berlin.

[18] The original SoLaR countries covered by the project were Finland, France, Germany, Italy, the Netherlands, Slovenia, and the UK. Cyprus, Hungary and Spain, as well as China, were subsequently invited to contribute to the current volume.

[19] The interview template and the case law template are annexed to this introduction, as Annex II and Annex III respectively.

national levels. In Chapter 3, Andreas Hofmann provides a crucial contribution to the literature on EU soft law by suggesting a taxonomy for soft law based on its connection with hard law. He uses the instruments selected by SoLaR as a case study to note that the only meaningful way to categorise the vast variety of shapes and forms that soft law can take is by distinguishing between soft law instruments that have a close connection to a piece of EU hard law (interpretative and decisional soft law) and soft law instruments that do not have such a connection (steering instruments). In Chapter 4, Miriam Hartlapp and Emilia Korkea-aho tackle methodological issues, noting how soft law is often seen as 'whatever-law' and Member States as a bunch of teenagers who could not care less about EU guidance. Bringing soft law under the scope of general implementation research, they propose a typology of Member State responses to EU soft law and illustrate, with references to SoLaR, how the socio-legal methods of implementation research can help explore the often-undetected effects of EU soft law in the Member States. In Chapter 5, Giulia Gentile ventures in a quest for specific ways in which EU soft law is implemented in the Member States, and confirms the potential for fragmentation and inconsistency. Her case study of environmental and competition soft law in the UK and France shows how the practices to receive EU guidance are fundamentally different and can yield problematic consequences from the perspective of legitimate expectations, legal certainty and sincere cooperation.

Part II of the book, 'Country Analyses', zooms in on the various jurisdictions studied, and examines the status and legal effects of soft law in the activities of national courts and administrations. This part is the result of a fruitful collaboration between the authors who have shared and discussed their findings for the past four years, working together on three main aspects.[20] The first issue analysed concerns the status and legal effects of EU soft law in the different jurisdictions. Second, the chapters distil whether soft law is reviewable by national courts and how national authorities and courts perceive such instruments. Third, this part offers an insight on whether the use of soft law by national courts and administrations contributes to fostering or undermining good governance.

In Chapter 6, Napoleon Xanthoulis and Anastasia Karatzia note that the recourse to EU (or national) soft law in the Cypriot legal system is a reality, but its role in litigation is rather insignificant, and administrative practice varies greatly depending on the field. In Finland, authorities and judges positively endorse soft law's guiding effects in a multitude of situations. In Chapter 7, Emilia Korkea-aho, Katri Havu, Päivi Leino-Sandberg and Liisa Tarkkila suggest that the positive approach is best explained by 'pragmatic legalism' that is less

[20] SoLaR produced four Working Papers, one in each of the four policy areas studied: https://papers.ssrn.com/sol3/papers.cfm?abstract_id=3668793; https://papers.ssrn.com/sol3/papers.cfm?abstract_id=3656418; https://papers.ssrn.com/sol3/papers.cfm?abstract_id=3667387; https://papers.ssrn.com/sol3/papers.cfm?abstract_id=3668981.

interested in abstract considerations of the nature of bindingness, but uses soft law if it has a guiding value in a concrete case. In Chapter 8, Nathalie Rubio and Oana Ştefan show that France's Supreme Administrative Court has been increasingly socialised to soft law, advocating for the recognition and judicial review of national soft law, and recently sending a landmark preliminary reference to the ECJ, questioning the validity of guidance from the European Banking Authority. The hope is that this might revolutionise the justiciability of such instruments more widely in the EU, especially since concerns about the legitimacy of soft law have been expressed by interviewees across the board. In Chapter 9, Miriam Hartlapp, Andreas Hofmann and Matthias Knauff observe that in Germany, the use of EU soft law by judges and administrators is driven by efficiency gains, and the reliance on EU guidance is most frequent in the fields of competition and the environment. In Chapter 10, the analysis conducted by Petra Láncos shows a negligible relevance of EU soft law in the Hungarian legal order, although such instruments are sometimes used in competition law enforcement and by the Office of the Green Ombudsman. This might be explained by the historical reluctance of judges and public officials to rely on 'external' sources. In Chapter 11, Jacopo Alberti and Mariolina Eliantonio show that in Italy, the national approach to EU soft law has generally received a good press from national courts and authorities, but its use seems to be rather pragmatic, 'utilitarian' and somewhat 'random'. In Chapter 12, Barbara Beijen concludes that EU soft law is of relevance in the Netherlands and in practice is considered binding. The downside is that important principles, such as legality or transparency, are at a loss. In Chapter 13, Matej Avbelj and Katarina Vatovec conclude that EU soft law is relied on mostly by the Slovenian administration, whereas courts show a positivist caution. Yet there are indications that such instruments are gaining momentum, as witnessed by the *Kotnik*[21] saga regarding potential constitutional clashes with the Banking Communication.[22] In Chapter 14, Luis Arroyo Jiménez and José María Rodríguez de Santiago conclude that EU soft law can have an important impact on Spanish administrative law, yet the courts tend to take such instruments into consideration only when they are invoked by the parties. In Chapter 15, Mary Dobbs and Oana Ştefan note that there is a certain degree of willingness to refer to soft law in UK administration and court practice wherever this is considered useful and appropriate (mostly in competition and environment). However, following Brexit, the application of EU soft law will remain at best haphazard in the UK.

In Chapter 16, the last chapter of this part, Francis Snyder contrasts the experiences of the EU Member States with the role of soft law in the Chinese legal

[21] Case C-526/14 *Tadej Kotnik and Others v Državni zbor Republike Slovenije* [2016] EU:C:2016:570.

[22] European Commission, 'Communication from the Commission on the application, from 1 August 2013, of State aid rules to support measures in favour of banks in the context of the financial crisis ('Banking Communication')' [2013] OJ C216/1.

system. He notes that the range and variety of soft law used in China are much greater than in Europe. While Chinese soft law is similar to soft law in many Western legal systems, he cautions against misleading first impressions and invites us to consider such instruments in their cultural, societal and historical context.

Part III, 'Evaluation', zooms out on key findings of the country reports. In Chapter 17, Mariolina Eliantonio tackles the question of the reviewability of soft law measures and concludes that national courts are not only more open than the Court of Justice of the European Union (CJEU) in admitting claims against soft law measures, but might even become the vector of change of the CJEU's approach to judicial review of soft law. In Chapter 18, Napoleon Xanthoulis untangles the complicated assessment of the Court to determine whether an act is capable of producing legally binding effects for the purposes of judicial review. His chapter delves into the two criteria used by the Court to this effect, discussing the interplay between the intention of the author and the perception of the concerned parties. He shows how the effects of soft law can come in different shades alongside a time-sensitive continuum. In Chapter 19, Oana Ştefan takes stock of the numerous interview findings that pointed out the lack of clarity of soft law instruments, as well as of the results of case law analysis showing diverging attitudes towards soft law. She draws wider conclusions with regard to the role of EU soft law in fostering (or undermining) the principles of transparency and the consistent application of EU law. In Chapter 20, Ulrika Mörth usefully places the soft law question against the wider background of the tension between output and input legitimacy in political systems. She offers an empirical analysis of the use of soft law by the Swedish government to show how soft law can expand the political sphere, while the 'democratic realm remains within the parliamentarian chain of command and control'.

One of the finalities of SoLaR was to draw up some form of policy recommendations for consideration by national courts. Our initial idea was that national courts in particular are struggling with the problems of application of EU soft law and that with a little help from SoLaR, at least some of the problems and issues in relation to EU soft law in the Member States could be alleviated. We see things slightly differently now. Our research has shown that EU soft law plays an important role in the everyday life of public administration at all levels of government. Soft law matters at the national level, yet it does not always constitute a mainstream source in the jurisdictions studied and is largely sector-dependent. National judges and national administrations across European capitals find soft law useful and informative, although most of the judges are not yet accustomed to these instruments. Administrators and judges often take issue with questions regarding the legitimacy, clarity and transparency of EU soft law. With some notable exceptions,[23] there is little hope that the lack of

[23] Conseil d'État, 4 December 2019, Fédération bancaire française (FBF), Case No 415550; Case C-911/19 *Fédération bancaire française (FBF) v Autorité de contrôle prudentiel et de résolution* (ACPR), request for a preliminary ruling from the Conseil d'État (France) lodged on 13 December 2019.

judicial scrutiny of soft law at the European level can be offset by national vigilance and potentially recourse to the preliminary reference procedure.[24]

These issues with legitimacy, clarity and transparency impede national administrators and judges from using soft law in the intended and optimal ways. These issues are not the result of national legal-cultural peculiarities or preferences (or failures to come to grips with EU soft law) and thus cannot be addressed by Member States, let alone by individual judges or authorities granting permits or financial assistance for major renewable energy projects, but would need to be addressed at the EU level.

This collection was never intended to be just about theoretical findings. Nor was it meant to be a collection of pieces of empirical evidence without a solid theoretical foundation to aid interpretation and analysis. Instead, it was intended to combine these two worlds. In our view, policy recommendations are children of a happy marriage between theoretical findings and empirical insights. These four policy recommendations are intended for the EU to ponder and constitute the main points to take away from the book:

1. *Improve the accessibility of soft law*. One of the most general concerns raised by courts and authorities in the Member States is the difficulty of finding relevant soft law measures. All non-binding rules adopted by the Commission (alone or in collaboration with others) should be publicly available on a dedicated Commission website. These rules should be easily searchable in a database or repository using one or more policy areas, year of adoption and keywords as search criteria.
2. *Provide translations of key guidance and encourage national dissemination and implementation of soft law*. If one is serious about EU soft law having a domestic impact, translations of at least the most important soft law measures should be provided. In particular, this concerns interpretative guidance intended to explain the terms of underlying binding secondary law. National dissemination and implementation should be encouraged and supported. Our research shows that national 'implementing' guidance that adapts EU soft law guidance to domestic circumstances increases the relevance and potential impact of EU soft law nationally.
3. *Adopt guidelines for the adoption of non-binding rules*. Soft law comes in a multiplicity of forms and from a multiplicity of sources. There are no rules on how soft law is prepared, and practices differ between institutions involved in soft law-making and between policy areas. Domestic actors are deeply concerned about the impact of EU soft law on democratic legitimacy and transparency. From the Member States' point of view, EU soft law often lacks a clear chain of accountability and raises questions

[24] AH Türk and N Xanthoulis, 'Legal Accountability of European Central Bank in Bank Supervision: A Case Study in Conceptualizing the Legal Effects of Union Acts' (2019) 26 *Maastricht Journal of European and Comparative Law* 151.

on the possibilities for realising democratic accountability. The use of soft law – especially if it is used instead of legislation – can undermine the role of national legislators. Clear procedural rules on how EU soft law is adopted would help to alleviate some of these concerns.

These guidelines should establish the basic procedural requirements of soft law-making and give guidance on the format of the soft law document:

Procedural requirements

- Public consultation.
- Involvement of civil society and other interested parties.
- Transparency of the process (including record-keeping and documentation requirements).

Format

- References to EU and national laws, related regulations and relevant policies.
- Purpose of the document.
- Process of adoption.
- Responsibilities and authorities for implementing the policy (eg, comply or explain requirements).
- Contact information for questions and resources available for assistance.

4. *Engage in a dialogue with Member States.* The definition of soft law is understood in different ways in different Member States, and the way in which national actors use soft law is influenced by their national legal and political cultures. An awareness of the differences in national conceptions of soft law will help make soft law that is perceived both legitimate and efficient by national actors.

These policy recommendations not only concern the particular instruments we studied in SoLaR, but also generally concern soft law in its emergency and non-emergency forms. Due respect for transparency, clarity, legitimacy and engagement in a dialogue is now more important than ever with a torrent of emergency soft law. This should be kept in mind when the pandemic soft law is just a faint memory, and the soft law we study is refreshingly boring again and deals with insurance guarantee schemes[25] or safe and secured parking places.[26] Perhaps the day shall come when doubts regarding rule-of-law credentials will no longer linger in dark corners of non-binding regulation and will not be likely to creep in, overshadowing responses to future crisis situations in a more harmonious EU.

[25] European Commission, 'White Paper on Insurance Guarantee Schemes' (COM/2010/0370 final).

[26] Opinion of the European Economic and Social Committee on the European Road Safety Policy and Professional Drivers – Safe and secured parking places [2007] OJ C175/88.

ANNEX I

SPECIFIC INSTRUMENTS INVESTIGATED IN EACH POLICY FIELD

FINANCIAL REGULATION

Soft law measure	*Year of publication*
Guidelines on the enforcement of financial information (ESMA/2014/1293)–21 April 2017	2017
Exemption for market making activities and primary market operations under Regulation (EU) 236/2012 of the European Parliament and the Council on short selling and certain aspects of Credit Default Swaps (ESMA/2013/74)–21 February 2017	2017
Joint Guidelines on complaints-handling for the securities (ESMA) and banking (EBA) sectors (JC 2014 43)–18 February 2015	2015
Guidelines on remuneration policies and practices (MiFID) (ESMA/2013/606)–7 October 2014	2014

ENVIRONMENTAL LAW

Environmental Directive	*Soft law measure*	*Year of publication*
Water Framework Directive	1. No 1 – Economics and the Environment – The Implementation Challenge of the Water Framework Directive	2003
	2. No 2 – Identification of Water Bodies	2003
	3. No 3 – Analysis of Pressures and Impacts	2003
	4. No 4 – Identification and Designation of Heavily Modified and Artificial Water Bodies	2003
	5. No 5 – Transitional and Coastal Waters – Typology, Reference Conditions and Classification Systems	2003
	6. No 6 – Towards a Guidance on Establishment of the Intercalibration Network and the Process on the Intercalibration Exercise	2003
	7. No 7 – Monitoring under the Water Framework Directive	2003
	8. No 8 – Public Participation in Relation to the Water Framework Directive	2003

	9. No 9 – Implementing the Geographical Information System Elements (GIS) of the Water Framework Directive	2003
	10. No 10 – Rivers and Lakes – Typology, Reference Conditions and Classification Systems	2003
	11. No 11 – Planning Processes	2003
	12. No 12 – The Role of Wetlands in the Water Framework Directive	2003
	13. No 13 – Overall Approach to the Classification of Ecological Status and Ecological Potential	2003
	14. No 14 – Guidance on the Intercalibration Process (2004–06)	2005
	15. No 15 – Groundwater Monitoring (WG C)	2007
	16. No 16 – Groundwater in Drinking Water Protected Areas	2007
	17. No 17 – Direct and indirect inputs in the light of the 2006/118/EC Directive	2007
	18. No 18 – Groundwater Status and Trend Assessment	2009
	19. No 19 – Surface water chemical monitoring	2009
	20. No 20 – Exemptions to the environmental objectives	2009
	21. No 21 – Guidance for reporting under the WFD	2009
	22. No 22 – Updated WISE GIS guidance (November 2008)	2009
	23. No 23 – Eutrophication Assessment in the Context of European Water Policies	2009
	24. No 24 – River Basin Management in a Changing Climate	2009
	25. No 25 – Chemical Monitoring of Sediment and Biota	2010
	26. No 26 – Risk Assessment and the Use of Conceptual Models for Groundwater	2010
	27. No 27 – Deriving Environmental Quality Standards	2011
	28. No 28 – Preparation of Priority Substances Emissions Inventory	2012
	29. No 29 – Reporting under the Floods Directive	2013
	30. No 30 – Procedure to fit new or updated classification methods to the results of a completed intercalibration exercise	2015

	31. No 31 – Ecological Flows (final version)	2015
	32. No 32 – Biota Monitoring	2014
	33. No 33 – Analytical Methods for Biota Monitoring	2014
	34. No 34 – Water Balances Guidance (final version subject to language and format checks)	2015
Habitats Directive	1. Guidance document: Managing Natura 2000 sites (2000)	2000
	2. Guidance document on the Assessment of Plans and Projects significantly affecting Natura 2000 sites (November 2001)	2002
	3. Guidance document on Article 6(4) of the 'Habitats Directive' 92/43/EEC	2007
	4. Guidance Natura 2000 and Forests	2015
	5. Guidance document 'Farming for Natura 2000'	2014
	6. Guidance on Aquaculture and Natura 2000	2012
	7. Inland waterway transport and Natura 2000	2012
	8. The implementation of the Birds and Habitats Directives in estuaries and coastal zones	2011
	9. Wind energy developments and Natura 2000	2011
	10. Non-energy mineral extraction and Natura 2000	2011
	11. Guidance document on Climate change and Natura 2000	2013
	12. Guidance document on the strict protection of animal species of Community interest under the Habitats Directive 92/43/EEC	2007
	13. Commission note on Designation of Special Areas of Conservation (SACs)	2012
	14. Commission note on setting conservation objectives for Natura 2000 sites	2012
	15. Commission note on establishing conservation measures for Natura 2000 sites	2013
Environmental Impact Assessment Directive	1. Commission guidance document on streamlining environmental assessments conducted under Article 2(3) of the EIA Directive	2016
	2. Streamlining environmental assessment procedures for energy infrastructure Projects of Common Interest (PCIs)	2013

	3. Guidance on the Application of the Environmental Impact Assessment Procedure for Large-Scale Transboundary Projects	2013
	4. Guidance on Integrating Climate Change and Biodiversity into Environmental Impact Assessment	2013
	5. Interpretation of definitions of project categories of Annex I and II of the EIA Directive	2015
	6. Interpretation of definitions of certain project categories of Annex I and II of the EIA Directive	2008
	7. Interpretation suggested by the Commission as regards the application of the EIA Directive to ancillary/associated works	2012
	8. Application of the EIA Directive to projects related to the exploration and exploitation of unconventional hydrocarbon	2012
	9. Application of EIA Directive to the rehabilitation of landfills	2010
	10. Clarification of the application of Article 2(3) of the EIA Directive	2006
	11. EIA – Guidance on Screening – 2001	2001
	12. EIA – Guidance on Scoping – 2001	2001
	13. EIA Review Check List – 2001	2001
	14. Guidelines on the Assessment of Indirect and Cumulative Impacts as well as Impact interactions	2001
	15. Communication from the Commission – Trans-European networks: Towards an integrated approach	2007
	16. Commission staff working document – Accompanying document to the Communication from the Commission Trans-European Networks: Toward and integrated approach	2007

COMPETITION LAW AND STATE AID

Soft law measure	*Year of publication*
Guidelines on Vertical Restraints (2010/C 130/01)	2010 and 2000
Communication from the Commission – Guidance on the Commission's Enforcement Priorities in Applying Article 82 of the EC Treaty to Abusive Exclusionary Conduct by Dominant Undertakings (2009/C 45/02)	2009

Guidelines on the Applicability of Article 101 of the Treaty on the Functioning of the European Union to Horizontal Co-operation Agreements (2011/C 11/01)	2011 and 2001
Guidelines on the Application of Article 81(3) of the Treaty (2004/C 101/08)	2004
Notice on Agreements of Minor Importance which do not Appreciably Restrict Competition under Article 101(1) of the Treaty on the Functioning of the European Union (*De Minimis* Notice) (2014/C 291/01)	2014 and 2001
Commission Notice on Cooperation within the Network of Competition Authorities (2004/C 101/03)	2004
Commission Notice on the Co-operation between the Commission and the courts of the EU Member States in the Application of Articles 81 and 82 EC (2004/C 101/04)	2004
Commission Communication on State Aid Elements in Sales of Land and Buildings by Public Authorities (97/C 209/03)	1997
Communication from the Commission on State Aid for Films and Other Audiovisual Works (2013/C 332/01)	2013
Commission Notice on the Enforcement of State Aid Law by National Courts (2009/C 85/01)	2009
Commission Notice on the Notion of State Aid as Referred to in Article 107(1) of the Treaty on the Functioning of the European Union (2016/C 262/01)	2016
Guidelines on State Aid for Environmental Protection and Energy 2014–2020 (2014/C 200/01)	2014
Communication from the Commission on the Application, from 1 January 2011, of State Aid Rules to Support Measures in Favour of Banks in the Context of the Financial Crisis (2010/C 329/07)	2010

SOCIAL POLICY

Soft law measure	*Year of publication*
Recommendation on investing in children (2013/112/EU)	2013
Buying Social. A Guide to Taking Account of Social Considerations in Public Procurement (European Commission 2010)	2010
Commission Recommendation on transparency in equal pay (2014/124/EU)	2014

ANNEX II

INTERVIEW TEMPLATE

1 *Prelude*

1.1 Short introduction

- Introduce yourself and SoLaR.
- Mention that SoLaR is an EU-funded, multi-disciplinary and cross-country collaborative network.

1.2 Why he/she was selected

- Expert working with implementation of EU law in the specific area (policy field/ specific instruments agreed by solar policy group).
- Explain that in each country 10–15 interviews are carried out.

1.3 Interview material

- Stress that the interview material will be used for scientific purposes only and assure full anonymity.
- Ask if the interviewee agrees to be recorded or if he/she prefers to talk without tape (in this case, take notes manually).

1.4 Overview of the interview

- Thank the interviewee to have granted the audience, indicate how long the talk will take approximately and give an overview of different aspects you would like to talk about: the context in which the interviewee uses EU soft law, effects and justiciability of soft law.

2 *Information on interviewee*

2.1 Could you briefly describe your professional background? Since when have you been on your current position?

2.2 How frequently do you deal with EU soft law instruments? In what kind of situations?

3 *Usage and effects of EU soft law*

Soft law has many different meanings; in the following when I talk about soft law, I refer to all types of EU instruments issued by the European Parliament, Commission or Council that are non-binding.

3.1 When dealing with soft law, what is your impression of how soft law is understood in your working environment? Is it considered as a valid source of law/having relevance for decision-making?

3.2 Thinking of the specific area, there are different EU soft law instruments:

- Which of these instruments do you use in your work? If not, why not?
- Check specifically for the instruments your policy group selected to investigate more closely.

3.3 Can you describe the process that led to the decision to use these instruments?

- Is it you who decides whether or not to use soft law?
- Interaction with colleagues in your department or in other departments when deciding to use EU soft law?

3.4 What influences/ motivates the usage?

- Need for clarification of hard law (especially where the underlying legislative framework is complex/technical)?
- Easing the implementation process?
- Moving interpretation in a specific direction; which one?
- Soft law has been invoked by the parties (applicants, stakeholders, organisations etc).
- Making sure you are 'doing the right thing' (vis-a-vis the Commission, the Federal Government, the higher authorities in the field).
- Peer pressure: other colleagues do that too.
- Cross-border peer pressure: you know (eg, from participating in European networks) that other authorities in similar positions in other Member States use soft law in similar situations.
- National 'legal' or 'practical' culture of using soft law?
- Now, if you think back, did this change over time?

3.5 Turning to the effects of the EU soft law on the specific area we mentioned, what are their practical and legal effects?

- How do they differ from/go beyond hard law in the area?
- Do they change rights and obligations of actors?
- Increase/decrease transparency?

3.6 Can you give me an example of an EU soft law instrument that is/was particularly relevant in your policy field? And one that is/was not?

- In practical terms?
- In legal terms?
- How would you explain the differences?

3.7 If you would be free to regulate in the specific area what type of instrument would you ideally use? Why?

4 *Judging EU soft law*

4.1 National administrations/courts do not always converge in their views – that is part of the game – but only in some cases does this translate into contestation of soft law. When is this the case?

- What are typical arguments in favour or against the use of soft law?

4.2 If we look into the literature we can differentiate between views on soft law that stress its positive sides (cheap, fast, flexible) and views that are more sceptical (lacking legitimacy and increasing uncertainty).

- Which side is closer to your own view on soft law? Why?

4.3 What do you think about soft law?

- Acts as a catalyst for successful international cooperation.
- Is well-suited to deal with the complexity of European affairs, their diversity.
- Is well-suited to regulate sensitive sectors.
- Works well in situations where swift action is imperative.
- Enhances discretion of some actors to the detriment of others (ie, Parliament versus executive).
- Is inappropriate for court use.
- Something else.

5 *Conclusion*

5.1 Now that we have talked about different aspects of EU soft law in your area, is there anything I forgot to ask that is important in this context?

3.4 Any documents or reports you would recommend?

3.5 Other people to talk to?

ANNEX III

GUIDANCE DOCUMENT FOR SoLaR MEMBERS: METHODOLOGY FOR CASE LAW SEARCH AND ANALYSIS

1. INTRODUCTION

In our application, we promised, as one of the main activities, to undertake research on the use of EU soft law by national courts in the selected policy areas. Furthermore, we promised that, in what we called 'the preparation (Year 1) phase', an analytical framework for further study would be established and most suitable methods for data collection and mapping of available data (case law, data sets, selection of appropriate bodies and institutions) would be developed.

This document is meant to provide guidance on the above-mentioned analytical framework and the methodology to be followed.

2. METHODOLOGY FOR CASE LAW RESEARCH

A. A Search Based on Keywords

The search for rulings will be carried out on the basis of preselected keywords, bearing in mind that the use of keywords should not be understood too strictly, as the aim is to maximise the results of the search.

Each policy team will agree on a set of keywords in accordance with the most reasonable approach for each policy. For the environmental law field, it might make most sense to search for the underlying hard law instrument (eg, the Habitats Directive), while in another policy field, the search could be based on the selected soft law instruments themselves.

B. Limitations to the Search

The search will be limited to supreme (ordinary and administrative) jurisdictions, as well as to specialised adjudicative bodies (eg, tribunals in the UK).

No temporal limitations are imposed.

Remember that the search that results in nil/very few hits is also a research result that needs to be reported.

3. ANALYTICAL FRAMEWORK FOR ANALYSIS

The following questions are to be analysed:

1. the status and legal/practical effects of soft law recognised by the court;
2. the justiciability of soft law and the way in which judicial review of such instruments is undertaken by the court;
3. the ways in which the use of soft law before the courts contributes to fostering or undermining general principles of law, such as legal certainty, transparency and consistent application of European law.

Part I

Normative Assumptions

2

Revisiting Soft Law
Governance, Regulation and Networks*

IMELDA MAHER

I. INTRODUCTION

SOFT LAW AND networks are key tools of governance, and they have major implications for EU law in the Member States. This chapter examines the relationship between governance, soft law and networks, using European competition law as a case study. In doing so, it explores how to describe governance, noting that there is an important conceptual divide between public and private forms of governance that in turn raises questions of the interplay between governance and regulation. It notes the discussion of soft regulation and suggests that the term may best describe norm creation in the private sphere, while soft law remains the preserve of the public sphere, although boundaries are fuzzy, as much regulation takes place in the shadow of publicly created norms. This leads to a discussion of the hybrid nature of soft law, in particular the approach of the European courts on the binding nature of soft law for EU courts and for national courts. Governance, soft law and networks are clearly interrelated. Governance tends to be the focus of the political scientists, soft law of the lawyers, and networks are perhaps shared to some degree, with Moran seeing the regulatory state as where governing becomes 'governance', which in turn is a matter of steering networks.[1]

This chapter explores networks, the challenges and opportunities they pose for governance, especially in a multi-level governance setting, and their role as

* Thanks to Ronan Riordan for research assistance, to the editors and to participants at the Fourth SoLaR Workshop, 'EU Competition and State Aid Soft Law and its Reception in the Member States', 11–12 October 2018, New University, Ljubljana, for their helpful feedback.

[1] M Moran, 'Understanding the Regulatory State' (2002) 32 *British Journal of Political Science* 391, 412.

sources of soft law at the EU level. Following a review of the shift to new governance in the EU in the early 2000s, the chapter takes competition law as a case study and analyses the interplay of networks and soft law for EU governance at the EU and national levels before concluding.

II. GOVERNANCE

It is difficult to define governance.[2] In the EU context, Poul Kjaer reminds us that while a general concept of governance has been introduced, it remains essentially empty, and the decisive step towards an overarching theory has not yet been made.[3] Burris, Kempa and Shearing provide a definition: organised efforts to manage the course of events in the social system, a definition that is so broad as to cover both government (statist and institutionalist) through to governance.[4] Colin Scott offers a narrower conception that separates out government from governance: the destabilisation of traditional government-centred governance, and the diffusion of governing capacity and legitimacy to a wider array of actors.[5] However, governance does not have to destabilise. Tools of governance such as soft law can complement the main tool of government: hard law.

The reference to diffusion is important in relation to soft law. The European Commission in its White Paper on Governance warned of the risk of the European Parliament being sidelined.[6] Arguably, the Commission could be concerned that coordination techniques, such as those of the open method of coordination,[7] might also sideline it, given that these techniques place greater emphasis on horizontal and state level policy learning.[8]

The challenge for governance methods, including soft law, is that the informality that is associated with the creation and operation of these techniques can undermine legitimacy. Legislatures may be sidelined, there may be a lack of transparency due to the diffuse nature of the creation of the norms, and the uncertainty surrounding their effects further renders accountability around them complex and difficult. In short, there is a tension between the normative demands and the functional attractiveness of soft law. In the context of the EU,

[2] AM Kjaer, *Governance* (Cambridge, Polity Press, 2004) 3.

[3] PF Kjaer, *Between Governing and Governance: On the Emergence, Function and Form of Europe's Post-national Constellation* (Oxford, Hart Publishing, 2010) 10.

[4] S Burris, M Kempa and C Shearing, 'Changes in Governance: A Cross-disciplinary Review of Current Scholarship' (2008) 41 *Arkon Law Review* 1, 3.

[5] C Scott, 'Governing without Law or Governing without Government? New-ish Governance and the Legitimacy of the EU' (2009) 15 *European Law Journal* 160, 164.

[6] European Commission, 'European Governance: A White Paper' COM (2001) 428 final.

[7] D Hodson and I Maher, 'The Open Method as New Form of Governance: The Case of Soft Economic Policy Co-ordination' (2001) 39 *Journal of Common Market Studies* 719.

[8] C Scott, 'The Governance of the European Union: The Potential for Multi-level Control' (2002) 8 *European Law Journal* 59.

this is further complicated by multi-level governance, where the links between national and EU public and private actors are complex.[9]

De Búrca and Scott provide a description of new governance in the context of the EU as the 'wide range of processes and practices that have a normative dimension but do not operate primarily or at all through the formal mechanism of traditional command-and-control type legal institutions'.[10] This is the narrowest of the three descriptions and the most legalistic. It sees a fairly clear demarcation between governance practices that lie beyond traditional government and puts law firmly on the side of government, although Joanne Scott has argued in favour of soft law forming the basis for judicial review before the Court of Justice of the European Union (CJEU) in the context of Member State guidelines in the environmental sphere that undermined primary legislation and were immune from legal challenge.[11] The lack of bindingness remains a challenge for the courts and, indeed, the difference between bindingness and legal effects can be seen as going to the heart of lawyers' understanding of soft law.[12] The argument in favour of the ability to challenge soft law before the courts weakens the firm demarcation initially suggested by de Búrca and Scott between traditional government (and legal institutions) and new governance.[13] Governance has become polycentric with a greater emphasis on function, especially in the context of the EU, which is a polity constrained by limited and limiting competences.

As for the relationship between governance and soft law, soft law can be seen as a primary mechanism within governance and as part of the experience of governance, but only as part. For example, much of the debate around governance, especially in the regulation literature, focuses on the public/private divide. The polycentric nature of governance means that there is much greater emphasis on the exercise of power by private actors, eg, corporations and insurance companies. The fuzzy boundaries between the public and private can be seen with credit-rating agencies, private firms whose impact on state economies during the fiscal crisis was such that they were eventually placed within a legal (public) framework within the EU.[14]

[9] Scott (n 5) 170; E Korkea-aho, 'EU Soft Law in Domestic Legal Systems: Flexibility and Diversity Guaranteed' (2009) 16 *Maastricht Journal of European and Comparative Law* 271.

[10] G de Búrca and J Scott, 'Introduction: New Governance, Law and Constitutionalism' in G de Búrca and J Scott (eds), *New Governance and Constitutionalism in Europe and the US* (Oxford, Hart Publishing, 2006) 3.

[11] J Scott, 'In Legal Limbo: Post-legislative Guidance as a Challenge for European Administrative Law' (2011) 48 *Common Market Law Review* 329.

[12] Korkea-aho (n 9) 275.

[13] O Ştefan, 'Helping Loose Ends Meet? The Judicial Acknowledgement of Soft Law as a Tool of Multi-level Governance' (2014) 21 *Maastricht Journal of European and Comparative Law* 359.

[14] Regulation (EC) No 1060/2009 on Credit Rating Agencies [2009] OJ L302/1, amended by Regulation (EU) No 462/2013 of the European Parliament and of the Council of 21 May 2013 [2013] OJ L146/1; H McVea, 'Credit Rating Agencies, the Subprime Mortgage Debacle and Global Governance: The EU Strikes Back' (2010) 59 *International and Comparative Law Quarterly* 701; A Darbellay, *Regulating Credit Rating Agencies* (Cheltenham, Edward Elgar, 2013).

This public/private divide, which is of primary concern in the regulation literature, raises the question of the source of soft law. Governance can take place through private actors issuing codes of practice, for example, in the advertising industry.[15] Would we call these codes of practice soft law? Or does the moniker 'law' ensure that the genus of soft law is always in the public and not the private domain? Senden notes that the Commission's 2001 Governance White Paper treats the open method of coordination (OMC) as separate from concepts of co-regulation (an EU framework within which private actors draw up codes of conduct and standards) and self-regulation (which is action exclusively within the private domain).[16] Jacobsson and Sahlin-Andersson in their discussion of transnational governance discuss soft regulation, a term which seems to suggest that soft law and some forms of regulation are conceptually blurred.[17] For them, soft regulation includes both the informal and the formal, given that recommendations to report and coordinate can, from an administrative point of view, appear highly formalised. They see soft regulation as being akin to regulated self-regulation, where rules develop incrementally in dialogue between the regulated and the regulator, creating ambiguity as to who is making the rules. Jacobsson also notes the 'remarkable softness in regulation' in the EU through the OMC.[18] The role of private actors in the development and implementation of soft law in the EU is emphasised as deserving more attention by Korkea-aho.[19] This may be because in the European context, soft law may be seen as reserved for public actors, while the term 'self-regulation' is reserved for private actors. With the adoption of guidelines in both domains, the origin of the rules may affect the nature of the potential legal effects of those measures, eg, private actors may not bind a public actor such as the Commission, which can bind itself through the principle of legitimate expectation when it issues soft law measures indicating how it will act in the future.[20]

Burris, Kempa and Shearing develop the notion of nodal governance and how the primary 'commodity' in governance is information, with a node representing an information point, its significance waxing and waning depending at any particular moment on the importance of that information for the particular governance issue.[21] This view of nodal governance highlights the importance

[15] European Advertising Standards Alliance, *Blue Book* (EASA, 2018), www.easa-alliance.org/products-services/publications/blue-book.

[16] LAJ Senden, 'Soft Law, Self-Regulation and Co-regulation in European Law: Where Do They Meet?' (2005) 9 *Electronic Journal of Comparative Law*.

[17] B Jacobsson and K Sahlin-Andersson, 'Dynamics of Soft Regulation' in M-L Djelic and K Sahlin-Andersson (eds), *Transnational Governance: Institutional Dynamics of Regulation* (Cambridge, Cambridge University Press, 2006) 253.

[18] B Jacobsson, 'Regulated Regulators: Global Trends of State Transformation' in M-L Djelic and K Sahlin-Andersson (eds), *Transnational Governance: Institutional Dynamics of Regulation* (Cambridge, Cambridge University Press, 2006).

[19] Korkea-aho (n 9).

[20] Joined Cases C-189/02 P, C-202/02 P, C-205–208/02 P and C-213/02 P *Dansk Rørindustri and Others v Commission* [2005] EU:C:2005:408, para 211.

[21] Burris, Kempa and Shearing (n 4).

of relationship and, with it, networks. Arguably, networks constitute another fundamental configuration of governance, with Rhodes in his seminal 1996 article on governance in the UK noting six possible definitions of governance, but ultimately identifying it as the management of self-organising, interorganisational networks.[22] Börzel defines policy networks (while noting that the definition is not uncontroversial) as a set of relatively stable relationships which are of non-hierarchical and interdependent nature linking a variety of actors, who share common interests with regard to a policy and exchange resources to pursue those interests, acknowledging that cooperation is the best way to achieve common goals.[23] Rhodes and Börzel both see networks as complementing, and alternatives to, governance through hierarchy (often associated with government) and markets (competition). Börzel identifies two different schools – interest intermediation and governance – with some overlap between them.

The interest intermediation school sees policy networks as generic for all kinds of relationships between public and private actors, with many different kinds of networks possible and categorised in different ways in the literature. She notes that there is a greater emphasis on heterogeneous interest networks, with homogeneous interest networks relatively neglected in the literature – although since then, we have seen a considerable amount of work undertaken on the burgeoning number of competition networks (see below). Börzel sees the governance school of networks as concerned with non-hierarchical coordination, including all actors involved in any way in the formulation and implementation of a policy. The emphasis is on informal interactions by actors with interdependent interests who strive to solve problems in a non-hierarchical manner. The challenge of horizontal self-coordination can be overcome when coordination takes place in the shadow of hierarchy or within network structures requiring trust and communication to produce effective outcomes.[24] Börzel goes on to note that networks do not directly serve decision-making, but are there for information, communications and influence in the preparation of decisions. The challenge is that they can be resistant to change. Levi-Faur reminds us of the major reorganisation of governance in the EU along two related axes: the emergence of agencies and network governance.[25]

Bell and Hindmoor remind us that from the perspective of the state, governments remain critical to governance and that governance is about state–society relations whatever arrangements are ultimately in place.[26] In other words,

[22] RAW Rhodes, 'The New Governance: Governing without Government' (1996) 44 *Political Studies* 652, 658.

[23] TA Börzel, 'Organizing Babylon: On the Different Conceptions of Policy Networks' (1998) 76 *Public Administration* 253, 254.

[24] ibid 261–62.

[25] D Levi-Faur, 'Regulatory Networks and Regulatory Agencification: Towards a Single European Regulatory Space' (2011) 18 *Journal of European Public Policy* 810.

[26] S Bell and A Hindmoor, *Rethinking Governance: The Centrality of the State in Modern Society* (Cambridge, Cambridge University Press, 2009) 10.

governance is not an alternative to government, as government is routinely and authoritatively implicated in all forms of governance.[27] At the same time, especially in the context of globalisation, Djelic and Sahlin-Andersson note that in exploring governance, the changing role of states and governments is a necessary focus.[28] As new forms of governance emerge, regard needs to be had to their institutional context. In the next section, we will explore governance in the EU. As new governance methods have developed nationally and internationally, so too have they become a feature of the EU.

III. SOFT LAW AND THE EU TURN TO NEW GOVERNANCE

Soft law can be defined as rules of conduct which, in principle, have no legally binding force, but which nevertheless may have practical effects.[29] And as Ştefan noted, Snyder has developed this definition by suggesting soft law may also have legal effects, for example, when the Court of Justice of the European Union (CJEU) is willing to give effect to it.[30] Terpan sees the concept as contested and not clear-cut, but, like Abbott and Snidal in their discussion of soft law in the context of international relations,[31] views law as a continuum from binding hard law to legal relevance, with soft law somewhere on that continuum.[32] Abbot and Snidal see soft law as combining both binding and non-binding norms, so their analysis captures the myriad variants on soft law in the EU. They frame what lawyers understand as soft law in terms of legalisation. Legalisation is a continuum depending on the intensity of three factors: obligation, precision and delegation.[33] This rationalist approach, while attractive in terms of the use of a continuum, was also criticised from a constructivist perspective by Finnemore and Toope who note the lack of discussion of processes and, more fundamentally, note the fuzzy nature of the concept of obligation.[34] Terpan sees obligation as depending on the source and content, as well as either the existence

[27] ibid 13.

[28] M-L Djelic and K Sahlin-Andersson, 'Introduction: A World of Governance: The Rise of Transnational Regulation' in M-L Djelic and K Sahlin-Andersson (eds), *Transnational Governance; Institutional Dynamics of Regulation* (Cambridge, Cambridge University Press, 2006) 7.

[29] F Snyder, 'The Effectiveness of European Community Law: Institutions, Processes, Tools and Techniques' (1993) 56 *Modern Law Review* 19, 32.

[30] Ştefan (n 13) 362.

[31] KW Abbott and D Snidal, 'Hard and Soft Law in International Governance' (2000) 54 *International Organization* 421.

[32] F Terpan, 'Soft Law in the European Union: The Changing Nature of EU Law' (2015) 21 *European Law Journal* 68, 70.

[33] KW Abbott, RO Keohane, A Moravcsik, A-M Slaughter and D Snidal, 'The Concept of Legalization' (2000) 54 *International Organization* 401.

[34] M Finnemore and SJ Toope, 'Alternatives to "Legalization": Richer Views of Law and Politics (2001) 55 *International Organization* 743, offering a critique of the 2000 special issue (n 31); this was part of a special issue on legalisation. See also J Goldstein, M Kahler, RO Keohane and A-M Slaughter, 'Response to Finnemore and Toope' (2001) 55 *International Organization* 759.

or strength of mechanisms for enforcement as determining how firm an obligation is in law.[35] He sees the two qualities of obligation and enforcement as allowing for soft law to be construed as its own category of law. Given the nature of either of these qualities can vary so much, having regard to them is certainly useful analytically, but not so much in terms of categorisation.

Trubek, Cottrell and Nance note that perspectives on soft law depend on theoretical orientation.[36] They discuss how Abbott and Snidal's rationalist approach (and, more specifically, rational institutionalism) assumes international institutions are set up by states to advance their mutual interests.[37] For Trubek et al, a rational choice approach to soft law helps to explain how soft law comes about. Constructivist perspectives with the emphasis on context, ideas and the role of collectively held understandings provide insights into how soft law may bring about a change in conduct. Thus, it is important to have regard to a range of factors in analysing soft law, including theoretical lens, level of law (international, supranational, domestic or regional) and sector.[38]

Trubek et al, seeking to resolve the thickness and variety of soft law in the EU (having explored governance in relation to fiscal governance and employment policy), point to hybridity, ie, where there is a mixture of hard and soft law within a field affecting the same actors. Terpan also points to the melange of hard norms and soft enforcement. This mix can be seen in fiscal policy, where soft obligations in the EU broad economic policy guidelines may ultimately trigger hard enforcement through the excessive deficit procedure (although the likelihood of such enforcement is remote, despite the introduction of extra safeguards such as reserve qualified majority voting in the Council of Ministers).[39] In the softer employment policy domain, where there is no hard enforcement, coordination still emanates from a treaty provision which is necessarily hard law.[40] He also notes the emergence of hybridity in relation to the OMC, where disbursement of cohesion funds, for example, can be linked to compliance with the objectives set under OMC, and monitoring and benchmarking as techniques can be incorporated into directives in relation to implementation review. Korkea-aho goes further than simply looking to the hybrid nature of the measures concerned, calling for attention to be paid to emerging institutional and legal links between EU institutions and Member States, and noting the role of non-state actors.[41]

[35] Terpan (n 32).

[36] DM Trubek, P Cottrell and M Nance, '"Soft Law", "Hard Law" and EU Integration' in G de Búrca and J Scott (eds), *New Governance and Constitutionalism in Europe and the US* (Oxford, Hart Publishing, 2006) 76.

[37] ibid 71.

[38] Terpan (n 32); J d'Aspremont, 'Softness in International Law: A Self-Serving Quest for New Legal Materials' (2008) 19 *European Journal of International Law* 1075.

[39] Articles 121 and 126 TFEU.

[40] ibid arts 146–50; K Armstrong, 'The Open Method of Coordination: Obstinate or Obsolete?' (2016) University of Cambridge Faculty of Law Research Paper No 45/2016.

[41] Korkea-aho (n 9) 273.

The coordination that these new methods were to facilitate between the EU and the Member States, and between Member States has materialised to varying degrees depending in particular on the policy field. Hence, Lodge[42] in an empirical study of two very different policy fields (pensions and information society) noted how in the absence of hierarchy (or, using the language of Trubek et al, hybridity of hard and soft law), very demanding prerequisites framing the policy and expected outcomes are needed for the governance method to succeed. Thus, the absence of hierarchy can dilute effectiveness, although where the EU carries no regulatory 'stick' with which to impose action on the Member States, it cannot be blamed where the governance initiative fails. Lodge also points to how the governance processes with multiple objectives can be confusing and policy learning between Member States is hampered where no meaningful comparison can be drawn between the data provided. These two examples highlight some of the flaws seen in the new governance approach of the EU, discussed in the next section.

IV. THE OVER-AMBITIOUS TURN TO NEW GOVERNANCE

The way in which the Lisbon Strategy developed highlights the significance of the policy field.[43] This Strategy was an attempt to address employment and social policy issues within the EU by consolidating a series of processes (Luxembourg dealing with employment, Cardiff dealing with structural policy and Cologne providing of macroeconomic dialogue).[44] The ambition of Lisbon was to create the most competitive and dynamic knowledge-based economy in the world capable of sustaining economic growth with more and better jobs and greater social cohesion within a 10-year timeframe. An environmental element was added subsequently.[45] The method through which this was to be achieved was coordination and the tool is the OMC, which combined guidelines, benchmarking, and monitoring and reporting.[46] There were no sanctions and, as it turned out, few legal effects. The OMC became synonymous with the emergence of new governance in the EU – new because it could be seen as a response to the strain that the Single European Act placed on the original EU governance model, with its emphasis on centralisation, functional segmentation and vertically integrated structures[47] articulated through formal binding rules. The response

[42] M Lodge, 'Comparing Non-hierarchical Governance in Action: The Open Method of Coordination in Pensions and Information Society' (2007) 45 *Journal of Common Market Studies* 343.

[43] European Council, 'Presidency Conclusions Press Release: Lisbon 24/03/2000' Nr 100/1/00.

[44] Hodson and Maher (n 7).

[45] European Council, 'Presidency Conclusions Press Release: Göteborg 15/6/2001' Nr 200/1/01.

[46] Hodson, and Maher (n 7).

[47] N Lebessis and J Paterson, 'Developing New Modes of Governance' in O de Schutter, N Lebessis and J Paterson (eds), *Governance in the European Union* (Luxembourg, Official Publications of the European Union, 2001) 268.

to this centralisation was the principle of subsidiarity in Maastricht.[48] OMC, with its emphasis on policy learning between national actors, is an articulation of that principle. Functional segmentation remains and we see coordination through OMC operating in different ways in different sectors.[49]

OMC is still part of the governance structures of the EU, especially in the employment and social policy fields,[50] but the Lisbon Strategy petered out discredited even before the fiscal crisis, with the Sapir Report[51] and the later Commission review[52] noting in particular its incoherence and ineffectiveness as the number of policy objectives proliferated. In fact, the European Parliament in its review noted that the strategy was called on to perform so many large and complex tasks that it could not really be reviewed.[53] In relation to the OMC itself, it is seen as a positive tool insofar as it highlights the need for monitoring where reforms are introduced and the importance of benchmarking. The weakness remains the lack of sanction of any sort, even where benchmarking and monitoring take place. Europe 2020[54] as the initial successor has greater focus, but the overlay of the European Pillar of Social Rights[55] once again raises the question of the proliferation of objectives, principles and values, although some lessons have been learnt with the introduction of scoreboards as a naming-and-shaming exercise proving useful. The most recent strategy is noticeably limited to four objectives.[56]

One positive outcome from the Lisbon Strategy is that it encouraged policy learning in part by Europeanising common problems.[57] The concept of Europeanisation arises because in the case of OMC, with its emphasis on shared guidelines, national reports and shared policy learning, this form of European coordination and soft law impacts on the domestic law and politics of the Member States. Europeanisation is a contested concept, with both a

[48] Article 5(3) TEU.

[49] Lodge (n 42).

[50] E Barcevičius, T Weishaupt and J Zeitlin (eds), *Assessing the Open Method of Coordination: Institutional Design and National Influence of EU Social Policy Coordination* (Basingstoke, Palgrave Macmillan, 2014).

[51] A Sapir, P Aghion, G Bertola, M Hellwig, J Pisani-Ferry, D Rosati, J Viñals, H Wallace, M Buti, M Nava and PM Smith, *An Agenda for a Growing Europe: The Sapir Report* (Oxford, Oxford University Press, 2004).

[52] European Commission, 'Staff Working Paper: Lisbon Strategy Evaluation Document' SEC(2010)414 final.

[53] European Parliament, *The Lisbon Strategy 2000–2010: An Analysis and Evaluation of the Methods Used and Results Achieved, Final Report* (Brussels, European Parliament, 2010).

[54] European Commission, 'Europe2020: A strategy for smart, sustainable and inclusive growth' COM(2010) 2020 final.

[55] European Parliament, Council and Commission, *European Pillar of Social Rights* (2017), ec.europa.eu/commission/sites/beta-political/files/social-summit-european-pillar-social-rights-booklet_en.pdf.

[56] European Council, *A New Strategic Agenda 2019–2024*, www.consilium.europa.eu/media/39914/a-new-strategic-agenda-2019-2024-en.pdf.

[57] European Parliament (n 53); J Krcek, 'Assessing the EU's "Lisbon Strategy": Failures & Successes' (2013) 5(9) *Inquiries*, www.inquiriesjournal.com/articles/754/assessing-the-eus-lisbon-strategy-failures-successes.

centralising analytical lens and a national lens.[58] Some analyses focus on how centralised institutions are developed and embedded in the EU. Hence, Risse, Cowles and Caporaso define Europeanisation as 'the emergence and development, at [a] European level, of distinct structures of governance'.[59] OMC and EU soft law could be seen as part of that phenomenon. At the domestic level, Saurugger provides a useful discussion of Europeanisation as causal and explanatory factors for understanding the incremental transformation and functional changes in national policies and laws.[60] She views this process as a circular and dynamic process, not a linear one, operating on the meso (national) and macro (EU) levels, with the EU influencing national policy and laws, and Member States similarly influencing EU policy and laws. Snyder notes that Europeanisation has led to the partial convergence of Member States, while conversely also resulting in new divergences between national legal systems, and one interesting question to be asked is to what extent EU soft law and the coordinating processes that facilitate this coordination result in convergence or divergences at the national level.[61]

V. COMPETITION LAW: THE INTERPLAY OF HARD LAW, SOFT LAW AND NETWORK

A. Soft Law: Supporting, Enforcing and Elaborating on Hard Law

At the time of the Lisbon Agenda, Hodson and Maher were at pains to point out that the OMC was not new; at best, it was new-ish.[62] This was for several reasons: first, as is clear from the European Council conclusions setting it up, it was a consolidation of existing processes; second, coordination through policy learning was a well-established technique of governance in the EU in justice and home affairs through the Trevi group, and in defence before the emergence of the common European security and defence regime, albeit a less open form of coordination in the latter, given security sensitivities. Korkea-aho also notes how soft law instruments were seen as part of the response to the legitimacy concerns of the EU raised at the 1992 Edinburgh Council.[63] Finally, the idea that

[58] H Kassim, 'The National Co-ordination of EU Policy: The Domestic Level' in H Kassim, G Peters and V Wright (eds), *The National Co-ordination of EU Policy* (Oxford, Oxford University Press, 2000) 235; U Mörth, 'Europeanization as Interpretation, Translation, and Editing of Public Policies' in K Featherstone and CM Radaelli (eds), *The Politics of Europeanization* (Oxford, Oxford University Press, 2003).

[59] M Risse, J Cowles and T Caporaso, *Transforming Europe: Europeanisation and Domestic Change* (Ithaca, Cornell University Press, 2001) 3.

[60] S Saurugger, 'Europeanisation in Times of Crisis' (2014) 12 *Political Studies Review* 181.

[61] F Snyder, *The Europeanisation of Law: The Legal Effects of European Integration* (Oxford, Hart Publishing, 2000).

[62] Hodson and Maher (n 7).

[63] Korkea-aho (n 9).

the emergence of soft law through the OMC process was in any way new simply ignored that bastion of soft law since the very early years of the EEC: competition law and policy. The failure to acknowledge that soft law was long-standing in the EU underlines the functional segmentation of the EU post the SEA and the relative isolation of scholarship on competition law.[64]

The first Competition Law Notice was issued on exclusive dealing contracts with agents in 1962, followed by the safe harbour notice for minor agreements in 1970,[65] setting a trend for soft law that was (relatively) uncontroversial in the field. In fact, it was the very formalistic approach of the Commission towards individual exemptions which stymied the effective implementation of the prohibitions in the treaties, leading to a radical change in 2003 with the move towards self-evaluation and the abolition of the notification system.[66] Gerber noted how the Commission in its early years used its decision-making to learn about competition practice and policy, having been given extraordinarily extensive powers.[67] A highly legalistic approach was supported by the Court, with competition law being seen as a key tool in the process of market integration.[68] In the second phase – roughly from the oil crisis to the Single Act – that early learning was set down in Block Exemption Regulations,[69] which were meant to reduce the notification burden on business and the Commission, but the high level of formalism rendered them of limited value, even when supported by soft law.

From a soft law perspective, what is interesting is that a hybrid model emerges at this time. The very detailed Notices accompanying the Block Exemptions were essential to the application of those Regulations.[70] Practitioner texts analysed not only the Regulations but also their accompanying Notices, where the Commission articulated its position on how the provisions of the Regulation

[64] DJ Gerber, 'Competition Law' in M Reimann and R Zimmermann (eds), *The Oxford Handbook of Comparative Law*, 2nd edn (Oxford, Oxford University Press, 2019) 5–7.

[65] European Commission, 'Notice on exclusive dealing contracts with commercial agents' [1962] OJ 139/2921; 'Notice on agreements, decisions and concerted practices of minor importance' [1970] OJ C64/1.

[66] I Maher, 'Competition Law Modernisation: An Evolutionary Tale?' in P Craig and G de Búrca (eds), *The Evolution of EU Law*, 2nd edn (Oxford, Oxford University Press, 2010).

[67] DJ Gerber, 'The Transformation of European Community Competition Law' (1994) 35 *Harvard International Law Journal* 1.

[68] Maher (n 66).

[69] See Council Regulation No 19/65/EEC on application of Article 85(3) of the Treaty to certain categories of agreements and concerted practices [1965] OJ 36/533, which led to, eg, Commission Regulation (EEC) No 1983/83 on the application of Article 85(3) of the Treaty to categories of exclusive distribution agreements [1983] OJ L173/1; Commission Regulation (EEC) No 1984/83 on the application of Article 85(3) of the Treaty to categories of exclusive purchasing agreements [1983] OJ L173/5; Commission Regulation (EEC) No 4087/88 on the application of Article 85(3) of the Treaty to categories of franchise agreements [1988] OJ L359/46; Commission Regulation (EC) No 240/96 on the application of Article 85(3) of the Treaty to certain categories of technology transfer agreements [1996] OJ L31/2 (as amended).

[70] See, eg, Commission notice concerning Commission Regulations (EEC) No 1983/83 and (EEC) No 1984/83 of 22 June 1983 on the application of Article 85(3) of the Treaty to categories of exclusive distribution and exclusive purchasing agreements [1983] OJ C101/84 P 2.

would be applied by it.[71] These soft law instruments were referred to from the early 1970s in the CJEU, although Ştefan reminds us that there were only 41 such references up until 2001.[72] The status of these Notices can be viewed under Terpan's categorisation. Their often-discursive style giving examples of what was allowed and not allowed meant that they did not look like legislation and hence lacked the precision expected of law. That said, to attempt to benefit from a block exemption in a manner that went contrary to the Notice would be ill-advised, suggesting that they were certainly of high legal relevance. As the Notices contain a 'without prejudice' clause vis-a-vis the court, this at least on the face of it suggested they were not binding.[73] However, regard should be had to context and actor. Hence, the Notices could be viewed as binding the Commission and it is arguable that for a legal adviser to ignore these Notices would constitute professional negligence, given how central they are to the application of the competition rules.

In the post-SEA phase, where more demands were to be made on competition law as market integration improved and market liberalisation increased, the chronic problems surrounding Commission enforcement led to further reliance on soft law, this time through the issuance of comfort letters or discomfort letters, where parties were told that files would not be pursued.[74] These letters were of legal relevance and probably binding on the Commission provided there was no change in circumstances, but were of no consequence before a national court or vis-a-vis third parties.[75] In other words, the legal effect depends greatly on the actor against whom the soft law measure is to be invoked and in what context.

It is helpful to categorise these various soft law measures in competition law: (1) supporting Notices designed to clarify and supplement a hard law measure (eg, Notices on Block Exemption Regulations); (2) measures designed to facilitate enforcement or, more accurately, to reduce the burden of enforcement. Here we find, for example, the Leniency Notice, the *De Minimis* Notice,[76] the now-defunct comfort letters and the guidelines on enforcement priorities for Article 102 TFEU;[77] and, finally, (3) soft law is used by the Commission as an exposition of law and policy, eg, the notice on market definition.[78] This last category is

[71] See, eg, V Korah and WA Rothnie, *Exclusive Distribution and the EEC Competition Rules: Regulations 1983/83 & 1984/83* (London, Sweet & Maxwell, 1992).

[72] O Ştefan, 'European Competition Soft Law in European Courts: A Matter of Hard Principles?' (2008) 14 *European Law Journal* 753.

[73] See, eg, European Commission, 'Guidelines on Vertical Restraints' SEC(2010) 411, para 1(4).

[74] D Stevens, 'The "Comfort Letter": Old Problems, New Developments' (1994) 15 *European Competition Law Review* 81.

[75] *Dansk Rørindustri and Others v Commission* (n 20).

[76] European Commission, 'Notice on Immunity from fines and reduction of fines in cartel cases' [2006] OJ C298/11, p 17, as amended, [2015] OJ C256/1.

[77] European Commission, 'Guidance on the Commission's enforcement priorities in applying Article 82 of the EC Treaty to abusive exclusionary conduct by dominant undertakings' [2009] OJ C45/7.

[78] European Commission, 'Notice on the definition of relevant market for the purposes of Community competition law' [1997] OJ C372/5.

the most controversial, as codification of existing law can move into expansion on and of that law.[79] For example, in the 2004 guidelines on the application of Article 101(3), the Commission noted that the guidelines aim to provide an analytical frame – a methodology for the application of the economic approach already referred to in previous guidelines from the Commission.[80] This is troubling. One soft law, a discursive measure, refers to another in a self-referential manner. Both soft law measures emanate from the same actor: the Commission. While there was consultation with stakeholders about the measures, the European Parliament was sidelined.

More fundamentally, as Georgieva reminds us, the ambiguity of soft law – its legal relevance, the uncertainty of its status as binding law and the importance of context for determining that status – serves to undermine certainty, which is a key concern in EU competition law.[81] She notes how those subjects of competition law (or at least their lawyers) have internalised soft law issued by the Commission in this sphere because of the close epistemic community of practitioners that exists. This gives soft law standing for subjects, but not necessarily for courts. The CJEU is not bound by soft law, with Ştefan arguing that reliance on the hard/soft divide is unhelpful and regard should be had primarily to the impact soft law may have in practice on the legal circumstances of individuals – ie, the scope of judicial protection of individuals vis-a-vis public power should be enlarged.[82] In other words, the formalism inherent in a binary divide between hard and soft law may be unhelpful, especially in an EU where regulatory space is increasingly characterised by the presence of soft law on a continuum of hybridity and legal relevance. Of course, the application of legal principles such as legitimate expectation go some way towards addressing a possible lacuna in judicial review by the Court, but it is arguable that they do not go far enough.

B. The European Competition Network: Enforcement and Cooperation

So, governance through soft law measures has been a feature of competition law in the EU since the 1960s.[83] A more recent development emerged in 2003

[79] ZR Georgieva, 'Soft Law in EU Competition Law and its Judicial Reception in Member States: A Theoretical Perspective' (2015) 16(2) *German Law Journal* 223.

[80] European Commission, 'Guidelines on the application of Article 81(3) of the Treaty' [2004] OJ C101/97, para 5, which refers to the earlier guidelines on vertical restraints, horizontal cooperation agreements and technology transfer agreements.

[81] Case T-115/94 *Opel Austria GmbH v Council of the European Union* [1997] EU:T:1997:3.

[82] Ştefan (n 13). See also Scott (n 11).

[83] Given the extent to which national competition regimes have aligned themselves with the EU competition law regime, soft law is also characteristic of those national regimes. See M Drahos, *Convergence of Competition Laws and Policies in the European Community* (The Hague, Kluwer, 2001); I Maher, 'Alignment of Competition Laws in the EC' (1996) 16(1) *Yearbook of European Law* 223.

with the establishment of the European Competition Network (ECN).[84] The EU required every Member State to designate a competition authority empowered to apply the EU competition rules. These authorities are members of the ECN.[85] Giving expression to the subsidiarity principle (Article 5(3) and Protocol 2 of the Treaty on European Union (TEU)), fundamentally addressing the enforcement burden (through self-regulation as well as decentralisation), the EU adopted a governance tool increasingly common in the EU: an agency network.[86] Agency networks have existed from the early days of the EU: a network of central bankers created in 1964 is the first identified by Levi-Faur.[87] The Trevi network was set up in 1975 (both now replaced by the European Central Bank and Europol). Levi-Faur sees the European Commission as a form of regulatory governance that is hierarchical and political, while agencies tend to be based on professional hierarchy of national experts and are more collegial. The ECN, unlike the first two networks mentioned above, represents a decentring of power away from the Commission to the national level, even though the Commission is a member of the network. The ECN must be viewed in the broader context of the emergence of these professional networks at the EU level in competition, as well as other fields such as energy[88] or telecoms.[89]

The ECN can also be seen as a response to the failure of that other tool of governance: soft law. The notice on cooperation with NCAs[90] had little impact, inhibited by the then-ongoing Commission monopoly on exemption under the treaties and in the absence of delegating legislation.[91] This is a case of soft law unable to have the effect required because of the underlying limitations of the hard law it was designed to supplement.

Relying on expertise and the shared objectives articulated in the EU prohibitions enforced by the national agencies, the most important currency is that of information.[92] Unusually among competition networks, the ECN members can share confidential information (subject to limitations linked to criminal

[84] Council Regulation (EC) No 1/2003 of 16 December 2002 on the implementation of the rules on competition laid down in Articles 81 and 82 of the Treaty [2003] OJ L1/1; European Commission, 'Notice on cooperation within the Network of Competition Authorities' [2004] OJ C101/43.

[85] Council Regulation 1/2003 (n 84) paras 11 and 35.

[86] I Maher and O Ştefan, 'Competition Law in Europe: The Challenge of a Network Constitution' in D Oliver, T Prosser and R Rawlings (eds), *The Regulatory State: Constitutional Implications* (Oxford, Oxford University Press, 2010).

[87] D Levi-Faur, 'Regulatory Networks and Regulatory Agencification: Towards a Single European Regulatory Space' (2011) 18 *Journal of European Public Policy* 810.

[88] I Maher and O Ştefan, 'Delegation of Powers and the Rule of Law: Energy Justice in EU Energy Regulation' (2019) 128 *Energy Policy* 84.

[89] M Blauberger and B Rittberger, 'Conceptualizing and Theorizing EU Regulatory Networks' (2015) 9 *Regulation & Governance* 36.

[90] European Commission, 'Notice on Cooperation between National Competition Authorities' [1997] OJ C313/3.

[91] I Maher, 'Functional and Normative Delegation to Non-majoritarian Institutions: The Case of the European Competition Network' (2009) 7 *Comparative European Politics* 414.

[92] Maher and Ştefan (n 86); I Maher, 'Competition Law Modernization: An Evolutionary Tale?' in Craig and de Búrca (n 66) 734.

enforcement).[93] This builds trust and mutual respect, and arguably improves enforcement strategies for all members – though this is not empirically proven. It can lead to policy convergence or what Slaughter calls informed divergence.[94] Networks where there is a high level of trust improve opportunities for policy learning, although there is a greater risk of groupthink.

The ECN is a hybrid regime combining both hard and soft laws. The Regulation provides for its existence[95] and this hard law measure is supplemented by two soft law measures: a joint declaration from the Council and the Commission,[96] and a Commission Notice.[97] That the Declaration was deemed necessary suggests a certain nervousness around its creation, but, as we know from Wilks' later analysis, such anxiety was misplaced with a well-functioning and cooperative network in place – a puzzle, but also fairly clear.[98] The agencies are implementing EU competition law under Regulation 1/2003[99] and also national laws largely based on the EU rules. The network is an enforcement network largely concerned with case allocation by national case officers, with subgroups existing for particular sectors or issues.

The decision as to which agency takes on a case is not a legally enforceable or reviewable act,[100] even though the decision as to which competition agency should pursue a case has significant legal effects, given that competition laws are criminalised in some Member States but not others. This case allocation exercise can be seen as a form of soft law, albeit one that is opaque.[101] There is an inbuilt sanction should any agency refuse to hand over a case or handle it badly, as the Commission is empowered under the Regulation to take over any case.[102] In principle, the best-placed national competition agency deals with the case, even if the case was already opened by another. If more than three agencies are involved, then the Commission can assume the case. The hotel bookings cases[103] show that the Commission can also perform a supportive role, leaving

[93] Council Regulation 1/2003 (n 84) art 12.

[94] A-M Slaughter, *A New World Order* (Princeton, Princeton University Press, 2004) 181.

[95] Council Regulation 1/2003 (n 84) art 11.

[96] Council and European Commission, 'Joint Statement of the Council and the Commission on the Functioning of the Network of Competition Authorities' [2002] Interinstitutional File 2000/0243(CNS).

[97] European Commission (n 84).

[98] S Wilks, 'Agencies, Networks, Discourses and the Trajectory of European Competition Enforcement' (2007) 3 *European Competition Journal* 437.

[99] Council Regulation 1/2003 (n 84).

[100] Case C-17/10 *Toshiba Corporation and Others* [2012] EU:C:2012:72, para 90.

[101] I Maher, 'Competition Law Networks and the Challenge of Transparency' (2019) UCD Working Papers in Law, Criminology & Socio-Legal Studies Research Paper No. 1/2019, ssrn.com/abstract=3339884, dx.doi.org/10.2139/ssrn.3339884.

[102] Council Regulation 1/2003 (n 84) art 11(6).

[103] *Skyscanner v CMA* [2014] CAT 16 (UK); Commitment Decision, *Competition and Consumer Commission v Booking.com* 6 October 2015 (Ireland); Konkurrensverket, *Booking.com* Decision 506/2013 15 April 2015 (Sweden); Autorité de al concurrence, Decision No 15-D-06, 15 April 2015, *Booking.com (France)*; Autorità Garange della Concorrenza e Mercato, 1779 – *Mercato dei Servizi Turistici-Prenotazioni Alberghiere*, 21 April 2015 (Italy).

the agencies to act individually – an approach that backfired with a German court decision[104] deviating from the competition agency decisions found in the other jurisdictions.[105]

The ECN, through the Heads of Agencies, can issue soft law measures and has done so, publishing recommendations and a draft leniency model.[106] More provocatively, its resolution following the CJEU judgment in *Pfleiderer*[107] set out clearly that the heads of the competition agencies thought effective protection of information received under leniency arrangements had to be protected and should not be discoverable for private damages actions.[108] This was at odds with the judgment of the Court, which was ultimately reversed through a directive.[109] In fact, the draft leniency model has also been superseded by hard law in the form of a directive which requires all states to have a leniency policy.[110] This recent legislation built on the ECN to bolster the tools and fines available to the agencies and to increase their independence. As a result of policy learning and effective enforcement, the existence of a soft tool of governance, the network is now being used to bolster the status of competition agencies within the states in their enforcement of EU competition law.

The ECN was introduced in part as a result of the systemic problem of the failure of earlier cooperation notices and a formalistic and centralised approach to law enforcement. Its operation continues based on mutual trust, information sharing and the allocation of cases, which does not constitute a reviewable decision for the courts. Following mutual learning and experience on leniency, and a unified but non-binding response to the very different approach of the CJEU to the confidentiality of information shared by parties when whistleblowing on cartels, soft law has been replaced by hard law, creating obligations for Member States, and the decision of the Court has been changed by legislation. The hybrid nature of competition law is underlined again with the preferred governance tool of the ECN retained and reinforced by legislation.

[104] Düsseldorf, OLG 9 Jan 2015, AZ.VI-Kart 1/14 (V).

[105] I Maher, 'The Challenge of European Competition Network Convergence in the Definition of Harm to Competition' in D Gerard, M Merol and B Meyring (eds), *The Notion of Restriction of Competition* (Brussels, Bruylant, 2017).

[106] European Competition Network, 'ECN Model Leniency Programme (as Revised in November 2012)', ec.europa.eu/competition/ecn/mlp_revised_2012_en.pdf.

[107] Case C-360/09, *Pfleiderer AG v Bundeskartellamt* [2011] EU:C:2011:389.

[108] European Competition Network (Resolution, 23 May 2012).

[109] Directive 2014/104/EU of the European Parliament and of the Council of 26 November 2014 on certain rules governing actions for damages under national law for infringements of the competition law provisions of the Member States and of the European Union [2014] OJ L349/1, art 6.

[110] Directive (EU) 2019/1 of the European Parliament and of the Council of 11 December 2018 to empower the competition authorities of the Member States to be more effective enforcers and to ensure the proper functioning of the internal market [2019] OJ L11/3, art 17.

C. National Autonomy in the Context of the Network

Korkea-aho notes how soft law can reduce legislative flexibility at the national level – even while viewed as increasing national autonomy.[111] This raises the question whether the move to a governance structure combining a network and soft law, such as the ECN, has the same effect. To answer this question, it is necessary first to disaggregate this notion of national autonomy. In other words, it is important to examine for whom autonomy is increased. Regulation 1/2003 has not increased national government autonomy, but has increased the autonomy of their competition agencies, to which Member States have delegated the enforcement of EU (and national) competition law. In 2003, national governments were simply required to ensure they designated a competition agency for the purposes of the Regulation and the ECN.[112] Sixteen years later, in Directive 2019/1, the independence of those agencies is now guaranteed,[113] correspondingly constraining national governments and their sway over those agencies.[114] At the same time, the agencies have been given more extensive enforcement powers to increase their effectiveness. Legislative flexibility has been reduced by formal legislation, reducing government autonomy, but markedly increasing agency autonomy.

Under the adumbration of competences in the Lisbon Treaties, competition law is listed as an exclusive competence.[115] Yet, as Townley has persuasively argued, this exclusivity is framed in terms of establishing the competition rules and 'the rest', ie, implementation and enforcement are shared competences.[116] In policy terms, coordinated diversity is important for the development of the field and to ensure effective responsiveness, albeit within a framework that avoids protectionism.[117] The EU (mainly the Commission, but with the oversight of the Member States through the Advisory Committee)[118] retains competence over policy formation. The national agencies as members of the ECN are giving effect to the EU rules through their coordinated enforcement practices that have now been augmented under Directive 2019/1.

This experience over a relatively short period of time casts the ECN as a form of pre-law arrangement. On the strength of a narrow legal base (two provisions in a regulation), without legal personality and with no formal law-making

[111] Korkea-aho (n 9) 273.

[112] Council Regulation 1/2003 (n 84) art 35.

[113] Directive 2019/1 (n 110) art 5(1).

[114] Maher (n 91).

[115] Article 3 TFEU.

[116] C Townley and AH Türk, 'The Constitutional Limits of EU Competition Law: United in Diversity' (2019) 64(2) *Antitrust Bulletin* 235, 245. For shared competence, see art 4(1) TFEU.

[117] C Townley, 'Coordinated Diversity: Revolutionary Suggestions for EU Competition Law (and for EU Law too)' (2014) 33 *Yearbook of European Law* 194; C Townley, *A Framework for European Competition Law: Co-ordinated Diversity* (London, Bloomsbury, 2018).

[118] Advisory Committee on Restrictive Practices and Dominant Positions. See Council Regulation 1/2003 (n 84) art 14.

powers, the ECN has proven to be an effective conduit for case allocation, increased alignment of competition law practice and information exchange. This governance experience then provided the context for greater formalisation through legislation simultaneously reducing (government) and increasing (agency) autonomy.

VI. CONCLUSION

The relationship between governance, soft law and networks is at best woolly, partly due to the multi-layered nature of each of these concepts. Governance incorporates both soft law and networks – both tools through which more horizontal learning-based norms of legal relevance are articulated. Soft law remains a complex and multi-faceted concept, and one generally reserved for actors in the public domain. In the EU, laws are often hybrid, with soft law combined with or emanating from a hard and binding legal norm. This hybridity can be clearly seen in the competition law sphere, where soft law has been evident since the early 1960s. The other main tool of EU governance is the network and through an exploration of soft law and networks in EU competition law, the extent to which soft law can support hard law is evident. The recent changes in the ECN show that an enforcement network with a formal legal base, but with no formal law-making powers, can still lead to the extension of powers by its member agencies at the expense of their own governments (albeit with those governments as the law-makers in the Council). Soft law and networks as tools of EU governance can shape and reshape legal norms and the exercise of public power.

3

Types of EU Soft Law and Their National Impact

ANDREAS HOFMANN

I. INTRODUCTION

THE PRIMARY CHARACTERISTIC of soft law is that it is not legally binding and (hence) cannot be legally enforced. This, however, is where the commonality between the myriad forms of soft law in the EU ends. Distinguishing EU soft law from EU hard law appears reasonably straightforward: hard law ultimately always has a legal basis in the EU treaties,[1] has binding legal force and can generally be judicially enforced. On the other hand, the lower boundary of the concept of EU soft law is much less clear – it is conceptually problematic to differentiate between soft law and no law at all. When even a speech by the President of the European Central Bank (ECB) can fundamentally re-align the expectations of market actors, a clear-cut definition of where soft law ends and no law begins will be difficult at best. Soft law comes in a vast array of formats, from statements of intent and vague policy recommendations to legal clarifications and complex technical specifications.

This chapter takes a closer look at EU soft law instruments and adopts a classification that primarily follows pragmatic criteria, based on a distinction initially introduced by Linda Senden.[2] The central criterion for this distinction is the soft law instrument's connection to hard law. Some soft law documents are companion pieces to hard law, while others have no such connection. This distinction should in principle allow predictions about the real-world impact of soft law instruments. This chapter applies this distinction to the soft law instruments studied in the European Network of Soft Law Research (SoLaR) project, themselves an illustration of the wide variety of soft law instruments at the EU level, and gives an outlook on how well this distinction holds up in explaining soft law impact at the national level. A final section concludes.

[1] Hard law can also have a basis in secondary legislation, which in turn is based on the treaties.
[2] L Senden, *Soft Law in European Community Law* (Oxford, Hart Publishing, 2004).

II. WHAT IS EU SOFT LAW?

EU soft law is a subset of the total output of the EU institutions. The other two elements of this output are hard law, mostly (but not all) in the form of legislation, and items that cannot be classified as legal at all (ie, non-legal material). Ever since EU soft law became a subject of academic attention,[3] repeated attempts have been made to present a workable definition that would make it possible to properly distinguish soft law from hard law on the one hand and from non-legal material on the other.[4] While no clear consensus exists, it is generally agreed that, ultimately, EU hard law has a legal basis in the EU treaties, has binding legal force and can generally be judicially enforced.[5] Prominent grey areas between soft and hard law include foreign policy and macroeconomic steering, as output in these fields can contain binding legal obligations that are not judicially enforceable.[6] Soft law typically lacks these characteristics – it does not necessarily have a legal basis in the treaties, it is not legally binding and hence it cannot be judicially enforced. It is perhaps more problematic to differentiate between soft law and non-legal matter.[7] As a minimum threshold, a document or statement needs to have been authored by an EU institution or agency and aim to influence the behaviour of a target audience. Soft law in this sense has been referred to as 'rules of conduct' that, while not legally binding, aim at a 'practical effect'.[8] This excludes, at the very least, trivial statements by individuals and purely informative material, such as annual reports or statistics. However, it is impossible to systematically exclude classes of documents and acts from this minimum threshold of soft law. After all, ECB President Mario Draghi's speech in July 2012, in which he announced that the ECB would do 'whatever it takes to preserve the euro', outlined the ECB's future conduct and aimed at calming investor anxiety.[9] As such, it fits the minimum soft law definition above and may have been the most effective piece of soft law ever produced.

[3] R Baldwin and J Houghton, 'Circular Arguments: The Status and Legitimacy of Administrative Rules' (1986) 2 *Public Law* 239; KC Wellens and GM Borchardt, 'Soft Law in European Community Law' (1989) 14 *EL Rev* 267; F Snyder, 'Soft Law and Institutional Practice in the European Community' in S Martin (ed), *The Construction of Europe* (Dordrecht, Kluwer, 1994) 197.

[4] For an overview of different definitions, see O Ştefan, M Avbelj, M Eliantonio, M Hartlapp, E Korkea-aho and N Rubio, 'EU Soft Law in the EU Legal Order: A Literature Review' (2019) SoLaR Working Paper, https://ssrn.com/abstract=3346629.

[5] Senden (n 2) 45; F Terpan, 'Soft Law in the European Union: The Changing Nature of EU Law' (2015) 21 *European Law Journal* 68, 76.

[6] S Saurugger and F Terpan, 'Studying Resistance to EU Norms in Foreign and Security Policy' (2015) 20 *European Foreign Affairs Review* 1.

[7] M Cini, 'The Soft Law Approach: Commission Rule-Making in the EU's State Aid Regime' (2001) 8 *Journal of European Public Policy* 192, 194.

[8] F Snyder, 'The Effectiveness of European Community Law: Institutions, Processes, Tools and Techniques' (1993) 56 *MLR* 19, 64; Senden (n 2) 112.

[9] Speech by Mario Draghi, President of the European Central Bank at the Global Investment Conference, London, 26 July 2012, www.ecb.europa.eu/press/key/date/2012/html/sp120726.en.html.

Some soft law does have a legal basis in the EU Treaties. The Treaties enumerate five types of legal acts by which the EU can exercise its competences (Article 288 of the Treaty on the Functioning of the European Union (TFEU)). Regulations, directives and decisions are legally binding, whereas 'recommendations and opinions shall have no binding force' (Article 288(5) TFEU). In this sense, the treaties themselves make a distinction between hard law and soft law. But just as regulations, directives and decisions are not an exhaustive list of sources of EU hard law (primary law itself and Court of the Justice of the European Union (CJEU) case law are also sources of hard law), soft law evidently comes in more guises than only recommendations and opinions. Just how much of the EU output is soft law is therefore difficult to quantify. One such attempt[10] used a random sample from the EU's 1997 'directory of legislation in force'[11] to conclude that regulations, directives and decisions (in the meaning of Article 288 TFEU) make up 67 per cent of the EU's legal acts, while recommendations and opinions together amount to about 5 per cent. The rest of the sample consisted of acts not listed in Article 288 TFEU, of which another small portion (6 per cent of the whole sample) were non-binding acts, such as Council resolutions and Commission communications.[12] This suggests that, in 1997,[13] about 11 per cent of what the compilers of the directory[14] term 'legislation in force' consisted of soft law[15] – a small but not insignificant part of the EU's legal output.

To this has to be added the hardly quantifiable array of non-binding acts that the Publications Office does not classify as 'legal acts', but that still fall under the definition of soft law. Some of these acts, such as Commission notices, are published in the C-series of the Official Journal (which contains 'information and notices'), but this series also contains a good amount of items that cannot be classified as either hard or soft law (such as euro exchange rates). In keeping with the ad hoc nature in which EU institutions often employ soft law, many other (likely most) soft law acts are not systematically accessible through the official EUR-Lex portal or any other single repository. There is a general impression that the output of EU soft law has grown significantly in recent times,[16] but empirical evidence remains difficult to assemble. EUR-Lex currently lists 37,175 legal acts as legislation in force,[17] of which only 614 are recommendations and

[10] A von Bogdandy, F Arndt and J Bast, 'Legal Instruments in European Union Law and Their Reform: A Systematic Approach on an Empirical Basis' (2004) 23 *Yearbook of European Law* 91.

[11] Available at: eur-lex.europa.eu.

[12] Von Bogdandy et al (n 10) 97.

[13] The authors state that a cursory sample from the 2001 directory returned similar results.

[14] EUR-Lex and the directory are managed by the Publications Office of the European Union, an inter-institutional office. It is not altogether transparent by what criteria the legal acts in the directory are compiled. Not all acts stem from the L-series of the Official Journal – some acts also appeared in the C-series; von Bogdandy et al, (n 10) 94.

[15] Another 9 per cent consisted of international agreements, a noted grey area.

[16] E Korkea-aho, *Adjudicating New Governance: Deliberative Democracy in the European Union* (Abingdon, Routledge, 2015); Terpan (n 5).

[17] Accessed through EUR-Lex advanced search, collection 'legal acts', limited to legislation in force.

417 are opinions; that is, while these two instruments made up 5 per cent of von Bogdandy et al.'s sample in 1997, they only make up 2.7 per cent of the current directory of legislation in force. This reduction could be an artefact of at times obscure book-keeping by the Publication Office, but it may also reflect a decline in the importance of the two formal soft law instruments listed in Article 288 TFEU relative to other legal acts. If the impression of a proliferation of soft law at the EU level is indeed correct, it will primarily comprise other more informal soft law instruments.

III. TYPES OF EU SOFT LAW

As the last paragraph indicates, EU soft law comes in a myriad of forms. In parallel with a definition of the outer limits of soft law, a number of attempts have been made to distinguish between different types of soft law.[18] While no taxonomy will ever successfully compartmentalise all forms of soft law, this chapter will draw on a distinction proposed by Linda Senden and will concentrate on two particular types of soft law (see Table 3.1) that are assumed to be particularly relevant in an analysis of the national impact of EU soft law, which is the subject of the SoLaR network and the country chapters in this volume.

Table 3.1 Two types of soft law

Type 1: close connection to hard law
interpretative soft law
decisional soft law
Type 2: weak or no connection to hard law
steering instruments

The first type comprises such soft law acts that, in the words of Linda Senden, 'provide guidance as to the interpretation and application of existing EU law'.[19] In other words, this type of soft law exists in close connection to a piece of hard law, to which it functions as a complement. This comprises interpretative guidelines issued by EU institutions, mostly the Commission,[20] relating to regulations, directives and in some instances CJEU case law.[21] Within this

[18] For an overview of different approaches, see Ştefan et al (n 4).

[19] Senden (n 2) 118.

[20] C van Dam, 'Guidance Documents of the European Commission: A Typology to Trace the Effects in the National Legal Order' (2017) 10 *Review of European Administrative Law* 75.

[21] See, eg, European Commission, 'Communication from the Commission concerning the consequences of the judgment given by the Court of Justice on 20 February 1979 in Case 120/78 (Cassis de Dijon)' [1980] OJ C256/2 or European Commission, 'Commission notice on access to justice in environmental matters' [2017] OJ C275/1.

type, Senden distinguishes two subtypes. The first subtype comprises acts that offer an interpretation of a piece of hard law for a third-party audience, such as a Commission document that outlines how protected areas should be managed under EU environmental legislation,[22] something which Senden calls 'interpretative' soft law.[23] The second subtype comprises acts that present an interpretation of a piece of hard law that guides the conduct of the author itself, such as Commission guidelines on how it interprets key terms in competition policy,[24] which it itself enforces (Senden calls this 'decisional' soft law).[25] The central characteristic of these subtypes of soft law is their close connection to hard law.

The other relevant type of soft law in turn comprises instruments that do not bear a close connection to hard law, but rather independently suggest a certain course of action, such as a Council recommendation on the integration of the long-term unemployed into the labour market.[26] This type of soft law outlines programmes and sets targets. It is often produced in fields where the EU has few legislative competences and therefore acts as an alternative to hard law (Senden calls this 'steering instruments').[27] To use recommendations (an important, but not the only soft law instrument of this type) as an example, 61 out of the 614 recommendations (about 10 per cent) listed in EUR-Lex under legislation in force pertain to the field of social policy,[28] where the EU has few legislative competences. In contrast, there are no recommendations of general application in the field of competition policy, a field of exclusive EU competence.[29] However, recommendations are also used in fields where the EU has legislative competences, such as the internal market (31 acts)[30] or environmental policy (38 acts).[31] Here, soft law may be a substitute where there is no political agreement on legislation.[32]

[22] See, eg, European Commission, *Managing Natura 2000 Sites: The Provisions of Article 6 of the 'Habitats' Directive 92/43/EEC* (Luxembourg, Office for Official Publications of the European Communities, 2000).

[23] Senden (n 2) 118.

[24] See, eg, European Commission, 'Communication from the Commission – Guidance on the Commission's enforcement priorities in applying Article 82 of the EC Treaty to abusive exclusionary conduct by dominant undertakings' [2009] OJ C45/7.

[25] Senden (n 2) 119.

[26] Council of the European Union, 'Council recommendation of 15 February 2016 on the integration of the long-term unemployed into the labour market' [2016] OJ C67/1.

[27] Senden (n 2) 119.

[28] Accessed through EUR-Lex advanced search, collection 'legal acts, limited to legislation in force, form: recommendations, directory code 05.20 (social policy)'.

[29] The directory code for competition policy is 08. The 15 Commission recommendations listed in the search results are directed at individual Member States (Portugal, France and Italy) and date from before 1988.

[30] Directory code 13.30 (Internal market: approximation of laws).

[31] Directory code 15.10 (environment).

[32] PL Láncos, 'Piercing the Soft Law Veil? The Hard Truth about Directive-Like Recommendations' (2020), https://papers.ssrn.com/sol3/papers.cfm?abstract_id=3670619.

IV. EU SOFT LAW IN SoLaR RESEARCH

In order to study the national use of EU soft law, the SoLaR project has selected a number of EU soft law instruments for in-depth investigation. These pieces of soft law are illustrative of the variety of instruments issued at the EU level. They stem from four policy fields: financial market regulation, competition policy, environmental protection and social policy. The selected instruments fall into different categories of soft law and differ both in terms of authorship and addressees. Based on the distinction introduced in the previous section, the following section provides details on these differences and how they might matter for the national use of the instruments.

A. Financial Market Regulation

All soft law instruments studied in the field of financial market regulation were authored by the European Securities and Markets Authority (ESMA).[33] ESMA is one of four institutions set up as part of the EU's system of financial supervision.[34] As a response to the international financial crisis, it was created in 2010 as an independent EU authority with the task of 'assisting competent national supervisory authorities in the consistent interpretation and application of Union rules and contributing to financial stability necessary for financial integration'. Its role is to supervise securities markets with a view to 'prevent regulatory arbitrage and guarantee a level playing field' by 'promoting supervisory convergence'.[35] For these purposes, ESMA is authorised to issue guidelines and recommendations addressed to the national supervisory bodies that it coordinates as well as directly to financial market participants. As soft law, these guidelines and regulations are not legally binding, but the addressees, both national authorities and market participants, are required to notify ESMA and justify their action in the event that they decide not to follow the soft law instruments. This 'comply or explain' mechanism, which is itself enshrined in hard law, guarantees at a minimum that national actors will be aware of the document and take at least some action; that is, this procedural component is enforceable, irrespective of the content of the soft law instrument. SoLaR selected four such guidelines for further investigation.

[33] For a detailed overview of research conducted, see M Avbelj (ed), 'EU Financial Regulation Soft Law in the Member States: Finland, France, Germany, Italy, the Netherlands, Slovenia and the UK' (2020) SoLaR Working Paper, https://papers.ssrn.com/sol3/papers.cfm?abstract_id=3668793.

[34] The other three institutions are the European Banking Authority (EBA), the European Insurance and Occupational Pensions Authority (EIOPA) and the European Systemic Risk Board (ESRB).

[35] Regulation (EU) No 1095/2010 of the European Parliament and of the Council of 24 November 2010 establishing a European Supervisory Authority [2010] OJ L331/84.

Table 3.2 Financial market regulation

Guidelines – exemptions for market-making activities and primary market operations under Regulation (EU) 236/2012 of the European Parliament and the Council on short selling and certain aspects of Credit Default Swaps	ESMA/2013/74
Guidelines – remuneration policies and practices (MiFID)	ESMA/2013/606
Guidelines on complaints handling for the securities (ESMA) and banking (EBA) sectors	JC/2014/43
ESMA guidelines on enforcement of financial information	ESMA/2014/1293

Three of these relate to a concrete piece of hard law, while the fourth does not. The guidelines on 'exemptions for market-making activities and primary market operations', which relate to the Short Selling Regulation,[36] and the 'guidelines on remuneration policies and practices', which relate to the Markets in Financial Instruments Directive',[37] are addressed to both financial market participants and national authorities, while the 'ESMA guidelines on enforcement of financial information', which relate to the Transparency Directive,[38] are addressed only to national authorities. The fourth soft law instrument, the 'guidelines on complaints handling for the securities and banking sectors', addressed only to national authorities, does not relate to a specific piece of hard law,[39] but, like the others, requires a report on compliance. The three pieces of soft law with a clear connection to financial market legislation can be classified as interpretative soft law as they address the behaviour of third parties and interpret specific aspects of legislation. The fourth has less clear connections to a specific piece of hard law, but is situated in the wider context of financial market legislation and shares with the others a hard procedural component. As such, it too is much more akin to interpretative soft law than a steering instrument. ESMA places these guidelines prominently on its website[40] and they are accessible through the ESMA library database. However, the instruments are not accessible through general EU law portals such as EUR-Lex and have not been published in the Official Journal.

[36] Regulation (EU) No 236/2012 of the European Parliament and of the Council of 14 March 2012 on short selling and certain aspects of credit default swaps [2012] OJ L86/1.

[37] Directive 2004/39/EC of the European Parliament and of the Council of 21 April 2004 on markets in financial instruments [2004] OJ L145/1.

[38] Directive 2004/109/EC of the European Parliament and of the Council of 15 December 2004 on the harmonisation of transparency requirements in relation to information about issuers whose securities are admitted to trading on a regulated market [2004] OJ L390/38.

[39] Unlike the others, the official ESMA table of guidelines does not list an 'overarching directive' for this document: www.esma.europa.eu/sites/default/files/library/esma_guidelines.pdf.

[40] www.esma.europa.eu.

B. Competition Policy

The soft law instruments selected for study in the field of competition are more numerous than the four instruments studied in the field of financial market regulation.[41] The selection comprised 13 instruments from the fields of state aid and anti-trust, in which the Commission is tasked with the direct enforcement of EU law vis-a-vis national authorities and third parties.

Table 3.3 Competition policy

Commission Communication on State aid elements in sales of land and buildings by public authorities	97/C 209/03
Commission Notice on cooperation within the Network of Competition Authorities	2004/C 101/03
Commission Notice on the cooperation between the Commission and the courts of the EU Member States in the application of Articles 81 and 82 EC	2004/C 101/04
Communication from the Commission – Notice – Guidelines on the application of Article 81(3) of the Treaty	2004/C 101/08
Communication from the Commission – Guidance on the Commission's enforcement priorities in applying Article 82 of the EC Treaty to abusive exclusionary conduct by dominant undertakings	2009/C 45/02
Commission notice on the enforcement of State aid law by national courts	2009/C 85/01
Guidelines on vertical restraints	2010/C 130/01
Communication from the Commission on the application, from 1 January 2011, of State aid rules to support measures in favour of banks in the context of the financial crisis	2010/C 329/07
Communication from the Commission – Guidelines on the applicability of Article 101 of the Treaty on the Functioning of the European Union to horizontal cooperation agreements	2011/C 11/01
Communication from the Commission on State aid for films and other audiovisual works	2013/C 332/01
Communication from the Commission – Guidelines on State aid for environmental protection and energy 2014–20	2014/C 200/01
Communication from the Commission – Notice on agreements of minor importance which do not appreciably restrict competition under Article 101(1) of the Treaty on the Functioning of the European Union	2014/C 291/01
Commission Notice on the notion of State aid as referred to in Article 107(1) of the Treaty on the Functioning of the European Union	2016/C 262/01

[41] For a detailed overview of research conducted, see O Ştefan (ed), 'EU Competition and State Aid Soft Law in the Member States: Finland, France, Germany, Italy, the Netherlands, Slovenia and the UK' (2020) SoLaR Working Paper, https://papers.ssrn.com/sol3/papers.cfm?abstract_id=3667387.

All of these soft law instruments are authored by the Commission and inform the target audience of the way in which the Commission intends to enforce EU law on state aid and antitrust. To illustrate this, the Commission's 1997 communication on 'state aid elements in sales of land and buildings by public authorities' states its purpose in the following way: 'The Commission has drawn up general guidance to Member States in order to make its general approach with regard to the problem of state aid through sales of land and buildings by public authorities transparent and to reduce the number of cases it has to examine.' All soft law instruments in this field have a close connection to hard law – much of it to primary law. They can therefore all be classified as decisional soft law. While they inform us of the author's (the Commission's) own conduct, they simultaneously address the behaviour of third parties – public authorities in state aid and private companies in antitrust – so that they reorient their behaviour in expectation of the Commission response. The distinction between interpretative and decisional soft law is therefore not entirely clear-cut.[42]

The chosen soft law instruments are also illustrative of the complexity of soft law nomenclature. While all instruments pursue the same objective, they come with a variety of labels. Commission 'notices' at least overlap with the nomenclature of the Official Journal C-series (for 'information and notices'), but 'communication', the hybrid 'communication – notice' and simply 'guidelines' conform to no official format. Nonetheless, all selected instruments were published in the Official Journal C-series.

C. Environmental Protection

The soft law instruments selected in the field of environmental protection are even more numerous than those in competition policy.[43] Rather than identifying a closed list of instruments, research in this field concentrated on the soft law produced at the EU level in connection with three central pieces of legislation in EU environmental law: the Environmental Impact Assessment Directive,[44] the Habitats Directive[45] and the Water Framework Directive.[46] By design, the

[42] Ştefan et al (n 4) 20.

[43] For a detailed overview of the research conducted, see M Eliantonio and G Lisi, 'EU Environmental Soft Law in the Member States: A Comparative Overview of Finland, France, Germany, Italy, the Netherlands, Slovenia and the UK' (2020) SoLaR Working Paper, https://papers.ssrn.com/sol3/papers.cfm?abstract_id=3656418.

[44] Originally Council Directive 85/337/EEC of 27 June 1985 on the assessment of the effects of certain public and private projects on the environment [1985] OJ L175/40, replaced by Directive 2011/92/EU of the European Parliament and of the Council of 13 December 2011 on the assessment of the effects of certain public and private projects on the environment [2011] OJ L26/1.

[45] Council Directive 92/43/EEC of 21 May 1992 on the conservation of natural habitats and of wild fauna and flora [1992] OJ L206/7.

[46] Directive 2000/60/EC of the European Parliament and of the Council of 23 October 2000 establishing a framework for Community action in the field of water policy [2000] OJ L327/1.

soft law under investigation in this field bears a close connection to hard law. Nonetheless, the instruments come from different authors and in a wide variety of formats.[47]

Table 3.4 Environmental protection

Soft law relating to Directive 2011/92/EU of 13 December 2011 on the assessment of the effects of certain public and private projects on the environment	Directive 85/337/EEC, 2011/92/EU
Soft law relating to Directive 92/43/EEC of 21 May 1992 on the conservation of natural habitats and of wild fauna and flora	Directive 92/43/EEC
Soft law relating to Directive 2000/60/EC of 23 October 2000 establishing a framework for Community action in the field of water policy	Directive 2000/60/EC

All of the soft law instruments relating to the environmental impact assessment directive are listed on the corresponding Commission website under the heading 'guidance and research'. The site states that the instruments 'can be of interest to authorities, developers, consultants, researchers, organisations and to the public'.[48] The earliest documents listed on the site (and hence in the SoLaR sample) stem from 1999 to 2001 and were primarily authored by external consultants under research contracts with the Commission. As an illustration, the 1999 'guidelines for the assessment of indirect and cumulative impacts', authored by the consultancy 'Hyder' under contract with the Commission, were compiled to 'advise practitioners … how to approach these kinds of impacts during the various stages of [impact assessment], how to adapt the approach to a specific project and [to suggest] methods and tools'. The earliest document authored by the Commission itself is a 'clarification of the application of article 2(3) of the EIA directive'. This article allows for exemptions from impact assessment requirements in 'exceptional cases'. The soft law instrument states that 'no indication is provided in the directive of how the term "exceptional cases" should be interpreted, and experience shows that doubts may arise as to when the provisions of this article can be legitimately invoked. The aim of this document is to assist Member States' authorities in deciding when and how [the article] should be applied'. The other soft law instruments pursue a similar purpose and come in formats such as 'communications from the Commission' (not published in the Official Journal), 'guidance notes', 'guidance documents' or simply 'guidance', 'interpretation' or 'booklet' (the latter on the 'most important rulings' of the Court of Justice on impact assessment). The only instrument in the sample

[47] See also M Eliantonio, 'Soft Law in Environmental Matters and the Role of the European Courts: Too Much or Too Little of it?' (2018) 37 *Yearbook of European Law* 496.

[48] ec.europa.eu/environment/eia/eia-support.htm.

that was published in the Official Journal C-series was a 2016 'Commission notice – Commission guidance document on streamlining environmental assessments' (OJ C273/1).

The soft law instruments in the sample relating to the Habitats Directive follow the template of those relating to the Impact Assessment Directive. They too are collected on the respective Commission websites under the heading 'guidance'[49] and come in multiple formats, including 'guidance documents' and 'Commission notes' (not 'notice', hence not published in the Official Journal). They too are partially authored by consultants under contract with the Commission. The sample contains three instruments that were published in the Official Journal C-series: a 2019 document entitled 'Managing Natura 2000 sites' (OJ C33/1), which was 'drafted following consultations with the nature protection authorities of the Member States and stakeholders', and two 'Commission notices' published back-to-back in 2018, the first entitled 'Guidance document on the requirements for hydropower in relation to EU nature legislation' (OJ C213/1) and the second 'Energy transmission infrastructure and EU nature legislation' (OJ C213/62). The content of the latter two in particular does not differ significantly from other guidance documents (such as 'Natura 2000 and forests' or 'Farming for Natura 2000') that were not published in the Official Journal – it is unclear which publication policy the Commission follows.

The soft law instruments studied in relation to the Water Framework Directive do not differ significantly in substance or purpose, but they differ in terms of authorship. Implementation of the Water Framework Directive takes place within a 'common implementation strategy' that includes several formalised 'working groups' and 'expert advisory fora',[50] which prepare 'guidance documents' that are signed off by both the Commission and the national water managers. The documents are consecutively numbered and published on the respective Commission website[51] (but not in the Official Journal). To date, 36 such instruments have been produced and included in the study.

The soft law instruments selected from these three subfields of environmental policy all share the purpose of giving practical guidance in the implementation of technically complex pieces of legislation, including the interpretation of ambiguous legal terms. The addressees are both national authorities and private parties (mostly developers). As such, all selected soft law in the field of environmental protection can clearly be classified as interpretative soft law.

[49] Separated by subject matter: 'Natura 2000 network' (ec.europa.eu/environment/nature/natura2000/management/guidance_en.htm) and 'species protection' (ec.europa.eu/environment/nature/conservation/species/guidance/index_en.htm).

[50] European Commission, 'Common implementation strategy for the water framework directive (2000/60/EC)', strategic document, 2 May 2001.

[51] ec.europa.eu/environment/water/water-framework/facts_figures/guidance_docs_en.htm.

D. Social Policy

Three soft law instruments were selected in the field of social policy.[52] These instruments include comparatively formal pieces of soft law, but they are at the same comparatively remote from EU hard law relative to the other instruments in the sample.

Table 3.5 Social policy

Buying social. A Guide to Taking Account of Social Considerations in Public Procurement	SEC(2010) 1258
Commission Recommendation of 20 February 2013 – Investing in children: breaking the cycle of disadvantage	2013/112/EU
Commission Recommendation of 7 March 2014 on strengthening the principle of equal pay between men and women through transparency	2014/124/EU

The Buying Social guide was initially adopted by the Commission as a staff working document in 2010 (and can as such be accessed in the Commission register of documents, but not EUR-Lex) and was reworked in 2011 into a book publication (with its own ISBN) by the Publication Office. The document states that 'the Commission has widely consulted public authorities in the Member States and many other interested parties and stakeholders' when drafting the instrument. The instrument states its purpose as '(a) to raise contracting authorities' awareness of the potential benefits of [socially responsible public procurement] and (b) to explain in a practical way the opportunities offered by the existing EU legal framework'. It provides guidance 'chiefly for public authorities', but expresses the hope 'that it will inspire private-sector purchasers too'. The instrument clearly has a connection to (hard) EU public procurement law and, as such, classifies as interpretative soft law. It differs from other such instruments in the sample, in that its contents represent a break from previous interpretations of the respective hard law – while previously the sole criterion for selecting tenders in EU public procurement law was the lowest price, the instrument encourages the consideration of social criteria.[53] It therefore presents an interesting case to investigate whether an established interpretation of hard law can be significantly altered through soft law.

The Commission recommendation on investing in children is one of only two soft law instruments in the sample that conform to a format listed in

[52] For a detailed overview of the research conducted, see M Hartlapp (ed), 'Studying EU Soft Law Effects in Social Policy' (2020) SoLaR Working Paper, https://papers.ssrn.com/sol3/papers.cfm?abstract_id=3668981.

[53] M Hartlapp, 'Soft Law Implementation in the EU Multilevel System: Legitimacy and Governance Efficiency Revisited' in N Behnke, J Broschek and J Sonnicksen (eds), *Configurations, Dynamics and Mechanisms of Multilevel Governance* (London, Palgrave Macmillan, 2019) 193, 203.

Article 288 TFEU. It is published in the 2013 Official Journal L-series for legislation (OJ L59/5) and appears in the directory of legislation in force on EUR-Lex. The instrument acknowledges that 'policies addressing child poverty are primarily the competence of Member States', but suggests that 'a common European framework can strengthen synergies across relevant policy areas, help Member States review their policies and learn from each other's experiences'. It therefore 'recommends that Member States organise and implement policies to address child poverty and social exclusion ... in accordance with the following guidelines'. It addresses a field with little legislative competences at the EU level and suggests a course of action in the absence of legislation. As such, it is a classic steering instrument.[54]

The other soft law instrument to conform to a format listed in Article 288 TFEU is the Commission recommendation on transparency in equal pay. It too was published in 2014 in the Official Journal L-series (OJ L 69/112) and is listed in the directory. The instrument addresses a field (gender discrimination and equal pay) in which EU hard law exists in both primary law and a specialised directive on the implementation of the principle of equal opportunities and equal treatment of men and women,[55] but this hard law does not specifically address the subject of the instrument – the transparency of wage categories, which the Commission finds 'essential for the effective application of the equal pay principle'. The recommendation therefore 'provides guidance to Member States to assist them in a better and more effective implementation of the equal pay principle in order to combat pay discrimination and to contribute to tackling the persistent gender pay gap'. Since it expands on rather than merely interpret existing hard law, this document can be classified as a steering instrument, albeit with some connection to hard law.

It would be difficult to claim that the selected soft law instruments in all four policy fields constitute a representative sample of EU soft law in general. While they are illustrative of the variety of soft law used in the EU and contain the most relevant formats, little can be said about representativeness in a numerical sense. The total population of EU soft law, after all, is largely unknown. What can be said is that the selected soft law instruments are representative of soft law issued *in their field*. The selected instruments therefore have a strong connection to hard law in fields where important EU hard law exists and where the EU has evident legislative competences. The only two steering instruments in the sample stem from the field of social policy, where the EU has comparatively few legislative competences and the existing corpus of hard law is much smaller.

The sample is clearly skewed towards interpretative and decisional soft law, and research results have correspondingly less to say about the national impact

[54] ibid 203.

[55] Directive 2006/54/EC of the European Parliament and of the Council of 5 July 2006 on the implementation of the principle of equal opportunities and equal treatment of men and women in matters of employment and occupation (recast) [2006] OJ L204/23.

of steering instruments, of which EU institutions have produced a lot. At the same time, this type of soft law most closely resembles the instruments used in the context of the 'open method of coordination' in employment and social policy and, more recently, the 'European semester', the national impact of which has been extensively studied.[56] However, future research could direct more attention to the national impact of soft law instruments that are atypical for their field – in particular, steering instruments (such as recommendations) in fields where the EU has strong legislative competences.

V. THE NATIONAL USE OF EU SOFT LAW

The SoLaR project set out to investigate how the selected pieces of EU soft law operate at the national level and how they are used by national administrations and the judiciary. There is reason to believe that the distinction between soft law that has a strong connection to hard law (interpretative and decisional soft law) and soft law that does not (steering instruments) will be particularly useful in addressing the questions asked by the SoLaR project. The first type – soft law with a close connection to hard law – should be more likely to be taken up by national authorities for several reasons. For one thing, the literature on 'new modes of governance' expects greater impact from soft law operating in the 'shadow of hierarchy'[57] as it is part of mutually interdependent relationships involving different types of public authority and problem-solving styles. Theories of the policy cycle typically expect a (hard) piece of EU legislation to initiate reform or policy change at the national level. As part of this process, guidance by soft law instruments may be welcomed by national actors tasked with implementation. Hard law typically comes with at least some degree of legal uncertainty and room for interpretation. 'Street level bureaucracy'[58] may welcome accompanying soft law as it reduces complexity. It is less likely that national actors will take up EU steering instruments without this connection to hard law. This can be because national actors may simply not be aware that the EU instrument exists. By its nature, soft law typically lacks deadlines for

[56] See, eg, S Bekker, 'EU Coordination of Welfare States after the Crisis: Further Interconnecting Soft and Hard Law' (2014) 19 *International Review of Public Administration* 296; CF Sabel and J Zeitlin, 'Learning from Difference: The New Architecture of Experimentalist Governance in the EU' (2008) 14 *European Law Journal* 271; I Maher, 'Law and the Open Method of Coordination: Towards a New Flexibility in European Policy-Making?' (2004) 2 *Zeitschrift für Staats und Europawissenschaften* 248; DM Trubek and LG Trubek, 'Hard and Soft Law in the Construction of Social Europe: The Role of the Open Method of Co-ordination' (2005) 11 *European Law Journal* 343.

[57] D Lehmkuhl, 'Cooperation and Hierarchy in EU Competition Policy' in I Tömmel and A Verdun (eds), *Innovative Governance in the European Union: The Politics of Multilevel Policy-making* (Boulder, Lynne Rienner, 2008) 103.

[58] M Lipsky, *Street-Level Bureaucracy: The Dilemmas of Individuals in the Public Service* (New York, Sage, 1980).

transpositions that would require action at the national level (but see the exceptions in financial market regulation). Moreover, soft law instruments that are issued without a link to hard law are more likely to reflect a lack of EU legislative competences or a lack of agreement between EU policy-makers. This might indicate greater resistance among national authorities to altering national rules. It can therefore be hypothesised that the actions of national authorities will more likely align with the content of soft law that has a close connection with hard law than with soft law that does not.

The results of the SoLaR project point in this direction.[59] While differences exist between countries, interview partners in national authorities, particularly those close to policy implementation 'on the ground', generally expressed a familiarity with interpretive and decisional soft law. They highlighted the advantages of the flexible nature of such soft law in adapting to current circumstances as well as its ability to deal with sensitive issues, while retaining a degree of national discretion that hard law lacks.[60] There is an appreciation of the practical guidance that interpretative soft law offers for complex and technical pieces of legislation, although at times soft law itself appears overly technical to practitioners.[61] Interpretative soft law is considered of high quality, which raises the bar for officials to argue against it.[62] A number of interviewees have described such soft law as 'de facto binding', as it is routinely followed by authorities as well as private actors who operate under the regulatory frameworks.[63] Courts also make frequent use of interpretative soft law. The analysis of national case law databases returned a large number of cases with concrete references to interpretative EU soft law, particularly in the fields of environmental and competition policy. This was confirmed in an interview with a Dutch administrative judge, who pointed out that such EU soft law might become binding on account of frequent references in case law.[64] Practitioners in policy fields with a high degree of exposure to EU rules, such as competition policy, use interpretative and decisional EU soft law reflexively, without much concern for its validity[65] or legitimacy.[66] Apart from its practical value as an implementation aid, interviewees also pointed out that adjusting their behaviour to interpretative soft law reduces the risk of becoming the subject of Commission infringement proceedings,[67] which is further evidence that the distinction between interpretative and decisional soft law is not always easy to maintain in practice.

[59] For Germany, see M Hartlapp and A Hofmann, 'The Use of EU Soft Law by National Courts and Bureaucrats: How Relation to Hard Law and Policy Maturity Matter' (2020) *West European Politics*.

[60] Avbelj (n 33) 21.

[61] Eliantonio and Lisi (n 43) 15–16.

[62] ibid 16.

[63] Avbelj (n 33) 20; Ştefan (n 41) 85.

[64] Ştefan (n 41) 26.

[65] ibid.

[66] ibid 85.

[67] Eliantonio and Lisi (n 43) 22, 57.

At the other end of the spectrum, the instrument with the least connection to hard law in the SoLaR sample of EU soft law, the Commission recommendation on investing in children, a steering instrument intended to induce policy change in national responses to child poverty, was used sparingly in the Member States in the study. Despite the fact that it was generally known among interview respondents, only authorities in Finland, France and Italy showed a concrete response, with national soft law instruments issued in France and Italy, and a hard piece of legislation in Finland that cues aspects of the recommendation concerning early childhood education and measures against child poverty.[68] For Finland and Italy, there are indications that national agencies and ombudspersons tasked with children's rights championed the national uptake of the EU soft law instrument. In the absence of such bodies, little usage was detected.[69] No court references to this steering instrument could be identified either.

VI. CONCLUSION

This chapter has presented characteristics of EU soft law in distinction from hard law and instruments that cannot be classified as legal at all. It has demonstrated that definitions of soft law produce grey areas in both directions, although it appeared more difficult to delineate soft law from no law at all. It has highlighted that EU soft law does not follow a predefined format. In fact, it is issued under many different labels; recommendations and opinions are officially recognised as soft law in the EU treaties, but other labels such as guidelines, guidance documents and notes are also frequently found. Nomenclature does not seem to follow consistent rules, as many such documents have very similar content. Likewise, there appear to be no consistent rules about where such soft law is published. Even soft law instruments authored by a single body, such as the Commission, is sometimes published in the Official Journal C-series and sometimes merely published on topical webpages or online repositories. Given this complexity, this chapter has proposed a simple typology, resting on a distinction between soft law instruments that have a close connection to a piece of EU hard law (interpretative and decisional soft law) and soft law instruments that do not have such a connection (steering instruments). Most soft law studied by the SoLaR network, the results of which are published in this volume, conform to the former type (interpretative and decisional soft law). They are typical instruments in areas with dense EU regulatory competences, such as environmental policy, competition policy and, more recently, financial market regulation. The only steering instruments in the SoLaR sample stem from the area of social policy, a policy field with traditionally fewer legislative competences and fewer

[68] Hartlapp (n 52) 16–17.
[69] ibid.

binding hard law instruments. In line with the expectations formulated in this chapter, research results from within the SoLaR network indicate that the first type of soft law (interpretive and decisional soft law) sees greater use by administrations and the judiciary at the national level than the second type. Certainly, more fine-grained empirical analysis as well as case selection more explicitly based on the distinction between the two types of soft law would provide more robust results in this regard. However, the insights presented in this chapter and throughout this volume should provide a fruitful basis for further investigation on what impact EU soft law has at the national level.

4

'Whatever-Law' and Teenage Member States? The National Reception of EU Soft Law and How to Study It

MIRIAM HARTLAPP AND EMILIA KORKEA-AHO

I. INTRODUCTION

SCHOLARS AND PRACTITIONERS broadly agree that EU non-binding instruments, commonly referred to as soft law, are on the rise.[1] What is more, this volume demonstrates that Member States abide by EU soft law. National compliance with soft law is, at least at a glance, hard to grasp, because the concept of compliance presupposes a formal requirement to adhere to a norm.

In the multi-level context of the EU, compliance with the law arises from the treaty-based requirement for Member States to implement directives on time and in accordance with the objectives of the directive in question.[2] However, compliance is not limited to changing what is said in law books. Norm implementation must be followed by behavioural 'law in action' compliance.[3] Neither formally applies to soft law. There is no enforceable requirement to implement or apply EU soft law. Deadlines and notification processes usually only concern hard law implementation. Nor are there third parties, such as national or supranational courts, to enforce 'in action' compliance by Member States with EU soft law.

[1] No comprehensive statistical data is available, acutely reflecting the complexities involved in studying soft law: how can statistical data be gathered on something that exists under so many different names and in so many forms? Some attempts have been made at measuring and systematising soft law. See A Hofmann, ch 3 in this volume; and A von Bogdandy, F Arndt and J Bast, 'Legal Instruments in European Union Law and Their Reform: A Systematic Approach on an Empirical Basis' (2004) 23 *Yearbook of European Law* 91.

[2] Article 288 TFEU.

[3] With the Commission as an ultimate guardian of this pursuant to art 257 TFEU.

This has implications for the conceptualisation and methodology of studies interested in terms of how and to what extent soft law is received at the national level. This volume paints an inconsistent and complex scene of national reception of soft law. Soft law can be incorporated into national legislation, it can be relied upon by the national decision-maker regularly – irrespective of the fact that it has never been implemented in letter or spirit – or it can be dealt with by civil servants frequently, yet never expressly referred to, being considered weak or superfluous. If this is the case, *how do we then map and systematically study the national reception of EU soft law?*

To address this question, we provide a conceptual and methodological contribution. We conceptualise the national reception of soft law as four distinct Member State options: (1) formally transpose and comply with soft law; (2) choose not to officially transpose but apply nevertheless; (3) ignore and passively resist soft law;[4] or (4) actively defy and take action deviating from the norm[5] – a typology we develop in more depth against our empirical findings towards the end of this chapter. This conceptualisation is general enough to offer comparison with, and allow analytical import from, hard law implementation research, while being specific enough to capture and differentiate the empirical effects of soft law.

Our conceptualisation, which relies on implementation research, requires justification because studies of EU implementation are focused on hard law, typically overlooking soft law as what we describe as 'whatever-law', often also implying the Member States' lack of active agency in the process. Analysing the national reception of soft law from a broader perspective of implementation research yields a nuanced image of how soft law is received nationally. Soft law matters nationally, but 'soft law Europe' is more differential than' hard law Europe'.[6] Not only does EU soft law come in different forms 'that largely escape succinct taxonomies',[7] but national responses to EU soft law also differ more than responses to hard law. While in some cases, EU soft law is taken seriously and its implementation into national law takes place much like the implementation of EU hard law, in other cases, soft law is neglected or even resisted – something which in the case of hard law would be against the treaties.

We explain this national variation with reference to the conceptional fuzziness of soft law compliance and the fact that our research methods bring to the forefront the differential situation on the ground. Where national actors do not

[4] For norm resistance, see S Saurugger and F Terpan, 'Studying Resistance to EU Norms in Foreign and Security Policy' (2015) 20 *European Foreign Affairs Review* 1.

[5] M Hartlapp, 'Soft Law Implementation in the EU Multilevel System: Legitimacy and Governance Efficiency Revisited' in N Behnke et al (eds), *Configurations, Dynamics and Mechanism of Multilevel Governance* (London, Palgrave Macmillan, 2019) 193.

[6] A Windhoff-Héritier et al, *Differential Europe: The European Union Impact on National Policymaking* (Lanham, MD, Rowman & Littlefield, 2001).

[7] M Hartlapp and A Hofmann, 'The Use of EU Soft Law by National Courts and Bureaucrats: How Relation to Hard Law and Policy Maturity Matter' has been published in the meantime: (2021) 44 *West European Politics* 134, DOI: 10.1080/01402382.2020.1738095.

have a clear-cut understanding of what constitutes a permissible and legitimate continuum of responses to EU soft law, the national reception of EU soft law is influenced by the role played by soft law in the national legal order as well as the legal, political and cultural context of the country. This is important and relevant to studies of hard law implementation, as well. The research on the implementation of framework directives has shown that a standard implementation story falls short of capturing national idiosyncrasies and country-specific (vested) interests involved in ensuring that open-ended provisions are correctly transposed and applied in Member States.[8] The diversity of soft law instruments and policy fields also plays a role, and the narratives of the national reception of soft law are policy field-specific. This suggests that in addition to widely discussed questions of efficiency and legitimacy, diversity is a third important dimension when appraising EU soft law.[9]

Another contribution is methodological and follows from the above conceptualisation. The study of national reception of EU soft law is a complicated task, for soft law compliance does not necessarily include changes in the legal or political governance of the Member States. How then should data be collected and utilised to understand national reception, let alone compare different reactions of countries? We argue that the methods that have been employed in studies on EU hard law compliance cannot easily be transferred to study and explain compliance with soft law. On the one hand, and unlike with the transposition of directives, there is no 'baseline compliance' (or non-compliance for that matter) against which we might be able to analyse and compare countries. On the other hand, there are usually no deadlines or formal notification processes for EU soft law. Hence, research on EU soft law must deploy a wide range of methods to detect and trace national effects. Drawing on socio-legal approaches and methods used by political scientists studying implementation, we argue that qualitative expert interviews and case law analysis are particularly suited to this task. Below we do not only discuss the methods used to obtain our findings, but we also connect our methodological choices to empirical results and theoretical findings.

Above we have used the terms 'reception', 'compliance' and 'implementation' almost interchangeably. For the purposes of this chapter, 'reception' is the broadest term, including all kinds of ways in which Member States respond to a regulatory trigger from Brussels, and it covers all of the four options identified in the above typology. 'Compliance' commonly refers to behaviour that positively conforms to a norm and in terms of our typology, it covers the first three of the four. This is obvious with respect to the first (official compliance) and second (de facto compliance) categories, but is less obvious in terms of the third category (ignorance). However, we conceptualise ignorance as a form of compliance,

[8] E Korkea-aho, 'Watering down the Court of Justice? The Dynamics between Network Implementation and Article 258 TFEU Litigation' (2014) 20 *European Law Journal*, 649.

[9] E Korkea-aho, 'EU Soft Law in Domestic Legal Systems: Flexibility and Diversity Guaranteed?' (2009) 16 *Maastricht Journal of European and Comparative Law* 271.

because our empirical data suggests that ignorance is frequently linked to situations in which a Member State already has the same or similar rules in place; in other words, an 'ignorant' Member State may already be fully compliant with EU soft law norms. Finally, 'implementation' means putting in place policies and rules and applying them.[10] Unlike compliance, the term 'implementation' refers to changes in law and practice, and cannot occur without active engagement with EU policies. While in most cases the outcome of this engagement will be new policies and actual application, we may, theoretically at least, envisage an implementation process that involves active defiance on the part of the Member State. Section II below will show that the choice of terms also reflects preferences of different research traditions, with the term 'compliance' more likely being used when talking about (hard) legislation. Soft law, if studied at all, is 'used', 'implemented' or 'received'.

The remainder of this chapter is organised as follows. Section II discusses the state of the art of EU compliance/implementation studies. Section III discusses the multi-method approach chosen for the SoLaR project. Section IV shows how our chosen methodology affords a systematic, comparative and contextual understanding of the empirical results and theoretical findings. Section V concludes.

II. NATIONAL RECEPTION OF SOFT LAW: A SEARCH FOR A FRAMEWORK

The national implementation of EU hard law is a perennial concern for the EU and the Commission as the guardian of the treaties.[11] In a bid to avoid going down the judicial route, the Commission tries to ensure implementation through a consensus-seeking dialogue with a potentially non-compliant Member State, and only in cases where the dialogue has fallen short of providing a credible solution to the problem does the Commission launch the infringement proceedings pursuant to Article 258 of the Treaty on the Functioning of the European Union (TFEU).[12] The Commission is keen to try out new tricks, ranging from scoreboards and peer reviews to information exchange systems,[13] or an informal problem-solving network SOLVIT.[14]

[10] The notion of 'transposition' is often used narrowly to refer to the legal process by which Member States adopt EU directives as part of national legal systems.

[11] EU Commission, EU Law: Better Results through Better Application, Brussels, 21.12.2016 C(2016) 8600 final. See also O Treib, 'Implementing and Complying with EU Governance Outputs' (2014) 9 *Living Reviews European Governance* 21; G Falkner et al, *Complying with Europe. EU Minimum Harmonisation and Soft Law in the Member States* (Cambridge, Cambridge University Press, 2005); M Haverland and M Romeijn, 'Do Member States Make European Policies Work?: Analysing the EU Transposition Deficit' (2007) 85 *Public Administration* 757. Many of these studies are part of the Europeanisation literature, focusing on instruments that are legally binding.

[12] The EU publishes annually a report on the application of EU law. For the latest 36th report, see https://ec.europa.eu/info/publications/2018-commission-report-monitoring-application-eu-law_en.

[13] https://ec.europa.eu/internal_market/imi-net/index_en.htm.

[14] http://ec.europa.eu/solvit/index_en.htm.

The combination of methodologies is a characteristic of the EU's complex implementation policy. First, the EU combines both coercive[15] and problem-solving strategies.[16] Second, it has learnt to carefully navigate between regional, national and supranational levels of government, and to motivate actors across this multi-level system to improve implementation. For instance, national courts play an important role in ensuring Member State implementation and enforcement of EU law.[17] Third, EU soft law is increasingly used to tackle compliance issues. In other words, soft law itself is becoming an enforcement tool for the implementation of hierarchically higher binding norms.[18] In addition to studies assessing how Member States have transposed EU directives, an interest in the 'law in action' research emerges and highlights the dilemma that even perfectly 'even rules' may result in 'uneven practices'.[19] This 'in action' strand has been spurred by the conviction that it is not enough to ensure that EU law is correctly paraphrased in domestic law books. Therefore, rather than assessing Member States' transposition of law, the focus should be on the application of law – that is, whether individuals are adequately informed about their rights or whether national authorities enforce and correctly apply EU law. This research has nevertheless remained a minority position in wider compliance studies, not least because it is research-intensive.

Neither implementation studies nor law in action research have paid much attention to the national reception of soft law, and studies on the compliance with EU soft law are few. An exception is the research on the Open Method of Coordination (OMC), a new governance regulatory instrument introduced by the Treaty of Amsterdam. There are no formal hoops to jump through in order to be compliant with the OMC, and its reception and national effects manifest themselves in many forms. Regarding the European Employment Strategy (EES), the OMC instrument was argued to be capable of defining what problems domestic policy-makers should address, identifying good policy options, limiting the number of policy options policy-makers should consider and helping

[15] M Dougan, 'From the Velvet Glove to the Iron Fist: Criminal Sanctions for the Enforcement of Union Law' in M Cremona (ed), *Compliance and the Enforcement of EU Law* (Oxford, Oxford University Press, 2012).

[16] M Hartlapp, 'On Enforcement, Management and Persuasion. Different Logics of Implementation Policy in the EU and the ILO' (2007) 45 *Journal of Common Market Studies* 653.

[17] See D Piqani, 'The Role of National Constitutional Courts in Issues of Compliance' and A Nollkaemper, 'The Role of National Courts in Inducing Compliance with International and European Law: A Comparison' in Cremona (n 15).

[18] O Ştefan, 'Soft Law and the Enforcement of EU Law' in A Jakab and D Kochenov (eds), *The Enforcement of EU Law and Values: Ensuring Member States' Compliance* (Oxford, Oxford University Press, 2017).

[19] E Versluis, 'Even Rules, Uneven Practices: Opening the "Black Box" of EU Law in Action' (2007) 30 *West European Politics* 50; A Zhelyazkova, C Kaya and R Schrama, 'Decoupling Practical and Legal Compliance: Analysis of Member States' Implementation of EU Policy' (2016) 55 *European Journal of Political Research* 827; N Dörrenbächer, 'Europe at the Frontline: Analysing Street-Level Motivations for the Use of European Union Migration Law' (2017) 24 *Journal of European Public Policy* 1328.

envisage potential courses of action to solve or lessen the effects of the problem in question.[20]

The EU's role as an enforcer of OMC policy norms is weak, as it cannot employ the usual coercive mechanisms available, including the courts. Research focuses on why the non-binding OMC is capable of affecting Member State policies and inculcating a national change. A range of explanations have been offered, ranging from mutually beneficial learning[21] through peer pressure, benchmarking and competition[22] to calling out.[23] In situations where there is little possibility of oversight from above (the Commission or the courts) or from the sides (Member States as peers), domestic preferences may be constrained by national politics, public opinion and organised civil society.[24] What is common to these situations is that influence remains conditional. EU norms work like a 'selective amplifier' of national interests,[25] because Member States do not simply adapt to the Brussels norm, but use whatever comes from Brussels in accordance with national preferences.[26]

Whilst research on the OMC has emphasised the instrumental logic by which Member States acknowledge the OMC norms, studies of Commission recommendations have pointed out that the persuasiveness of soft law also matters and that the implementation of a Commission recommendation depends on how convincingly it is articulated.[27] Thick consensus[28] and successful deliberation[29]

[20] S Regent, 'The Open-Method of Coordination: A New Supranational Form of Governance?' (2003) 9 *European Law Journal* 190; D Ashiagbor, 'Soft Harmonisation: The "Open Method of Coordination" in the European Employment Strategy' (2004) 10 *European Public Law* 305; C de La Porte and P Nanz, 'The OMC – a Deliberative-Democratic Mode of Governance?: The Cases of Employment and Pensions' (2004) 11 *Journal of European Public Policy* 267. These debates have moved on to discuss the integration of soft and hard governance in the European Semester; see, eg, S Bekker, 'EU Coordination of Welfare States after the Crisis: Further Interconnecting Soft and Hard Law' (2014) 19 *International Review of Public Administration* 296.

[21] CF Sabel and J Zeitlin, 'Learning from Difference: The New Architecture of Experimentalist Governance in the EU' (2008) 14 *European Law Journal* 271.

[22] S Borrás and K Jacobsson, 'The Open Method of Co-ordination and New Governance Patterns in the EU' (2004) 11 *Journal of European Public Policy* 185.

[23] L Tholoniat, 'The Career of the Open Method of Coordination: Lessons from a "Soft" EU Instrument' (2010) 33 *West European Politics* 93.

[24] P Van Wolleghem, 'Why Implement without a Tangible Threat? The Effect of a Soft Instrument on National Migrant Integration Policies' (2017) 55 *Journal of Common Market Studies* 1127.

[25] J Visser, 'The OMC as a Selective Amplifier for National Strategies of Reform: What the Netherlands Want to Learn from Europe' in L Magnusson (ed), *The Open Method of Coordination in Action: The European Employment and Social Inclusion Strategies* (Berlin, Peter Lang, 2005) 173.

[26] C Woll and S Jacquot, 'Using Europe: Strategic Action in Multi-level Politics' (2010) 8 *Comparative European Politics* 110.

[27] C Andone and S Greco, 'Evading the Burden of Proof in European Union Soft Law Instruments: The Case of Commission Recommendations' (2018) 31 *International Journal for the Semiotics of Law* 79.

[28] J Pauwelyn et al, 'When Structures Become Shackles: Stagnation and Dynamics in International Lawmaking' (2014) 25 *European Journal of International Law* 733.

[29] E Korkea-aho, *Adjudicating New Governance: Deliberative Democracy in the European Union* (Abingdon, Routledge, 2015).

are indicators of persuasive influence. Implementation of norms runs through the recognition of norms following a logic of appropriateness.[30]

While the literature on EU implementation and compliance provides insights into mechanisms through which EU norms are received in Member States, the transfer of its findings and methods to study how soft law is nationally received has some significant caveats. The first is the question of generalisability.[31] EU soft law takes many more forms than OMCs or Commission recommendations.[32] Opinions, codes of conduct, communications, notices, guidelines and resolutions do not typically come with benchmarking or peer-review processes, rendering instrumental mechanisms of uptake at the national level more unlikely for these instruments.[33] Many soft law instruments also lack the interactive and iterative elements, making it rather unlikely that persuasive mechanisms operate across the broad spectrum of EU soft law instruments. Compliance with EU soft law seems to depend on the interaction between characteristics of the policy instrument in question and national-level interests and processes. Second, and as mentioned above, without tangible deadlines or a formal notification process, it is difficult to analyse and compare how Member States fare in implementing EU norms. In order to address both of these caveats, it is necessary to revisit the methodology of soft law studies.

III. HOW SHOULD THE RECEPTION OF SOFT LAW BE STUDIED? METHODOLOGICAL ASPECTS

The methodology of the European Network on Soft Law Research (SoLaR) was inspired by socio-legal approaches and political science implementation studies. Besides traditional legal research relying on textual analysis, our work draws on socio-legal studies in two ways. First, in the tradition of socio-legal research that seeks to understand law in its political, legal, cultural and social contexts, we have also analysed soft law as an integral element of the broader normative environment in which it is intended to operate. Not only does law regulate what is happening in political, legal, cultural and social contexts, but these contexts also produce and shape soft law, its effects and reception. Second, socio-legal

[30] J March and J Olsen, 'The Institutional Dynamics of International Political Orders' (1998) 52 *International Organization* 94.

[31] M Hartlapp, 'Learning about Policy Learning: Reflections on the European Employment Strategy' (2009) 13 *European Integration Online Papers*.

[32] *cf* Hofmann, ch 3 in this volume. For the national effects of different types of soft law, see Z Georgieva, 'Soft Law in EU Competition Law and its Reception in Member States' Courts: An Empirical Study on National Judicial Attitudes to Atypical Legal Instruments in EU Competition Law' (PhD thesis, Tilburg University, 2018); C van Dam, 'Guidance Documents of the European Commission: A Typology to Trace the Effects in the National Legal Order' (2017) 10(2) *Review of European Administrative Law* 75.

[33] However, in areas of exclusive competence such as State aid, the Commission casts a long shadow of hierarchy which affects Member State choices.

research is methodologically inclusive and uses methods of social sciences.[34] The socio-legal approach adopted within the SoLaR network is triangular and consists of literature review, case law analysis of national court rulings, and the collection of interview data from experts working in national administrations and the judicial branch. Immediately below, our focus is on interviews and case law research in a multi-lingual and multi-country project.

A. Expert Interviews

The network produced 111 interviews with judges and civil servants.[35] Numbers differ slightly between the Member States, but are sufficient to explore the research question raised and to bring out important differences between policy fields and national practices. In order to successfully conduct interviews in a multi-country research project, the coordinators of the SoLaR network agreed on a semi-structured template to guide those conducting interviews in the selected legal systems.[36] This template was then translated into national languages by national policy teams. Each national team was expected to equally include judges and civil servants, but some adjustments to the ratio were made depending on the characteristics of the policy field.

The SoLaR interviews are 'expert interviews' and due regard was paid to the constraints of this methodology.[37] A key consideration is the difference between an 'expert' and a 'layperson'. Experts are people who have specialised knowledge, gained through extensive learning or training, whereas laypeople have everyday knowledge that draws on (lived) experience. This definition of experts applies to judges and civil servants on which SoLaR focused.[38] Substantial knowledge such as the extensive knowledge of EU water law guidance documents is not the only dimension of expertise, since the 'expert is not interviewed as an individual; the interview context is organisational or institutional'.[39] Many of our questions

[34] L Webley, 'Qualitative Approaches to Empirical Legal Research' in P Cane and HM Kritzer (eds), *The Oxford Handbook of Empirical Legal Research* (Oxford, Oxford University Press, 2010).

[35] Finland (18), the UK (8), the Netherlands (19), Slovenia (18), France (13), Italy (17) and Germany (18). Besides the original seven SoLaR countries, the contributors for Spain, Hungary and Cyprus conducted 11, 6 and 0 interviews, bringing the total up to 128.

[36] Annex II.

[37] M Meuser and U Nagel, 'ExpertInneninterviews – vielfach erprobt, wenig bedacht. Ein Beitrag zur qualitativen Methodendisckussion' in D Garz and K Kraimer (eds), *Qualitativ-empirische Sozialforschung. Konzepte, Methoden, Analysen* (Opladen, Westdeutscher Verlag) 441.

[38] Each policy team was responsible for locating the experts they wanted to interview. In a multi-country project, this involves an element of discretion that cannot be entirely removed. However, leaving the decision to the national teams was also the most reliable way to gain access to relevant people. Apart from Finland, all other teams encountered problems in securing access. In the UK, despite numerous efforts, no judge agreed to interviews. If the search for interviewees was met with refusals (partially or wholly), a short explanation was submitted in the relevant policy report.

[39] G Abels and M Behrens, 'Interviewing Experts in Political Science: A Reflection on Gender and Policy Effects Based on Secondary Analysis' in A Bogner et al (eds), *Interviewing Experts* (Basingstoke, Palgrave Macmillan, 2009) 140.

were designed to excavate a broader institutional culture of EU soft law use, underpinning individual respondents' answers.

Expert interviews can be applied to different research contexts. First, the 'exploratory expert interviews' help 'the researcher to develop a clearer idea of the problem or as a preliminary move in the identification of a final interview guide'.[40] Second, the expert can provide systematic and comprehensive information in a 'systematising expert interview', a widely used research strategy. Third, the 'theory-generating interview' helps the researcher formulate a theory of the phenomenon.[41] The SoLaR interviews fell into the first category of exploratory expert interviews, and were used to gather information and to make sense of a field of scarce empirical knowledge. The interviewed judges and civil servants as experts offered valuable information on processes through which soft law enters the national system and insights on the motivations of actors, potential conflicts and questions of power related to soft law. However, the interviews also helped us systematise the field. Where the SoLaR literature review – the first step in the three-year project[42] – provided us with theoretical assumptions about the use of EU soft law in national systems, they were incorporated into and systematically assessed in the interviews. These assumptions involve, inter alia, legal tradition, exposure of the actor/policy field to EU influence, or differences between the types of instruments. As with expert interviews, the SoLaR interviews were also semi-structured with a set of open-ended questions allowing for 'free' answers covering factors specific to one or several countries or legal cultures. Insights from the interviews have been anonymously reported and discussed in the SoLaR Working Papers (all available on SSRN).

The value of expert interviews in studying soft law is illustrated by the following example. While EU hard law is typically transposed via a legislative process, EU soft law is frequently 'implemented' outside the legislative process. Capturing the variety of implementation instruments and processes is a challenge to the 'classical' methodology of EU implementation studies relying on detecting legislative changes. Data collection by systematically contacting actors in responsible ministries and agencies instead provided a solid basis to assess the reception of soft law at the national level. Therefore, rather than trying to establish whether the Member State had 'transposed' or applied the soft law measure in question, we asked our interviewees: 'Which of these instruments do you use in your work?'[43]

[40] A Bogner and W Menz, 'The Theory-Generating Expert Interview: Epistemological Interest, Forms of Knowledge, Interaction' in Bogner et al (n 39) 47.

[41] ibid 48. For the use of expert interviews in EU legal research, see also E Korkea-aho and P Leino-Sandberg, 'Interviewing Lawyers: A Reflection on Interviews as a Legal Research Method in European law' (2019) 12(1) *European Journal of Legal Studies* 17.

[42] O Ştefan et al, 'EU Soft Law in the EU Legal Order: A Literature Review' (2019) SoLaR Working Paper, https://ssrn.com/abstract=3346629.

[43] Annex II.

B. Case Law Research

Our case law research located and evaluated national rulings where judges explicitly mentioned EU soft law. We did not aim at a quantitative analysis of soft law references. Rather, the aim was to shed light on the ways in which judges use soft law; in other words, to increase a qualitative understanding of the role of soft law in national judgments. The multi-lingual character of our team enabled us to cross the language barrier that usually afflicts multi-country research and prevents researchers from fully exploiting national publicly available databases. The search for rulings was carried out based on selected keywords that were agreed upon according to the most workable approach for each policy area. For instance, in the environmental law field, the search was conducted using hard law instruments such as the Habitats Directive or the Water Framework Directive as keywords, while in the context of competition law and State aid, the search was based on the selected soft law instruments themselves. The keywords were translated into national languages. However, in countries such as Finland and Slovenia, national judgments occasionally cited Commission documents in English without necessarily translating them, so the search included the keywords both in the national language and in English.[44]

The search was limited to supreme (ordinary and administrative) jurisdictions as well as to specialised courts (eg, the Competition Appeals Tribunal in the UK).[45] Based on pilot searches, it was decided that no temporal limitations were necessary, as the number of cases was manageable.[46] Once the judgments were retrieved, they were analysed by national policy teams. The questions that each team asked were: (1) the status and legal/practical effects of soft law recognised by the court; (2) the justiciability of soft law and the way in which judicial review of such instruments is undertaken by the court; and (3) the ways in which the use of soft law before the courts contributes to fostering or undermining general principles of law, such as legal certainty, transparency and the consistent application of EU law. If the search for cases was performed with no results, a short explanation was submitted, including information on keywords that were used. Some ideas as to why the search did not yield any results were also provided.

Just like the interviewing technique, this data collection method also addressed a gap identified at the intersection of EU implementation and compliance studies, notably the need to pay more attention to what happens on the ground.

[44] Keywords can be found in the SoLaR Working Papers, available on SSRN.

[45] In the context of environmental law, some national teams also searched the case law of lower courts.

[46] The only exception was competition law and State aid, where the number of cases would have been too much without a temporal limitation. For further details, see O Ştefan (ed), 'EU Competition and State Aid Soft Law in the Member States: Finland, France, Germany, Italy, the Netherlands, Slovenia and the UK' (2020) SoLaR Working Paper, https://papers.ssrn.com/sol3/papers.cfm?abstract_id=3667387.

IV. EMPIRICAL INSIGHTS ON METHODOLOGY

The above methodology yielded important insights in at least three respects. First, it helped capture the different ways in which EU soft law is received in the Member States and offered new insights into what explains the observed differences in the national reception of EU soft law. Second, it demonstrated that the academic distinction between legal and practical effects of soft law is less relevant on the ground than what the common perception about the distinction is. Third, it increased our understanding about the usefulness of interviews in soft law research, especially when combined with case law research. We will discuss each in turn.

A. Typology of Reception

At the beginning of this chapter, we posited that Member State reception of soft law is differential. We also suggested that a more nuanced understanding of different perspectives of compliance and implementation literatures as well as between hard and soft law research is helpful in terms of directing our attention to these differences. As shown by our empirical data, there are at least four options through which EU soft law is received at the national level: (1) formal compliance; (2) de facto compliance; (3) ignorance or passive resistance; and (4) active defiance. While they are analytically distinct, our empirical cases might yield aspects of different reception types as they evolve over time.

i. Formal Compliance

Member States have several choices in relation to formally complying with EU soft law. In the following, we will elaborate the main characteristics of these choices and provide some examples. More can be found in other chapters in this volume:[47]

- Hard law incorporation by 'transposing' EU soft law into national legislation (the Buying Social guide in Italy; the integration of the EU Recommendation on Equal Pay into the French Code du Travail; Slovenian competition legislation; Spanish Water Planning legislation).
- Soft law incorporation by reproducing EU soft law in the form of traditional national soft law (environment circulars in the UK; BaFin circulars (*Rundschreiben*) in Germany; the Hungarian Competition Authority's guidance).

[47] This is borrowed from, and expanded on, O Ştefan in ch 19 in this volume. Because all the examples are from chapters in this volume, we do not provide specific references to each.

- Hybrid incorporation by using combinations of hard and soft law to 'transpose' EU soft law (traces of the EU antitrust Guidelines on fines can be found in the French Code de commerce; however, the Competition Authority has also set up its own guidelines for setting fines).
- The inclusion – and sometimes translation – of EU soft law into a loose group of manuals, guidebooks, databases etc (Finland's public procurement guidelines; the UK interactive handbooks by the Financial Conduct Authority; the FFH-VP-Info database of the Federal Agency for Nature Conservation (Bundesamt für Naturschutz) containing information on habitats impact assessment procedures; Italian non-binding manuals paraphrasing habitats guidance documents).
- Q&As and press releases (especially, in the field of financial regulation, press releases by the French financial authority (Autorité des marchés financier (AMF)).
- The inclusion of EU soft law by references to it on national websites (the French social security website Cleiss; the websites of the French Competition Authority and the Ministère de l'Economie et des Finances with references to competition and State aid soft law instruments; the website of the Cyprus financial authority CySec).

Whether soft law is incorporated into legislation, nationally recognised soft law, some other form of non-binding guidance or a combination of them depends on the policy instrument and the policy sector. The concrete examples enumerated above show that formal compliance occurs particularly in two policy fields: financial policy and competition law and State aid. One reason may be that there are procedural measures to encourage formal compliance in these fields.

For instance, the European Securities and Markets Authority (ESMA) issues soft law guidelines and recommendations. The competent authorities and financial institutions 'shall make every effort to comply with those guidelines and recommendations' and are called upon to provide reasons for non-compliance.[48] This is an example of a new type of soft law that comes with normative elements that strongly induce compliance. ESMA publishes compliance tables on its website, setting out the list of competent authorities that comply or intend to comply with ESMA's guidelines. While this does not provide, strictly speaking, for a binding enforcement mechanism, ESMA can use other soft enforcement tools to foster compliance of national authorities, such as 'calling out' through compliance tables, or peer reviews according to Article 30 of the ESMA Regulation.[49] Hence, these soft law measures

[48] Article 16 of Regulation (EU) No 1095/2010 of the European Parliament and of the Council of 24 November 2010 establishing a European Supervisory Authority (European Securities and Markets Authority).

[49] S Post, 'EU Soft Law Effects in Financial Regulation: Insights from the United Kingdom' in M Avbelj (ed), 'EU Financial Regulation Soft Law in the Member States: Finland, France, Germany, Italy, the Netherlands, Slovenia and the UK' (2020) SoLaR Working Paper, https://papers.ssrn.com/sol3/papers.cfm?abstract_id=3668793.

are not 'soft' after all,[50] because procedural requirements effectively curtail the room for a Member State authority to neglect EU soft law. The use of 'procedural sticks' likely varies strongly between policy areas and possibly over time,[51] but since there is no available data on how systematically the EU uses deadlines or 'comply or explain' requirements with soft law measures, the proceduralisation of soft law is hard to substantiate.

Another point to note about the above list is that EU soft law is rarely incorporated verbatim, and many Member States appear to adapt EU soft law in light of national circumstances – a process which we have called the 'nationalisation' or 'translation' of EU soft law. An example of this is EU State aid manual published by the Department for Business, Energy and Industrial Strategy (BEIS), which the UK authorities not only duly transposed into national legislation, but, whilst doing so, also translated it from formal EU documentation into a more practical guide to the rules.[52]

ii. De Facto Compliance

Besides formal compliance, we found evidence of situations where EU soft law has not been officially incorporated in any of the ways listed above, but is nevertheless complied with. Many of the concrete situations where we witnessed de facto compliance concerned administrative decision-making, yet we also identified situations where de facto compliance occurred in national policy-making. In Finland, for instance, EU recommendations in the context of social policy – a policy area that falls within the shared competence of Member States – provide a window of opportunity (and some leverage too) to critically appraise domestic legislation against EU guidance and to identify spaces for improvement.[53]

Our empirical material suggests that national decision-makers use EU soft law even when it is not formally incorporated into national hard or soft law such as circulars in Germany or *lignes directrices* in France. Thus, even where no formal process has been initiated to incorporate or acknowledge EU soft law, it may be capable of altering general practice and specific decisions in the national administrations. In Slovenia, EU law in general was described as being read in detail among administrative actors. The awareness of EU soft law instruments was also high, and administrative actors understood soft law as a tool that

[50] M van Rijsbergen, 'On the Enforceability of EU Agencies' Soft Law at the National Level: The Case of the European Securities and Markets Authority' (2014) 10(5) *Utrecht Law Review* 116.

[51] Many Commission recommendations also entail some form of the notification process with a deadline; see, eg, the Recommendation on Transparency in Equal Pay that requires national authorities to report national measures within a fixed timeframe.

[52] O Ştefan and A Biondi with I Dereme, 'National Report on the UK: The Use of EU Soft Law by National Courts and Administration in the Field of EU Competition and State Aid Law' in Ştefan (n 46).

[53] E Korkea-aho, 'The Finnish Report on the Reception of Social Soft Law' in M Hartlapp (ed), 'Studying EU Soft Law Effects in Social Policy' (2020) SoLaR Working Paper, https://papers.ssrn.com/sol3/papers.cfm?abstract_id=3668981.

allows a de-formalisation of procedures and gives 'a direction on how to think in the legal framework, which is set by binding regulations'.[54] Similar sentiments were expressed among Finnish authorities and judges. Many of the EU soft law measures were not formally introduced into or made part of the national legal order, yet the experts were aware of the terms of EU soft law.[55]

De facto compliance was detected in the UK too, where many of the EU soft law instruments have not been formally incorporated, arguably in the interests of simplification and transparency.[56] However, UK courts have faith in national authorities and assert that they would know which rules to apply. The High Court noted that 'it might be confidently expected that Natural England were aware of the terms of the Habitats Directive, the Commission Guidance and the Habitats Regulations, given that they were the authority responsible'.[57] An informed decision-maker would know which guidance to consider and where to find it.

iii. Ignorance and Passive Resistance

Of all possible options, ignorance is usually portrayed as something that is particularly appealing to Member States. Why would Member States bother reacting to 'whatever-law', especially if there is no legal requirement to do so or supranational authorities to monitor performance? Contrary to initial expectations of finding plenty of evidence for the 'teenage Member States notion', we found hardly any examples of Member State ignorance or passive resistance. We argue that this is because EU soft law requires action on the part of recipient, be it positive (formal or de facto compliance) or negative (active defiance). The lack of ignorance may also explain why our empirical data involves examples of 'window-dressing', that is, a Member State masquerading a national policy measure – a measure it had already taken some time ago or would have taken irrespective of the EU – as a tailored regulatory response to, and the implementation of, the EU soft law measure.

The existence of window-dressing was confirmed by comparing our empirical insights with the results contained in official reports of the Commission.[58] Several Member States reported changes that had either taken place earlier than the reception of EU soft law should have taken place or that were causally

[54] G Justinek, 'National Report on Slovenia: The Use of EU Soft Law by National Courts and Administration in the Field of EU Social Policy' in Hartlapp (n 53).

[55] E Korkea-aho et al, ch 7 in this volume.

[56] M Dobbs and O Ştefan, ch 15 in this volume.

[57] See, eg, *Morge v Hampshire County Council* [2009] EWHC 2940 (Admin) (17 November 2009) [60].

[58] H Frazer and E Marlier, 'Progress across Europe in the Implementation of the 2013 EU Recommendation on "Investing in Children: Breaking the Cycle of Disadvantage" – A Study of National Policies' (2017) European Commission, DG Employment, Social Affairs and Inclusion/ Directorate C – Social Affairs/ Unit C.2.

unrelated to the soft law instrument. For instance, our analysis of the reception of the recommendation investing in children[59] showed that Germany and the Netherlands continued their respective national agendas without adapting to the underlying idea of the EU recommendation. Despite the absence of national efforts to implement the recommendation, both countries reported a range of policy instruments as ensuring compliance with the recommendation.[60] It is likely that the use of procedural sticks – 'comply or explain' mechanisms or deadlines for reporting national responses – increases the occurrence of window-dressing.[61]

iv. Active Defiance

Some Finnish environmental authorities reported having raised opposition to EU soft law documents, especially where they felt that the Commission was trying to use them as an unauthorised/unlawful benchmark in infringement proceedings.[62] German civil servants reported that the recommendation investing in children had not been nationally implemented. The interviewed officials explained that the decision not to 'implement' was that the Recommendation deviated from an earlier EU policy that had been in line with the German family-oriented view on policies for children. Consequently, the German authorities decided to proceed with their national policy, despite the fact that it departed from the EU soft law instrument.[63] However, as noted above, this Recommendation was one of the policy instruments that led the German authorities to window-dress national policy measures as implementing the agenda set forth in the Recommendation.

Sometimes an act of active defiance may take place in court. In Hungary, what was seen as mushrooming in the application of EU competition soft norms in domestic competition law cases prompted the Hungarian Supreme Court (Kuria) to make an effort to rein in the unwelcome development. The Kuria declared that the 'judicial practice placing a Commission guideline that is not even a legal act of the Union, into the centre of the judgment's reasoning' is

[59] EU Recommendation Investing in Children: Breaking the Cycle of Disadvantage (2013/112/EU).

[60] M Hartlapp, 'The National Report on Germany: The Use of EU Soft Law by National Courts and Administration in the Field of EU Social Policy' in Hartlapp (n 53); B Beijen, 'National Report on the Netherlands: The Use of EU Soft Law by National Courts and Administration in the Field of EU Social Policy' in Hartlapp (n 53).

[61] Procedural sticks might not function in a comparable manner across policy fields. For instance, window-dressing in a comply or explain scenario might lead to legal action and redress, something that will not happen in social policy.

[62] E Korkea-aho, 'National Report on Finland: The Use of EU Soft Law by National Courts and Administration in the Field of EU Environmental Law' in M Eliantonio and G Lisi (eds), 'EU Environmental Soft Law in the Member States: A Comparative Overview of Finland, France, Germany, Italy, the Netherlands, Slovenia and the UK' (2020) SoLaR Working Paper, https://papers.ssrn.com/sol3/papers.cfm?abstract_id=3656418.

[63] Hartlapp (n 60).

mistaken,[64] which clearly not only discourages lower courts from using soft law but also signals that the active defiance is a viable category of national reception.

B. The Difference between Legal and Practical Effects

The second empirical insight on the SoLaR methodology relates to the *difference between legal and practical effects* – the distinction often drawn especially in legal research on soft law. The legal effects of soft law have been seen to consist of providing a 'normative framework for future negotiations', 'concretizing the duty of institutional cooperation' or 'producing a stand-still effect on the non-conforming conduct of a State or institutions'.[65] Practical effects are harder to pinpoint, but some have argued that they include substantial changes in the policies of the Member States to whom the soft law measure is addressed, and they can inculcate the change in policy principles.[66]

As far as national *policy-making* is concerned, our argument is that the difference between legal and practical effects does not capture the actual choices facing Member States. Our empirical findings suggest that in practice, Member States' options when 'implementing' EU soft law are effectively limited to 'liking it or lumping it',[67] de facto complying or ignoring in the above typology. On the one hand, there is little space for Member States not to 'like' or non-comply with soft law, which has led to situations where Member States strategically window-dress causally non-related measures as soft law compliance. On the other hand, Member States are in principle free to 'lump' and ignore soft law coming from the EU, but in many cases, they cannot do so without giving good reasons, as demonstrated by, for example, ESMA's comply or explain obligations.

With respect to national *administrative and judicial decision-making*, our data suggests that rather than legal and practical effects, EU soft law has 'official' and 'non-official' effects. A case in point is Germany, where the legal system has been dismissive of soft law.[68] Both the Federal Constitutional Court (Bundesverfassungsgericht (BVerfG)) and the Federal Administrative

[64] P Láncos, ch 10 in this volume. For the concept of 'explicit rejection' in the field of competition soft law, see Z Georgieva, 'The Judicial Reception of Competition Soft Law in the Netherlands and the UK' (2016) 12(1) *European Competition Journal* 54; or in the Italian country report, J Alberti and F Croci, 'National Report on Italy: The Use of EU Soft Law by National Courts And Administration in The Field of EU Competition and State Aid Law' in Ştefan (n 46).

[65] O Ştefan, *Soft Law in Court: Competition Law, State Aid and the Court of Justice of the European Union* (Alphen aan den Rijn, Wolters Kluwer, 2013) 16.

[66] K Jacobsson, 'Between Deliberation and Discipline: Soft Governance in EU Employment Policy' in U Mörth (ed), *Soft law in Governance and Regulation: An Interdisciplinary Analysis* (Cheltenham, Edward Elgar, 2004) 81.

[67] This means that a person must accept a situation they do not like because it cannot be changed. UK Parliament Speaker John Bercow used the phrase in Parliament's Brexit discussions in September 2019.

[68] *cf* M Hartlapp, A Hofmann and M Knauff, ch 9 in this volume.

Court (Bundesverwaltungsgericht (BVerwG)) ruled that soft law does not bind courts.[69] Yet, once we had identified references to EU soft law in national case law, we asked judges about their use of EU soft law. In environmental policy, the interviewees explained that the Federal Administrative Court referred to EU soft law documents in numerous cases, often concerning prominent infrastructure projects, such as the dredging of rivers around Hamburg and Bremen harbours or the extension of the runway at Münster Airport.[70] The reasons given by the interviewees for this divergence between the official resistance and non-official use of law were many: the authoritative nature of EU documents as they come from the source close to original legislation and a willingness to signal to the CJEU that their argument is 'on the right level' in order to counter suspicion that national courts block the intrusion of EU rules, as well as the helpful expert information contained in EU soft law.[71]

C. Taking a Method to the Field: Interviews

The third and final insight concerns the need to understand whether the methodological approach of the SoLaR delivered the results expected.

Consider the EU Buying Social guide that most Member States officially 'transposed' into national legal systems. In Slovenia, the Ministry for Public Administration responsible for public procurement published the EU's Buying Social guide on its website, and the interviews confirm that it is well known and widely used among national officials.[72] In the Netherlands, the Ministry of Internal Affairs created a legal leaflet that explicitly refers to the EU Buying Social guide, and the Dutch Public Procurement Expertise Centre (Pianoo), a body directly linked to the government, introduces the EU Buying Social guide on its webpage.[73] Finland adopted non-binding guidance, including the publication of an English-language Guide to Socially Responsible Public Procurement and a Handbook of Government Procurements that mentions the EU's Buying Social guide in the list of further reading. The Finnish interviewees reported that the EU guide was very influential and widely read during the preparation

[69] Bundesverfassungsgericht, order of 31.5.1988–1 BvR 520/83, BVerfGE 78, 214 ref 37.

[70] 'The references to soft law are very specific and acknowledge their value in the interpretation of hard law'; 'This document [CIS document 2], while not binding, nonetheless has special importance (*besonderes Gewicht*) for the interpretation [of the WFD]' (BVerwG 9 A 18/15, 10.11.2016); 'Regarding the interpretation and implementation of art. 6.3 [of the Habitats Directive], permitting authorities would be well advised to consult the Commission's interpretative document Managing Natura 2000 Sites, irrespective of the fact that an authoritative interpretation can only be given by the CJEU' (BVerwG, 4 B 70/02, 05.03.2003).

[71] A Hofmann, 'National Report on Germany: The Use of EU Soft Law by National Courts and Administration in the Field of EU Environmental Policy' in Eliantonio and Lisi (n 62).

[72] Justinek (n 54).

[73] Beijen (n 60).

of Finnish soft law.[74] In Italy, the Ministry of the Environment adopted a Guide for the integration of social aspects in public tenders via a decree in June 2012.[75] In Germany and France, national guidance documents on social criteria were published in temporal proximity to the publication of the EU Buying Social guide. The developments in France are more difficult to categorise because guidance documents on social criteria seem to have been 'transposed' nationally, but have been declared non-binding by administrative courts.[76] However, what is clear is that applying the methodology typically used in transposition studies with its focus on legislative change would have masked the diverse effects of EU soft law at the national level. Neither the wide usage across all the countries nor the variety of forms of national reception would have become visible without interviews.

Even in situations where Member States 'transposed' EU soft law into national legislation, our methodology could provide new insights. In some cases, the interviewees reported legislative processes that had been initiated to give EU soft law a binding effect at the national level. Good examples are provided by the transposition of the Commission Recommendation on Transparency in Equal Pay via the pay transparency law in Germany (Entgelttransparenzgesetz) or the transposition of non-binding ESMA guidelines into hard law in a number of countries such as Finland, Germany and Slovenia.[77] In these cases, the EU law instrument, despite its soft character, provided additional incentives for transposition (a notification deadline for the Commission Recommendation and 'comply or explain' mechanisms associated with ESMA guidelines), and the officials we interviewed explained that these additional incentives made a difference in the national reception of EU soft law.

V. CONCLUSION

Our most striking finding is the wide variety of national responses to EU soft law. It most certainly is not 'whatever-law', raising lukewarm emotions from Member States. While in some cases, EU soft law compliance is taken as a given and its 'transposition' into national (hard or soft) law takes place much as it does for EU directives, other cases are characterised by window-dressing or even resistance. Significant differences prevail across countries, policy areas

[74] Korkea-aho (n 53).

[75] F Spera and M Eliantonio, 'National Report on Italy: The Use of EU Soft Law by National Courts and Administration in the Field of EU Social Policy' in Hartlapp (n 53).

[76] Hartlapp (n 60); and O André, 'National Report on France: The Use of the EU Soft Law by National Courts and Administration in the Field of EU Social Policy' in Hartlapp (n 53).

[77] For the German example, see Hartlapp (n 60); and for ESMA's guidelines, see the overview given in M Avbelj, 'EU Financial Regulation Soft Law in the Member States: Finland, France, Germany, Italy, the Netherlands, Slovenia and the UK' in Avbelj (49).

and whether we discuss administrative or judicial functions. In fact, 'soft law Europe' is more differential than Europe seen through a hard law lens. This seems logical, if we acknowledge the conceptual fuzziness around the notion of soft law compliance. Where actors do not have a clear-cut understanding of what compliance with soft law requires from them, their response will be developed on a case-by-case basis. It is likely to be influenced not only by the specificities of the issues or instrument at hand, but also by the role soft law plays in the national legal system, as well as by the approach of the Member State to EU integration.

Member States have very different views on the place of soft law in the national legal hierarchy. While in some countries, the notion of soft law did not exist prior to the EU starting to increasingly adopt soft law instruments, others have a long tradition of resorting to guidance instruments or using administrative instruments to steer societies.[78] For instance, both the Finnish and German interviewees noted that soft law is historically unknown as a legal category. Both countries have administrative guidelines and circulars, but their function has been more limited than that of current EU soft law. Even in the absence of a domestic soft law category, Member States have quickly adapted to EU soft law, giving it a unique role in the hierarchy of legal norms. Despite the fact that soft law has not been an important legal category, Finland's approach to soft law is the most positive and pragmatic among the countries we studied. Judges and civil servants seem to pay little attention to the difference between legal and practical effects. For them, and quite irrespective of the policy field we studied, the distinction between legal and practical effects was largely irrelevant. They reported on the use of EU soft law when it is 'useful' and 'necessary'. This is in all likelihood explained by 'pragmatic legalism' that characterises the Finnish legal culture more broadly.[79] Decision-makers are not interested in abstract considerations of the nature of bindingness, but rather in careful consideration of all the elements that ultimately constitute the right decision in the case at hand.

Besides legal-cultural considerations, our data suggests that the size and the self-perceived role of the Member State in the EU also matter. This preliminary observation fits the findings of the research on EU hard law implementation, according to which larger Member States and those that perceive themselves as exporters rather than recipients of EU norms are less keen to implement.[80] This pattern was (although patchily) also observed in our empirical data. In the context of social policy, interviewees from the French Cour de Cassation admitted that they rarely used EU hard law and entirely neglected EU soft law. Soft law was considered potentially useful, providing information and guidance for judicial or administrative interpretation – but without legal value.[81] On the contrary,

[78] Ştefan et al (n 42).
[79] See Korkea-aho et al, ch 7 in this volume.
[80] Falkner et al (n 11).
[81] André (n 76).

in Slovenia, the interviewees stressed the importance of EU law for their actions, even where EU law is soft. Slovenia has been portrayed as the best pupil in class and a role model for all Central and Eastern European states, both those that are already members and those aspiring to become members.[82] Similarly, Finland's small size and general acceptance of EU integration has paved the way for the smooth reception of EU soft law.[83] However, both explanatory factors, especially the latter (the size and pro-European consensus), require more research. For instance, it needs to be analysed whether and, if so, to what extent positive sentiments about the EU measured through Eurobarometer surveys are reflected in the national reception and use of soft law.

In sum, diversity becomes a defining characteristic of EU soft law reception. Consequently, any judgement of EU soft law should reflect not only on efficiency and legitimacy, but should also assess diversity – either critically as the increasingly uneven playing field or positively as a means for the accommodation of (growing) heterogeneity in the EU. Finally, with the observation that diversity is a core characteristic of national soft law reception comes the quest to use diverse methodologies. It is by opening up to different data sources and collection techniques that we are able to capture the range of national-level processes and outcomes.

[82] See Avbelj and Vatovec, ch 13 in this volume.

[83] Policy area differences still persist. As far as many EU social policy initiatives are concerned, it was easy for Finland to accept soft law, as EU soft law in that area was going in a direction that Finland approved of.

5

'Verba Volant, Quoque (Soft Law) Scripta?'

An Analysis of the Legal Effects of National Soft Law Implementing EU Soft Law in France and the UK

GIULIA GENTILE

I. INTRODUCTION

EU SOFT LAW is not subject to transposition duties by the Member States.[1] Yet national authorities have increasingly adopted soft law acts to implement EU soft law in a variety of policy areas, such as competition and environment. As argued by Hartlapp, national implementation practices result in efficiency gains, while the implementation of EU soft law by the Member States demonstrates that EU soft law has legal effects.[2]

This chapter provides insights into the effects of selected soft law measures issued by the French and UK authorities to implement EU Commission soft law in competition and environmental policies. The contribution of this chapter to the existing literature and the European Network of Soft Law Research (SoLaR) project is twofold. First, the chapter conducts a textual analysis of the chosen

[1] While transposition is required to make EU directives applicable at the national level by way of adoption of national measures, implementation is concerned with non-conformity and incorrect application cases. For an overview of the difference between transposition and implementation, see www.europarl.europa.eu/RegData/etudes/BRIE/2018/608841/IPOL_BRI(2018)608841_EN.pdf. In certain instances, the implementation of EU soft law is required, see, eg, EIOPA guidelines on the implementation of the Solvency II Directive.

[2] M Hartlapp, 'Soft Law Implementation in the EU Multilevel System: Legitimacy and Governance Efficiency Revisited' in N Behnke, J Broschek and J Sonnicksen (eds), *Configurations, Dynamics and Mechanisms of Multilevel Governance* (New York, Springer International Publishing, 2019).

national implementing measures and closely assesses their wording. Second, it discusses the legal effects of national implementing soft law with regard to (a) the potential effect on third parties, (b) the influence on the discretion of the issuing authority and (c) the use made by national courts. This analysis reaches two main findings. First, the legal effects of national implementing soft law are unsettled and thus increase unpredictability and uncertainty associated with EU soft law. Second, there is a risk of fragmentation of legal effects between EU soft law and national implementing soft law, decreasing legal certainty and hindering good governance.

Ancient wisdom offers guidance to rationalise the role and effects of EU and national soft law and suggests a way forward. According to the Latin proverb,[3] spoken words (*verba*) 'fly away' (*volant*) and thus have no influence on individuals' behaviour, while written words (*scripta*) will 'remain' (*manent*) and influence legal conduct. How can we then ensure that the wording of EU soft law measures 'stays' and does not 'fly away'? This chapter argues that EU institutions, jointly with national authorities and courts, should strive to enhance the uniformity of the effects of soft law measures at the EU level and in Member States. In particular, EU and national authorities ought to ensure that soft law is treated as 'written words' (*scripta*), the meaning and effects of which 'remain' (*manent*) in the legal orders of the EU and its Member States.

The rest of the chapter proceeds as follows. First, an overview is given of the selected EU policy areas and the legal effects of EU soft law measures issued in these fields are described. Second, the national implementation of specific EU soft law measures in the areas of competition and environment law in France and the UK are discussed, along with the legal consequences of national implementing soft law. Some final remarks and suggestions on how to address the fragmentation of the legal effects of EU and national soft law are provided in the conclusion.

II. METHODOLOGY

This chapter analyses selected national soft law measures adopted in France and the UK to implement EU Commission soft law on competition (excluding State aid) and environmental matters. Both of these fields fall within the scope of the SoLaR project, have attracted attention in literature[4] and represent, respectively, exclusive and shared EU competences. Accordingly, they reflect different levels of

[3] The full version of the Latin proverb is 'Verba volant, scripta manent' ('Spoken words fly away, written words remain').

[4] See, among others, O Ştefan, 'European Competition Soft Law in European Courts: A Matter of Hard Principles?' (2008) 14 *European Law Journal* 753; E Korkea-aho, 'EU Soft Law in Domestic Legal Systems: Flexibility and Diversity Guaranteed?' (2009) 16 *Maastricht Journal of European and Comparative Law* 271; T Devine and M Eliantonio, 'EU Soft Law in the Hands of National Authorities: The Case Study of the UK Competition and Markets Authority' (2018) 11 *Review of European Administrative Law* 49.

centralisation of EU policies and distinct types of EU soft law. EU and national competition authorities (NCAs) rely on a robust organisation with extensive powers, directed and overseen by the Commission. In contrast, the EU and Member State environmental authorities cooperate within less structured and more informal networks. As a result, soft law in these areas also serves different purposes. EU competition soft law is classified as decisional-interpretative, whilst soft law issued in the domain of environmental law and policy primarily intends to guide the implementation of relevant policies and offer interpretative guidance to (national) decision-makers.[5]

The legal orders of France and the UK[6] are taken as textbook examples of common and civil law systems. In the French system, the divide between hard law and soft law remains controversial in the academic literature and case law. Labelling acts that do not stem from the legislative process as 'law' is problematic, as it runs against the principle of parliamentary sovereignty, according to which the Parliament issues laws that are the expression of the will of the people.[7] In a common law system, such as the UK, a more encompassing notion of law exists[8] and the question of the legal effects or bindingness of an act issued by national authorities has not occupied English courts or scholars.

Interestingly – but understandably, given the lack of the duty to transpose – national authorities in the selected jurisdictions have not implemented the same EU soft law acts. Therefore, since a top-down selection (ie, choosing the EU soft law measure and researching the implementing measures in France and the UK) was not possible, a bottom-up approach was followed instead (ie, researching among national acts and selecting measures[9] that have implemented EU soft law).

This chapter focuses on French and UK soft law implementing measures that include references to EU soft law or provide details concerning the relationship between the national implementation instrument and the original EU soft law measure. This selection method ensures that the sample comprises national acts that are specifically intended to give effects to EU soft law. Among the plethora of existing national soft law measures, the author has selected and analysed acts that best illustrate the diversity of soft law implementation practices in France and the UK. The sample is neither systematic nor exhaustive, but is intended to

[5] See A Hofmann, ch 3 in this volume.

[6] The UK left the EU on 31 January 2020. The analysis included in the chapter pre-dates Brexit day.

[7] See N Rubio and O Ştefan, ch 8 in this volume. See also C Thibierge, 'Le droit souple, réflexion sur les textures du droit' (2003) 4 *Revue trimestrielle de droit civil* 599.

[8] Judicial decisions constituting common law are classified among the UK legal sources. Among the sources of UK law, scholars also include constitutional conventions, which are not strictly speaking legal documents. See B Hilaire, *Understanding Public Law* (Abingdon, Taylor & Francis, 2009) 9. See also M Dobbs and O Ştefan, ch 15 in this volume, as well as N Xanthoulis and A Karatzia, ch 6 in this volume.

[9] The chapter analyses a total of eight implementing measures, four in the area of competition law (two in France and two in the UK) and four in the area of environmental policy (two in France and two in the UK).

highlight certain important aspects for both jurisdictions. The lack of soft law in France and the UK giving effects to the *same* EU soft law measure is a testament to the fragmented implementation of EU soft law in the Member States.

III. EU COMPETITION SOFT LAW

Competition law falls within the exclusive competences of the EU.[10] The expansion of this particular EU competence was proactively driven by the Commission Directorate-General for Competition (DG Comp), which has a central role in investigating potential violations in this field.[11] Article 5 of Regulation 1/2003 has devolved competence in handling competition cases to the NCAs,[12] which, jointly with the Commission, exercise oversight powers and enforce EU and national competition law. Cooperation also occurs at a horizontal level amongst Member State competition authorities. The European Competition Network (ECN), composed of the Commission and NCAs, operates as a coordination mechanism for the enforcement of EU competition law.

Over the years, the Commission has issued numerous soft law acts in the field of competition law[13] in the form of notices, recommendations, opinions or communications,[14] with the operation of the ECN itself regulated primarily through soft law.[15] Despite a wealth of soft law in this area, there is still uncertainty surrounding the effects of EU competition soft law. For instance, soft law measures may contain caveats mentioning that they do not bind the Commission.[16] Yet, EU courts have not been deterred from relying on those acts in their reasoning[17] or from establishing that soft law instruments bind the discretion of their author, and that national courts should consider EU soft law

[10] Article 3 TFEU. See also C Townley and AH Türk, 'The Constitutional Limits of EU Competition Law: United in Diversity' (2019) 64 *Antitrust Bulletin* 235.

[11] See DJ Gerber, *Law and Competition in Twentieth-Century Europe: Protecting Prometheus* (Oxford, Oxford University Press, 2001).

[12] Council Regulation (EC) No 1/2003 of 16 December 2002 on the implementation of the rules on competition laid down in Articles 81 and 82 of the Treaty [2003] OJ L1/1.

[13] See I Maher, 'Competition Law Modernization: Evolutionary Tale?' in P Craig and G de Búrca (eds), *Evolution of EU Law* (Oxford, Oxford University Press, 2011). See also I Maher, ch 2 in this volume.

[14] Information gathered through EUR-Lex, https://bit.ly/35cGSog.

[15] See, eg, 'Notice on cooperation within the Network of Competition Authorities' [2004] OJ C101/43; European Commission, 'Commission Notice on the handling of complaints by the Commission under Articles 81 and 82 of the EC Treaty' [2004] OJ C101/65.

[16] See, eg, European Commission, 'Commission Notice on Immunity from fines and reduction of fines in cartel cases' [2016] OJ C298/17. Its introduction specifies that the notice is a 'documentation tool and has no legal effects'. The effects of EU soft law in the field of EU state aid have been discussed in O Ştefan, *Soft Law in Court: Competition Law, State Aid and the Court of Justice of the European Union* (Dordrecht, Kluwer Law International, 2013).

[17] See, eg, Case-19/77 *Miller International Schallplatten GmbH v EC Commission* [1978] EU:C:1978:19. Also, in Case T-79/12 *Cisco & Messaget Spa v Commission* [2013] EU:T:2013:635, the General Court (GC) relied on the guidelines of the Commission on horizontal mergers as an interpretative tool to apply Regulation 139/2004, jointly with the relevant case law.

when judging.[18] At the national level, Georgieva finds that EU competition soft law may gain effects as a vessel for general principles of EU law.[19] Despite these developments, the scope and nature of legal effects of EU competition soft law are not completely determined.

A. National Soft Law Measures Implementing EU Competition Soft Law in France

The Autorité de la concurrence (AdC) is the competent authority to assess anti-competitive practices occurring on French territory and to issue relevant sanctions. As noted above, French scholars and judges have expressed sceptical views on soft law, 'as it could be dangerous and affect the integrity of the legal order'.[20] These critical opinions have not prevented the AdC from implementing EU soft law measures through national (soft law) acts. But the ambiguity concerning the legal effects of EU competition soft law is interestingly reflected in the AdC's implementing measures. To illustrate this point, the following paragraphs discuss, in turn, the AdC's measures implementing the ECN leniency programme model and the Commission guidelines on non-horizontal and horizontal concentrations.

Leniency programmes[21] were first created at the EU level through a 1996 Commission communication.[22] These do not have 'legislative force' and do not bind Member States.[23] In 2001, leniency programmes were introduced under the French Commerce Code.[24] The EU regulatory framework of leniency programmes changed with the creation of the ECN in 2003, and the adoption of the ECN model leniency programme, which is, like earlier leniency programmes, non-binding and cannot create any legitimate expectations.[25] The absence of binding

[18] Case C-322/88 *Grimaldi* [1989] EU:C:1989:646. See also Case C-526/14 *Kotnik* [2016] EU:C:2016:570. See E Korkea-aho, 'National Courts and European Soft Law: Is *Grimaldi* Still Good Law?' (2018) 37 *Yearbook of European Law* 470.

[19] Z Georgieva, 'Soft Law in EU Competition Law and its Judicial Reception in Member States: A Theoretical Perspective' (2014) TILEC Discussion Paper.

[20] Translation from French; see PM Eisemann, 'Les Gentlemen's agreements comme source du droit international' (1979) *Journal du droit international* 326, cited in F Chatzistavrou, 'L'usage du soft law dans le système juridique international et ses implications sémantiques et pratiques sur la notion de règle de droit' (2005) 15 *Le Portique* 79.

[21] Leniency programmes allow for reductions of sanctions linked to competition infringements under certain conditions, such as the cooperation of companies with the national or European authorities in the identification of anti-competitive behaviour.

[22] European Commission, 'Communication de la Commission concernant la non-imposition d'amendes ou la réduction de leur montant dans les affaires portant sur des ententes' [1996] OJ C207/4.

[23] Case C-557/12 *Pfleiderer* [2011] EU:C:2011:389, para 21.

[24] L 464-2 and R 464-5 of the French Commercial Code, introduced with the loi du 15 mai 2001 sur les nouvelles régulations économiques.

[25] 'ECN Model Leniency Programme Report on Assessment of the State of Convergence', https://ec.europa.eu/competition/ecn/model_leniency_programme.pdf; see paras 4 and 5.

effects is meant to keep leniency procedures as flexible as possible and to provide national authorities with discretion. Following the changes at the EU level, in 2006 the AdC issued a 'Communiqué de procédure' laying down the substantive and procedural requirements to initiate a leniency programme under French law.[26] The French communication gives guidance to market operators on how the AdC implements these programmes. The text of the communication remains silent as to its legal effects, but the relevant provisions of the Code of Commerce and the ECN model leniency programme are extensively mentioned. The communication also identifies the AdC's effort to 'homogenise' the enforcement of leniency programmes in the light of the ECN model.[27] In 2012, the AdC issued a brochure, addressed to the general public, explaining the functioning of leniency procedure. The brochure mentions explicitly that it is devoid of level value.[28]

By endorsing the ECN programme and implementing it via national soft law, the AdC has introduced a new tool of national governance modelled on the European example. The adoption of a soft law communication instead of legislation to lay down the procedural requirements of leniency programmes contributes to broadening the discretion of the AdC. The AdC's soft law also increases flexibility in setting leniency programmes.

Overall, the French implementation of the EU leniency programmes only partially resembles the initial EU measure. While both the Commission and the AdC primarily use soft law, the French legal order also regulates leniency programmes through hard law. Although there is presently no case law on the French leniency programmes, the presence of hard law in this field resolves the issue of the breadth of the AdC's discretion. The discretion of the AdC in enforcing leniency programme must respect the boundaries set by the Code de Commerce – a piece of hard law. This also means that any violation of hard law provisions by the AdC is amenable to judicial control. The co-existence of hard and soft law in this field nevertheless raises a concern: if national hard and soft law on leniency programmes are not applied harmoniously with the European leniency model, the efforts to 'homogenise' European and national leniency programmes are held back. If national implementing measures are enforced independently from the ECN model, problems in terms of uniform application of EU law may arise.[29] Furthermore, the policy objectives envisaged and set out in the ECN model leniency programme may be frustrated if national implementing measures diverge from EU measures.

Another example is the Lignes directrices de l'Autorité de la concurrence relatives au contrôle des concentrations (hereinafter 'AdC Lignes directices').[30] As explained in their preface, these guidelines complement the existing national

[26] The communication was revised in 2012 and in 2015.

[27] 'ECN Model Leniency Programme' (n 25) para 5.

[28] www.autoritedelaconcurrence.fr/doc/brochure_clemence_nov12.pdf.

[29] Interestingly, in the *avis* issued by the AdC concerning national leniency programmes, there is no mention of the European leniency programme model.

[30] www.autoritedelaconcurrence.fr/sites/default/files/ld_concentrations_juill13.pdf.

and EU legislation, and lay down the EU-inspired conditions to evaluate anticompetitive mergers. Through the guidelines, the AdC has also identified additional situations that are not regulated under the original Commission communications.[31] The AdC Lignes directrices mention the Commission guidelines on non-horizontal[32] and horizontal[33] concentrations to interpret legal concepts[34] and to set a minimum threshold for national policies.[35] A series of disclaimers included in the AdC Lignes directrices provide insights on their intended legal nature. Paragraph 13 specifies that this guidance is devoid of any 'normative purpose'[36] and merely provides companies with 'a pedagogical presentation on its scope, on the progress of the procedure before the Authority and the objectives, criteria and methods used for the analyses on the merits [of merger transactions]'. However, paragraph 14 indicates that the AdC Lignes directrices may be applied against individuals in the context of competition enforcement; indeed, they have been relied on by AdC when it has evaluated alleged anticompetitive behaviour, jointly with hard law provisions.[37]

It is unclear whether the AdC Lignes directrices can be invoked independently, without reference to hard law, against individuals before French courts. The issue of the effects of the AdC Lignes directrices becomes even more complex when we consider their impact on the discretion of the AdC. The AdC declares that it 'undertakes to apply the guidelines each time it examines a transaction, provided that no circumstances particular to this transaction or any consideration of general interest justify derogations therefrom'.[38] This statement raises more questions than answers.

Legal scholars and practitioners have argued that the wording of AdC Lignes directrices creates legal ambiguity as to their use by the AdC and national courts.[39] Moreover, due to many 'vague' concepts in the AdC Lignes directrices,

[31] See, eg, 'Communication consolidée sur la competénce de la Commission en vertu du règlement (CE) no 139/2004 du Conseil relatif au contrôle des opérations de concentration entre entreprises' [2009] OJ C43/10; European Commission, 'Communication de la Commission relative aux restrictions directement liées et nécessaires à la réalisation des opérations de concentration' [2005] OJ C56/24.

[32] 'Guidelines on the assessment of non-horizontal mergers under the Council Regulation on the control of concentrations between undertakings' [2008] OJ C265/6.

[33] 'Guidelines on the assessment of horizontal mergers under the Council Regulation on the control of concentrations between undertakings' [2004] OJ C31/5.

[34] AdC Lignes directrices, paras 324 and 386 concerning the notion of horizontal merger and related issues.

[35] These Commission guidelines have been applied by the General Court in *Cisco Systems Inc* to assess whether the Commission respected the limits of its discretion. See *Cisco & Messaget Spa v Commission* (n 17).

[36] This notion seems to indicate that the guidelines do not wish to create obligations of legislative nature – thus, binding erga omnes.

[37] Décision n° 10-DCC-198 du 30 décembre 2010 relative à la création d'une entreprise commune par Veolia Environnement et la Caisse des Dépôts et Consignations.

[38] AdC Lignes directrices, para 14.

[39] Nathalie Pétrignet et al, 'Projet de révision des lignes directrices en matière de contrôle des concentrations', 25 March 2013, https://cms.law/fr/fra/publication/flash-info-concurrence-projet-de-revision-des-lignes-directrices-en-matiere-de-controle-des-concentrations.

market operators ultimately bear the risk of inconsistent interpretations.[40] The Conseil d'Etat case law has attempted to provide some degree of certainty and to remove risks for market operators, noting that the AdC Lignes directrices can be used to assess whether the authority has respected the limits of its discretion. This case law makes no reference to the original EU soft law measure.[41] Consequently, the fact that the national measures are of EU inspiration is immaterial in establishing its legal effects. In this respect, one may legitimately ask whether a divergent interpretation of the AdC Lignes directrices from the original EU soft law acts constitutes a breach of the EU principle of consistent interpretation. Being implementing measures of EU acts, it could be argued that the AdC Lignes directrices should be interpreted in the light of the original EU soft law measure under the *Von Colson* doctrine.[42]

B. National Soft Law Measures Implementing EU Competition Soft Law in the UK

UK competition law is populated by a plethora of hard and soft law acts. In addition to the provisions stemming from the EU Treaties, a primary legal source is the UK Competition Act 1998, establishing the competences of the Competition and Market Authority (CMA). Section 60 provides that national courts should ensure that there is no inconsistency between the EU and UK law when applying that Act. The basis for implementation practices of EU competition soft law in the UK is the Enterprises Act 2002. Section 106 provides that the CMA has powers to adopt soft law measures in the form of advice and guidance documents.[43] The adoption of soft law is thus authorised by a national legislative provision. On the basis of this authorisation, the CMA has adopted multiple soft law measures. When implementing EU soft law, CMA acts refer to the original EU soft law and regulate their interplay with EU measures. Several CMA acts also replicate the content of EU soft law.

The study of the implementation of EU competition soft law in the UK will focus on two measures: the 'Mergers: Guidance on the CMA's jurisdiction and procedure' and the 'Vertical Agreements: understanding competition law' guidance adopted by the Office of Fair Trading (OFT). These acts, which are discussed below, implement the Commission Consolidated Jurisdictional Notice and the Commission's 'Guidelines on Vertical Restraints', respectively.

[40] ibid.
[41] Conseil d'État, 3ème – 8ème chambres réunies, 25/05/2018, 404382.
[42] Case C-14/83 *Von Colson* [1984] EU:C:1984:153. See also *Grimaldi* and *Kotnik* (n 18).
[43] See, eg, s 31D(1) of the Competition Act 1998, which requires the CMA to prepare and publish guidance on the circumstances in which it may be appropriate to accept binding commitments.

The purpose of the 'Mergers: Guidance on the CMA's jurisdiction and procedure'[44] is to set rules on mergers involving companies active in the UK and covered by the provisions of the Enterprise Act. It briefly addresses mergers falling within the ambit of Commission competence under the EU Merger Regulation[45] and the relationship between domestic and European merger control systems. This national guidance cannot supersede any EU legislation or guidance,[46] and is to be applied flexibly, with the Authority able to depart from it if need be.[47] Furthermore, the guidance cannot be considered as a comprehensive document, 'nor can it be cited as a definitive interpretation of the law'.[48] The content of the CMA guidance effectively reproduces the content of the Commission Consolidated Jurisdictional Notice under Council Regulation (EC) No 139/2004 on the control of concentrations between undertakings.[49]

In other national instruments, the connection with EU soft law has been acknowledged even more explicitly. An example is the 'Vertical Agreements guidance adopted by the OFT, the authority preceding the CMA.[50] This guideline explains how the authority would apply Article 101 of the Treaty on the Functioning of the European Union (TFEU) and the prohibition to vertical agreements, describing the application of the Commission's Block Exemption for Vertical Agreements and the treatment of vertical agreements. In this guidance document, the OFT has stated that it has taken into account the European Commission's Notice 'Guidelines on Vertical Restraints'[51] as a reference point.[52] As a result, the OFT Guidelines on Vertical Restraints should be read and applied together with the European Commission Notice on Guidelines on Vertical Restraints.[53] However, the CMA guidance also indicates that: 'Anyone in doubt about how they may be affected by the EC Treaty, the Competition Act 1998 or the Enterprise Act 2002 should seek legal advice.'[54]

Thus, the CMA's and OFT soft law measures are instruments addressed to companies in order to facilitate the interpretation of EU and national competition rules. The interaction between the EU and UK competition soft law is

[44] https://assets.publishing.service.gov.uk/government/uploads/system/uploads/attachment_data/file/384055/CMA2__Mergers__Guidance.pdf.

[45] Council Regulation (EC) No 139/2004 of 20 January 2004 on the control of concentrations between undertakings (the EC Merger Regulation) [2004] OJ L24/1.

[46] See n 44, para 1.5.

[47] ibid para 1.6.

[48] ibid para 1.5.

[49] European Commission, 'Commission Consolidated Jurisdictional Notice under Council Regulation (EC) No 139/2004 on the control of concentrations between undertakings' [2008] OJ C95/1.

[50] https://assets.publishing.service.gov.uk/government/uploads/system/uploads/attachment_data/file/284430/oft419.pdf.

[51] https://ec.europa.eu/competition/antitrust/legislation/guidelines_vertical_en.pdf.

[52] See n 50, para 4.6. The same also applies for other guidance; see, eg, https://assets.publishing.service.gov.uk/government/uploads/system/uploads/attachment_data/file/284396/oft401.pdf.

[53] 'Guidelines on Vertical Restraints' [2010] OJ C130/1.

[54] See n 50, at 1.

clearly governed by the principle of consistent interpretation, reaffirmed at the national level under section 60 of the Competition Act and, more specifically, in the analysed national soft law acts.[55] Such principle ensures consistency between the EU and UK levels of governance.[56]

In order to assess and identify the legal effects of the CMA's soft law, attention should be paid to the competence of the CMA to adopt soft law measures under the Enterprise Act. Under this legislation, the authority is empowered to issue guidance concerning competition policies to the public. Therefore, such competence would be devoid of purpose if CMA soft law acts could not produce legal effects at least in the form of interpretative documents. As a consequence, CMA's soft law measures should be presumed to produce legal effects in the light of the CMA's competences. Another question is whether they can be invoked against individuals, as in France. First, it should be noted that the CMA relies on its guidance documents when issuing decisions against third parties.[57] Second, in case *Société Coopérative de Production SeaFrance SA v The Competition and Markets Authority et al*,[58] the UK Supreme Court (UKSC) interpreted the 2014 CMA Merger guidelines discussed above. In the judgment, these guidelines were used to evaluate the effects of the cessation of business and determine the way in which the CMA assesses the relevant circumstances. The UKSC did not interpret the CMA guidelines in the light of the original EU soft law. However, the judgment confirms that CMA soft law acts produce legal effects on third parties, both as legal basis for CMA's decisions and as an interpretative document. In addition, the CMA soft law has a 'self-binding' effect on the authority's discretion.

By way of a preliminary conclusion, the effects of UK competition soft law seem clearer and more coherent than those of French competition soft law. Indeed, the CMA has not excluded the 'normative purpose' (ie, binding nature) of its soft law measures. Consequently, no contradiction has arisen between the wording of the CMA soft law and the way in which it has been applied by the CMA – a contradiction that we have observed in relation to some of the analysed French competition soft law.

Yet the concerns raised for the AdC's soft law also apply to the CMA measures. The CMA wields an extensive margin of discretion in the implementation and application of EU policies set in soft law acts.[59] If the national implementing

[55] *cf* 'Vertical Agreements', https://assets.publishing.service.gov.uk/government/uploads/system/uploads/attachment_data/file/284430/oft419.pdf.

[56] As required by the principle of supremacy, if a conflict between national soft law and EU hard and soft law arises, the latter must prevail. How the CMA guidances will be applied after Brexit remains to be seen.

[57] See, eg, https://assets.publishing.service.gov.uk/media/5a71fe2be5274a7f9c5862d4/provisional_findings_report.pdf.

[58] *Société Coopérative de Production SeaFrance SA v The Competition and Markets Authority et al* [2015] UKSC 75.

[59] The same circumstances could also arise for other NCAs when implementing EU soft law and applying relevant national measures.

acts have binding effects not envisaged for the original EU measures, the former will 'overachieve' the policy results set at the EU level.[60] As a result, the application of the CMA soft law by the national authority without taking into account the legal effects of the original EU soft law will lead to the fragmentation of the effects between EU soft law and national implementing acts. The fragmentation of legal effects of EU soft law may also arise in the context of judicial interpretation of CMA soft law. If CMA's soft law is applied or interpreted by UK courts as having effects that are different from those of the EU original measures, the courts will also contribute to the fragmentation of the legal effects of soft law.

IV. EU ENVIRONMENTAL SOFT LAW

Both the EU and its Member States share legislative competences in environment. The EU environmental administrative structure is not centralised and relies on a number of EU and national entities, unlike the competition law model, where the Commission plays a *primus inter pares* role. EU soft law is also different in the context of environmental law and policy. EU environmental measures often take the form of framework legislation. Soft law may be used to complement these frameworks and detail the content of EU environmental policies. Overall, environmental soft law has an interpretative function aimed at fostering the implementation of complex pieces of EU environmental legislation.[61]

EU environmental soft law is abundant, amounting to more than 150 EU instruments in the form of recommendations, opinions and communications.[62] The wealth of EU environmental soft law is partly due to the substantial Commission's soft law-making powers stemming from EU hard law. For instance, Directive 2008/98 provides the Commission with the power to adopt guidance documents addressed to the Member States concerning the reduction of environmental impact and waste.[63] As discussed by Eliantonio, EU environmental soft law has rarely been interpreted by the ECJ and is mostly cited by Advocates General (AGs), who use it as an interpretative tool.[64] The case law on environmental guidance documents demonstrates that there is no uniform approach in relation to their effects. While the non-binding nature of these documents

[60] EU soft law measures implemented by the CMA may provide that they do not have binding effects. See, eg, the 'Commission's notice on Immunity from fines and reduction of fines in cartel cases', implemented in the UK through the 'CMA's guidance as to the appropriate amount of a penalty'. The Commission notice is explicitly deprived of binding effects on the Commission.

[61] M Eliantonio, 'Soft Law in Environmental Matters and the Role of the European Courts: Too Much or Too Little of it?' (2018) 37 *Yearbook of European Law* 496.

[62] Compiled by the author from https://eur-lex.europa.eu.

[63] Directive 2008/98/EC of the European Parliament and of the Council of 19 November 2008 on waste and repealing certain Directives [2008] OJ L312/3, arts 8 and 38.

[64] Eliantonio (n 61).

is accepted in some cases,[65] the existence of legal effects does not seem to be explicitly excluded.[66]

A. National Soft Law Measures Implementing EU Environmental Soft Law in France

The protection of the environment is at the core of numerous soft law acts issued by the Agence de l'Environnement et de la Maîtrise de l'Énergie (ADEME). This authority has a broad mandate to gather information, mobilise the public, advise in the adoption of policies and assist in their implementation.[67] The ADEME works under the supervision of the Ministry of Ecological and Solidarity Transition (METS).[68] Both the ADEME and the METS issue national guidance documents (*circulaires* and *lignes directrices nationales*), which deal with similar themes to Commission guidance documents on environmental policy.[69] Some of the ADEME and METS guidelines expressly refer to these Commission documents. For instance, the French guidelines concerning the Environmental Impact Assessment Directive cite relevant EU soft law and include weblinks to EU guidance documents.[70] Other soft law acts by the ADEME or the METS implement national hard law[71] or are preparatory documents for the adoption of local strategies[72] giving effects to EU policies.[73] Two examples of French environmental soft law will be discussed below: the ADEME measures implementing the EU circular economy plan and the METS 'Lignes directrices nationales sur la séquence éviter, réduire et compenser les impacts sur les milieux naturels' (hereinafter 'METS Lignes directrices').

[65] See, eg, Case C-461/13 *Bund für Umwelt und Naturschutz Deutschland* [2014] EU:C:2014:2324, Opinion of AG Jääskinen.

[66] Eliantonio (n 61); J Scott, 'In Legal Limbo: Post-legislative Guidance as a Challenge for European Administrative Law' (2011) 48 *Common Market Law Review* 329.

[67] www.ademe.fr/en/about-ademe.

[68] Décret n° 2017-1071 du 24 mai 2017 relatif aux attributions du ministre d'Etat, ministre de la transition écologique et solidaire, JORF n°0123 du 25 mai 2017 texte n° 10 sets out the competences of this minister.

[69] G Lisi et al, 'National Report on France: The Use of EU Soft Law by National Courts and Administration in the Field of EU Environmental Law' in M Eliantonio and G Lisi (eds), 'EU Environmental Soft Law in the Member States: A Comparative Overview of Finland, France, Germany, Italy, the Netherlands, Slovenia and the UK' (2020) SoLaR Working Paper, https://papers.ssrn.com/sol3/papers.cfm?abstract_id=3656418.

[70] This is confirmed by Lisi et al (ibid).

[71] See ADEME 'Méthanisation' (November 2016), www.ademe.fr/sites/default/files/assets/documents/avis_ademe_methanisation_novembre_2016.pdf. The document specifies that the methanisation should be one of the initiatives to achieve the objectives of the law on the green transition.

[72] See, eg, ADEME, *Guide Méthodologique du Développement des Stratégies Régionales d'Économie Circulaire en France* (2014). This guide is mainly intended for elected officials and agents to mobilise support in view of the entry into force of the law on the green transition.

[73] See, eg, 'Lignes directrices encadrant l'adoption de décisions d'autorisation de mise à disposition sur le marché de produits biocides', implementing Regulation (EU) No 528/2012.

In 2014, the Commission adopted the 'Communication setting out the action plan for a circular economy',[74] but at present its effects remain unclear. The circular economy policy was positively received in France, with the Law concerning the energetic transition for the green growth enacted in 2015.[75] The legislation provides the ADEME with powers to adopt recommendations and guidelines on the disposal of waste as implementing acts of the circular economy plans. The ADEME has exercised this competence by adopting guidelines[76] to guide the public in the achievement of circular economy objectives. The language used in the ADEME documents is informative and educative.[77] To a large extent, ADEME soft law on circular economy reproduces the educative-informative content included in similar EU soft law measures. As an example, the ADEME has published a *fiche tecnique*[78] on the EU system of ecolabelling. The document states that it seeks to diffuse information concerning the European Ecolabelling system in France, and contains links to the Commission website and the relevant guidance on the EU system on ecolabelling.[79] In addition, it sets out EU environmental legislation and the interaction of the EU policies with relevant national measures.

The METS Lignes directices date back to 2013.[80] They are based on EU directives,[81] but reference and take note of Commission guidance.[82] They address 'the concerned operators' such as state entities, companies and associations, and lay down principles and harmonised methods at the national level on the implementation of the 'avoid, reduce and compensate' sequence[83] under EU and national legislation.[84] The guidelines specify that their nature is methodological and they 'propose non-normative methods'.[85]

[74] 'Communication from the Commission to the European Parliament, the Council, the European Economic And Social Committee and the Committee of the Regions Towards a Circular Economy: A zero waste programme for Europe' COM(2014)398.

[75] Loi relative à transition énergétique pour la croissance verte. The connection between this legislation and the Commission initiative is further confirmed by the following document: www.ecologique-solidaire.gouv.fr/sites/default/files/9-1-17_PLAN_DECHET_2016-2025_pour_BAT.pdf.

[76] See ADEME 'L'économie Circulaire en 10 Questions' (2009), www.ademe.fr/leconomie-circulaire-10-questions and www.ademe.fr/faire-dechets-0.

[77] They employ expressions such as 'Utilisez le papier avec modération' and 'Respectez les doses recommandées'.

[78] www.ademe.fr/sites/default/files/assets/documents/fiche-technique-ecolabel-europeen-201901.pdf.

[79] ibid 1.

[80] www.side.developpement-durable.gouv.fr.

[81] see pages 11 and 21 of the METS Lignes directices.

[82] ibid 78, 122 and 139.

[83] Lignes directrices nationales sur la séquence éviter, réduire et compenser les impacts sur les milieux naturels. Service de l'économie, de l'évaluation et de l'intégration du développement durable (Paris, Ministère de l'écologie, 2013).

[84] see n 83, at 4 ('Les recommandations méthodologiques de chaque fiche proposent des modalités possibles de mise en œuvre des textes législatifs et réglementaires existants, y compris sur la base d'exemples').

[85] www.ecologique-solidaire.gouv.fr/eviter-reduire-et-compenser-impacts-sur-lenvironnement#: ~: text=Le%20minist%C3%A8re%20d%C3%A9finit%20la%20politique,par%20la%20diffusion%20d'%C3%A9l%C3%A9ments.

Both the ADEME and METS soft law is primarily addressed to citizens and businesses. The ADEME guidelines in particular attempt to influence individual behaviour by addressing the general public. The ADEME and METS acts are also among the instruments guiding the activities of the French authorities competent to enforce environmental law, that is, regional bodies and the so-called *préfets*.[86]

While it is not yet established whether this soft law could be applied as self-standing instruments against individuals, one could argue that the ADEME and METS acts may be invoked together with liability rules applicable in the field of environmental law concerning matters such as waste disposal.[87] In such a scenario, these soft law acts could be used as interpretative instruments to detail the content of obligations set out in EU and national legislation. If so, the need to obtain judicial protection in relation to these soft law acts is pronounced.[88] Then again, the 'self-binding' effect of French environmental soft law is limited. Due to their 'educative' nature, these soft law measures could in principle bind their author only if the authority had sanctioning powers, which is not currently the case. For instance, the ADEME is not directly involved in the enforcement of environmental law, since its role is mainly advisory and educative. It cannot adopt decisions or issue measures that are binding on third parties based on its own soft law. Accordingly, the ADEME does not exercise any discretion in its relationship with individuals, and thus the question of whether its discretion is bound by its soft law becomes void. The same discussion also applies to the METS, which does not possess enforcement powers either.

To date, French courts have not exhaustively addressed the question of the legal effects of environmental soft law produced by the ADEME and the METS. In 2014, the Court of Appeal of Nancy held that the METS Lignes directices analysed above do not have 'normative' value (ie, binding force).[89] The Court of Appeal did not consider the fact that these guidelines form part of the implementation measures of EU hard and soft law. Nor did it consider the presence of national hard law in interpreting the legal effects of the guidelines. However, this particular judgment was issued by a lower court, and a higher court might reach a different conclusion. A different interpretation of the legal effects of ADEME

[86] In France, the *préfets* are the main authorities in charge of enforcing environmental law. For an overview of the environmental administration in France, see https://uk.practicallaw.thomsonreuters.com/Document/I9e2e9fb2a29d11e79bef99c0ee06c731/View/FullText.html?originationContext=docHeader&contextData=(sc.Default)&transitionType=Document&needToInjectTerms=False&firstPage=true&bhcp=1.

[87] See art 1246 of the French Civil Code, regulating the action for liability for environmental damage.

[88] ADEME, 'Caractérisation de la Problématique des Déchets Sauvages' (February 2019), www.ademe.fr/sites/default/files/assets/documents/rapport-caracterisation-problematique-dechets-sauvages-2019.pdf.

[89] Cour Administrative d'Appel de Nancy, 1ère chambre – formation à 3, 12/06/2014, 13NC00244, Inédit au recueil Lebon. The judgment refers to the concept of 'normative value', which seems to correspond to the EU notion of 'legally binding' effects.

acts is nevertheless likely in the light of the jurisprudential trends in France. In recent years, French courts have been increasingly open towards acknowledging the legal effects of soft law acts.[90] Be that as it may, in this case too, we observe the risk of fragmentation of legal effects of EU soft law and national implementing measures, since the effects of national soft law are interpreted without taking those of the EU original measures into account.

B. National Soft Law Measures Implementing EU Environmental Soft Law in the UK

From an organisational perspective, UK environmental governance is more fragmented than the French system. The UK Environment Agency (UKEA) is the main body responsible for enforcing and issuing environmental permits. In addition, other authorities oversee the implementation of environmental policies in the different regions of the UK.[91] The UKEA has issued several soft law measures, which in most cases are adopted to implement EU soft or hard law. The following analysis focuses on two UKEA soft law acts: the 'Guidance on the legal definition of waste and its application' and 'European Union Emissions Trading System (EU ETS) Phase III – Guidance for installations', implementing the Commission's Guidance document on the Waste Framework Directive and the Commission's Monitoring and Reporting Regulation (MRR) Guidance document, respectively.

The 2012 'Guidance on the legal definition of waste and its application'[92] is part of measures adopted by the UK to transpose[93] the Waste Framework Directive.[94] It also implements EU soft law instruments concerning the circular economy. It states the following: 'This guidance is published alongside the Commission guidance interpreting the key provisions of the Directive … and takes account of the Directive's definitions and provisions.'[95] The final part of the guidance seeks to make the principles established in the EU and national case law on the definition of waste more accessible to the public. The guidance specifies that they do not change the legal definition of waste, and they do not take precedence over the case law on the definition's interpretation. They only provide clarifications on that case law according to the competent authorities'

[90] E Honorat, 'Innover et tenir bon' in *La scène juridique: harmonies en mouvement. Mélanges en l'honneur de Bernard Stirn* (Paris, Éditions Dalloz, 2019) 327.

[91] For example, the Natural Resources Wales and the Scottish Environment Protection Agency.

[92] UK Environmental Agency, 'Guidance on the Legal Definition of Waste and its Application, 8, https://assets.publishing.service.gov.uk/government/uploads/system/uploads/attachment_data/file/69590/pb13813-waste-legal-def-guide.pdf.

[93] ibid.

[94] Directive 2008/98/EC of the European Parliament and of the Council of 19 November 2008 on waste and repealing certain Directives [2008] OJ L312/3.

[95] UK Environmental Agency (n 92) 8.

knowledge at the time of publication of the guidance. They also include details on how operators should use them. First, businesses and other organisations remain responsible for ensuring compliance with the law on waste, and the courts are in charge of interpreting it. Second, in the event of a disagreement between a competent authority and a third party as to whether a particular substance is waste, legal advice should be sought.[96] This guidance serves as an interpretative tool for waste operators that must comply with it.[97] It is not clear whether the guidance binds the discretion of the UKEA.[98]

A second example of UK environmental soft law implementing EU soft law is the 'European Union Emissions Trading System (EU ETS) Phase III – Guidance for installations', which was adopted by the UKEA in 2018.[99] The original EU guidance clearly specifies that it lacks legally binding effects.[100] The UKEA document serves various objectives. First, it describes the main provisions of the greenhouse emissions regulations. Second, it sets out the understanding of the views of the UK Department for Business, Energy and Industrial Strategy (BEIS) on how the regulations should be applied and how particular provisions should be interpreted. Third, it sets out the regulators' understanding of BEIS's views on how particular provisions in relevant European legislation should be read. The guidance also explains the conditions under which to obtain a permit under the UK regulations. In addition, it gives directions on how to make applications (including permit applications) and how to comply with the permit terms. It uses prescriptive language addressed to relevant operators on how to obtain the permits and the applicable requirements.[101] In particular, it clarifies that the use of the word 'must' indicate a legal requirement.[102] The guidance aims at complementing existing EU legislation, as it lists the obligations under the UK regulations and applicable European legislation.

Two features of the UKEA EU ETS soft law suggest that this document produces legal effects towards third parties: the prescriptive wording, aimed at influencing the behaviour of third parties, and the clear link[103] with national hard law and EU legislation. The presence of legal effects is confirmed by the

[96] ibid 13.

[97] ibid.

[98] UK regulators have to comply with the Regulators' Code, which sets out the power to adopt guidance and advice to the public, and the general principles of UK administrative law, including legality and proportionality. See https://assets.publishing.service.gov.uk/government/uploads/system/uploads/attachment_data/file/300126/14-705-regulators-code.pdf.

[99] https://assets.publishing.service.gov.uk/government/uploads/system/uploads/attachment_data/file/714272/EU-ETS-Phase-III-Guidance_for_installations.pdf.

[100] European Commission, 'Guidance Document – The Monitoring and Reporting Regulation – General guidance for installations', MRR Guidance document No 1, updated version of 27 November 2017, 1.

[101] See n 99, arts 16 ff.

[102] ibid p 3.

[103] The relevant EU and national legislation is extensively mentioned in the considered UK environmental soft law instruments.

fact that the UKEA has robust sanctioning powers and can punish violations of its soft law measures. However, if the UKEA EU ETS guidance is seen as enforceable, a twofold risk will arise. First, to the extent that the EU original measure has no binding effects, the legal effects of EU soft law and those of national implementing soft law will differ. Second, the enforceable nature of the UKEA EU ETS soft law may overachieve the objectives set in the original EU soft law.

Whether or not this guidance document binds the UKEA is uncertain. No guidance from the UK courts' case law exists concerning the legal effects of any UKEA soft law.

V. AN ANALYSIS

The picture that emerges from the analysis of implementation practices of EU soft law in France and the UK is complex.

In France, EU competition and environmental soft law has been implemented through a combination of soft and hard law. In terms of legal effects, French authorities' soft law measures implementing EU soft law reproduce to a large extent the uncertainties surrounding the original EU soft law. A textual analysis of the implementing soft law reveals incoherencies in the practice of the French competition authority. The greatest problem is that the wording of soft law measures does not correspond to the way in which these acts are used in practice. For example, the AdC has included caveats excluding the 'normative' purpose of its soft law documents, but has itself invoked them against individuals. Indeed, the AdC has relied on its 'non-binding' guidelines when issuing merger decisions. Similarly, French courts have interpreted the AdC's soft law measures as binding on their author, but have not settled whether they may be invoked against third parties before national courts.

A degree of uncertainty arises in the environmental field too. For example, the ADEME guidance documents implementing the Commission communications on the circular economy utilise a prescriptive language aimed at motivating citizens. Yet it is not clear whether they can be enforced against individuals. This option is not entirely ruled out, because the ADEME acts are capable of guiding the enforcement of environmental law by the French competent authorities. The same observation with regard to individuals applies to METS soft law. Then again, self-binding effects for the issuing authority seem unlikely, because neither the ADEME nor the METS has enforcement powers of its own. With respect to case law, a French lower court has excluded the 'normative nature' of national environmental soft law.[104]

[104] See Cour Administrative d'Appel de Nancy (n 89).

Overall, French courts have not taken a clear stance on the effects of national soft law measures implementing EU soft law and have not interpreted the national acts in light of the original EU measures.

In the UK, the question of the binding nature of soft law has occupied neither regulators nor judges. In the area of competition law, UK legislation and soft law guidance include clauses requiring courts and sector operators to solve potential conflicts between EU acts (including soft law) and national implementing measures in favour of the former (eg, section 60 of the Competition Act). Such clauses play a crucial role in ensuring coherence between the EU and the UK legal orders. The wording of the UK soft law does not rule out legal effects towards individuals. For this reason, there are no contradictions between the language used in those acts and the way in which these measures are applied or interpreted. The national legislative framework (eg, the competence of the CMA to issue soft law acts) and the enforcement powers of UK national authorities (eg, the UKEA sanctioning powers) suggest that UK soft law – both competition and environmental – is binding towards third parties. Whether or not UK soft law acts self-bind their authors is open to debate. However, such effects cannot be excluded in the absence of clear indications to the contrary.

Overall, UK courts have interpreted the effects of national soft law on a case-by-case basis and have relied on soft law acts, mainly in the competition field, as interpretative tools. No UK court has interpreted UKEA environmental soft law acts so far.

In a comparative analysis, the French implementing soft law is by and large faithful to the original EU soft law, and the terminology of the French soft law reflects, to a large extent, that of the original EU measure and rules out the existence of legal effects. UK soft law seems instead to be written to have legally binding effects, unlike the original EU soft law that UK soft law implements. Consequently, UK soft law may run the risk of overachieving what EU soft law, deprived of legal effects, requires. Such a risk exists, for instance, in relation to the UKEA EU ETS Guidance, the wording of which is prescriptive and implies binding effects, while the EU original document is deprived of legally binding effects.

Yet, for both UK and French soft law implementing EU soft law, the same concern arises: these national acts may be *interpreted or applied* as producing legal effects different from those of the EU original measure.

Even where EU soft law is considered as lacking legal effects, national implementing measures can be interpreted and applied by courts and regulators in a binding manner. An example is provided by the AdC Lignes directrices, the wording of which creates significant unpredictability for market operators. The document rules out its 'normative purpose'. Yet the Lignes directrices have been relied on by AdC when the authority has evaluated alleged anti-competitive behaviour. Similarly, UK soft law acts implementing EU environmental soft law may be considered as having binding effects, while the original EU soft law is not binding. This fragmentation of legal effects of EU and national soft law is problematic for two reasons. First, when the legal effects of national measures diverge from those intended by the original EU measure, national soft law implementing acts could interfere with the expected policy goals established at the EU level. Second, the fragmentation of legal effects across different policy levels adversely affects legal certainty, the principle of uniform application and legitimate expectations, as well as the sincere cooperation between EU and national authorities provided under Article 4(3) of the Treaty on European Union (TEU).[105]

There are no easy fixes. In order to 'harmonise' the effects deriving from EU soft law measures across the Member States, one possible solution would be to apply national implementing (soft or hard) law consistently with EU soft law. But the principle of consistent interpretation can only partially address the fragmentation of the legal effects of EU soft law and national implementing measures. Namely, the unclear wording of EU soft law instruments and their inconsistent use by EU institutions may lead national authorities to implement EU soft law in a manner that does not correspond to the letter and spirit of the original soft law measure, but reflects a national understanding of soft law. Consequently, divergent national implementing measures generate effects that are different from those envisaged by European institutions – a situation that cannot be remedied by the principle of consistent interpretation.[106]

The following question arises: how can we then ensure that the wording (*scripta*) of soft law measures 'stays' (*manent*) and does not 'fly away' (*volant*)? Some suggestions are offered in the concluding remarks.

VI. CONCLUDING REMARKS

This chapter has analysed the effects of selected EU soft law measures by authorities in France and the UK to implement EU competition and environmental soft law. Implementation practices in France and the UK are different; furthermore, the effects of national soft law implementing EU soft law may diverge from those of the original EU soft law. The diversity of implementation practices and the (resulting) fragmentation of legal effects between EU soft law and national implementing measures are problematic for a number of reasons. They hinder legal certainty and the principle of legitimate expectations, as well as the sincere cooperation between EU and national authorities, guaranteed under Article 4(3) TEU. Ensuring a consistent interpretation of national implementing measures in the light of EU soft law is not a perfect solution to the problem. When the wording of the original EU soft law measure is unclear or

[105] The uniform application of EU law is a well-established principle in the ECJ case law. See, eg, Case C-510/10 *TV2 Danmark A/S v NCB* [2012] EU:C:2012:244.

[106] A similar view has been expressed in Korkea-aho (n 18).

its use by EU institutions is inconsistent, national authorities are often at a loss as to how to implement EU soft law. Consequently, the principle of consistent interpretation is not workable.

European and national authorities should instead strive to enhance the uniformity of the effects of soft law measures. But they should not embark on this effort in a non-coordinated fashion; rather, they should cooperate. Possible ways to do so include, among other things, institutional meetings involving EU and national authorities to determine the effects of EU soft law instruments and relevant implementing measures. A further option is the alignment of the wording of national soft law instruments with that used in the original EU soft law act, coupled with the duty of both EU and national authorities to apply soft law in line with the chosen wording. In particular, both EU and national entities should ensure that EU soft law is considered as 'written words' (*scripta*), whose meaning and effects are to 'remain' (*manent*) in the legal orders of the Member States.

Part II

Country Analyses

6

EU Soft Law in Cyprus
In Search of Role and Value

NAPOLEON XANTHOULIS AND ANASTASIA KARATZIA*

I. INTRODUCTION

THIS CHAPTER AIMS to identify and evaluate the use and effects of EU soft in two policy fields, namely competition law and financial regulation within the Cypriot legal order.[1] In carrying out this research, we apply a mixed methodology. With respect to competition law, we analyse the decisions of the national competition authority and the case law of the Cypriot courts. Furthermore, we draw on the Cypriot competition authority's own perceptions about EU soft law – as these were recorded in the authority's answer to a questionnaire – to evaluate the latter's normative and practical impact in the domestic administrative practice.[2] With respect to financial regulation, we carry out an empirical analysis of the published instruments issued by the competent Cypriot regulator and review the relevant case law.[3]

The chapter is structured as follows: In section II, we briefly describe the basics of the Cypriot legal system, tracing the historical roots of its hybrid nature. In section III, we explore the normative role of soft law. We focus on Cypriot 'circulars', the main instrument giving effect to EU soft law in the Cypriot administrative practice, and analyse their legal effects and reviewability in light of the case law of Cypriot courts. Section IV presents our two case studies. We begin by offering an overview of the interaction between EU soft law and the Cypriot public administration. Thereafter, we explore the use of EU soft

* We would like to thank the Cyprus Commission for the Protection of Competition for responding to our questionnaire.

[1] Due to space constraints, environmental law and social policy are not covered.

[2] The questionnaire was based on the SoLaR template, annexed to this volume as Annex II. Our analysis is largely focused on administrative practice, as there is limited case law on soft law in the fields of financial regulation and competition law.

[3] The Cypriot financial regulator declined to be interviewed.

law instruments by the Cypriot public authorities in the fields of competition law and financial regulation and discuss our findings. We identify a lack of uniform approach to EU soft law within the Cypriot administrative practice in the two fields of policy and explore the respective implications in our concluding remarks.

II. CYPRUS: A HYBRID LEGAL SYSTEM

Built upon the dual foundations of common law and civil law, Cyprus is generally classified among the so-called 'mixed' legal systems.[4] Although Cyprus' constitutional and administrative law is dominated by the continental tradition, the rules and principles of private law are largely governed by the common law doctrine.[5] There is a strict hierarchy of norms, at the top of which we find a Constitution in the form of a single written document. At the same time, the general principles of administrative law developed under the continental doctrine. Somewhat paradoxically, Cypriot courts today still receive guidance from pre-1960 English common law principles, even if these are no longer in force in the UK. Similarly, the case law of other common law jurisdictions is still regarded as persuasive authority in Cypriot litigation.[6]

The fusion of civil law and common law expands beyond the normative design of the Cypriot legal system, influencing its governance and institutional practice. The Cyprus Supreme Court endorses Greek-inspired administrative law principles whilst operating under common law-based procedural rules. Judicial decisions enjoy strong precedential value and the Supreme Court of Cyprus retains the power to reverse its own judgments. This fusion of civil law and common law-based authorities in judicial practice often obscures the method of interpretation of legal norms and leads to an inconsistent use of terms and concepts in judicial reasoning. Overall, the Cypriot legal system can be described as a dynamic amalgamation of different normative traditions, constantly interacting and transforming the legal landscape, with EU law playing an important role.

Cyprus' membership of the EU brought about a fundamental change in the domestic normative order.[7] Following the examples of other Member States, the

[4] N Hatzimihail, 'Cyprus as a Mixed Legal System' (2013) 6 *Journal of Civil Law Studies* 37. By the term 'mixed legal system', we refer to 'political entities where two or more systems apply cumulatively or interactively, but also entities where there is a juxtaposition of systems as a result of more or less clearly defined fields of application', as defined in V Palmer, 'Mixed Legal Systems' in M Bussani and U Mattei (eds), *The Cambridge Companion to Comparative Law* (Cambridge, Cambridge University Press, 2012) 379. See also V Palmer (ed), *Mixed Jurisdictions Worldwide: The Third Legal Family*, 2nd edn (Cambridge, Cambridge University Press, 2012).

[5] S Farran et al (eds), *A Study of Mixed Legal Systems: Endangers, Entrenched or Blended* (Abingdon, Routledge, 2016) 238.

[6] ibid 89.

[7] For a general overview, see C Lycourgos, 'Cyprus Public Law as Affected by Accession to the EU' in C Kombos (ed), *Studies in European Public Law* (Athens, Sakkoulas, 2010).

Cypriot Constitution contains an explicit provision[8] recognising the primacy of EU law over domestic law, including national constitutional provisions, in line with the normative hierarchy signalled by the European Court of Justice in *Costa v Enel*.[9] The need to comply with EU law requirements has also led to the creation of many independent regulatory authorities, each responsible for different policy areas, such as consumer protection, personal data protection, competition, children's rights, energy and state aid, amongst others. For example, the Preamble to the Law that establishes the Cypriot Competition Authority[10] explicitly mentions that the Law is amended for the purposes of applying Regulation 1/2003 in Cyprus.[11]

The Guidance issued by the Legal Service of the Republic in 2017 on drafting and harmonising national legislation sheds light on the transposition of EU law in the national legal order.[12] The Guidance mainly deals with the transposition of EU Regulations and Directives, and briefly refers to the transposition of Decisions and Framework Decisions.[13] Although this Guidance is informative about the transposition of EU law in the national legal order, it does not mention EU soft law. Moreover, to our knowledge, there is no overarching national transposition mechanism concerning EU soft law. Hence, even though the binding effect of 'hard' EU norms was never questioned within the Cypriot legal order, assessing the equivalent normative and practical influence of the so-called 'soft law' instruments adopted by EU institutions is a more difficult exercise. We will discuss the transposition of EU soft law in the areas of competition law and financial regulation in section IV as part of our case studies in these two policy areas.

III. CYPRIOT 'SOFT LAW' INSTRUMENTS: THE CASE OF 'CIRCULARS'

As such, soft law is not a recognised legal category in the Cypriot legal order. Judicial decisions do not refer to the term 'soft law' to describe national or EU instruments that may be normative in nature, but do not have binding force. Equally, the Cypriot legal scholarship does not typically engage with the soft law discourse when analysing executive power. This is not to say that there are

[8] Cyprus Constitution, art 1A.

[9] Case C-6/64 *Costa v ENEL* [1964] ECR 585.

[10] Protection of Competition Law 13(I)/2008 as amended.

[11] Council Regulation (EC) No 1/2003 of 16 December 2002 on the implementation of the rules on competition laid down in Arts 81 and 82 of the Treaty [2003] OJ L1/1.

[12] Republic of Cyprus Legal Service, 'Guidelines on Drafting National and Harmonizing Legislation', 27–30, www.law.gov.cy/law/lawoffice.nsf/All/795A0B23299892BAC22580DE0029E003?OpenDocument.

[13] For example, the Guidance stipulates that the drafter should clarify any unclear provisions of a Directive by studying the Directive in other official languages, Court of Justice of the European Union (CJEU) case law, relevant Commission guidelines and by asking the Commission itself for clarification.

no soft law instruments in Cyprus. In carrying out its conferred powers, the Cypriot administration regularly adopts opinions, recommendations, policy frameworks, guidelines and other types of instruments which do not have binding effects per se. However, following the classic continental legal tradition, courts and academic commentators generally prefer to analyse the effects of executive power by assessing their capacity to produce legal effects in the course of which they apply a substantive assessment. Hence, we first discuss how the courts conduct this substantive assessment in judicial review before discussing circulars in more detail.

A. Judicial Review and the Substantive Assessment of Legal Effects

According to Article 146(1) of the Constitution of Cyprus, concerned persons can bring a direct annulment action against any decision, act or omission of any organ, authority or person, exercising executive or administrative authority. The consistent case law of Cypriot courts has interpreted this provision as introducing two cumulative criteria for determining whether an act falls within the scope of judicial review. First, the contested measure must be 'administrative' (*διοικητική*) in nature. In many cases, the courts investigate whether the measure entails a 'public objective'[14] that would enable it to belong to the domain of public law rather than private law.[15] Second, an act must be 'executable' or of 'executive character' (*εκτελεστή πράξη*), in the sense that it must be capable of producing binding legal effects. A measure is regarded as having binding legal force where it is found to impose an obligation or determine the rights of a person.[16]

Only administrative acts specifying and individualising the scope of generally applicable norms can be subject to judicial review directly in annulment actions. By contrast, regulatory acts fall outside the scope of judicial review because they normally create norms of general application and are not typically directed to specific persons. Being quasi-legislative in nature, the normative scope of regulatory acts is not exhausted to individual instances, but can apply to innumerable present or future factual scenarios.[17] Unlike individual administrative acts, regulatory acts cannot be challenged directly before a court.[18] However, their validity can be reviewed indirectly as an incidental matter when raised in the course of an annulment action against a binding administrative act that was adopted by virtue of that regulatory act.

[14] *Savvas Yianni Valana and the Republic of Cyprus* (Case No 138/61), 9 April 1962; *Ναυτικός Όμιλος Πάφου v Αρχής Λιμένων* (1992) 1 ΑΑΔ 882, 893–94.

[15] *Achilleas Hadjikyriacou and Theologia Hadjiapostolou*, 3 RSCC F, 89. See also *Antoniou and Others v Republic* (1984) 3 CLR 623; and *Machlouzarides v Republic* (1985) 3 CLR 2342.

[16] *Κυπριακή Δημοκρατία v Sunoil Bukering Ltd* (Appeal No 1064) (1994) 3 ΑΑΔ 26, 21 January 1994.

[17] *Lanitis Farm Ltd v Republic* (1982) 3 CLR 124.

[18] *Παπαφιλίππου v Republic* (Case No 5/61) (1961) 1 RSCC 62, 26 April 1961; *Police v Hondrou* (Case No 133/61) (1962) 3 RSCC 82, 6 April 1962.

Cypriot courts endorse a substantive approach for determining whether an act is capable of producing binding legal effects vis-a-vis a person. This means that rather than focusing on the label of an instrument, Cypriot courts are ready to examine the content of the act in the light of its wording, subject matter and context.[19] An act is regarded as normative in nature if it brings about a change in the legal position of a person by either imposing duties or determining rights. The same methodology applies for assessing the legal effects of acts that can be described as 'soft law' instruments.

B. Circulars

The closest instrument in the Cypriot administrative practice that partially resembles the nature and function of what the literature broadly refers to as soft law is a 'circular' (Εγκύκλιοι). Circulars are measures which are commonly adopted by the Cypriot government and public service in the exercise of their conferred powers; in Cyprus, they are typically associated with the Franco-Greek administrative culture, but can be found in other jurisdictions (eg, France and Italy).[20]

Circulars can be divided into two basic categories in terms of the manner via which they produce legal effects: 'internal circulars' and 'external circulars'. Internal circulars are those normally directed to subordinate administrative bodies; as such, they are regarded as 'internal' to the public service's function. Sometimes, the Cypriot legislator imposes a duty on a public authority to issue a circular on a specific subject matter, eg, for the purposes of implementing and specifying a piece of legislation.[21] At other times, the legislator may empower a public authority to adopt an internal circular without imposing a strict duty to do so.[22] Finally, a public authority may decide to adopt a circular in the absence of explicit powers, relying on the authority's broad discretionary powers in the exercise of executive power.[23] The objectives of internal circulars also differ. Some circulars intend to regulate the conduct and practice of public officials taking the form of instructions or warnings, whilst others are merely informative in nature.[24] Circulars are also used for clarifying the scope or application of certain norms, expressing opinions and recommendations pertaining to the

[19] An exhaustive analysis falls outside the scope of this chapter. For examples of the Cypriot courts' approach, see the case law cited in nn 18–29.

[20] See N Rubio and O Ştefan, ch 8 in this volume and Jacopo Alberti and Mariolina Eliantonio, ch 11 in this volume on France and Italy, respectively.

[21] See, eg, *Άριστος Αριστείδης ν Κυπριακής Δημοκρατίας* (Appeal No 848) (1991) 3 ΑΑΔ 588, 6 November 1991.

[22] See, eg, *CP Envirosystems Ltd v Κυπριακής Δημοκρατίας* (Case No 322/96) (1997) 4 ΑΑΔ 3120, 12 December 1997.

[23] See, eg, *Σωτήρης Σωτηριάδης v Κυπριακής Δημοκρατίας* (Case No 310/91) (1992) 4 ΑΑΔ 2599, 24 July 1992.

[24] See, eg, *Άριστος Αριστείδης v Κυπριακής Δημοκρατίας* (n 21).

manner in which the administration should perform its tasks, or outlining the future course of action.[25]

Whether an 'internal' circular produces legal effects is determined by the Cypriot courts based on a substantive assessment if and when the circular is challenged before the courts. Due to their 'internal' function, such circulars have an impact on the powers and duties of public bodies, but not private persons. This means that they are unable to directly affect the legal position of persons external to the administration;[26] when these circulars do produce legal effects, these do not penetrate the walls of Cypriot bureaucracy. On this basis, the case law of the Cypriot courts has consistently held that persons outside the administration cannot contest the legality of internal circulars via direct annulment actions. This does not mean that circulars escape the principle of legality. Cypriot courts are empowered to review the validity of an internal circular indirectly if the circular has led to the adoption of a subsequent act with binding effects vis-a-vis persons.[27]

Different consequences may result from a finding of invalidity of an internal circular. In most cases, the invalidity of internal circulars would automatically invalidate any other act subsequently adopted on the basis of that circular. An exception to this rule is where the adoption of the final act was based on some other lawful authority, in which case the Court would uphold the validity of the final act.[28] Moreover, even if a party acted in violation of a circular when concluding an agreement with another private party (whose legal position was not affected by that circular), the validity of such an agreement may remain unaffected.[29]

The second category of circulars covers instruments capable of producing external legal effects. Such circulars can change the legal position of persons that are outside the administration. In turn, there appear to be two types of circumstances that can give rise to external legal effects. First, a court may conclude that an act issued in the form of 'circular' is de facto a decision with binding force. When this happens, the court would scrutinise the circular directly.[30] Second, a circular may be regarded as entailing self-imposed commitments on behalf of

[25] *Dr Andreas Vorkas and Others* v *The Republic of Cyprus* (Case No 204/83) (1984) 3 ΑΑΔ 757, 22 June 1984.

[26] *Βάσος Σολωμού ν Κυπριακής Δημοκρατίας* (Case No 1080/91) (1995) 4 ΑΑΔ 2002, 3 October 1995.

[27] *S Kyriakou Euromarket Ltd ν Κυπριακής Δημοκρατίας* (Case No 375/96) (1997) 4 ΑΑΔ 3191, 15 December 1997. See also *Ανδρέας Σ Κακουρή* v *Κυπριακής Δημοκρατίας* (Case No 631/90) (1991) 4 ΑΑΔ 2762, 26 July 1991.

[28] See, inter alia, in this respect, *Pikis v The Republic* (Case No 12/66) (1967) 3 CLR 562, 575, 22 September 1967; *Spyrou (No 1) v The Republic* (Case Nos 80/71, 96/71, 100/71, 145/71–147/71, 164/71, 166/71, 195/71, 196/71, 203/71–205/71) (1973) 3 CLR 478, 484, 11 September 1973; *Akinita Anthoupolis Ltd v The Republic* (Case No 362/78) (1980) 3 CLR 296, 303, 14 June 1980; *Paraskevopoulou v The Republic* (Case No 374/78) (1980) 3 CLR 647, 661, 662, 4 December 1980.

[29] *Στέλιος Μαρκίδης ν Εθνική Τράπεζα της Ελλάδος (Κύπρου) Λτδ* (Appeal No 303/2008) (2012) 1 ΑΑΔ 324, 8 March 2012; *Μαρία Συρίμη ν Παγκυπριακή Χρηματοδοτήσεις Δημόσια Εταιρεία Λτδ* (Appeal No 315/2007) (2010) 1 ΑΑΔ 1131, 12 July 2010.

[30] *Άριστος Αριστείδη ν Δημοκρατίας* (n 21).

the issuing public authority. Such acts then arguably produce dual legal effects. From the perspective of the author of these circulars, they impose a duty on the issuing administrative authority to comply with the normative content of the circular. Sometimes, the scope of this self-imposed duty would require that authority to either comply with its commitments or explain the reasons why departing from them is justifiable. From the perspective of other parties, these circulars trigger the right of affected persons to the protection of their legitimate expectations, namely an expectation that the public authority would fulfil its declared commitments.[31] Circulars with external legal effects that create norms of general application would be the same as Regulatory Acts.[32]

The multiple functions of circulars in the Cypriot administrative practice make it difficult to classify 'hard law' and 'soft law' measures within the Cypriot legal order. In addition to the above categorisation of 'internal' and 'external' circulars, one can add the circulars that have a quasi-binding effect on their addressees in terms of the consequences of non-compliance. An example can be found in the area of financial regulation, where the Cyprus Securities and Exchange Commission (CySec) is the competent authority. Article 25(1)(c)(ii) of the CySec Law[33] gives the power to CySec to collect information from persons who fall within the competence of CySec for the purposes of statistical analyses and risk management. In order to facilitate the collection of this information, Article 25(1)(c)(iii) allows CySec to determine the applicable procedure through issuing a circular. In order to characterise such a circular as soft law, we would have to argue that non-compliance with CySec's request for information as stipulated in the circular itself has no legal consequences. Yet, Article 37(5) gives CySec the power to impose administrative penalties to regulated entities that do not comply with a relevant circular. The power of an administrative body to impose penalties for not complying with a circular precludes an absolute categorisation of circulars as soft, non-binding measures. Instead, when put together with the above examples of circulars, it reinforces our understanding of a circular as a multi-purpose instrument, which only sometimes resembles what we generally perceive as soft law.

As such, the research of circulars issued by the competent national authorities was a key element in our attempt to understand the position and the role of EU soft law in the context of competition and financial regulation law in Cyprus. We now turn to the findings from our two case studies on EU soft law within the Cypriot administrative and judicial practice in the fields of competition law and financial regulation. The following section begins with some general remarks about EU soft law in Cypriot public administration, before focusing on the case studies.

[31] *CP Envirosystems Ltd v Κυπριακής Δημοκρατίας* (n 22). This seems to have been also implied in *Σωτήρης Σωτηριάδης v Κυπριακής Δημοκρατίας* (n 23); *S Kyriakou Euromarket Ltd v Κυπριακής Δημοκρατίας* (n 27).

[32] *China Wanbao Engineering Corporation v Κυπριακής Δημοκρατίας* (Case No 794/95) (1997) 4 ΑΑΔ 2084, 11 September 1997.

[33] Ο περί Επιτροπής Κεφαλαιαγοράς Κύπρου Νόμος του 2009 (*N* 73(I)/2009).

IV. EU SOFT LAW IN COMPETITION LAW AND FINANCIAL REGULATION IN CYPRUS

A. General Remarks

The Cypriot public administration does not seem to have a uniform approach towards EU soft law. The approach of the administrative bodies differs regarding the impact of soft law on the operations of the administration, as well as the implementation and communication of soft law to the public. The precise impact of EU soft law on the conduct of public officials in Cyprus remains relatively unknown and unexplored. As one commentator puts it: 'Whether government actors have initiated regulatory changes because they are "appropriate", or due to the risk of reputational damage, is not possible to determine.'[34] In certain fields, EU soft law has been seen as a source of clarification and guidance, which – contrary to some national 'soft law' measures mentioned previously – does not create binding obligations on the authority itself.[35] Elsewhere, the choice of soft law for regulating employment affairs has resulted in a high degree of compliance by the concerned parties, who rarely deviate from its normative scope, even if no legal sanctions are in place.[36] There is also evidence that in certain policy areas such as taxation, Cypriot officials treat specific EU soft law as a normative source that creates expectations of compliance.[37]

Regarding the way in which soft law is communicated to the public, the difference in the approach of the administration is apparent when we compare the practice of the Commission for the Protection of Competition (CPC) to that of the Office of the Commissioner for State Aid Control (hereinafter the 'Office'), which is an independent government official, and to that of CySec. On the website of the Office, there are several soft law instruments in the field of State aid, some of which take the form of circulars.[38] A number of these circulars aim to inform other public authorities (and, by virtue of their publication, the wider public) of new developments in EU soft law.[39] A similar practice is applied by CySec, which publishes circulars relating to soft law measures issued by the European Supervisory Agencies.[40] By way of contrast, the CPC has not made public any circular for the purpose of communicating or implementing EU soft law in the field of competition law. As we will see below, this does not mean that the CPC does not use such measures. An interesting question, which is yet to be explored, is whether the different approaches between Cypriot

[34] P Henriksen Ringstad, 'Between Soft Law and a Hard Place: EU Influence on Taxation Policies in Cyprus before, during and after the Bank Crisis' (Master's thesis, Department of Political Science, Faculty of Social Sciences, University of Oslo, 2014) 54–55.

[35] Questionnaire answered by the Cyprus CPC.

[36] A Emilianides and C Ioannou, *Labour Law in Cyprus* (Dordrecht, Kluwer, 2019) para 112.

[37] Henriksen Ringstad (n 34) 55.

[38] www.publicaid.gov.cy/publicaid/publicaid.nsf/csac11_gr/csac11_gr?OpenDocument.

[39] See, eg, 'Εγκύκλιος Αρ. 68 Νέες Κατευθυντήριες Γραμμές της Ευρωπαϊκής Επιτροπής για τις Κρατικές Ενισχύσεις Περιφερειακού Χαρακτήρα της περιόδου 2014–2020'.

[40] www.cysec.gov.cy/en-GB/home, 'Latest Circulars'.

public authorities with respect to the implementation (or not) of EU soft law instruments in the form of Cypriot circulars reflects a potential corresponding difference in the impact of EU soft law on the domestic administrative practice.

In the remainder of this chapter, we explore the impact of EU soft law instruments that are adopted in the field of competition law on the practice of the Cypriot competition authority (the CPC) and in the field of financial regulation in the practice of CySec. Our analysis is largely focused on administrative practice, as there was limited relevant case law in these two fields. Before proceeding with the analysis, a note on methodology is necessary.

B. Methodology

In respect of competition law, our research drew upon four sources. First, we conducted desk-based research on the legal framework establishing the CPC. Second, we recorded the experiences and views of the CPC itself as expressed in the single, authorised, written response by the CPC to our questionnaire which was based on the template of the European Network of Soft Law Research (SoLaR) for the face-to-face interviews.[41] Third, we analysed all the publicly available decisions of the CPC which refer to EU soft law instruments. Our entire dataset consisted of 496 decisions of the CPC from 2009 until 2019 that are recorded online, including decisions relating to Articles 101 and 102 of the Treaty on the Functioning of the European Union (TFEU) (or the respective national law) and decisions relating to merger control.[42] Through this method of triangulation, we have sought to identify the role and value of EU soft law in the decision-making process of the CPC. Finally, we researched the jurisprudence of Cypriot courts referring to EU soft law in competition law. We should also note that, in Cyprus, the responsibility for State aid does not belong to the CPC, but to the Office for the Commissioner for State Aid Control. Although we contacted the Office, we never received a response, so our findings with respect to competition law below do not include EU soft law on State aid.

Regarding financial regulation, we did not receive any response from CySec to our request to forward a questionnaire to relevant public officials or interview them in person. Hence, our findings derive from the research of the CySec practices, which are available on the CySec website. The website includes circulars issued by CySec since 2003. We collected all these publicly available CySec circulars into a database and identified those circulars that refer to: (i) EU binding instruments (eg, Regulations, Directives and Delegated Regulations); (ii) any type of EU soft law (eg, European Securities and Markets Authority

[41] The CPC agreed to respond to our invitation to an interview by answering a written questionnaire as an institution instead of having face-to-face interviews.

[42] The dataset includes all the published Decisions of the CPC, including those overruled by the Supreme Court: www.competition.gov.cy/competition/competition.nsf/index_en/index_en?OpenDocument.

(ESMA) Guidelines and European Supervisory Authorities (ESAs) Joint Committee Guidelines), including but not limited to the measures included in the SoLaR sample; (iii) Cypriot national law; and (iv) international instruments (eg, Financial Action Task Force Best Practices), including circulars mentioning measures from more than one of these categories. Finally, we researched the jurisprudence of Cypriot courts referring to EU soft law in financial regulation.

Out of 544 circulars that we recorded,[43] 70 refer to EU soft law, with 50 referring to Guidelines adopted by ESMA, the European Banking Authority (EBA) or the ESAs Joint Committees,[44] 10 refer to ESMA's Public Statements, and the rest are other documents such as ESMA or EBA Opinions, Publications or Briefings.[45] Focusing on the 50 circulars that refer to Guidelines, we intend to provide insight into the relevance and role of such Guidelines – as EU soft law measures – in the practice of CySec. Our database allowed for comparisons of circulars referring to Guidelines with circulars referring to legally binding EU and national instruments.

Below we will sketch the main findings in the fields of competition law and financial regulation. Our analysis shows that EU soft law increasingly strengthens its presence in the Cypriot administrative practice, but has yet to establish itself in the reasoning process of Cypriot courts. Furthermore, there are qualitative differences in the approach of the targeted Cypriot authorities in the use of EU soft law. This divergence can be explained, at least in part, with reference to the functions of EU soft law in the examined policy areas.

C. EU Soft Law in Cypriot Competition Law

The main legislative basis for the application of competition law in Cyprus is the Protection of Competition Law 13(I)/2008 as amended by Law No 41(I)/2014. This transposes Regulation 1/2003 into the domestic legal order and sets the powers of the CPC, as the national competent authority under the Regulation.[46] In its activity, the CPC is assisted by its internal administration (hereinafter the 'Service'). The Service is responsible for collecting data, reporting complaints and submitting suggestions to the CPC. It facilitates the CPC in the exercise of its powers and duties, which includes preparing drafts of the CPC decisions, carrying out investigations and communicating with external parties on behalf of the CPC.

[43] We excluded CySec circulars that simply announced the results of qualifying exams that CySec organises. The dataset is valid as of 1 March 2020.

[44] This number includes circulars that invite the regulated entities to contribute to public consultations for the drafting of new Guidelines.

[45] In particular, the dataset includes one Joint Supervisory Statement, one Supervisory Briefing, two ESMA Publications, two ESMA/EBA Opinions, one ESMA Briefing and one Consultation Paper that is not about Guidelines.

[46] Article 23. The Competition Commission was established under the Law on the Protection of Competition of 1989 (repealed) and was re-instituted under the 2008 Law on the Protection of Competition.

In its written response to our questionnaire, the CPC paints a picture of the use of soft law by the CPC that corresponds to the traditional understanding of soft law in the context of EU law as instruments that provide guidance and clarification pertaining to the interpretation of norms and the expected practices.[47] The organisation is often guided by EU soft law both during the investigation of submitted complaints and during *ex officio* investigations in relation to infringements of competition law. According to the CPC, the most frequently used instruments are the 'Guidelines on Vertical Restraints', the 'Guidelines on Horizontal Cooperation Agreements' and the 'Commission Communication in Applying Article 82'. The 'Guidelines on the Application of Article 81(3)' and the *De Minimis* Notice have also been used over time, while it appears that the 'Commission Notice on Cooperation within the Network of Competition Authorities' is also used, in accordance with the organisation's obligations under Regulation 1/2003.

A look into the dataset of the CPC decisions reveals that, out of the total 108 references to EU soft law instruments that we identified, the 'Commission Notice on the Definition of the Relevant Market' is the most often-cited measure (51.8 per cent), followed by the 'Guidelines on Vertical Restraints' (13.8 per cent).

Figure 6.1 References to specific EU soft law instruments in CPC decisions

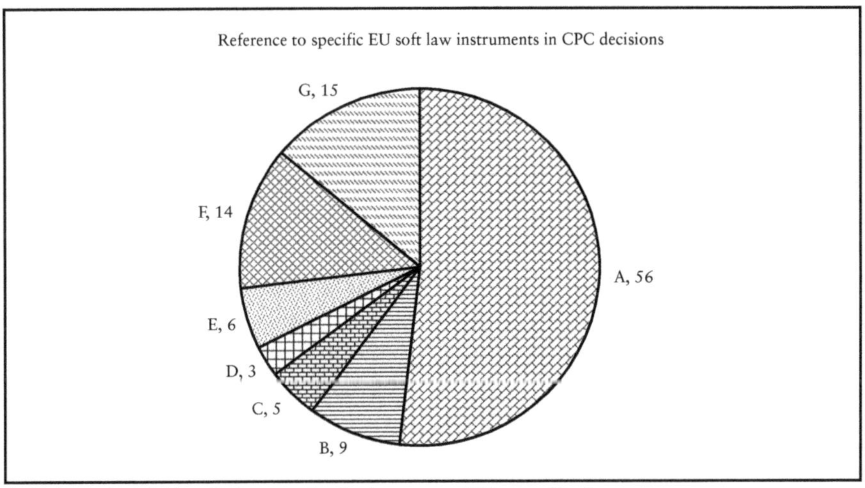

A Notice on the definition of relevant market for the purpoce of EU competition law

B Guidelines on Vertical Restraints

C Guidelines on the application of Article 81(3) TEC (current Article 101(3) TFEU)

D Guidelines on the applicability of Article 101 TFEU to horizontal co-operation agreements

E Guidelines on the method of setting fines imposed pursuant to Article 23(2)(a) of Regulation No 1/2003

F Guidance on the Commissioon's enforcement priorities in applying Article 82 TEC (current Article 102 TFEU) to

G Guidelines on the effect on trade concept contained in Articles 81 and 82 TEC (current Articles 101 and 102 TFEU)

[47] The CPC's written response to our questionnaire (on file with the authors). We received the response on 2 September 2019.

However, according to the CPC's replies to our questions, the choice of soft law instruments, as well as the intensity of their use, is not predetermined. Instead, the use of such measures is assessed on a case-by-case basis and depends on whether there is an actual need to resort to soft law. It is the investigating team of the CPC that will assess whether any of the EU Notices or Guidelines are relevant and whether they can offer useful guidance during the investigation process of a case at hand. Beyond the level of investigations, the decision-making body of the organisation may also be guided by soft law in formulating the substance of its decisions. In all circumstances, the decision as to whether to use soft law is taken objectively. When asked about the influences that motivate the use of EU soft law by the organisation, CPC replied that its decisions to resort to soft law instruments are not influenced by the manner in which the same instruments are treated in other jurisdictions or by the ideological or political underpinnings of individual officials involved in a case.[48]

As regards the frequency of the use of EU soft law in the CPC decisions, there appears to be no clear pattern. Figure 6.2 shows that the number of CPC decisions per year where reference is made to EU soft law has decreased in the last few years. However, a closer look at our dataset revealed that although the number of CPC decisions referring to soft law instruments has decreased, there is more variety to the EU soft law instrument to which the CPC refers. Having said that, we would treat this finding with caution, given that the choice of instrument also depends on the subject matter of the cases that the CPC addresses at any given time.

Figure 6.2 Number of CPC decisions per year referring to EU soft law

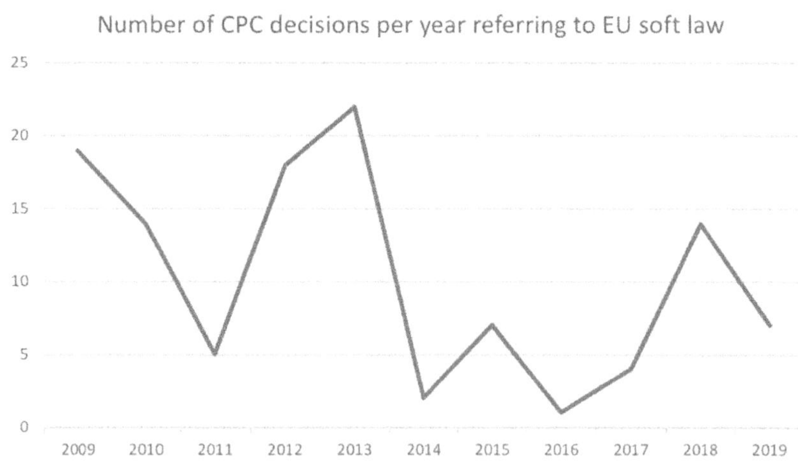

[48] The CPC's written response to our questionnaire (on file with the authors).

Overall, the CPC considers EU competition soft law as a useful normative component of the European competition policy and as an instrument that must be used in line with the application of the EU's wider policy framework. In the eyes of the CPC, EU soft law measures provide clarity and guidance, and enhance transparency in the application of competition law, while ensuring a homogeneous application of competition policy across Member States. Furthermore, soft law has the capacity to act as a catalyst for successful international cooperation and it is well suited to address the complexity and diversity of European affairs. Moreover, due to its ability to provide guidance and a level playing field for all parties concerned, soft law operates effectively in situations that mandate swift action.[49]

Interestingly, the CPC noted certain limits to the role and usefulness of EU soft law in the field of competition policy. For instance, the CPC's reply to the questionnaire clearly indicated that CPC sees EU hard law as taking precedence over any EU soft law instrument. In the view of the CPC, although soft law plays a useful role in clarifying EU or national norms and providing guidance both to the organisation and to the courts, it is less appropriate than hard law in regulating sensitive sectors. According to the CPC, EU soft law is not capable of affecting the rights or obligations of relevant stakeholders.[50] The position of EU soft law as serving a guiding role is reflected in the CPC decisions. Some of the expressions used in decisions referring to the Commission's Guidelines or Communications include 'the [CPC], *drawing guidance* from the case law and the Commission Guidelines on Vertical Restraints' 'the [CPC], *guided* from the Commission Communication on the Enforcement of Art. 81(3)' and 'the [CPC], *taking into consideration* the Guidelines'. Notably, in one of its decisions, the CPC clarified that Guidelines issued by the European Commission do not bind the CPC, but provide guidance as to the matter at hand.[51] By way of contrast, CPC has pointed out in its answer to our questionnaire that national soft law differs from EU soft law, in that the former is binding on the administrative body that issues it.[52]

So far, no EU soft law instrument in the field of competition law has been incorporated into the Cypriot legal order in the form of national – hard or soft – instrument. As a result, whenever the CPC refers to EU soft law, it cites the original EU instrument. Moreover, it does not appear that soft law in the field of competition has created legal friction in Cyprus so far: there is no reason to think that EU soft law works in favour of some actors to the detriment of others and there have not yet been cases where a national court reviewed or annulled

[49] ibid.
[50] ibid.
[51] ΕΠΑ 54/2012.
[52] The CPC's written response to our questionnaire (on file with the authors).

the use of EU soft law.[53] We identified only two cases where EU soft law measures were mentioned in court rulings.[54]

Unlike the picture in administrative practice, EU soft law has yet to finds its place in Cypriot case law. The lack of case law referring to competition soft law can be explained with reference to the jurisdiction of the Cypriot Administrative Courts (and the Supreme Court on appeal) to review measures adopted by the CPC. The jurisdiction of the courts in such administrative cases is limited to a procedural review of CPC decisions, as opposed to a substantive review of the merits of these decisions. As a result, the majority of the cases that arise before the Cypriot courts deal with issues such as the legality of the composition of the committee that adopted the decision, and whether the decision was taken in line with the principles of good administration.[55] Due to procedural limitations on the scope of judicial review, the cases that typically arise before the Cypriot courts do not allow the establishment of judicial precedent with respect to the interpretation and application of competition law rules or clarification as to the use of EU soft law by the CPC. There is a chance that such issues will arise following the transposition of the Damages Directive into Cyprus law, which may trigger civil claims involving EU soft law measures. We have not identified any such cases during our research.[56]

D. EU Soft Law in Cypriot Financial Regulation

The Law governing the activities of CySec makes it clear that the ESMA Guidelines and Recommendations are considered to be non-binding.[57] Article 25(3) requires CySec to participate in ESMA's activities and to evaluate, when transposing EU law, 'the non-binding Guidelines and Recommendations of ESMA' (our translation). This is a notable provision when considered alongside observations

[53] *Αρχή Τηλεπικοινωνιών Κύπρου εναντίον Επιτροπής Προστασίας Ανταγωνισμού* (Case No 2004/2012), 29 September 2015; *Αρχή Τηλεπικοινωνιών Κύπρου εναντίον Επιτροπής Προστασίας του Ανταγωνισμού* (Case No 2019/2012), 25 July 2016; *FISSLER GMBH εναντίον Επιτροπής Προστασίας του Ανταγωνισμού* (Case No 2056/2012), 12 September 2016.

[54] *Αρχή Τηλεπικοινωνιών Κύπρου ν Επιτροπής Προστασίας Ανταγωνισμού* (n 53), making reference to the 'Notice on the application of the competition rules to access agreements in the telecommunications sector – framework, relevant markets and principles' [1998] OJ C265/2. Also note that in *Τηλεπικοινωνιών Κύπρου ν Επιτροπής Προστασίας του Ανταγωνισμού* (n 53), the Supreme Court of Cyprus made reference to the argument of the parties which was based, amongst other things, on the 'Commission guidelines on market analysis and the assessment of significant market power under the Community regulatory framework for electronic communications networks and services' [2002] OJ C165/6, although without elaborating further.

[55] Decisions taken by public bodies should be in line with the Law governing the General Administrative Principles codified in Ο περί των Γενικών Αρχών του Διοικητικού Δικαίου Νόμος του 1999 (158(I)/1999).

[56] It should be noted here that the electronic database of Cypriot case law does not include the civil law cases below the level of the Supreme Court, so there is a chance that there have been some decisions dealing with damages claims.

[57] Ο περί Επιτροπής Κεφαλαιαγοράς Κύπρου Νόμος του 2009 (N 73(I)/2009) Άρθρο 25(3).

from the practice of national authorities in other Member States according to which these authorities perceive ESA guidelines to be de facto binding and transpose them through binding national measures.[58] As such, Article 25(3) gives rise to the question of whether, and to what extent, the letter of the law is reflected in the practice of CySec.

The first step in examining the above question is to consider how ESMA Guidelines are incorporated into the national regulatory framework. A number of ESMA Guidelines are presented as part of the regulatory frameworks governing fields that fall under CySec's regulatory competence.[59] For example, where CySec sets out the regulatory framework on short selling law, it states all the relevant EU Regulations, Commission Delegated Regulations, Commission Implementing Regulations and the ESMA 'Guidelines on Exemption for market making activities and primary market operations'[60] with a direct link to the Guidelines. In other fields, the Guidelines are presented as part of a legal package containing not only EU laws but also national legislation.[61] The Central Bank of Cyprus (CBC), which is responsible for regulation dealing specifically with banks, also mentions ESA Guidelines within the applicable legal framework. The CBC online database offers a tool for searching legislation, CBC Directives and ESA Guidelines pertaining to licensing and supervision, financial stability and other areas.[62] The database includes the Joint EBA and ESMA Guidelines on complaints-handling for the securities and banking sectors[63] for which the CBC website mentions: 'The abovementioned Guidelines have been issued jointly by ESMA and EBA and have been fully endorsed by the Central Bank of Cyprus (CBC).'[64]

On at least one occasion, a CySec Directive refers specifically to the ESA Joint Guidelines that relate to the scope of the particular legal instrument. Article 12.4 of the Directive of CySec for the Prevention and Suppression of Money Laundering and Terrorist Finding states that: 'The Obliged Entities when assessing the money laundering and terrorist financing risks and when applying risk-based measures and procedures, should take into account, among

[58] T Tridimas, 'Indeterminacy, Legal Uncertainty, and Discretion in EU Law' in J Mendes (ed), *EU Executive Discretion and the Limits of Law* (Oxford, Oxford University Press, 2019) 62; M Avbelj (ed), 'Soft Law Financial Regulation in the Member States: Finland, France, Germany, Italy, the Netherlands, Slovenia and the UK' (2020) SoLaR Working Paper, https://papers.ssrn.com/sol3/papers.cfm?abstract_id=3668793.

[59] www.cysec.gov.cy/en-GB/legislation/services-markets/epey.

[60] ESMA, 'Exemption for market making activities and primary market operations under Regulation (EU) 236/2012 of the European Parliament and the Council on short selling and certain aspects of Credit Default Swaps' [2013] ESMA/2013/74.

[61] See, eg, CySec's explanation of the regulatory framework governing investment services law: www.cysec.gov.cy/en-GB/legislation/services-markets/epey.

[62] www.centralbank.cy/en/legal-framework.

[63] EBA and ESMA, 'Guidelines for complaints-handling for the securities (ESMA) and banking (EBA) sectors' [2018] JC 2018 35.

[64] Central Bank of Cyprus, announcement 6 February 2020, www.centralbank.cy/en/announcements/complaints-by-customers-of-credit-acquiring-companies-cacs-06-02-2020.

others, the Joint Guidelines and the Guidelines issued by the Financial Action Task Force (FATF).' Our understanding is that this creates an obligation for the regulated entities to consider the Guidelines as opposed to an obligation to comply with them per se.

The second step is to examine how CySec takes into account these Guidelines in its practice. CySec communicates these Guidelines to the relevant stakeholders in different ways through the adoption and publication of circulars. In some instances, the Circulars serve the purpose of informing the regulated entities of the issuing of new Guidelines. On other occasions, the Circulars inform the addressees about existing Guidelines. Very often, the Circulars contain a clear statement that CySec adopts the Guidelines. For example, Circular C338[65] explicitly mentions that 'CySec adopts the guidelines by incorporating them into its supervisory practices' and reminds the addressees of their obligations, which are not based on the guidance itself, but on the underlying regulation on complaints handling.[66]

On some occasions, the Circulars which refer to ESMA Guidelines state what they expect from the regulated entities as a result of these soft law measures. It should be noted that not all Circulars refer to the legal effects of the ESMA Guidelines. Those that do refer to legal effects demonstrate a pattern of the wording used by CySec to communicate to the regulated entities the effects that arise from these soft law measures: most of the Circulars use expressions that are consistent with the wording of the ESAs Regulation. Article 16 of the ESMA Regulation states that: 'The competent authorities and financial market participants *shall make every effort to comply* with those guidelines and recommendations' (emphasis added).[67] The most frequently found wording in CySec's Circulars is that regulated entities 'shall/should make every effort to comply' with the Guidelines as these are adopted by CySec. Expressions connoting expectation of or encouragement by CySec towards the recipients to comply with the Guidelines – or at least to take them into consideration – are also used in the Circulars. Some examples are: 'CySec expects [the regulated entities] to fully comply', 'CySec urges the financial market participants to whom these Guidelines apply to make every effort to comply with the Guidelines', 'CySec encourages the Cyprus Investment Firms to take measures to apply the Guidelines as soon as possible' and 'CySec expects persons responsible for the prospectus to consider these Guidelines when preparing a prospectus'.

The variation in the wording of CySec Circulars has implications with respect to the type of legal effects that these Circulars can produce. Since a concerned party is required to consider or make efforts to comply with a Circular,

[65] Repealing the 'Guidelines published for complaints-handling for the securities (ESMA) and banking (EBA) sectors' published on 27 May 2014 (JC 2014 43).

[66] Article 26 of Regulation 2017/5653.

[67] Circular 'C231: Joint Guidelines on the prudential assessment of acquisitions and increases of qualifying holdings in the financial sector'.

it can be argued that this Circular is capable of producing a legally binding obligation – albeit limited and relatively imprecise – vis-a-vis these parties. In order to fulfil the scope of this obligation, a concerned party would either have to take steps to be in line with the normative content of the Circular or to justify its non-compliance with the same. Such an obligation appears to mirror what typically applies to the case of ESMA Guidelines under Article 16 of the ESMA Regulation. By contrast, where a CySec Circular includes prescriptive phrases that go so far as an 'expectation of full compliance', it is possible for concerned parties to perceive the CySec Circular in question as if it required unconditional compliance. In other words, it seems to produce binding legal effects similar to those typically seen in regulations, orders and decisions. By way of comparison, Circulars referring to CySec's obligations arising from EU hard law such as a regulation use expressions such as 'The Commission *must* strictly apply the provisions of the Regulation'[68] or 'The Regulations are binding in their entirety and directly applicable in all Member States. The Commission requests ALL Regulated Entities to comply with the Regulations'.[69]

At other times, the ESMA Guidelines constitute the basis on which CySec then builds its own guidance for the regulated entities. An example of this is the ESMA Guidelines on remuneration policies and practices. In June 2013, with a Circular, CySec informed the Cyprus Investment Firms (CIFs) and the Fund Management Companies that ESMA had published the said Guidelines. The Circular provided the link to the Guidelines and a brief description of their purpose, and stated that CySec would issue its own guidelines based on those of ESMA.[70] This can be connected to a subsequent circular, which contains CySec's Guidelines on remuneration policies and practices. This Circular is informative about the way in which CySec perceives guidelines that it publishes, as it states that: 'Guidelines do not reflect absolute obligations. For this reason, the word "should" is often used. However, the words "must" or "are required" are used when describing a requirement of the Law.'[71] It could therefore be argued that national soft law in the form of Guidelines issued by CySec is understood by CySec not to be capable of giving rise to a legally binding obligation. The legal status of such national soft law would ultimately be determined by Cypriot courts on the basis of a substantive assessment if and when a relevant case arises.

CySec therefore uses the word 'should' with respect to the content of national Guidelines and the word 'must' for requirements deriving from national law.

[68] Circular 'CI144-2014-22: Capital adequacy and exposures of the Cyprus Investment Firms'.

[69] Circular 'CI144-2014-29: Council Regulations (*EU*) No.959/2014, No.960/2014 and No.961/2014 concerning restrictive measures in respect of actions undermining or threatening the territorial integrity, sovereignty and independence of Ukraine'. See also Circular 'C279: Discretions of Regulation (EU) No 1286/2014 on key information documents for packaged retail and insurance-based investment products (PRIIPs)', which states: 'CySEC emphasizes that all regulated entities should comply with the Regulation and any legislative acts are issued in accordance to it.'

[70] See, eg, Circular 'CI144-2013-18: Guidelines on remuneration policies and practices'.

[71] Circular 'C031: Guidelines GD-IF-07 Guidelines on remuneration policies and practices', para 3.

The difference in the wording of 'should' and 'must' that CySec makes between national Guidelines and national law can be parallelised with the difference in the wording of Circulars referring to 'EU hard law' and 'EU soft law'. By way of contrast to Circulars mentioning ESA Guidelines, as we described them above, Circulars that refer to EU Regulations (as an example of EU hard law) often include expressions such as: 'The Commission requests all entities to comply', 'CySec will not hesitate to use enforcement powers to uphold compliance', 'Regulated entities/Cyprus Investment Firms not complying will encounter enforcement action' and 'CySec emphasises that all regulated entities should comply with the Regulation'. Similar expressions are used in Circulars referring to national hard laws.[72]

Finally, regarding judicial practice, in a series of cases concerning the failure of one of the country's biggest banks in 2013 and the criminal liability of the bank's executives, the Supreme Court of Cyprus referred to the Guidance issued by the Committee of European Securities Regulators (CERS), which was the predecessor of ESMA.[73] The Guidance, inter alia, provides examples of behaviour that constitutes market abuse. The Court referred to the Guidance in the process of defining the 'spreading false or misleading information' under the national law[74] adopted to transpose the EU Directive on insider dealing and market manipulation (market abuse).[75] The case is a clear example of Guidelines being used in judicial practice to assist with the interpretation of national legislation. At the same time, it is an exception to the dominant trend in judicial practice not to make substantial use of EU soft law in the examined areas. So far, in the three cases where the selected guidelines of ESMA were briefly referred to,[76] the Cypriot courts did not elaborate on their legal or factual significance, as these instruments were not central to the main disputed issues.

[72] See, eg, Circular 'C204: Freedom to provide investment and ancillary services and/or perform investment activities in a third country', which concerns compliance with the Investment Services and Activities and Regulated Markets Law of 2007 and states that 'CySEC therefore draws the attention to all CIFs, that the relevant legislation provides that CySEC, within its supervisory powers, may take the necessary supervisory decisions, including the imposition of appropriate administrative sanctions and/or the restriction of the CIF's access to provide investment and ancillary services and/or perform investment activities in a third country and/or other administrative measures; in case of noncompliance with this Circular'.

[73] CERS Guidance on 'Market Abuse Directive Level 3 – first set of CESR guidance and information on the common operation of the Directive', www.esma.europa.eu/sites/default/files/library/2015/11/04_505b.pdf; Cyprus Supreme Court Criminal Appeals (Nos 2/2018 and 3/2018) *Iliadi v Republic and Bank of Cyprus v Republic*, Decision of 12 September 2018.

[74] Article 20(1)(c) of Πράξεων Προσώπων που Κατέχουν Εμπιστευτικές Πληροφορίες και των Πράξεων χειραγώγησης της Αγοράς (Κατάχρηση Αγοράς) Νόμος του 2005, N 116(*I*)/2005. The Preamble to the Law mentions that it was partly adopted to transpose EU legislation.

[75] Directive 2003/6/EC of the European Parliament and of the Council of 28 January 2003 on insider dealing and market manipulation (market abuse) [2003] OJ L96/1.

[76] See, eg, *Στυλιανίδης v Επιτροπή Κεφαλαιαγοράς Κύπρου* (Case No 905/2014), 22 November 2019; *Ξενοφώντος v Τράπεζα Κύπρου Δημόσια Εταιρεία Λτδ και Κεντρική Τράπεζα Κύπρου* (Case No 2503/2014), 11 July 2018; *Ελένης Χριστοδουλίδου v Sea Star Capital PLC κ.α.* (Case No 5852/2016), 14 October 2016.

V. CONCLUDING REMARKS

Although Cypriot law has not reserved official space for the term 'soft law', the use of national and EU instruments of such nature in the Cypriot legal system is a reality. At the same time, EU soft law has yet to play a significant role in judicial decision-making in the examined policy areas. Although there may be more than one reason why Cypriot judges do not refer to EU soft law, it is clear that the limitations on the scope of judicial review make it difficult for the Cypriot courts to engage with and apply the substantive rules – hard and soft – governing the administrative decision the legality of which is put into question.

In the absence of a legal category of soft law in the Cypriot legal system, 'circulars' can be regarded as the most prominent example of national soft law. Although EU competition soft law has not yet affected judicial practice, the Cypriot competition authority frequently refers to EU soft law instruments. The responses of the CPC to our questionnaire indicate that it does not consider EU competition soft law to have binding normative force, and there is no evidence that it is treated as such in the CPC practice. EU competition soft law remains a normative source that informs and guides the CPC in the exercise of its conferred powers; yet, the CPC appears to prioritise retaining wide discretion as to whether or not it will be guided by such instruments and to what extent in individual cases.

The CPC follows a case-by-case approach, making recourse to EU soft law in its decisions to the extent that this is appropriate and depending on the subject matter of the case at hand. By contrast, in the field of financial regulation, EU soft law has a more significant role. By using 'circulars', CySec integrates EU soft law into the Cypriot legal order and occasionally communicates the content of such EU instruments to concerned parties. These circulars expect the regulated entities to comply or to make their best efforts to comply. Sometimes the wording used by CySec might lead the concerned parties to perceive these Guidelines as requiring full and unconditional compliance. To ease the risk of possible discrepancies between CySec's intended legal effects and respective perceptions of concerned parties, CySec could apply a more consistent approach to the terms used in its Guidelines. A more harmonised administrative practice in this respect can contribute to CySec's regulatory efficiency and promote legal certainty by enabling stakeholders to better identify their requirements under CySec's Guidelines.

There is no uniform approach to EU soft law within the Cypriot administrative practice. The absence of a harmonised approach towards EU soft law across the Cypriot public administration is not surprising. Divergence can be attributed to the different functions of EU soft law in the two policy areas. At the EU level, financial regulation is highly centralised and regulated; by contrast, competition law remains relatively decentralised, leaving a significant degree of discretion to national authorities. In this sense, a different degree of divergence reflects the different regulatory models that characterise both policy fields.

More importantly, such a disparity preserves flexibility in the exercise of administrative discretion by acknowledging the regulatory nuances between EU soft law instruments, reinforcing the view that EU soft law is not a unified legal category.

Naturally, this chapter has important limitations. Our findings relied heavily on the empirical analysis of the administrative instruments with respect to the CPC and even more so with respect to CySec. Despite the wealth of information that our analysis of CySec's circulars has offered, important questions remain unanswered. What is the rationale for CySec applying a differential approach between national and EU financial regulation soft law? What are the possible enforcement implications – if any – for regulated entities that do not make an effort to comply with ESMA Guidelines? And what exactly is perceived by CySec as a 'best efforts' obligation? With respect to competition law, what is the reason underlying the CPC decision not to integrate EU soft law into the domestic legal order?

Future researchers could complement our effort by gaining insights from individual public officials on the perceptions and use of EU soft law in their daily administrative practice. Similarly, it would be useful to conduct interviews with Cypriot judges to acquire a better understanding on their readiness to be influenced by EU soft law, in what manner and under what conditions. Finally, researchers can draw comparisons between the approaches of Cypriot authorities to EU soft law in the policy fields that we examined and other policy fields.

7

The Finnish Soft Law Puzzle

How Can a Rule-Bound Parliamentary Democracy Be Reconciled with EU Soft Law?

EMILIA KORKEA-AHO, KATRI HAVU, PÄIVI LEINO-SANDBERG AND LIISA TARKKILA

I. INTRODUCTION

THIS CHAPTER ASSESSES the impact and application of EU soft law by Finnish judges and authorities. The starting point for our research is the notion that Finland is traditionally described as a country with a strong emphasis on formal law and support for parliamentary democracy.[1] Thus, the logical assumption at the outset seems to be that Finnish judges and civil servants, who are imbued with these values, are sceptical of soft law as non-binding executive 'law', given its lack of formality and approval by parliamentary procedures. Yet this chapter contradicts this view by investigating administrative practice and the Finnish supreme courts' case law in four European Network of Soft Law Research (SoLaR) policy fields. Against 'theoretical' odds, Finnish civil servants and judges use EU soft law regularly, endorsing its guiding effects in a multitude of situations. Civil servants also report that they apply soft law without discussing or challenging its contents or nature as applicable law. No significant differences exist between the investigated policy fields. The Finnish approach to EU soft law is positive, pragmatic and constructive. The level of institutional legitimacy accorded by the Finnish authorities to EU soft law seems to distinguish Finland from many other countries discussed in this volume.

[1] A Siaroff, 'Corporatism in 24 Industrial Democracies: Meaning and Measurement' (1999) 36 *European Journal of Political Research* 175, 179.

This 'Finnish soft law puzzle' is examined in four sections. Section II briefly describes the key role of legislation and the doctrine on the sources of law, since soft law – as a descriptive and conceptual category – has traditionally been discussed in relation to this doctrine. The Finnish soft law research has been, and still is, limited. The efforts of Finnish academic commentaries have mostly been directed at the EU, the international level,[2] or the national impacts of EU soft law, as in this project. Unsurprisingly then, soft law has defied a settled translation in Finnish. Sometimes soft law is literally translated as soft regulation (*pehmeä sääntely*), but it is not unusual to find the term 'soft law' in an otherwise Finnish-language text.[3] The findings of the interviews conducted with judges and civil servants are presented in section III. We have conducted a total of 18 interviews with Finnish judges and administrative officials acting across the four policy fields.[4] Drawing on these interviews as well as case law research, we describe how and on what grounds Finnish authorities use non-binding norms. In section IV, we examine why Finnish authorities comply with EU soft law, in the absence of a clear legal obligation to do so and their inculcation in a legal culture that has traditionally emphasised legislative obedience. By way of a conclusion in section V, we suggest that the Finnish judges and civil servants' constructive engagement with soft law is best explained by a mix of historical reverence for preparatory works to legislation and 'pragmatic legalism'. This approach is less interested in abstract considerations of the nature of bindingness, but rather builds on a careful consideration of all the elements that ultimately contribute to the adoption of 'the right decision' in the case.

II. EU SOFT LAW AND THE FINNISH LEGAL SYSTEM

The position of EU soft law in the Finnish legal system cannot be understood without understanding the doctrine of the sources on law, ranking the Acts of

[2] J Klabbers, 'The undesirability of Soft Law' (1998) 67 *Nordic Journal of International Law* 381; J Klabbers, 'The Redundancy of Soft Law' (1996) 65 *Nordic Journal of International Law* 167; E Korkea-aho, 'Laws in Progress? Reconceptualizing Accountability Strategies in the Era of Framework Norms' (2013) 2 *Transnational Environmental Law* 363; E Korkea-aho, 'Legal Interpretation of EU Framework Directives: A Soft Law Approach' (2015) 40 *European Law Review* 70; J Alaranta, 'Täytäntöönpanohankkeet reach-asetuksen konkretisointimekanismina' (2009) *Ympäristöpolitiikan ja -oikeuden vuosikirja* 203.

[3] Finnish-language judgments may also cite EU soft law measures in English without translating them into Finnish. See, eg, KHO:2017:182 or KHO:2017:161. The former concerns the protection of wolves. The Finnish Supreme Administrative Court referred the case to the European Court of Justice, also inquiring on interpretation of the Commission Habitats guidance. The Court did not mention the guidance; see Case C-674/17 *Luonnonsuojeluyhdistys Tapiola Pohjois-Savo – Kainuu ry v Risto Mustonen and Others* [2019] EU:C:2019:851.

[4] These 18 interviews were completed in the period from March 2017 to April 2019 and were spread as follows: five interviews in the context of environmental policy, five in social policy, four in relation to financial policy and four in the context of competition and State aid. Out of 18 respondents, six are judges and 12 work in administration. The larger proportion of civil servants is explained by the fact that in the context of financial policy, all the respondents are civil servants. For the methodology, see M Hartlapp and E Korkea-aho, ch 4 in this volume.

Parliament highest in the hierarchy of norms. We first discuss the choice for legislation as a constitutional requirement and, second, how (if at all) Finland transposes EU soft law into national law. In section II.C, we elucidate on the doctrine on the sources of law and what it means from the point of view of the application of law.

A. The Key Role of Acts of Parliament

The Constitution of Finland does not have a clause on categories of legal acts, unlike, for instance, the EU treaties which specifically mention the types of acts the EU institutions can adopt in Article 288 of the Treaty on the Functioning of the European Union (TFEU). The hierarchy of norms is nevertheless clear, in that when the Constitution refers to 'law' (*laki*), this is understood as a reference to Acts of Parliament. The government has limited delegated powers to issue Decrees (*asetus*) that must have a legal basis in the Constitution or in an Act of Parliament and be compatible with them. Section 80 of the Constitution lays down that the President of the Republic together with the Government, the Government on its own, or Ministries can issue Decrees.[5]

The primary role of legislation is visible in the Constitution. Namely, Section 80 of the Constitution requires that certain matters shall be laid down by Acts of Parliament, not by government Decrees or soft law. The division into 'legislative' and 'non-legislative' matters is also a key consideration in upholding parliamentary democracy and, the role of the Parliament of Finland (Eduskunta).[6] In the Finnish legal system, the distinction between legislative and non-legislative matters is primarily a substantive one, not a procedural one as in the EU, where the nature of a legal instrument is defined with reference to the procedure in which it has been approved. In Finland, a matter is legislative in nature if it affects the rights and obligations of private individuals or if the Constitution otherwise requires an Act to be adopted. Further, the Parliament's Constitutional Law Committee has clarified that a matter is of a legislative nature if it affects the foundations of an individual's rights or obligations, the same matter is currently regulated in an Act of Parliament or there is a general understanding that the matter should be regulated by an Act of Parliament.[7]

There is no mention in the Constitution of other types of regulation than Acts of Parliament and Decrees. However, Ministries and central authorities can issue non-binding letters of instruction (*ohjauskirje*) to their subordinate

[5] The Constitution of Finland (731/1999), 11 June 1999, translation available at: https://www.finlex.fi/fi/laki/kaannokset/1999/en19990731.pdf.

[6] Opinions of the Constitutional Law Committee 11/2000 vp and 12/2000 vp. See also V-P Viljanen, 'Onko eduskunnan asema lainsäädäntövallan käyttäjänä muuttunut?' (2005) *Lakimies* 1050, 1059–61.

[7] Opinion of the Constitutional Law Committee 11/2000 vp.

administration and share information on good practices.[8] Public authorities can issue these letters of instruction, even if the power to issue such measures has not been specifically provided by law. Ministries can issue letters of instruction on the basis of Section 68 of the Constitution that makes each Ministry, within its purview, responsible for the preparation of matters to be considered by the government and for the appropriate functioning of administration. Other agencies, such as regional state administrative agencies, can also issue letters as provided for by law. Usually there is no express basis in the law to do so, and the authority to issue instructions is implied by virtue of a general competence of the authority. Letters of instruction are internal measures and they are not meant to have effects outside the administration.[9]

B. The Finnish Transposition of EU Soft Law

There is no general guidance as to whether and how EU soft law acts are transposed in Finland. Practices vary depending on the policy context and the specific issue. The Finnish Ministry of Justice has prepared an EU law guide for legislative drafting, *Lainlaatijan EU-opas*. The guide makes note of non-binding rules that 'may have an impact, inter alia, on the interpretation of a specific article of the EU Treaty or EU act'. This kind of instrument can 'also be addressed, for example, to a particular EU Member State. Although such an instrument does not, in principle, have legal effects binding on a Member State, it can still have a significant practical impact on the activities in the Member State'.[10]

With respect to the transposition of EU soft law in Finland, the above distinction between legislative and non-legislative is important. Those matters that are deemed to have a legislative character must be transposed via Acts of Parliament. Conversely, non-binding acts cannot be used in matters that have a legislative character; instead, they are frequently used in non-legislative matters. Although most EU law obligations are transposed into domestic law through Acts of Parliament, government Decrees and soft law are also used to give effect to EU law. For instance, Finland implemented the so-called Plastic Carrier Bag Directive (2015/720/EU) by adopting a framework agreement with the Federation of Finnish Commerce.[11]

[8] Public authorities can also issue internal administrative regulations (*hallinnon sisäinen määräys*). They are legally binding instruments; see Lainkirjoittajan opas, 13.9, http://lainkirjoittaja.finlex.fi/13-saadosten-lajit-ja-saadostaso/13-9.

[9] For their use during the Coronavirus epidemic, see E Korkea-aho and M Scheinin '"Could You, Would You, Should You?" The Use of Non-binding Guidelines and Recommendations during the Coronavirus Epidemic in Finland' (2020) *European Journal of Risk Regulation* (forthcoming).

[10] Section 1.3.4 of Lainlaatijan EU-opas, last updated 29 June 2017, eu-opas.finlex.fi (our translation).

[11] For the agreement in English, see http://kassi-info.fi/wp-content/uploads/2016/10/Plastic_Carrier_Bag_Agreement.pdf.

Apart from failing to give guidance on how EU soft law should be transposed nationally, the guide does not specify *whether* EU soft law should also be transposed into national law. Not surprisingly, then, our findings, gleaned from the analysis of soft law instruments in the four policy fields, attest to a diversity of strategies in relation to the status of EU soft law in Finland.

Social policy stood out by its tendency to what we call 'nationalise' EU soft law. By this, we mean that domestic actors 'translate' EU soft law norms into national non-binding guidelines, explaining them to a domestic audience. The most conspicuous examples of this were provided by public procurement guidelines. For instance, the EU's Buying Social guide was incorporated into national soft law documents in a bid to give a national context to the EU recommendation on social aspects in public procurement. The Buying Social guide was seen as too general to provide concrete guidance to national public procurement authorities.[12] Clear examples of the 'transposition' of soft law also occurred in the context of financial policy. According to the information published on the European Securities and Markets Authority (ESMA) website, Finland is in full compliance with all ESMA guidelines.[13] The Finnish Financial Supervisory Authority has nationally 'transposed' (*saattaa kansallisesti voimaan*) many of the ESMA guidelines by adopting its own guidelines (*ohje*) and has published them on its website.[14] In these national guidelines, the Financial Supervisory Authority does not 'nationalise' EU rules by giving its own version of the guidance, but rather simply recommends that relevant actors comply with the ESMA guidelines, which are available on the Finnish Authority's website.[15]

EU soft law may also be transposed into national law by incorporating it into government proposals. For instance, in the government proposal relating to the Shareholder Rights Directive II (EU 2017/828), Commission soft law was referred to as an important source for a government Decree.[16] However, we did not find evidence of such practice in relation to the SoLaR instruments.

In the other two fields, EU soft law is not regularly subject to the process of 'nationalisation'. In the context of environmental law, EU guidance documents co-exist with national soft law documents usually prepared by – or under the

[12] E Korkea-aho, 'The Finnish Report on the Reception of Social Soft Law' in M Hartlapp (ed), 'Studying EU Soft Law Effects in Social Policy' (2020) SoLaR Working Paper, https://papers.ssrn.com/sol3/papers.cfm?abstract_id=3668981.

[13] www.esma.europa.eu/document-types/compliance-table.

[14] See, eg, 'ESMA/2013/74 Concerning Short-Selling' (Finanssivalvonta), www.finanssivalvonta.fi/tiedotteet-ja-julkaisut/valvottavatiedotteet/2013/markkinatakausta-ja-ensimarkkinaoperaatioiden-poikkeuksia-koskeva-ohje-voimaan-19.6.2013; or 'ESMA/EBA (JC 2014 43)' (Finanssivalvonta), www.finanssivalvonta.fi/tiedotteet-ja-julkaisut/valvottavatiedotteet/2014/muutetut-maaraykset-ja-ohjeet-32013-asiakasvalitusten-kasittelysta-voimaan-27.10.2014. Then again, the Finnish authority did not adopt guidelines to transpose ESMA Guidelines 2014/1293.

[15] https://www.finanssivalvonta.fi/en.

[16] See Government Proposal HE 305/2018 vp, 53 and 155. The government Decree was, nevertheless, adopted without reference to the guidelines simply because the Commission guidelines were not available.

auspices of – the Ministry of the Environment. The interviewed (environmental) judges reported that they prefer national guidance documents to EU ones. In their view, since the judgment's audience is Finnish, it makes sense to rely on guidance which is linguistically and legal-culturally closest to this particular audience. However, if the case concerns the interpretation of a particular EU directive in the national context, then the courts use EU guidance, as explicitly remarked by the interviewed judges.[17] In the field of competition law and State aid, EU soft law plays a central role and is commonly cited directly by national authorities when drafting legislative proposals or deciding cases. EU soft law is not transposed in the strict sense of the word. Some national guidance documents exist in parallel to EU documents, for example, regarding the setting of fines for competition infringements.[18] In general, few national documents exist and they do not attempt to repeat the exact contents of EU documents. The presence of original EU documents themselves is prominent.

C. The Doctrine on the Sources of Law as Guidance on the Application of Law

Besides requiring that certain matters shall be laid down by Acts of Parliament, the Constitution of Finland also requires those who exercise public powers to observe the law. According to the Constitution, 'the exercise of public powers shall be based on an Act. In all public activity, the law shall be strictly observed'.[19] In addition to national legislation, the term 'law' should be interpreted broadly to cover EU law, the European Convention on Human Rights and other international obligations.[20] It is the constitutional duty of the authorities that apply the law to ensure that all public decision-making is based on the law, the emphasis being on the Acts of Parliament. Nonetheless, just as the government as a lawmaker can use non-binding acts, the law-applying authority can also consider soft law.

[17] E Korkea-aho, 'National Report on Finland: The Use of EU Soft Law by National Courts and Administration in the Field of EU Environmental Law' in M Eliantonio and G Lisi (eds), 'EU Environmental Soft Law in the Member States: A Comparative Overview of Finland, France, Germany, Italy, the Netherlands, Slovenia and the UK' (2020) SoLaR Working Paper, https://papers.ssrn.com/sol3/papers.cfm?abstract_id=3656418.

[18] The Finnish Competition and Consumer Authority, 'Suuntaviivat seuraamusmaksusta vapautumiseksi ja seuraamusmaksun alentamiseksi kartellitapauksissa (2016)', www.kkv.fi/globalassets/kkv-suomi/julkaisut/suuntaviivat/suuntaviivat-2016-leniency.pdf.

[19] Section 2(3) of the Constitution of Finland.

[20] Finland is a country of mitigated dualism, which means that a domestic Act (or in some cases Decree) is required for making international obligations as part of the Finnish legal order (incorporation), but such practice is extensive and not exceptional, resulting in what some authors call de facto monism; see M Scheinin, *Ihmisoikeudet Suomen oikeudessa* (Helsinki, Suomalainen Lakimiesyhdistys, 1991). For the position of EU law in Finland, see T Ojanen, 'EU Law and the Response of the Constitutional Law Committee of the Finnish Parliament' 2007 (52) *Scandinavian Studies in Law* 203, 206.

The relevance of soft law as a non-binding source of law for law-applying authorities is acknowledged in the doctrine on the sources of law (*oikeuslähdeoppi*). The doctrine on the sources of law involves a typified decision-making model that moves in an orderly fashion from the strongest to the weakest source. Standing at the apex is the statutory law that is considered to be strongly normative. Consequently, its neglect in adjudication or administrative decision-making can constitute a violation of official duty. The second category of legal sources consists of two different kinds of normative material: first, preparatory legislative work, also known by the French name *travaux préparatoires*, providing information on the legislator's intention; and, second, court decisions, usually those of the Supreme Court and the Supreme Administrative Court.[21] They are also regarded as being normatively binding, but in a weaker sense. The crucial difference between strongly binding and weakly binding sources relates to the consequences of the action: failure to adhere to a weakly binding source is not considered to be a violation of official duty. Instead, it is likely that the decision that has either failed or refused to observe either one of these two weaker sources is appealed and subsequently overturned by a court at a higher level.[22]

Soft law most logically belongs to the third category of admissible or permissible legal sources. These are not binding but permissible legal sources which may be used to provide interpretation support and bolster the court's findings with additional arguments. This group of sources is diverse, ranging from legal scholarship and comparative insights to the so-called factual arguments. Factual arguments, known across the Nordic countries, include an array of psychological and social considerations, ethical and moral viewpoints, as well as soft law measures of various kinds. They are 'particularly important when the courts encounter a novel case' and they influence the courts' interpretations of legislation and 'their choices between conflicting considerations and differing doctrinal views'.[23] Interestingly, they may sometimes disrupt 'the hierarchy of the sources of law'.[24] Although this happens rarely and has – as far as the authors are aware – never occurred in relation to non-binding norms, there is an inbuilt mechanism in the Finnish legal system to give weight to arguments that potentially contradict legislative texts.

Although much of the above emphasises the key role of Acts of Parliament, it is important to keep in mind self-regulatory models – as an exception to regulatory state-dependence – have also blossomed in Finland as well as in other Nordic

[21] Finland does not have a constitutional court, and the primary control mechanism for ensuring the constitutionality of legislation is the (abstract) review carried out by the Constitutional Law Committee of Parliament.

[22] A Aarnio, *Laintulkinnan teoria: Yleisen oikeustieteen oppikirja* (Helsinki, WSOY, 1989); H Tolonen, *Oikeuslähdeoppi* (Helsinki, WSOY, 2003).

[23] O Lando, 'A Short Survey of the Laws of the Nordic Countries: The Laws in General and Contract Law in Particular' in O Lando et al (eds), *Restatement of Nordic Contract Law* (Copenhagen, DJØF Publishing, 2016) 13, 22.

[24] ibid.

countries. The system of self-regulation not only includes norm-generation but also mechanisms for norm-application, in the form of councils or other such bodies that control the respect for rules and investigate alleged violations. These models can be found in corporate governance and financial markets sectors, and professional services such as accounting, media and advertising.[25]

As the above also implies, the doctrine on the sources of law is primarily occupied with a formal status of the norm, not its real-life impact.[26] Moreover, the doctrine as well as the research on the doctrine dates back to before Finland joined the EU in 1995.[27] Consequently, it does not differentiate between EU and domestic legal sources beyond the fact that it recognises EU law as a source of law. Does EU soft law constitute part of admissible sources together with other factual arguments or is its position stronger than that of national soft law? As seen below, the interviews suggest that Finnish judges and authorities consider EU soft law to be more than simply a permissible legal source. In some observations, EU soft law is compared to the *travaux préparatoires*, that is, a weakly binding source, the disregard of which may have to at least be justified. This stronger sense of duty attached to EU soft law is of course implied and pushed for by the EU too. One such mechanism is the 'comply-or-explain' duty in the field of financial regulation.[28]

III. SOFT LAW IN ACTION? JUDICIAL AND ADMINISTRATIVE PRACTICES IN FINLAND

This section offers a thematic overview of case law research and the interview findings from all four policy fields. Although the policy instruments we have studied are different from one another and as such reflect the peculiarities of the four policy fields from which they originate, the interview findings are largely consistent across the policy fields. This enables a summary analysis. All the interviewees are referred to as 'her'.

[25] For self-regulation in the area of financial markets, see the information on the website of the Finnish Financial Supervisory Authority: www.finanssivalvonta.fi/en/regulation/financial-market-legislation/self-regulation.

[26] Allan Rosas, at the time a professor of international and constitutional law, and later a judge at the Court of Justice of the European Union (CJEU), published an article in 1993 on soft law as a source of fundamental rights law. He argued that soft law is used to denote formal existence and the bindingness of a legal norm, while its real-life impact is of lesser importance. See A Rosas, '"Soft Law" ihmisoikeuksien lähteenä' in A Rosas (ed), *Oikeus, demokratia, informaatio* (Helsinki, Lakimiesliiton Kustannus, 1993) 66.

[27] For recent attempts to revitalise the discussion, see J Karhu, 'Oikeudellinen kokemus oikeuslähteenä' 2019 7–8 *Lakimies* 1068.

[28] See, eg, art 20 of Directive 2013/34/EU of the European Parliament and of the Council of 26 June 2013 on annual financial statements, consolidated financial statements and related reports of certain types of undertakings [2013] OJ L182/19.

A. Status and Effects of Soft Law in Judicial Practice

For the Finnish judges, EU soft law constitutes first and foremost an interpretation aid. Non-binding norms assist the courts in clarifying and interpreting the law. Thus, soft law forms a crucial element in judicial decision-making striving to take all the relevant aspects into account.[29] It cannot be invoked as a 'stand-alone' provision upon which the judicial decision could be based and, in this sense, it is rather seen to give additional support to the court's conclusion. The majority of the interviewed judges explain that they use soft law *ex officio*. This means that even in cases where the parties do not refer to soft law, the judges systematically go through all normative material (including soft law) that they consider relevant to the case at hand.[30] This indicates that the national courts are more familiar with soft law sources than a reading of the judgments may suggest. If a particular soft law instrument has relevance for the case, it is usually paraphrased alongside legislation in the 'Applicable legal rules' (*Sovellettavat oikeusohjeet*) section of the ruling. Our empirical evidence includes only one interview where the judge refuted the idea of *ex officio* consideration and observed a certain degree of confusion in relation to the effects of soft law in her working environment.[31]

Ex officio consideration of soft law may be argued to be a statutory obligation. The Administrative Judicial Procedure Act (586/1996) applies to the judicial procedure in general administrative courts. Section 33(2) lays down that 'the appellate authority shall on its own initiative obtain evidence in so far as the impartiality and fairness of the procedure and the nature of the case so require'.[32] Similarly, Section 31 of the Administrative Procedure Act (434/2003) establishes that 'an authority shall ensure that a matter is sufficiently and appropriately examined, by acquiring the information and evidence necessary for a decision to be made on the matter'. Such information and evidence is understood to cover soft law too. The national courts' duty to proactively adhere to EU soft law is also explicated in the 1988 *Grimaldi* judgment.[33] None of the interviewed Finnish judges referred specifically to the case by name, but one interviewee stressed more generally that the Commission does not adopt soft

[29] See the interviews reported in Korkea-aho (n 17). Some respondents in the competition and State aid field referred to soft law as 'background information'; see K Havu and L Tarkkila, 'National Report on Finland: The Use of EU Soft Law by National Courts and Administration in the Field of EU Competition and State Aid Law' in O Ştefan (ed), 'EU Competition and State Aid Soft Law in the Member States: Finland, France, Germany, Italy, the Netherlands, Slovenia and the UK' (2020) SoLaR Working Paper, https://papers.ssrn.com/sol3/papers.cfm?abstract_id=3667387.

[30] Korkea-aho (n 17) 30.

[31] Havu and Tarkkila (n 29).

[32] See also O Mäenpää and N Fenger, 'Public Administration and Good Governance' in P Letto-Vanamo et al (eds), *Nordic Law in European Context* (Cham, Springer, 2019) 163, 176.

[33] Case C-322/88 *Salvatore Grimaldi v Fonds des maladies professionnelles* [1989] EU:C:1989:646. See also E Korkea-aho, 'Is *Grimaldi* Still Good Law?' (2018) 37 *Yearbook of European Law* 470.

law 'in vain', and in situations where it has adopted soft law, the national courts should apply it.[34]

The interviewed judges gave little regard to the differences between practical and legal effects, nor did they necessarily explicitly reiterate the non-bindingness of soft law. For instance, we looked for references by the Finnish Supreme Administrative Court to the Commission soft law documents in the context of the Water Framework Directive, the Habitats Directive and the Environmental Impact Assessment Directive. The Commission has published these documents in a bid to help national authorities interpret the underlying EU secondary law. Out of a total of 12 judgments where we identified references to Commission soft law guidance,[35] the Supreme Administrative Court explicitly mentioned the non-binding nature of EU guidance in only five judgments. In the remaining seven judgments, the non-binding nature of EU soft law guidance was assumed but not explicitly mentioned. This may be explained by the fact that none of the interviewed judges reported any controversies in relation to the use of soft law. For them, soft law, be it national or EU, forms a helpful source of interpretation, which they use when resolving cases brought to them. They themselves describe their view of soft law as 'fairly pragmatic'.[36]

Pragmatism is evident across all policy fields. In the field of competition and State aid, the Market Court and the Supreme Administrative Court are the responsible courts. The Supreme Administrative Court is the court that adjudicates these matters as the last instance. One or several of the specific EU soft law documents studied within this project were mentioned in 26 of its rulings. However, only a handful of the judgments involve elaborate discussions on the nature of non-binding documents as soft law or the normative nature of these instruments. Discussions on the soft law documents in these judgments almost exclusively focus on the substance of the soft law, without an express analysis of whether soft law documents should be used in legal reasoning or what the justifications for their inclusion in the judgments are in the first place.[37]

However, in the context of social policy, an interviewed judge emphasised the special nature of this policy sector and the potential unsuitability of soft law norms in social law adjudication. The area is, in her view, sensitive to fundamental and human rights concerns, and hence many issues in relation to social law and policy need to be legislated upon. There is a need for hard, binding law to grant rights to individuals and limit the authorities' discretion. This returns to the above-mentioned constitutional law requirement: if the matter affects the rights and obligations of private individuals, it can only be laid down in

[34] Korkea-aho (n 17) 34.

[35] There were 10 references to the Habitats Directive and two to the EIA. See ibid 27.

[36] ibid 32. The indifference to debates on legal and practical effects also characterises Finnish research on soft law.

[37] Havu and Tarkkila (n 29).

parliamentary acts. Furthermore, she pointed out that judicially relevant social policy soft law is national and that many EU recommendations are intended for national legislatures whose task it is to decide on the available resources.[38]

B. Administrative Practice: Status and Effects

The Finnish authorities share the same degree of pragmatism as judges do. For them, the use of soft law in decision-making is both 'a mandate and obligation'.[39] In addition, the relevance of soft law is emphasised by the fact that civil servants may also be involved in its creation or the maintenance of soft law policies through participation in various EU bodies and networks.[40] However, some differences between various policy fields were observed.

The most 'soft law-happy' voices were raised by officials dealing with environmental permits. For them, whilst decisions are in principle made in accordance with applicable law, these officials consider non-binding rules as being part of the overall assessment (*kokonaisharkinta*). Soft law comes in useful when the law leaves a wide array of options for the decision-maker that entail the exercise of discretion and where a choice must be made between several possible options. Moreover, soft law has a systematising effect: it helps officials issuing environmental permits to better structure their decisions by explaining all the relevant factors and considered interests, and how they have balanced these in their decision-making. Like judges, these officials are not interested in differentiating between legal and practical effects, nor do they attempt to define soft law.[41]

With regard to administrative (environmental) decision-making, it is worth noting that an administrative decision may be challenged by an appeal as provided by the Administrative Judicial Procedure Act (586/1996). According to section 5(1), any measure used for solving or dismissing a case may be challenged by an appeal. If the authority has used soft law and has done so erroneously or unfairly against complainants, to appeal against the decision also contesting the use of non-binding norms in the case is possible. However, we have not identified any cases where an explicit reference to these norms has been made. This finding supports the notion that soft law is used not as a decisive but as a complementary or additional argument to strengthen the reasoning behind a decision.

[38] Korkea-aho (n 12) 38.

[39] Korkea-aho (n 17) 31.

[40] This came through strongly in interviews conducted with financial policy authorities, but was also mentioned in the environmental law field. Some of the financial policy interviewees pointed to the lack of resources of small national authorities when it comes to participation in the preparation of guidance. See P Leino and E Korkea-aho, 'SoLaR Financial Regulation – Country Report on Finland' in M Avbelj (ed), 'EU Financial Regulation Soft Law in the Member States: Finland, France, Germany, Italy, the Netherlands, Slovenia and the UK' (2020) SolaR Working Paper, https://papers.ssrn.com/sol3/papers.cfm?abstract_id=3668793.

[41] Korkea-aho (n 17) 32.

In the context of social policy, EU soft law is welcomed as a positive reminder. According to an interviewed national civil servant, EU recommendations provide a window of opportunity (and some leverage too) to critically appraise domestic legislation against EU guidance and to identify spaces for improvement.[42] This field provides examples of how the institution of an ombudsman uses soft law. In Finland, specific supervisory organs or ombudsmen control the legality of legal acts in public administration. The institution of an ombudsman may have a general remit (such as the Parliamentary Ombudsman) or a specific remit, such as Ombudsmen for Children or Equality. For the specialised ombudsmen in particular, EU soft law provides additional arguments to persuade the government to increase funding or to advocate policy changes. For instance, the former Ombudsman for Children who also acted as Chairman of the European Network of Ombudsmen for Children, together with the chairman of the children's NGO Eurochild, cited the Commission recommendation on child poverty in the opinion piece for the newspaper.[43] The Finnish Ombudsman for Equality also relied on EU recommendations in his report on pay openness published by the Ministry of Social Affairs and Health in 2018.[44] At least in these two instances, the ombudsmen justified their message with an international non-binding norm enabling them to exert pressure on the Finnish government's agenda.

Some of the interviewed authorities in ministries and agencies are more sceptical of soft law. They see it as a tool for the Commission or other EU administrative authority to make (questionable) inroads into Member State autonomy. Critical voices were especially pronounced among policy-makers working on finance.[45] Scepticism and concern about the effects of financial soft law on competences seems to find some support in the *Eduskunta* as well. The Parliament has been critical about the extensive use of delegated acts and EU agency guidance, sometimes overturning national legislative choices.[46] Parliamentary criticism is fuelled by the fact that the EU sometimes uses soft law in matters that are considered to be of a legislative nature in Finland and hence require the Parliament's approval. The domestic law-making process then has to

[42] Korkea-aho (n 12) 37.

[43] Available in Finnish: www.ts.fi/mielipiteet/lukijoilta/3974023/Lukijalta+Lasten+oikeudet+EUn+talouspolitiikkaan.

[44] Available in Finnish: julkaisut.valtioneuvosto.fi/bitstream/handle/10024/161103/R_41_18_Selvitys_palkka-avoimuudesta.pdf, 17 and 23–24.

[45] Leino and Korkea-aho (n 40).

[46] See P Leino, 'Accountability Dilemmas of Regulating Financial Markets through the European Supervisory Agencies' in C Harlow et al (eds), *Research Handbook on EU Administrative Law* (Cheltenham, Edward Elgar, 2017). The Finnish Parliament has been particularly critical about the regulatory and decision-making functions of the European Central Bank (ECB). Its Committee on Economic Affairs has repeatedly pointed out how the ECB's technical regulation and guidance has a significant impact on national actors, but leaves national parliaments out of the loop without channels of influence. The Parliament has placed both the Bank of Finland and the Financial Inspection Authority under an obligation to develop new ways of cooperation between the national parliament, government ministries and the regulated industry. See Finnish Parliament, TaVM 12/2014 vp – K 13/2014 and TaVL 16/2014 vp – E 32/2014 vp.

navigate the system as best it can. Sometimes the problems cannot be resolved in the legislative process, and uncertainties trickle down to the stage of applying law, which explains the criticism among civil servants.

IV. THE FINNISH SOFT LAW PUZZLE

We have argued above that in Finland, national courts and administrations use soft law eagerly and almost in an 'automated' manner. In this section we discuss the reasons for this, especially given that the Finnish legal culture has traditionally emphasised obedience to formal Acts of Parliament.

A characteristic of the Finnish legal system is the strict adherence to law, legal principles, transparency, equality and an absence of formalism.[47] The key role of legalism was cemented in the struggles against the Tsarist autocracy, and legalistic attitudes are underpinned by a paternalistic political culture stressing law and public order.[48] In a legalistic approach, an administration's executive powers must possess an express basis in the law. Accordingly, decision-making power cannot be based solely on administrative regulations, guidelines, instructions or plans. Administrative regulations and directives can guide decision-making to the extent that 'this kind of supervision is based on a sufficiently precise rule establishing the power to issue such directives. In addition, internal administrative policy or strategy are to be complied with within the bounds set by law'.[49] Legalism, as interpreted in Finland, would seem to indicate a large dose of scepticism towards soft law forms of law-making. Nevertheless, Finnish legalism is pragmatic enough to offset some of the more sceptical perceptions on non-binding rules. There has traditionally been little interest and a general disbelief in the capacity of meta-level argumentations to clarify what law is or should be.[50] None of the 18 interviewees paid much attention to the nature of bindingness or the difference between legal and practical effects; instead, they emphasised that they use soft law if it is useful in a concrete case.

[47] K Zeigert and H Kötz, *An Introduction to Comparative Law*, 3rd edn (Oxford, Clarendon Press, 1998); P Letto-Vanamo and D Tamm, 'Nordic Legal Mind' in P Letto-Vanamo et al (eds), *Nordic Law in European Context* (Cham, Springer, 2019).

[48] Letto-Vanamo and Tamm (n 47) 7. This is not only a historical curiosity. Even today, Finnish statutory regulation as regards political parties and civil society is more specific than in other Nordic countries. See N Bolleyer, *The State and Civil Society: Regulating Interest Groups, Parties and Public-Benefit Organisations in Contemporary Democracies* (Oxford, Oxford University Press, 2018) 219.

[49] Mäenpää and Fenger (n 32) 166. They argue that the shift from 'executive government to public governance' – that is, administration using 'partnership and association' and hybrid forms of problem-solving mechanisms – is still to be explored in Finland (at 167).

[50] Whether there is a connection between Scandinavian legal realism and the liberal welfare state is debated. Due to the legalistic heritage of the nineteenth century, Finnish legal thinking was slow to accept the new realistic trends; see H Pihlajamäki, 'Against Metaphysics in Law: The Historical Background of American and Scandinavian Legal Realism Compared' (2004) 52 *American Journal of Comparative Law* 469.

Legalism and an associated reverence for the law is sometimes associated with the idea (often repeated in the popular media) that Finland implements everything that comes from Brussels too keenly and strives to be 'the best pupil in the EU'. It is true that Finland tends to view EU integration positively and has, as a main rule, traditionally implemented EU obligations without much debate.[51] This pattern has been changing. In 2017, the Finnish National Audit Office reviewed national implementation processes following repeated criticism from the Commission.[52] The Audit Office concluded that while Finland's implementation record is still good and above the EU Member State average, Finland has been struggling to transpose directives on time.[53] However, this is primarily a question of delays, not incorrect transposition as such.

Therefore, this discussion should perhaps not be taken as a sign of 'awkwardness' with the EU.[54] A certain respect for EU norms is also reflected in the interviews. It was repeatedly mentioned that EU soft law functions to specify the law and complement the legislative framework.[55] The interviewed environmental law judges explained that they use EU soft law with a view to ensuring – for their part – that the directive in question is interpreted in the same way in all Member States, keeping in line with the idea of uniform EU law.[56]

Another issue that has relevance for the impact of EU soft law in Finland is the central position of Acts of Parliament. Finns have great respect for their national Parliament as a democratically chosen legislator, which is reflected in the formal recognition of preparatory legislative work as an important source of law.[57] The Finnish government proposals (*hallituksen esitys*) are long, detailed and thorough. According to Bernitz (with references to both Finland and Sweden), the preparatory legislative material, primarily the Government Bills to Parliament proposing the legislation, often contained detailed explanations of the way in which the different provisions within the proposed statute are to be understood and interpreted. Normally, the courts are inclined to attach great importance to the interpretations recommended in the preparatory legislative material, although these are never binding in a formal legal sense.[58]

[51] G Falkner et al, *Complying with Europe: EU Harmonisation and Soft Law in the Member States* (Cambridge, Cambridge University Press, 2005).

[52] See in particular European Commission, 'Annual Reports on Monitoring the Application of EU Law, 2010–15, ec.europa.eu/info/publications/annual-reports-monitoring-application-eu-law_en.

[53] For the English-speaking summary, see www.vtv.fi/en/publications/implementation-of-eu-legislation.

[54] For the awkwardness argument, see A Brianson and M Stegmann McCallion (eds), *Nordic States and European Integration: Awkward Partners in the North* (London, Palgrave Macmillan, 2018). For the impact of EU integration on the Nordic cooperation, see P Leino and L Leppävirta, 'Does Staying Together Mean Playing Together? The Influence of EU Law on Co-operation between EU and Non-EU States: The Nordic Example' (2018) 43 *European Law Review* 295.

[55] Korkea-aho (n 17) 33; and Havu and Tarkkila (n 29).

[56] Korkea-aho (n 17).

[57] J Husa, 'Constitutional Mentality' in Letto-Vanamo et al (n 47) 43.

[58] U Bernitz, 'What is Scandinavian Law? Concept, Characteristics, Future' (2007) 50 *Scandinavian Studies in Law* 14, 20.

The frequent use of interpretations recommended in the preparatory material by courts was raised by many of the interviewees in the context of environmental law. For them, soft law has more relevance in the interpretation of EU law than in the national context, as there are no *travaux préparatoires* in the former.[59] In interpreting national law, the courts often look back to preparatory works of legislation to gain a better sense of the legislator's intentions. In relation to EU law, such works are more difficult to access. Soft law may be a useful substitute to preparatory works, assisting both judges and administrative officials to interpret the law's provisions in line with legislative intentions.[60] However, the importance attached to preparatory works does not mean that the courts follow the legislator's will slavishly. The years spent building the welfare state have paved the way for a goal-oriented and value-based legal reasoning – something now considered commonplace. Husa points out that Finnish courts seek to find a 'general argumentative base for justificatory purposes',[61] and in settling the case, they can freely consider relevant arguments and their weight.

The traditionally significant role of preparatory works in national law offers a key explanation for the ease with which the Finnish judges and authorities also use non-binding EU norms to find out the EU legislator's initial intentions. This 'easiness' masks a tension. The significance of preparatory works namely lies in their emphasis on constitutional democracy: '*travaux préparatoires* should be taken into account because they form a part of a democratic and rationally justifiable legislative procedure'.[62] Indeed, some interviewees expressed concern about the democratic pedigree of soft law and the strengthened law-making role of the Commission. In the environmental context where public participation has gained particular importance, the question was raised as to whether all relevant parties have been heard in the adoption of non-binding guidance.[63] However, they concluded that as long as soft law only complements but does not replace the legislation it is meant to specify, it cannot be seen as threatening the democratic control of the legislative process.[64]

Consequently, the potential tension between parliamentary democracy and soft law is avoided by emphasising soft law's secondary – and subordinate – role

[59] The increased significance of impact assessments in EU law-making may necessitate a new assessment in the future.

[60] Korkea-aho (n 17) 34. Note also the above-mentioned (n 29) comment on soft law as 'background information'.

[61] Husa (n 57) 44.

[62] A Peczenik and G Bergholz, 'Statutory Interpretation in Sweden' in N McCormick and R Summers (eds), *Interpreting Statutes* (Aldershot, Dartmouth, 1991) 311, 328.

[63] Korkea-aho (n 17) 34.

[64] This same point about the dynamic link between legislation and soft law is also made in environmental law research. See T Määttä, 'Näkökulmia sääntelytarkkuuteen: Lainsäädäntölähtöisestä analyysistä elävään oikeuteen' in J Tala (ed), *Sääntelytarkkuuden ongelmia* (Helsinki, Hakapaino Oy, 2010) 51, 71. For the same argument from democratic theory, see H Frykman and U Mörth, 'Soft Law and Three Notions of Democracy: The Case of the EU' in U Mörth (ed), *Soft Law in Governance and Regulation: An Interdisciplinary Analysis* (Cheltenham, Edward Elgar, 2004) 155, 161.

to legislation. The interviewees from competition and State aid commented that in providing additional details, soft law increases transparency and hence public support for the democratic process.[65] Two of the respondents also suggested that soft law is, in fact, at least somewhat 'democratic', as the process of drafting EU soft law involves discussions with Member State representatives.[66]

V. CONCLUSION

This chapter has shown how the attitudes in Finland towards law are legalistic but pragmatic towards soft law. In order to explain this potentially puzzling situation, we have emphasised two things in particular. First, preparatory works enjoy an established and non-controversial role in the Finnish legal system. For Finns, EU soft law in many ways serves the same function as government proposals – both are useful in giving information on the intention of the legislator. Second, soft law is approached from a pragmatic angle. While domestic actors are well informed of the more theoretical aspects involved in the adoption and use of soft law (binding/non-binding, legal/practical), they are reluctant to engage in metaphilosophical debates and instead emphasise that non-binding rules are used depending on their guiding value in a concrete case. This, which we have called 'pragmatic legalism', is summarised by Niilo Jääskinen, the Finnish judge in the European Court of Justice, as follows: 'Nobody is perfect. There is good soft law and bad soft law'.[67] This statement also reveals a risk that is not only inherent in the Finnish approach, but more generally in the different national approaches to soft law: in the end, the determination of the value of soft law is dependent on national courts or other adjudicating authorities.

[65] Havu and Tarkkila (n 29).

[66] ibid.

[67] N Jääskinen, Observation made in the SoLaR Final Conference, Aix-Marseille, 17–18 October 2019.

8

No Longer Small Enough to Fall through the Cracks

A French Story of Adaptation to the *Petites Sources* of EU Law

NATHALIE RUBIO AND OANA ŞTEFAN

I. INTRODUCTION

THIS CHAPTER EXPLORES the capacity of the French legal system to adapt and accommodate EU soft law.[1] Such an issue is topical for three reasons. The first, is because France, a founding Member State, has been straddling between its role of promoter of European integration and, at least up until 2016, its status as not the most compliant EU Member State.[2] A French

[1] This chapter draws on research work undertaken by the Aix-Marseille SoLaR team (Nathalie Rubio, Olivier André, Eric Oliva, Marie Lamoureux, Sandrine Maljean-Dubois and Eve Truilhé) and by Vanessa Richard. It relies on the following field working papers: G Lisi, M Eliantonio, S Maljean-Dubois and E Thuilhé-Marengo, 'National Report on France: The Use of EU Soft Law by National Courts and Administration in the Field of EU Environmental Law' in M Eliantonio, G Lisi (eds), 'EU Environmental Soft Law in the Member States' (2020) SoLaR Working Paper, https://papers.ssrn.com/sol3/papers.cfm?abstract_id=3656418; M Lamoureux and N Rubio, 'National Report for France: The Use of EU Soft Law by National Courts and Administration in the Field of EU Competition law and State Aid' in O Ştefan (ed), 'EU Competition and State Aid Soft Law in the Member States' (2020) SoLaR Working Paper, https://papers.ssrn.com/sol3/papers.cfm?abstract_id=2356227; E Oliva, 'National Report on France: The Use of ESMA's Guidelines by the French Authorities and Courts for the Regulation of Financial markets' in M Avbelj (ed), 'EU Financial Regulation Soft Law in the Member States' (2020) SoLaR Working Paper, https://papers.ssrn.com/sol3/papers.cfm?abstract_id=3668793; O André, 'National Report on France: The Use of EU soft law by National Courts and Administration in the Field of EU Social Policy' in M Hartlapp (ed), 'Studying EU Soft Law Effects in Social Policy' (2020) SoLaR Working Paper, https://papers.ssrn.com/sol3/papers.cfm?abstract_id=3668981.

[2] The three Member States against which the Commission received the highest number of complaints are Italy, Spain and France: European Commission, 'Commission Staff Working Document Accompanying the Document "Monitoring the Application of European Union Law"

case study on the reception of EU soft law can thus potentially reveal everything from full compliance, a cherry-picking attitude with regard to EU soft law, or rejection of such instruments. Second, the French legal system belongs to the continental legal tradition. Rooted in Romano-Germanic law, the French legal system is identified as a legal system which is written, centralised and based on formal law, codification and parliamentary democracy.[3] In principle, such characteristics would make it unlikely for the domestic legal system to naturally accommodate soft law. Like Italy or Hungary,[4] France has not yet developed a soft law culture nationally, with the exception of administrative circulars.[5] Third, this research takes place at a crucial moment in French doctrinal and case law development. Perhaps paradoxically, France is now at the forefront of soft law practice, with the Conseil d'État (French Administrative Supreme Court) showing a positive attitude towards such instruments.

In the landmark *Numericable* and *Fairvesta* decisions, the Conseil allowed annulment actions against, respectively, a position statement of the French Competition Authority and a press release of the French Financial Market Authority.[6] Such instruments would not be considered justiciable according to the traditional view that only instruments producing legal effects can be reviewed. Following these decisions, the previously EU-reticent Conseil d'État has been singled out in recent case law from the Court of Justice of the European Union (CJEU) for its flexible approach with regards to soft law. This is because it 'mapped the ground in a comprehensive report which offered, inter alia, a definition of soft law … it also built on that study by devising a new judicial test focusing on economic effects and the existence of significant influence on the behaviour of the addressees of the instrument'.[7]

As shown in our research, civil servants and judges do not seem overtly reluctant to rely on soft law, contrary to the expectation that such an attitude would be atypical in a rule-bound parliamentary democracy.[8] The European Network of Soft Law Research (SoLaR) methodology was employed for this chapter, with two caveats. The first is that French legal practitioners are not very familiar with

2018 Annual Report, Part I: General Statistical Overview' (4 July 2019) 12, https://ec.europa.eu/info/sites/info/files/report-2018-commission-staff-working-document-monitoring-application-eu-law-general-statistical-overview-part1_0.pdf.

[3] R Legeais, *Grands systèmes de droit contemporains, Approche comparative*, 3rd edn (Paris, LexisNexis, 2016) 30–37.

[4] J Alberti and M Eliantonio, ch 11 in this volume; and P Láncos, ch 10 in this volume.

[5] Conseil d'État, *Le droit souple*, Annual Study 2013 (Paris, La documentation Française, 2013) 59 and 70; Conseil d'État, 18 December 2002, *Duvignières*, no 233618; M Lombard et al (eds), *Droit administrative* (Paris, Dalloz, 2019) 58–65; F Melleray, 'Brèves observations sur les "petites" sources du droit administratif' (2009) *Actualité juridique de droit administratif* 917; C Testard, 'Le droit souple, une "petite" source canalisée' (2019) *Actualité juridique de droit administratif* 934.

[6] Rulings of 21 March 2016, *Numericable*, no 390023 and *Société Fairvesta International GmBH*, no 368082.

[7] Case C-16/16 *Kingdom of Belgium v European Commission* [2018] EU:C:2018:79, Opinion of AG Bobek, para 85.

[8] E Korkea-aho et al, ch 7 in this volume.

socio-legal research and conducting interviews was not straightforward. Only 13 judges and public servants responded, despite numerous invitations to interview across the fields of research. Second, although the wind of change is currently also blowing on French ground,[9] court language has been, traditionally and notoriously, brief.[10] Indeed, one can hardly retrieve any express references to soft law in French judgments, although various combinations of keywords were used to interrogate the public databases.[11] This chapter looks at the ways in which EU soft law is integrated into the French legal order, before exploring the judicial attitude towards such instruments. It outlines various French specificities which might prove inspiring for authorities and courts at different levels of EU governance when issuing or applying soft law.

II. THE RECEPTION OF EU SOFT LAW IN FRANCE: A STORY OF FRAGMENTATION AND OPENNESS

The reliance on EU soft law by the French administration in general, and the implementation of soft law in particular, is not systematic and occurs through a wide variety of ways, depending on the policy field, the actors involved and the specificities of each instrument. Our study reveals two main points to take away. First, a multitude of actors are involved in the reception of EU soft law and rely on different types of instruments to translate EU soft law in the French legal order. Courts, ministries and independent administrative authorities all contribute to the implementation of EU soft law in France or, indeed, to the application of EU soft law in individual cases. While the contribution of courts is addressed in section III, the current section looks at the ministries and independent administrative authorities. Second, administrative practice and legal academia show an increasingly open attitude towards the evolution of legal sources and the variety thereof.

[9] P Deumier, 'Motivation enrichie: bilan et perspectives' *D.* 2017, 1783; P Deumier and P Puig 'Quand le droit souple rencontre le juge dur' (2016) *Revue trimestrielle de droit civil* 571.

[10] B Markesinis and J Fedtke, *Engaging with Public Law* (Oxford, Hart Publishing, 2009); JL Halpérien, 'Les styles judiciaires, des traditions nationales?' (2015) *Droit et société* 491.

[11] Legifrance: www.legifrance.gouv.fr. Legifrance is the French government official platform for online legal texts. It provides access, in French, to laws and decrees published in the *Journal officiel*, important court rulings (especially from both civil and administrative Supreme Courts), collective labour agreements, standards issued by European institutions, and international treaties and agreements to which France is a party. 'Ariane Web': www.conseil-etat.fr. This case law database gives access to more than 230,000 documents: decisions and contentious opinion of the Conseil d'État and the administrative appellate courts, commentaries of these decisions and opinions having been retained for their contribution to the case law, as well as a selection of conclusions of public *rapporteurs*. 'Lexis 360' and 'Lamyline reflex' contain a wide range (albeit non-exhaustive) of lower court decisions. For the lists of keywords for each sector and specific websites, see the SoLaR working papers (n 1).

A. The Implementation of EU Soft Law by French Administration: A Scattered Picture

The implementation of EU soft law in the French legal order can be classified into four broad categories. First, soft law can be integrated into hard law. In competition, the *De Minimis* Notice,[12] as well as the leniency notice,[13] were integrated into the Code de commerce, which is the basic law regulating trade.[14] In social law, the Recommendation on equal pay[15] was integrated into the Code du travail.[16]

Second, EU soft law is implemented through national soft law or hybrid combinations. Indeed, EU soft law can be translated through specific national soft law instruments such as 'circulaires', but also through national hard law, for instance, the French Codes. Traces of the antitrust Guidelines on fines[17] can be found in the Code de commerce;[18] however, the Competition Authority has also set up its own guidelines for setting fines.[19] A Prime Minister Act from 2019[20] (an administrative *circulaire*), guides the action of the administration in relation to State aid and, together with Article 1511-1-1 of the Code general des collectivités territoriales, is meant to gather together all the relevant EU legislation.[21] The Ministère de l'Economie et des Finances (Ministry for the Economy and Finance) also published a Vade-mecum,[22] including various sectoral EU soft law and the notice on the notion of aid.[23] In the field of environmental law, the

[12] European Commission, 'Communication from the Commission – Notice on Agreements of Minor Importance which do not appreciably restrict Competition under Article 101(1) of the Treaty on the Functioning of the European Union (*De Minimis* Notice)' [2014] OJ C291/1.

[13] European Commission, 'Commission Notice on Immunity from fines and reduction of fines in cartel cases' [2006] OJ C144/23.

[14] Article L 464-6-1 and 2 of the Code de commerce incorporates market share thresholds into French law; art L. 464-2 and art R.464-5 of the Code de commerce incorporate the Leniency Notice.

[15] European Commission, 'Commission Recommendation of 7 March 2014 on strengthening the principle of equal pay between men and women through transparency' [2014] OJ L69/112.

[16] Article L 3221-2 of the Code du Travail (Labour Code) stipulates that work of equal value must lead to equal pay.

[17] 'Guidelines on the method of setting fines imposed pursuant to Article 23(2)(a) of Regulation No 1/2003' [2006] OJ C210/ 2.

[18] Articles L 420-1 to L 420-7 and L 464-2 of the Code de commerce.

[19] Autorité de la concurrence, 'Communiqué du 16 mai 2011 relatif à la méthode de détermination des sanctions pécuniaires', www.autoritedelaconcurrence.fr.

[20] Circulaire du Premier Ministre, 'Application des règles européennes de concurrence relatives aux aides publiques aux activités économiques' no 6060/SG (5 February 2019), http://circulaires.legifrance.gouv.fr/pdf/2019/02/cir_44368.pdf.

[21] ibid 43 (list of EU soft and hard law). For instance, EU soft law: European Commission, 'Commission Notice on the notion of State aid as referred to in Article 107(1) of the Treaty on the Functioning of the European Union' [2016] OJ C262/1; and also EU hard law: arts 107 and 108 TFEU; and Council Regulation (EU) No 2015/1589 ([2015] OJ L248/9) and Regulation (EU) No 733/2013 ([2013] OJ L204/11).

[22] Ministère de l'économie, 'Vade-mecum des aides d'État Edition 2019', www.economie.gouv.fr/daj/vade-mecum-des-aides-detat-edition-2019.

[23] See the list of all EU communications, guidelines and regulations in the 'Annex' of the Vade-mecum. In particular, in the scope of SoLaR research, the Vade-mecum cites European Commission (n 21).

French government has adopted its own guidance in relation to the EU instruments studied by the SoLaR project. This was in the form of *circulaires* and/or *lignes directrices nationales*, which have the same function and deal with similar issues as the relevant EU guidance documents.[24]

The third way to integrate soft law into the French legal order is through web references. The French Competition Authority and the Ministère de l'Economie et des Finances both refer on their website to various competition and State aid soft law instruments.[25] In the field of environmental law, a limited number of EU guidance documents relating to the Habitats Directive can be found on the governmental website of Natura 2000 sites, under the tabs 'Guides Europe' and 'Autres guides de référence'.[26] Most of these documents are available only in English, such as the Guidance document on Climate Change and Natura 2000,[27] and some have been translated into French, such as the Guidance on the requirements for hydropower in relation to Natura 2000.[28] In social law, the CLEISS website,[29] which is managed by the government, describes social security regimes throughout the world and especially within the EU. The fact that some soft law is not translated into French, together with the incorporation of soft law instruments without directly referring to the source, raises well-known issues relating to access to soft law instruments, as described elsewhere in this volume.[30]

Finally, a fourth way to integrate soft law is specific to financial supervision,[31] given the comply-or-explain obligation in relation to EU guidance, as provided for in Article 16 of the European Securities and Markets Authority (ESMA) Regulation.[32] The Authority of Financial Markets (Autorité des marchés financiers (AMF)) has several options in this regard. First, it could choose a mere

[24] In addition to arts L 414-4 and R 414-19 of the Code de l'environnement, see Ministre d'Etat, ministre de l'écologie, de l'énergie, du développement durable et de la mer, en charge des technologies vertes et des négociations sur le climat, 'Circulaire du 15 avril 2010 relative à l'évaluation des incidences Natura 2000', http://circulaire.legifrance.gouv.fr/pdf/2010/05/cir_31044.pdf. In addition to art L 122-1 of the Code de l'environnement, see Commissariat général au développement durable, 'Évaluation environnementale Guide d'interprétation de la réforme du 3 août 2016', www.ecologique-solidaire.gouv.fr/sites/default/files/Th%C3%A9ma%20%20Guide%20d%E2%80%99interpr%C3%A9tation%20de%20la%20r%C3%A9forme%20du%203%20ao%C3%BBt%202016.pdf.

[25] www.autoritedelaconcurrence.fr/fr/textes-de-reference; www.economie.gouv.fr/daj.

[26] www.ecologique-solidaire.gouv.fr/levaluation-environnementale; www.natura2000.fr/documentation/references-bibliographiques/guide-methodologique-pour-evaluation-incidences.

[27] Guidance document on Climate Change and Natura 2000, www.natura2000.fr/documentation/references-bibliographiques/guidelines-climate-change-and-natura-2000.

[28] Guidance on the requirements for hydropower in relation to Natura 2000, www.natura2000.fr/documentation/references-bibliographiques/orientations-pour-hydroelectricite-lien-avec-natura-2000.

[29] CLEISS stands for Centre des Liaisons Européennes et Internationales de Sécurité Sociale. See www.cleiss.fr.

[30] See O Ştefan, ch 19 in this volume.

[31] Oliva (n 1) 42.

[32] Regulation (EU) No 1095/2010 of the European Parliament and of the Council of 24 November 2010 establishing a European Supervisory Authority (European Securities and Markets Authority), amending Decision No 716/2009/EC and repealing Commission Decision 2009/77/EC [2010] OJ L331/84 (hereinafter 'ESMA Regulation').

declaration of conformity, with or without issuing a press release. Second, it could follow a case-by-case approach, which would potentially offer more leeway, while triggering the need to explain its actions in every case by reference to national provisions or the need for consultation. Finally, it could choose the more ambitious approach of transposing the guidelines into national legislation and regulations.[33]

The approach usually chosen by the AMF consists in using the guidelines only when the AMF Board decides to apply them.[34] In a press release, the AMF informed the stakeholders that the AMF Board members henceforth apply the ESMA guidelines.[35] These are mainly used to clarify certain practices by using the definitions provided by ESMA.[36] Most of the time, they are used to interpret the provisions of the AMF Regulation, which is a legally binding instrument.[37] This is yet another example of hybridity par excellence, as such a technique ensures that the AMF Regulation, which is national hard law, is constantly adapted to the soft guidance produced by ESMA.

Practices to implement EU soft law are thus diverse, with an important number of instruments translated into the French legal order, including through direct appropriation in a manner that might result in obliterating their EU origins.

B. Embracing the *Petites Sources*: An Increasingly Open Attitude to Soft Law

Contrary to such varied ways to implement EU soft law, the general attitude towards soft law is positive, which might challenge traditional views on the categories of legal sources in France. This happens both at the level of administrative authorities and in legal scholarship, with the Conseil d'État recently rubber-stamping soft law and confirming a new 'soft law-friendly' approach both for French practice and for academia.

Some ministries rely on EU soft law in their day-to-day activity more than others, depending on the field, with similar experiences being recorded

[33] AMF, 'Atelier 2: Un an après la mise en place de l'ESMA: impact de la doctrine et articulation avec la réglementation AMF' (19 March 2013), www.amf-france.org/fr/actualites-publications/evenements-de-lamf/colloques-et-conferences-de-lamf/13e-journee-de-formation-des-rcci-et-des-rcsi-atelier-ndeg-2-un-apres-la-mise-en-place-de-lesma.

[34] ibid 29. For instance, 'AMF Decides to Apply ESMA Guidelines on Risk Factors under the Prospectus Regulation (ESMA31-62-1293 FR)', AMF press release 29, November 2019.

[35] www.amf-france.org/fr/actualites-publications/communiques/communiques-de-lamf. See also AMF recommendations called 'doctrine'.

[36] AMF (n 33) 30. For instance, see the AMF press release about the ESMA guidelines on MiFID II product governance requirement (Directive 2014/65/EU on markets in financial instruments), 12 April 2018.

[37] AMF General Regulation, https://reglement-general.amf-france.org/eli/fr/aai/amf/rg/notes/fr.html.

in the Netherlands.[38] Interviews show that the Ministère de l'Economie et des Finances is very involved in the application of State aid law. Such an attitude can be explained by the fact that failure to follow the policies set out by the European Commission in State aid might lead to a recovery order against France, which would have important implications for the recipient, as well as for the economy. A civil servant from the Ministry told the SoLaR team that they are dealing daily with EU soft law instruments, as it is their responsibility to verify whether a measure can constitute State aid or not. When in doubt, the civil servants are expected to warn the national authorities involved and to get in touch with the Commission for a first informal dialogue.[39] Conversely, ministries dealing with social matters or the environment engage less often with soft law. The civil servants for social policy who were interviewed admitted that while they do deal with EU law frequently, they simply consider soft law to be too weak or superfluous to engage with.[40] In the field of the environment, the approaches vary depending on the background, culture, position and tasks of the civil servants, with some resorting to soft law on a daily basis.[41]

Similar field distribution can be noted at the level of independent administrative authorities, with authorities dealing with competition and financial regulation soft law being by far the most involved in implementation. These are the Autorité de la concurrence (French Competition Authority), the AMF, and the Autorité de contrôle prudentiel et des résolutions Prudential Supervision and Resolution Authority (ACPR)). The output from these authorities is fairly transparent and publicly available online, hence facilitating research. Our interviewees from the administrative authorities agreed that EU soft law is necessary and useful in their work. For instance, in the field of competition and State aid law, the civil servants we interviewed very frequently use European soft law instruments, which constitute important sources in their everyday practice. However, they stressed that European soft law instruments are scrutinised on a case-by-case basis whenever the issue falls within the scope of European law.[42]

In the field of environmental law, the interviewed civil servants agreed that soft law is a valid source of law that is relevant for decision-making. Administrators feel compelled to follow soft law documents issued by the Commission, acting in the shadow of hierarchy. Thus, the interviewees strongly believe that the Commission expects EU guidance to be followed and that failure to comply might result in a lawsuit against the national administration.[43] In any case, EU environmental soft law is generally considered to be a more

[38] On the Netherlands, see B Beijen, ch 12 in this volume.
[39] Lamoureux and Rubio (n 1).
[40] André (n 1) 50.
[41] Lisi et al (n 1) 45.
[42] Lamoureux and Rubio (n 1) 67.
[43] Lisi et al (n 1) 45.

precious source for the interpretation of EU hard law than in the other policy areas considered in the SoLaR project.[44] EU soft law should be carefully considered by lawyers when engaging in litigation, and not to do so is considered a strategical mistake.[45] The factors that motivate the use of EU environmental soft law in France include the need for the clarification of hard law, which is essential in such a specialised, complex and technical field; the facilitation of the implementation processes; and the desire to avoid litigation, while striving to 'do the right thing' vis-a-vis the Commission and the government.[46]

The French legal literature has reflected on EU soft law, although it has not yet recognised it as a source of law *stricto sensu*. Embracing wholeheartedly (EU or non-EU) soft law would be unusual, given that the French system is grounded in the basic principle of legality, in the sense that administrative acts must comply with higher norms. The principle of legality (*principe de légalité*) is nowadays understood broadly and as relating not only to laws, but also to constitutional norms, international and European norms, and the general principles of law defined by case law and regulations.[47] French law belongs to the Romano-Germanic tradition characterised by a certain formalism regarding the sources of law, which might be resistant to newer legal sources such as soft law. French legal theorists have called for a clear delineation from hard law, with Weil noting that the legal character of a norm cannot be a matter of scale – either a norm is law or it is not law at all.[48] Similarly, according to Thibierge, an exploration of 'flexible law' reveals three categories that are dependent on content ('vague law', characterised by the lack of detail), binding legal force ('soft law', that is, law without legal obligation), and enforcement ('slack law', meaning unenforceable law).[49] Moreover, research on soft law has been conducted by international and EU legal scholars working in French universities,[50] and less so by academics interested in the fields of national law. Until five years ago, soft

[44] ibid.

[45] ibid.

[46] ibid.

[47] Lombard et al (n 5) 23; P Weil and D Pouyaud, *Droit administratif* (Paris, Presses universitaires de France, 2017) 82–86.

[48] P Weil, 'Vers une normativité relative en droit international?' (1982) *Revue Générale de Droit International Public* 5.

[49] C Thibierge, 'Le droit souple, réflexion sur les textures du droit' (2003) *Revue trimestrielle de droit civil* 599.

[50] F Terpan, 'Soft Law in the European Union: The Changing Nature of EU Law' (2015) 21 *European Law Journal* 68; F Berrod, 'L'utilisation de la soft law comme méthode de conception du droit européen de la concurrence' (2015) *Revue de l'Union Européenne* 283; F Snyder, 'Soft Law' in D O'Keeffe, N Neuwahl and J Monar (eds), *Butterworths Expert Guide to the European Union* (London, Butterworths, 1996) 277–78; F Snyder, 'Soft Law and Institutional Practice in the European Community' in SD Martin (ed), *The Construction of Europe: Essays in Honour of Emile NOEL* (Deventer, Kluwer, 1994) 197–225; F Snyder, 'Soft Law and Institutional Practice in the European Community' (June 1993) EUI Working Paper LAW No 93/5; L Idot, 'A propos de l'internationalisation du droit. Réflexions sur la soft law en droit de la concurrence' (2007) 2 *Concurrences* 1.

law was not even mentioned in general handbooks of French public law and, as in Germany, played a very minor role in doctrine and legal education alike.[51] Recently, however, some experts in administrative law conceded to soft law the role of a 'small' source of law,[52] and civil law scholars are assigning a more important position to soft law in their studies.[53]

This discussion shows that the administration is open to soft law, and this is matched to a certain extent in academia. In that regard, the recent position of the Conseil d'État on the matter is highly relevant. With its composite function, the Conseil navigates between the worlds of administration and the judiciary, while at the same time informing academic discourse. In an Annual Study from 2013,[54] it found that soft law is 'a phenomenon theorized and valued by the legal literature'.[55] The findings of the study were carried forward in the case law, with the Conseil issuing a judicial definition for soft law. Accordingly, soft law comprises 'the set of instruments fulfilling the three following criteria: 1) they must have as an object to modify or guide the behaviour of their addressees by leading to their adherence; 2) they do not create in themselves rights or obligations for their addresses; 3) they represent, by their content and the way that they are structured, a degree of formalisation and structure which brings them closer to looking like rules of law'.[56] This definition has now been largely taken up by French academics.[57]

Finally, the Conseil d'État finds that the distinction between hard and soft law relates to a difference in scale rather than a difference in nature.[58] On the basis of the legal literature and the diversity of instruments, actors and fields, the Conseil notes that soft norms belong to a 'graduated normative scale' between soft and hard law,[59] rubber-stamping the idea that various forms of legalisation are situated alongside a continuum.[60] Readers of this book would probably agree that such openness to soft law is unprecedented. The question is to what extent is this approach matched in the case law of other French courts dealing with EU soft law, an issue to which this chapter now turns.

[51] M Hartlapp, A Hofmann and M Knauff, ch 9 in this volume.

[52] Lombard et al (n 5) 58–64; Melleray (n 5) 917; Testard (n 5) 934.

[53] P Deumier and JM Sorel (eds), *Regards croisés sur la soft law en droit interne, européen et international* (Paris, LGDJ, 2018).

[54] Conseil d'État (n 5).

[55] ibid 52–55 (our translation).

[56] Rulings of 21 March 2016, *Numericable*, no 390023 and *Société Fairvesta International GmBH*, no 368082.

[57] P Deumier and P Puig, 'Quand le droit souple rencontre le juge dur' (2016) *Revue trimestrielle de droit civil* 573; P Jestaz, 'La norme dans la doctrine privatiste du XXème siècle' (2020) *Revue trimestrielle de droit civil* 42–43; F Melleray, 'Le contrôle juridictionnel des actes de droit souple' (2016) *Revue française de droit administratif* 681–82.

[58] Conseil d'État (n 5) 63.

[59] ibid 69.

[60] ibid 191.

III. THE APPLICATION OF EU SOFT LAW BY FRENCH COURTS

The French dual system of jurisdiction consists of two separate orders: the administrative order, overseen by the Conseil d'État, and the civil order, overseen by the Cour de Cassation (French Supreme Court). The existence of these two different orders is rooted in French history, and was designed to prevent the ordinary judge from interfering with administrative matters. The justification of this duality is also based on the necessity of having two different legal systems, and thus an autonomous administrative law dealing with the general interest. Only an administrative judge can quash or amend the decisions made by authorities exercising executive powers. Despite the massive differences between the disputes that each order of jurisdiction deals with, our research shows common trends in the attitudes of civil and administrative judges towards soft law.

A. Soft Law is Everywhere: The Different Types of Litigation Concerning Soft Law

The distribution between the different orders and levels of jurisdiction depends on the nature of the contested national act, the object of the dispute and the parties to the dispute. Thus, civil and administrative courts have, in principle, jurisdiction over appeals against the decisions of independent administrative authorities, such as the Competition Authority and the Financial Market Authority. Administrative courts have jurisdiction over illegality proceedings, often as first instance and last resort, while both civil and administrative courts have jurisdiction over liability proceedings. Finally, civil courts have in principle jurisdiction over disputes between legal persons governed by private law.

Like other Member States, French courts cannot review European soft law; in other words, no allegation against EU guidance documents can be brought directly or indirectly before national judges. Indeed, national judges are not competent to review EU norms and have nothing to do with the softness of the acts. National soft law is justiciable before French courts. The Conseil d'État acknowledged jurisdiction to review national soft law and is constantly expanding the notion of reviewable acts.[61] Similarly, the civil courts are willing to take into account national competition soft law, while acknowledging their status

[61] In the *Fairvesta/Numericable* case (21 March 2016, Case Nos 368082, 368083 and 368084), the Conseil d'État recognised the admissibility of a judicial proceeding against national soft law acts. This position was confirmed by other subsequent cases: Conseil d'État, 20 June 2016, *FFSA*, Case No 384297; Conseil d'État, 30 June 2016, *CASA*, Case No 383822; Conseil d'État, 13 July 2016, *Société GDF Suez*, Case No 388150; Conseil d'État, 10 November 2016, *Mme Z et al*, Case No 384691; Conseil d'État, 20 March 2017, *Région Aquitaine-Limousin-Poitou-Charente*, Case No 401751; Conseil d'État, 13 December 2017, *Société Bouygues Telecom et al*, Case No 401799. Most recently in *GISTI* (12 June 2020, Case No 418142, A), justiciability was expanded to most of the soft law acts of general application issued by public authorities.

and flexibility.[62] Thus, even though national French courts are unlikely to review EU soft law, French judges could eventually engage in a dialogue with their counterparts in Luxembourg questioning the validity of EU soft law through the preliminary reference procedure. In the most recent *Fédération bancaire française* case, which is pending at the time of writing, the Conseil d'Etat sent such a preliminary reference question with regard to the validity of European Banking Authority guidance.[63]

Very few lower court judgments expressly refer to EU soft law. SoLaR only retrieved a few relevant cases of the Supreme Courts: there is no such decision in the environmental, social and financial fields;[64] two judgments deal with competition soft law and three with State aid. We also found 40 relevant decisions of the appellate courts in the field of competition law, out of which 28 mention EU soft law only in passing.[65]

These findings have to be read in the methodological context of this research. On the positive side, access to information was straightforward. French court rulings are published and are easily available in databases, which is not necessarily the case in other jurisdictions covered by the SoLaR project.[66] Searches based on keywords and/or the title/identifier of a text were therefore sufficient to retrieve the relevant judgments. However, the caveat to this relates to French judgment writing techniques. Indeed, it is rather difficult to determine whether a soft law instrument was taken into account, given the traditionally concise form of French judgments. This was even the case when soft law was directly or indirectly invoked by the parties. However, as mentioned by one of the judges we interviewed, even when EU soft law is not expressly mentioned in the ruling, it may very well have been considered at the preparatory stage.[67] We fully endorse the current reform requiring fuller argumentation and substantiation of the decisions of the Cour de Cassation and of the Conseil d'État. This will not only entail higher levels of legal certainty for the litigants, but would also enable researchers to explore French judicial reasoning in more depth.[68]

[62] Cour de Cassation, chambre commerciale, 18 October 2016, Case No 15-10.384; Cour de Cassation, chambre commerciale, 8 November 2017, Case No 16-17.226.

[63] Conseil d'État, 4 December 2019, *Fédération bancaire française (FBF)*, Case No 415550; ECJ, Request for a preliminary ruling from the Conseil d'État (France) lodged on 13 December 2019 – *Fédération bancaire française (FBF) v Autorité de contrôle prudentiel et de résolution* (ACPR) (Case C-911/19).

[64] Lisi et al (n 1); Oliva (n 1); André (n 1).

[65] Lamoureux and Rubio (n 1).

[66] M Avbelj and K Vatovec, ch 13 in this volume; Láncos, ch 10 in this volume.

[67] Lamoureux and Rubio (n 1) 67.

[68] Cour de Cassation, 'Rapport de la commission de réflexion sur la réforme de la cour de cassation' (April 2017) 129, https://www.courdecassation.fr/IMG/Rapport%20sur%20la%20r%C3%A9forme%20de%20la%20Cour%20de%20cassation.pdf; Conseil d'État, 'Vademecum sur la rédaction des décisions de la juridiction administrative', 2018, 4–16, https://www.conseil-etat.fr/actualites/actualites/juridiction-administrative-nouveaux-modes-de-redaction-des-decisions#:~:text=Le%20Conseil%20d'%C3%89tat%20publie,la%20motivation%20de%20ces%20d%C3%A9cisions.

B. The Convergent Judicial Approach to Soft Law

Our study shows that in France, the civil and the administrative courts converge with regard to their attitude towards soft law. Thus, both the Conseil État and the Cour de Cassation have devoted a study to the soft law phenomenon. As mentioned above, in its 2013 Annual Study, the Conseil d'État describes the role of soft law, gives instructions for using national soft law instruments and proposes a new typology. In its 2018 Annual Study, the Cour de Cassation pays more attention to the application of the Commission's guidelines in the field of competition law. It thus emphasises the specificity of soft law, which 'lays out the principles' determined by the European judge and gives 'methodologies'.[69]

Our research revealed two important trends:[70] first, soft law sometimes forms part of legal reasoning; and, second, soft law is an additional element used as a supplement to other legal sources, such as the case law of the European Court of Justice (ECJ). The examples drawn from different fields of research below will reflect these trends.

In *Expedia*,[71] the Cour de Cassation decided that the Competition Authority could engage proceedings against an agreement containing hardcore restrictions to competition, even though the market share fell below the impunity thresholds mentioned in a *De Minimis* Notice of the Commission.[72] The case, which also reached the ECJ in preliminary reference,[73] led the Commission to revise its notice, showing that the evolution of EU soft law is also inspired by national practice. In *Total*,[74] the Cour de Cassation recalled that while Commission guidance was not binding on the Competition Authority or national courts, it could be part of the reasoning in a case. Consequently, the Appellate Court was right to take such guidance into consideration and was entitled to refer to it in judgments.

In the field of State aid law, we found no discussion as to the soft nature of the instruments, with courts working directly with the substance of EU guidance. The judgments analysed reveal that EU soft law is used by the French judge in the same manner as hard law and is generally applied in cases.[75] Soft law is often used as a legal ground to explain specific EU terms and can sometimes be very

[69] Cour de Cassation, *Le rôle normatif de la Cour de cassation*, Annual Study 2018 (Paris, La documentation Française, 2019) 206, www.courdecassation.fr/IMG///2019-01-18_Etude_2018.pdf.

[70] There is no ruling in the field covered by the SoLaR research regarding social and financial legal matters.

[71] Case C-226/11 *Expedia Inc v Autorité de la concurrence and Others* [2012] EU:C:2012:795, para 27: 'it also follows from the objectives pursued by the *De Minimis* Notice, as mentioned in para 4 thereof, that it is not intended to be binding on the competition authorities and the courts of the Member States'. See also Cass Com, 16 April 2013, Case No 10-14.881, *Bull Civ* IV, n° 64.

[72] Cour de Cassation (n 69) 207.

[73] C-911/19 *FBF* (pending).

[74] Cass Com, 20 January 2015, Case Nos 13-16745, 13-16764, 13-16765, 13-16955, *Bull civ* IV, no 8.

[75] Conseil d'État, 9 March 2016, *Association Vent de Colère!*, Case No 384092.

helpful for the parties.[76] Interestingly, the Conseil d'État refrains from assessing the legality of national acts against Commission guidance on State aid, on the grounds of respecting the exclusive competence of the EU Commission in this area.[77] This latter finding gives even more substance to the concern that many EU soft law instruments are largely unchecked, given that neither the national courts nor the ECJ itself engage in judicial review.[78]

In the field of environmental law, there is no relevant case from the Supreme Courts, but two lower court judgments can to some extent be considered relevant for the purposes of our analysis. Both judgments relate to the protection of a site of Community importance under the Habitats Directive. In one judgment, the Lyon Administrative Appellate Court mentioned in its reasoning a provision of the Directive 'as construed by the European Commission',[79] without specifying which interpretation issued by the Commission they precisely referred to, and which document or guidance provided this interpretation.[80] Similarly, in another judgment, while analysing whether a site of Community importance had correctly been designated by French authorities, the Marseille Administrative Appellate Court referred to the form of the document used for the designation of the site and to the way in which it had been compiled in line with the Commission's expectations.[81] Yet, the judgment does not give any further details or references in this regard.[82]

This brief account of the judicial attitude to soft law in France shows that while express references and discussions of EU guidance in the case law are scarce, courts do engage with such instruments at different levels and orders of jurisdiction. Our limited interview material, as well as the above-mentioned environmental cases, might point to the suspicion that many of the soft law discussions happen behind the scenes, with potentially more guidance documents used in practice by the courts than might be apparent from word searches on publicly available databases.

IV. EVALUATION: IS THERE ANY ROLE FOR THE GENERAL PRINCIPLES OF LAW?

The SoLaR research shows that France matches the SoLaR findings regarding the application of EU soft law in other Member States, as can be seen elsewhere

[76] See the *Valeo* case, where the Conseil d'État adopted a different interpretation of a soft law act's provisions than the lower court: Conseil d'État, 26 July 2018, Case No 403009.

[77] Conseil d'État, 13 April 2018, *Association Vent de Colère!*, Case No 401755; Conseil d'État, 27 October 2016, *Société Efnovia*, Case No 392494.

[78] Cour administrative d'appel de Paris, 12 May 2014, *SIDE*, Case No 12PA00767.

[79] 'Telle qu'interprétée par la Commission européenne.'

[80] Cour Administrative d'Appel de Lyon, 21 March 2017, Case No 14LY03096.

[81] 'Rédigé en la forme prévue par la Commission européenne.'

[82] Cour Administrative d'Appel de Marseille, 28 March 2011, Case No 09MA02029.

in this volume. There is therefore no French exceptionalism compared with the other Members States across the fields. Somewhat paradoxically, EU soft law is not considered as a legal source, it is not considered to be legally binding, but it might have legal effects, and it is taken into account by both the administration and judges. This confirms a certain lack of clarity with regard to the effects of such instruments, which, together with legitimacy issues, constitute primary drawbacks surrounding EU soft law. The question is whether, in the application of EU soft law in France, general principles of law are thwarted or, conversely, enhanced.

The answer is nuanced. Although our interviewees have mentioned some drawbacks of soft law, they acknowledged that the use of EU soft law has many advantages.[83] It was mentioned that soft law is flexible, quick and well suited to deal with the complexity and diversity of issues in each Member State. EU soft law fills the gaps, allows an easier harmonisation of technical provisions and has the potential to facilitate the implementation process for civil servants and, more broadly, for all stakeholders, as it can help overcome national and local hurdles to the implementation of EU instruments. Globally, EU soft law instruments are used to supplement and/or clarify relevant hard law norms, codifying case law and Commission decisions in complex areas.

In relation to State aid, the civil servants we interviewed concurred that soft law ensures legal certainty and increases transparency and predictability, helping a common method of implementation of EU hard law. With regard to the role of soft law to ensure consistency in the application of the law across the Member States, while mentioned by some courts in their annual studies, such a principle cannot be traced in the rulings analysed.[84] In the field of competition law, one of the interviewees found it regrettable that some European soft law instruments are sometimes unclear or contain contradictory information. They considered that these drawbacks render soft law unhelpful and inefficient.

In relation to the environment, the interviewees emphasised that soft law lacks legitimacy and transparency because it is not generated in cooperation with Member States.[85] Environmental soft law would be more acceptable if it were the result of a more inclusive process.[86] Otherwise, soft law only increases the discretion of some actors (ie, the European Commission) to the detriment of others (ie, national authorities). Conversely, in competition, some interviewees were fond of the output legitimacy of soft law and its high specialisation; however, some more nuanced views were also expressed, purporting that legitimacy could become a problem if soft law is treated as hard law.[87]

[83] Lisi et al (n 1) 45 et seq; André (n 1) 49 et seq; Lamoureux and Rubio (n 1) 67 et seq.
[84] *cf* the *MasterCard* case: M Dobbs and O Ştefan, ch 15 in this volume.
[85] Lisi et al (n 1) 46.
[86] M Eliantonio, E Korkea-aho and O Ştefan, ch 1 in this volume.
[87] Lamoureux and Rubio (n 1) 68.

In social law,[88] the opinion of the interviewees was that EU soft law is still largely symbolic, but is useful in order to understand a policy goal or, if necessary, to clarify the substance of a hard law rule. The implementation of such instruments remains plausible, but the main usefulness of soft law is still seen in its informative or guidance role. The interviewees unanimously call for a better dissemination of soft law and, at the same time, ask for an educational effort from European institutions in this respect: the EU must issue understandable laws. Rules would spread more easily if they were accessible and intelligible.

The balance between the positive and the negative effects of soft law is therefore unsurprisingly difficult to strike. Depending on the field, some general principles of law are promoted at the expense of others, which is perhaps inevitable in the multi-governance setting of the EU, confirming previous hypotheses.[89]

V. CONCLUSION

Our research shows that there is both judicial and administrative awareness towards EU soft law in France, and a plurality of legal sources are being used by civil servants and judges nowadays. The core concern remains the quality of soft law,[90] which calls for clarification and accessibility, as reflected in recent case law developments, scholarly studies and ongoing national revisions. Facing such challenges, the hope rests – as is perhaps inevitable for a legal chapter – with the courts. The question is whether the openness to judicial review of national soft law by French courts will revolutionise justiciability of EU soft law in France and elsewhere in Europe. With a first step taken in the Fédération bancaire française, the ball is now in the court of the CJEU.[91]

[88] André (n 1) 51.

[89] O Ştefan, 'Helping Loose Ends Meet? The Judicial Acknowledgement of Soft Law as a Tool of Multi-level Governance' (2014) 21 *Maastricht Journal of European and Comparative Law* 359.

[90] Conseil d'État, *Simplification et qualité du droit*, Annual Study 2016 (Paris, La documentation Française, 2016), www.vie-publique.fr/sites/default/files/rapport/pdf/164000610.pdf.

[91] M Eliantonio, ch 17 in this volume.

9

Soft Law in Germany

Still Opposing Dynamics in Status and Effect

MIRIAM HARTLAPP, ANDREAS HOFMANN AND MATTHIAS KNAUFF*

I. INTRODUCTION

IN COMPARATIVE CLASSIFICATIONS, the historic origins of the German administrative system are often linked to the Prussian State. The system is characterised as functionally differentiated, with administrative rules forming part of the *Rechtsstaat*. There are strong federal elements accompanied by detailed rules on the division of power, resulting in a strong tradition of administrative law.[1] The legal system, in turn, follows the civil law tradition. Courts are specialised – there is no single supreme court, but a number of specialised federal high courts at the top of the judicial hierarchy.[2] This chapter takes as a starting point the opposing dynamics that result from the status and effect of soft law in the German administration and the judicial system. In theory, there is no place for soft law in the legal order. In practice, however, the administration has frequently used soft law as a steering tool both to regulate its inner workings in a complex federal polity and to ensure the effective implementation and consistent application of hard law. Against this background, the chapter

* This chapter draws on work we have published separately, in particular M Hartlapp and A Hofmann, 'The Use of EU Soft Law by National Courts and Bureaucrats: How Relation to Hard Law and Policy Maturity Matter' now published: (2021) 44 *West European Politics* 134, DOI: 10.1080/01402382.2020.1738095; and M Knauff, *Der Regelungsverbund: Recht und Soft Law im Mehrebenensystem* (Tübingen, Mohr Siebeck, 2010).

[1] A von Bogdandy and PM Huber, 'Evolution and Gestalt of the German State' in A von Bogdandy, M Huber and S Cassese (eds), *The Administrative State: Max Planck Handbooks in European Public Law* (Oxford, Oxford University Press, 2017).

[2] ibid 228; S Brouard and C Hönnige, 'Constitutional Courts as Veto Players: Lessons from the United States, France and Germany' (2017) 56 *European Journal of Political Research* 529.

asks whether the opposing dynamics are still prevalent in today's reception of concrete EU soft law instruments. Do administrative and legal actors use EU soft law differently?

To address this question, the next section describes the status and role of soft law in both spheres in more detail. The discussion then turns to a comparative assessment of soft law implementation in four different policy fields. The use that bureaucrats and judges make of EU instruments differs substantially across these policy fields. EU soft law is widely used both in environmental policy and competition law. In the field of financial market regulation, administrative actors pragmatically take up EU soft law where it helps to address the daily problems of market functioning. The use of EU soft law is comparatively contained in social policy. The differences between the policy fields seem to be influenced by the differential imprint that federal competences have on the administration as well as by the extent to which specialised courts are asked to rule on conflicts that involve an EU legal dimension. The chapter concludes by discussing, first, the motivations of actors in the legal and administrative sphere to use soft law that highlight why differences prevail in some areas and, second, possible drivers that overcome the opposing dynamics of EU soft law reception in the German case.

II. STATUS AND EFFECTS OF SOFT LAW IN GERMANY

German law does not acknowledge the term 'soft law' – in fact, no sensible German translation of the term exists. However, the concept of administrative rules (*Verwaltungsvorschriften*) is explicitly referred to in the German Constitution (Articles 84(2) and 85(2)). Legislation also often contains authorisations for the adoption of administrative rules. For example, paragraph 59 of the German Weapons Act[3] allows the Ministry of the Interior to adopt administrative rules on the carrying of firearms by its officers.

In relation to soft law stemming from the EU level, the German legislator has gradually made inroads into the German legal order in two ways. Some legislative acts now contain references to European Commission guidelines, such as paragraph 1 of the Ordinance on Transparency in energy and electricity tax law.[4] Even more important is the transposition of EU soft law into German binding law. For example, following a controversy between the German government and the European Commission about whether an exemption from a renewable energy surcharge for major industry classified as State aid, the German legislator felt compelled to adapt the Renewable Energies Act[5] to conform with the Commission Guidelines on State Aid for Environmental Protection and Energy.[6]

[3] Waffengesetz [2002] BGBl I S 3970.

[4] Energiesteuer- und Stromsteuer-Transparenzverordnung [2016] BGBl I S 1158.

[5] Gesetz für den Ausbau erneuerbarer Energien [2014] BGBl I S 1066.

[6] European Commission, 'Communication from the Commission – Guidelines on State aid for environmental protection and energy 2014–2020' [2014] OJ C200/1.

In contrast to the federal legal order, the States have historically embraced soft law. One prominent example in the context of constitutional law is the 1957 agreement (Lindauer Abkommen)[7] between the federal government and the States to solve a constitutional uncertainty about the competence to conclude international treaties. Another example is the 1950 non-codified agreement (Königsteiner Vereinbarung) between the prime ministers of the States on the order of the presidency in the federal upper legislative chamber (Bundesrat). More so than in constitutional law, soft law has been and continues to be important in the context of administrative law. Administrative rules are well known – although often qualified not as soft law, but as 'internal' law (*Innenrecht*) – and have widely been used regardless of the potential lack of legal bases.[8] With regard to content and function, German academic lawyers distinguish between organisational and procedural rules and service instructions (*Organisations-, Verfahrens- und Dienstvorschriften*), interpreting rules (*norminterpretierende Verwaltungsvorschriften*), discretion-guiding administrative provisions (*ermessenslenkende Verwaltungsvorschriften*) and technical circulars (*normkonkretisierende Verwaltungsvorschriften*).[9] In addition to administrative rules, other forms of soft law entered administrative practice in recent years, as administrative bodies discovered soft law as a means of rule-making. In particular, the federal agency for networks in electricity, gas, telecommunications, post and railway (Bundesnetzagentur) and the federal competition authority (Bundeskartellamt) have begun to use soft law instruments like guidelines and notices as steering instruments. It is apparent that Commission guidelines and communications serve as a blueprint for German agency rule-making. Another important development is the improved transparency of soft law-making in Germany. Authorities now usually publish new forms of non-binding rules in order to secure their intended effects. Administrative rules, too, have their own online repository.[10]

Turning to case law, we observe a change from a traditional neglect of national soft law to an increasing opening up to EU soft law.[11] However, in general, the German judiciary is still very reluctant to accept soft law as a legal yardstick. According to the Federal Constitutional Court (Bundesverfassungsgericht), administrative rules must not interfere with fundamental rights as they do not

[7] Deutscher Bundestag, Schlußbericht der Enquete-Kommission Verfassungsreform [1976] Drucksache 7/5924, 236.

[8] F Fleiner, *Institutionen des deutschen Verwaltungsrechts*, 8th edn (Tübingen, Mohr, 1928) 61 ff; W Jellinek, *Verwaltungsrecht*, 3rd edn (Berlin, Springer, 1931) 126. See, in detail, F Ossenbühl, *Verwaltungsvorschriften und Grundgesetz* (Bad Homburg, Gehlen, 1968) 34 ff.

[9] A Rogmann, *Die Bindungswirkung von Verwaltungsvorschriften* (Göttingen, Heymanns, 1998) 16; T Sauerland, *Die Verwaltungsvorschrift im System der Rechtsquellen* (Berlin, Duncker & Humblot, 2005) 63; M Trips, *Das Verfahren der exekutiven Rechtsetzung. Möglichkeiten und Erfordernisse der Aufnahme eines allgemeinen Verfahrens für Verordnungen, Satzungen und Verwaltungsvorschriften in das Verwaltungsverfahrensgesetz* (Baden-Baden, Nomos, 2006) 85.

[10] www.verwaltungsvorschriften-im-internet.de.

[11] Von Bogdandy and Huber (n 1) 226.

satisfy the constitutional requirement of a statutory provision.[12] In this vein, a higher regional court (Oberlandesgericht Düsseldorf) recently stated that the guidelines of the Bundesnetzagentur have no legal relevance and need to be qualified as mere legal opinions.[13] At the same time, the multitude of soft law instruments used at the EU level forces the German legal profession to deal with such forms of regulation. Legal practitioners find themselves increasingly unable to provide appropriate legal advice without considering soft law.[14]

In parallel, interest in soft law has increased among German academic lawyers. A search for 'soft law' in commentaries and journals in the leading legal database Juris[15] returns about 500 matches for the period between 2000 and 2019. Beyond a mere quantitative increase, two recent habilitation theses – by Nadja Braun Binder[16] and Matthias Knauff[17] – and several doctoral dissertations on specific forms of (mainly EU) soft law[18] indicate that, for the first time, soft law has become an object of intense legal research in Germany. Moreover, a (more) positive approach in legal doctrine towards soft law is developing,[19] albeit alongside many critical voices.[20] Unlike before, soft law today is perceived as an object of interest in German jurisprudence.

[12] Bundesverfassungsgericht [2006] 2 BvR 1673, 2402/04, BVerfGE 116, 69.

[13] OLG Düsseldorf [2017] VI-3 Kart 148/15 (V).

[14] Trips (n 9) 84.

[15] www.juris.de.

[16] N Braun-Binder, *Rechtsangleichung in der EU im Bereich der direkten Steuern* (Tübingen, Mohr Siebeck, 2017).

[17] M Knauff, *Der Regelungsverbund: Recht und Soft Law im Mehrebenensystem* (Tübingen, Mohr Siebeck, 2010).

[18] H Adam, *Die Mitteilungen der Kommission: Verwaltungsvorschriften des Europäischen Gemeinschaftsrechts? Eine Untersuchung zur rechtsdogmatischen Einordnung eines Instruments der Kommission zur Steuerung der Durchführung des Gemeinschaftsrechts* (Baden-Baden, Nomos, 1999); J Marquier, *Soft Law: Das Beispiel des OSZE-Prozesses. Ein Beitrag zur völkerrechtlichen Rechtsquellenlehre* (Diss. jur. Bonn, 2003); B Häberle, *Die Kronzeugenmitteilung der Europäischen Kommission im EG-Kartellrecht* (Baden-Baden, Nomos, 2005); DK Walzel, *Bindungswirkungen ungeregelter Vollzugsinstrumente der EU-Kommission – mit Schwerpunkt auf Mitteilungen, Bekanntmachungen, Leitlinien und Rahmen der Kommission im EG-Wettbewerbsrecht* (Baden-Baden, Heymann, 2008); DE Arndt, *Sinn und Unsinn von Soft Law. Prolegomena zur Zukunft eines indeterminierten Paradigmas* (Baden-Baden, Nomos, 2011); M Brohm, *Die 'Mitteilungen' der Kommission im europäischen Verwaltungs- und Wirtschaftsraum. Typologie, Rechtsnatur und Bindungswirkung für die Behörden der Mitgliedstaaten* (Baden-Baden, Nomos, 2012); M Goldmann, *Internationale öffentliche Gewalt. Handlungsformen internationaler Institutionen im Zeitalter der Globalisierung* (Berlin, Springer-Verlag, 2015); C Giersch, *Das internationale Soft Law. Eine völkerrechtsdogmatische und völkerrechtssoziologische Bestandsaufnahme* (Berlin, LIT Verlag, 2016); M Schramm, *Einseitiges informelles Verwaltungshandeln im Regulierungsrecht* (Heidelberg, Mohr Siebeck, 2016); F Strauß, *Soft Law als Steuerungsinstrument in der Bankenaufsicht. Eine Untersuchung im Völkerrecht, europäischen Unionsrecht und deutschen Verfassungsrecht am Beispiel der Basler Akkorde* (Baden-Baden, Nomos, 2016); JE Dickschen, *Empfehlungen und Leitlinien als Handlungsform der Europäischen Finanzaufsichtsbehörden. Eine dogmatische Vermessung* (Berlin, Springer, 2017); J Trunk, 'Leitlinien als "neues" Steuerungsinstrument im Völkerrecht – entwickelt unter anderem am Beispiel der "Freiwilligen Leitlinien für die verantwortungsvolle Verwaltung von Boden- und Landnutzungsrechten, Fischgründen und Wäldern"' (Diss jur, Hamburg, 2019).

[19] E Schmidt-Aßmann, *Verwaltungsrechtliche Dogmatik* (Heidelberg, Mohr Siebeck, 2013) 54.

[20] W Weiß, 'Das Leitlinien(un)wesen der Kommission verletzt den Vertrag von Lissabon' (2010) 21(7) *Europaisches wirtschafts und steuerrecht* 257; Arndt (n 18).

In sum, the growing importance of soft law as well as the willingness among many relevant protagonists in German legal circles to engage with soft law – with the possible exception of the courts – is strongly related to developments at the EU level. Still, soft law is not yet fully accepted and integrated into legal doctrine, and is thus of minor importance in legal education, despite the fact that it shows concrete effects, particularly in some of the policy areas described below. Without a more active role being taken by the legislator, it will take a long time until soft law will have become an integral part of the German legal order – if at all – despite its increasing and wide-ranging practical effects.

III. BETWEEN SCEPTICAL JUDGES AND PRAGMATIC BUREAUCRATS: THE POLICY FIELD-SPECIFIC USE OF SOFT LAW INSTRUMENTS

In the European Network of Soft Law Research (SoLaR) project, we explored how German authorities and courts use EU soft law instruments in four policy areas (financial market regulation and environmental, social and competition policy). Below we summarise insights from our case studies that are based on an analysis of German administrative and judicial documents as well as 18 interviews that have been conducted between December 2017 and July 2018. Interviewees worked in federal and State ministries, subordinate agencies and local administrative units. Two of the interviewees were judges. Semi-structured interviews were carried out face-to-face or over the phone, each lasting between 20 and 60 minutes. In addition, we conducted a systematic keyword search of court rulings at the highest federal level (civil and administrative) to find out whether and, if so, how German highest courts refer to soft law instruments. The results are presented according to policy fields. The differences between them are quite pronounced. We will discuss these differences both in light of competence allocation between the Länder and the federal level, and differences in the degree to which specialised courts are routinely exposed to EU law.

A. Financial Market Regulation

Financial markets are regulated at the central level in Germany. The four European Securities and Markets Authority (ESMA) guidelines on Enforcement of financial information (ESMA/2014/1293), Exemption for market making activities and primary market operations (ESMA/2013/74, under the Short Selling Regulation), Complaints handling for the securities and banking sectors (ESMA/EBA/2014/43) and Remuneration policies and practices (ESMA/2013/606) have all been used in Germany. The Federal Financial Supervisory Authority (Bundesanstalt für Finanzdienstleistungsaufsicht (BaFin)) issued soft law circulars and information sheets addressed at market participants. These circulars transposed the ESMA guidelines on Enforcement of financial information, Exemption for market making activities and Complaints-handling.

In addition, two of the four ESMA guidelines (on short selling and remuneration) are codified in national legislation.[21] Unlike soft law in the other studied policy fields, national authorities must notify ESMA whether they intend to comply with ESMA guidelines or, where they do not, must give reasons for non-compliance within two months of publication.[22]

On the one hand, this comply or explain mechanism (which is enshrined in EU hard law) increases pressure to align practices with the requirements of the ESMA guidelines. On the other hand, de facto notification turns EU soft law into a requirement that market participants have to fulfil vis-a-vis the national authorities.[23] This mechanism ensures that national standards are explicitly linked to soft EU standards or that the EU standards are transposed into binding or non-binding national law. For this reason, ESMA soft law is routinely used at the national level.[24]

Our interviewees considered guidelines to be lighter instruments that are easier and faster to adopt than hard legislation. Fast-changing requirements and rapid new developments render soft law a welcome or even a necessary policy instrument. Compared to complex negotiations and lengthy procedures in the legislative process that often continue for years, guidelines as well as a rapidly growing collection of frequently asked questions (FAQs) address questions of interpretation that typically emerge at the national level. This position was stressed in particular by officials working in the competent agency who were close to the day-to-day functioning of financial markets. Officials working in the ministry, in turn, were more concerned about keeping control over competence allocation in a quickly evolving policy field. In sum, EU soft law is frequently used in day-to-day administrative practices.[25]

The addressees of the soft law measures that we studied are usually legal or natural persons acting on financial markets. Annual reports issued by BaFin[26] highlight that two-thirds of the legal conflicts that reach them are initiated by insurers, followed by banks and securities companies. Courts are unlikely to make direct reference to EU soft law, as they will typically refer to the national (hard or soft) transposition instruments. Thus, it is not surprising that the soft law instruments we studied did not seem to have played a role before the judiciary. Moreover, interviewees were generally dismissive of the idea that EU soft

[21] WA 25-Wp 5700-2012/0006 [2013]; Leerverkaufs-Anzeigeverordnung [2014] BGBl I S 386; Wertpapierhandelsgesetz [1998] BGBl I S 2708.

[22] Regulation (EU) No 1095/2010 of the European Parliament and of the Council of 24 November 2010 establishing a European Supervisory Authority [2010] OJ L331/84.

[23] T Becker, 'ESMA Leitlinien "Vergütungsgrundsätze und – verfahren (MiFID)" und BT 8 der MaComp – neue Vergütungsvorgaben für Wertpapierdienstleistungsunternehmen' (2014) *Zeitschrift für Bank und Kapitalmarktrecht* 151.

[24] M Hartlapp and A Schwerdtfeger, 'Studying EU Soft Law Effects in Financial Regulation: Insights from Germany' in M Avbelj (ed), 'EU Financial Regulation Soft Law in the Member States: Finland, France, Germany, Italy, the Netherlands, Slovenia and the UK' (2020) SoLaR Working Paper, https://papers.ssrn.com/sol3/papers.cfm?abstract_id=3668793, 62.

[25] ibid 64–65.

[26] www.bafin.de/DE/PublikationenDaten/Jahresbericht/jahresbericht_node.html.

law could be used by national courts. However, our systematic search returned two court decisions that refer to ESMA in a broader context: A judgment of the Federal Administrative Court (Bundesverwaltungsgericht) referred to a common position agreed by members of the predecessor to ESMA (the Committee of European Securities Regulators (CESR)) to support the interpretation of a legislative provision.[27] After pointing to its non-binding character, the Court underlined that the common position represents the legal opinion of the relevant national authorities and therefore does entail the presumption to be correct. In another decision, the Federal Court of Justice (Bundesgerichtshof) stated that the power delegated to ESMA to issue guidelines comprises only the elaboration and concretisation of indicators relevant for norm interpretation. Norm requirements cannot take the form of soft law.[28] This interpretation questions ESMA's authority to formulate rules via soft law-making. Important as these cases are, they concern competences at the EU level to formulate norms rather than their implementation at the national level.[29]

In sum, our explorative analysis shows that EU soft law on financial market regulation is widely used by pragmatic administrative actors to resolve questions of day-to-day policy implementation. Where the adoption of hard law is lengthy and cumbersome, national-level actors embrace EU soft law for its potential to solve problems they encounter in their day-to-day market interactions. German courts, at least for the time being, seem to be more reluctant to embrace this type of soft law. This might be due to the limited value of additional EU guidance following the transposition of EU soft law at the national level as well as a general reluctance of courts in this policy field to consider ESMA soft law.

B. Environmental Policy

Our analysis of the use of soft law instruments in this field focused on guidelines concerning the Habitats Directive and guidance documents concerning the Water Framework Directive (WFD).[30] The EU Habitats Directive was implemented in German federal legislation through a revision of the Federal Nature Conservation Act in 1998.[31] State legislation was also amended. Virtually all implementation activities of the Habitats Directive were undertaken at the State level, ie, the designation of Natura 2000 sites, the legal framework for their protected status and the adoption of management plans. Shortly after the

[27] Bundesverwaltungsgericht [2011] 7 C 6/10, para 26.

[28] Bundesgerichtshof [2017] 5 StR 532/16, para 21.

[29] Hartlapp and Schwerdtfeger (n 24) 66.

[30] Council Directive 92/43/EEC of 21 May 1992 on the conservation of natural habitats and of wild fauna and flora [1992] OJ L206/7 and Directive 2000/60/EC of the European Parliament and of the Council of 23 October 2000 establishing a framework for Community action in the field of water policy [2000] OJ L327/1.

[31] Bundesnaturschutzgesetz [1998] BGBl I S 889.

Habitats Directive had passed the legislative process at the EU level, the Federal Agency for Nature Conservation (Bundesamt für Naturschutz) began work on national soft law interpretative guidelines in an attempt at standardisation, since all German States worked with different classifications and standards.

The WFD was implemented in federal legislation through a revision of the Federal Water Act in 2009.[32] State legislation was also revised. The resulting system for water management is multi-tiered. International river management cooperation is a federal competence. Water management in Germany is organised in 10 river areas, two of which are wholly national.[33] Cross-State coordination, including the setting-up of river basin management plans, is undertaken in river management areas. Concrete implementation of water management measures belongs to the State level. The main body for the coordination of water management between the federal and State levels is the Bund-Länder Arbeitsgemeinschaft Wasser (LAWA), which includes representatives from the Federal Ministry for the Environment and all State ministries. LAWA is itself the central source of soft law guidance on the implementation of water management policies. It is here that EU guidance documents are adapted into non-binding national guidance documents that are the primary reference points for implementation at the State level.

More specifically, interview partners in national administrations stressed that EU soft law documents are highly relevant in the implementation of hard law directives and assist in dealing with application problems. They highlighted that the advantage of soft law lies in its ability to flexibly respond to such problems, in particular where legal requirements remain abstract. Waiting for a hard law clarification is impracticable in practice, and hence soft law guidance is considered particularly helpful. Soft law documents are frequently referred to in scientific assessment procedures and form the basis of concrete measures. In the event of conflicts about the legality of such measures, soft law can be referred to as a justification for the measures taken by authorities. While not legally binding, they were said to convince by their scientific merit. An interview partner highlighted that soft law in the form of Commission notes is particularly relevant, since these notes are reference points for Commission enforcement of EU environmental law.

German courts are routinely confronted with both the Habitats Directive and the WFD. For the most part, the courts deal with the directives in the permitting processes, where either an applicant challenges the responsible authority's decision not to grant a construction permit or an environmental

[32] Wasserhaushaltsgesetz [2009] BGBl I S 2585.

[33] A Hofmann, 'National Report on Germany: The Use of EU Soft Law by National Courts and Administration in the Field of EU Environmental Law' in M Eliantonio and G Lisi (eds), 'EU Environmental Soft Law in the Member States: A Comparative Overview of Finland, France, Germany, Italy, the Netherlands, Slovenia and the UK' (2020) SoLaR Working Paper, https://papers.ssrn.com/sol3/papers.cfm?abstract_id=3656418.

group challenges the authority's decision to grant it. These cases are processed within the administrative court system. The Federal Administrative Court referred to EU soft law documents in numerous cases, often concerning prominent infrastructure projects, such as the dredging of rivers around Hamburg and Bremen harbours or the extension of the runway at Münster Airport. The references to soft law were very specific and acknowledged the value of soft law in the interpretation of hard law: 'This document [CIS document 2], while not binding, nonetheless has special importance [*besonderes Gewicht*] for the interpretation [of the WFD]',[34] or 'regarding the interpretation and implementation of art. 6.3 [of the Habitats Directive], permitting authorities would be well advised to consult the Commission's interpretative document Managing Natura 2000 Sites, irrespective of the fact that an authoritative interpretation can only be given by the CJEU [Court of Justice of the European Union]'.[35]

An interview partner at the Federal Administrative Court stated three primary reasons why the Court refers to EU soft law in its Habitats Directive case law. First, German courts cite all sorts of sources (literature, expert opinion, foreign courts etc). Among these sources, EU soft law documents are relatively authoritative because they are close to EU institutions as the source of the original legislation. As such, they are difficult to ignore. Second, courts refer to EU soft law to signal to the CJEU that their argument is 'on the right level', in order to counter suspicions that national courts block the national reception of EU rules. Finally, EU environmental soft law documents are informative. The level of expertise is substantively helpful. This quality raises the bar to argue against the interpretation offered in them.

In sum, in the field of environmental policy, the soft law instruments under investigation were extensively used by administrations and courts – cutting across the opposing dynamics of the two spheres regarding soft law implementation in Germany. In the policy area with far-reaching federal competences, actors at the national and subnational levels routinely referred to EU hard and soft law. Moreover, the interviewees reported a strong interest in using the soft law instruments to avoid implementation conflict over EU hard law. Clearly, in environmental policy, pragmatic practice dominates legalistic considerations of soft law's legal status.

C. Social Policy

The first instrument studied, a Commission Recommendation on investing in children (2013/112/EU), was not implemented at the national level in Germany. Interviewees reported that the recommendation is very vague and of a general

[34] Bundesverwaltungsgericht [2016] 9 A 18/15.
[35] Bundesverwaltungsgericht [2003] 4 B 70/02.

nature, and hence of little help in national policy-making. In addition, it marks a shift in EU policy, with the Commission turning from an 'alliance for families' towards investing in children. Since the German approach has continued to focus on families, actors in the administration lacked substantial incentives to follow this new direction and did not opt for implementation. Nor could usage by courts be traced.[36]

Second, the EU guide Buying Social finds its equivalent in the national guideline Considering social criteria in public procurement issued by the German Association of Cities and Towns, together with the federal executive, in 2001. Pre-dating the EU soft law instrument by some months, the national guide was motivated by the wish to implement a policy shift. Interviewees reported that they had wanted to push public actors in smaller cities to implement social goals in public procurement. Others, however, stressed that the connection to existing EU hard law on public procurement rendered the implementation of the EU Buying Social guide difficult because hard and soft law differed in substance. For much of the integration process, the EU rules stipulated that contracts can only be awarded to bidders with the lowest price, and EU case law[37] had prohibited the national practice to award contracts only to those bidders that granted pay at least at the level of locally applicable collective agreements. The soft law instrument is the first instrument that explicitly called for (re)consideration of social criteria in public procurement. One interviewee found EU soft law that diverges from existing interpretations helpful in policy development. Others were more concerned and stated that tenderers and bidders were very sensitive to legal controversies that risk prolonging public procurement procedures for months or years. In this context, interviewees that offered professional counsel on public procurement pointed to the legal uncertainty that was created by the EU soft law instrument. And in the event of doubt, they advised their clients to stick to legislation.[38] Thus, the differences in the regulatory objectives of the hard and soft instruments constrained a broader reception of the EU guide Buying Social at the national level.

Legal conflicts in this area concern a failure of a public authority to issue a call for tenders, incorrect tenders and incorrect awards. Typically, potential or de facto competitors launch these cases. Sometimes conflicts are solved via extra-judicial procedures with district level arbitration. Yet, judicial conflicts remain frequent, involving local procurement chambers at first and higher regional

[36] M Hartlapp, 'Studying EU Soft Law Effects in Social Policy: Insights from Germany' in M Hartlapp (ed), 'Studying EU Soft Law Effects in Social Policy' (2020) SoLaR Working Paper, https://papers.ssrn.com/sol3/papers.cfm?abstract_id=3668981, 56–57.

[37] Case C-346/06 *Rüffert* [2008] ECR I-1989.

[38] Since the last reform in 2014/16, procurement law has become more open towards 'social procurement'; see, eg, D Hattenhauer and C Butzert, 'Die Etablierung ökologischer, sozialer, innovativer und qualitativer Aspekte im Vergabeverfahren' (2017) *ZfBR* 129.

courts later on.[39] Interviewees explained that, for arbitration as well as adjudication, national law – which implements EU hard law – is more relevant than EU soft law. This is in line with the doubts raised by administrative actors about the legal uncertainty created by soft law in time-sensitive procurement processes.[40] Yet, in the wider context of public procurement cases, EU soft law sometimes features in judgments relating to public procurement decisions.[41]

For the third instrument, the Recommendation on Transparency in equal pay (2014/124/EU), supplementing the Equal Treatment Directive,[42] clearly pushed for implementation. Prior to the publication of the recommendation, the German Social Democratic Party (SPD) and the Christian Democrats (CDU) had negotiated and signed a coalition agreement that included provisions on equal pay transparency and was influenced by existing EU hard law on the issue. The subsequent law on transparency in pay[43] was adopted much later on 30 June 2017. National legislative negotiations proved lengthy, since the ministries involved were headed by members of different coalition partners. Within these negotiations, definitions about 'work of equal value' and 'assessment criteria for comparing different jobs' were modelled on the EU soft law instrument.[44]

Administrative actors in favour of equal pay policies described the EU soft law instrument as helpful in pushing their points through at the domestic level. The national law is accompanied by two soft law guides that give practical advice to assist in implementation, both of which reference EU soft law. One guide addresses employees (eg, defining concepts such as work of equal value or pay), whereas the other addresses employers as well as works councils (eg, detailing the steps to secure the rights endowed by legislation) (both adopted in 2017). Thus, the EU soft law instrument was implemented in both a hard and soft form. Judicial conflicts about equal pay are frequently dealt with by specialised labour courts, but no reference to the recommendation had been made at the time of investigation. As the law was only adopted in 2017, there might be cases over time with conflicts in lower courts needing some time to work their way through the legal hierarchy.

In sum, social policy showed great variation in terms of soft law usage. A very soft recommendation on investing in children was dismissed by administrative actors who showed no inclination to take up substantial steering coming from Brussels. In the other two cases, EU soft law was used by national actors who were interested in EU instruments to improve and alter national practices.

[39] Hartlapp and Hofmann (n1).

[40] Hartlapp (n 36) 55.

[41] Knauff (n 17) 194.

[42] Directive 2006/54/EC of the European Parliament and of the Council of 5 July 2006 on the implementation of the principle of equal opportunities and equal treatment of men and women in matters of employment and occupation (recast) [2006] OJ L204/23.

[43] Entgelttransparenzgesetz [2017] BGBl I S 2152.

[44] Hartlapp (n 36) 57.

However, for public procurement, substantial contradictions between hard and soft EU instruments rendered broad national reception difficult. Overall, national actors made limited use of EU soft law in the social policy field. We observe little pragmatic use in the administration and even less in courts.

D. Competition Policy

Our analysis of the implementation of soft law instruments in the field of competition policy focused on guidelines concerning antitrust and State aid law. State aid is entirely governed by EU law, it is an exclusive EU competence, and aid-granting authorities are directly subject to EU rules. No distinct German law exists in this field. Competition law has a long tradition in Germany that precedes EU rules,[45] but the German law is now harmonised with EU rules to the extent that much of the wording is identical to the relevant EU treaty articles (Articles 101 and 102 of the Treaty on the Functioning of the European Union (TFEU)). The selected soft law instruments are all authored by the Commission and concern such issues as the legality of horizontal cooperation agreements between firms (competition law) or the sale of buildings and lands by public authorities (State aid). They offer the Commission's interpretation of hard law and inform market actors of the Commission's own enforcement of competition rules.

A unit within the Federal Ministry for Economic Affairs is responsible for the coordination of compliance with EU State aid rules for all aid-granting authorities. However, it has no direct competence to direct the behaviour of regional and local authorities. This unit has begun to issue its own soft law guidelines in 2014 as part of a new compliance management system.[46] The German guidelines are based on the EU soft law. Among these are recommendations for the implementation of EU State aid law in Germany, a handbook on state aid (mainly a German translation of the 'State aid manual' drafted by the UK Department for Business, Innovation and Skills) and a State aid checklist. These documents reference Commission documents, as well as EU soft law tools such as General block exemption regulation (GBER) checklists and the eState aid-WIKI and FAQs.

The national competition authority is the Bundeskartellamt, which oversees competition rules for companies active in the German market (under the threshold for direct involvement of the Commission). At the State level, the Landeskartellbehörden enforce competition rules for regional markets. As part of administrative law, the Bundeskartellamt regularly issues its own guidelines

[45] Gesetz gegen Wettbewerbsbeschränkungen [1957] BGBl I S 1081.
[46] www.bmwi.de/Redaktion/DE/Artikel/Europa/beihilfenkontrollpolitik.html.

on aspects pertaining to its own practices that are not governed by EU law, such as fines.[47]

German courts are involved in the adjudication of competition law disputes in several ways. In competition law cases, private actors either challenge decisions by competition authorities or they sue competitors for damages incurred from alleged anti-competitive practices. Both types of cases go through the civil court system. The latter type, essentially decentralised enforcement of EU competition rules, has recently gained greater prominence. In State aid law, only the Commission has competence to decide on the compatibility of State aid with EU law. However, private actors can take aid-granting authorities to court for not following appropriate procedures, including the reporting of State aid to the Commission. In 2011, the Federal Court of Justice decided that private actors could also sue aid-granting authorities for damages incurred as a consequence of not following these obligations.[48] A Commission notice and a handbook on the enforcement of State aid law by national courts – both soft law instruments – give guidance on decentralised enforcement, but their implementation was not part of this investigation.

Interview partners stated that they know and use EU soft law as German and EU competition rules are identical in many points and use the same standards (eg, the concept of 'substantial lessening of competition' in merger control or 'improving the production of goods' or 'promoting technical or economic progress' as grounds for exemptions). Thus, guidelines interpreting European law help in the interpretation of national law too. National authorities use the guidelines regularly. An interview partner at the Landeskartellbehörde stated that in competition law control, German authorities generally follow the Commission, including its soft law that is regularly consulted. The interviewee mentioned some exceptions, such as the Commission's 'efficient competitor test', where the Commission will sometimes defer action when consumer prices are positively affected. This is not the approach of the German Bundeskartellamt. In general, the interview partner saw no reasons to deviate from Commission guidelines if they apply to the case at hand. In this sense, the interview partner described them as 'factually binding', ie, binding for practical purposes. The interview partner also found soft law guidelines substantively helpful, as competition law has many legal terms in need of greater definition (such as 'dominance' and 'abuse'). Soft law allows for a flexible and adaptable mode of addressing these problems and enables the creation of common standards for the European market.

German courts refer to EU soft law on a regular basis. The most important ones are the Commission Communication on State aid elements in sales of land and buildings by public authorities and the Guidelines on Vertical restraints

[47] Hartlapp and Hofmann (n 1) 147.
[48] Bundesgerichtshof [2011] I ZR 136/09.

in competition law. An interview partner at the Higher Regional Court of Düsseldorf, the first court of appeal for decisions of the Bundeskartellamt (and hence the busiest competition law jurisdiction), stated that this court regards soft law guidelines as no more but also no less than a scholarly opinion, which needs to be taken seriously. His view of the soft law instruments was moderately critical. The judges know that soft law guidelines exist and take them into account, but they do not feel bound by them. The interview partner stated that it does not hurt to consult the guidelines, but that the court independently arrives at its own opinion, and the guidelines do not usually help the court in its legal interpretation. There are cases where the Court has explicitly decided not to follow the interpretation offered in guidelines.[49] However, among the cases surveyed, an explicit disagreement appeared to be the exception, not the rule. The interview partner doubted the usefulness of issuing guidelines before a substantial body of case law has developed. According to this person, the legal field needed to grow in order to develop an understanding of the problems that emerge, and it is only after a body of case law exists that guidelines (based on this case law) can be useful.

In sum, in the field of competition law, actors in the bureaucracy and judiciary reported great awareness of EU hard and soft law. The supplementary soft law instruments under investigation were extensively used by administrations and courts, and the behaviour of both largely aligned with the content of EU soft law instruments. We contend that this alignment of administrative effect and usage in courts is supported by the general importance of EU competition law for the legal order in Germany.

IV. CONCLUSION: CAUGHT BETWEEN WEAK LEGAL AND STRONG PRACTICAL RELEVANCE

This chapter has explored how German administrative authorities and courts use EU soft law, and how they consider questions of governance efficiency and a potential lack of legitimacy. We found that extensive use was made of EU soft law instruments by both German administration and courts in environmental and competition policy. In financial market regulation, administrative actors regularly made use of EU soft law, but we found few references in court documents. This might be due to the relative novelty of EU regulation in this field. Finally, we found little use of EU soft law in the social policy field, both among the administration and the courts.

Evidence from our interviews suggests that efficiency gains are frequently a main driver of EU soft law usage. Actors involved in the day-to-day implementation of financial market regulation, environmental and competition policy perceived soft law instruments as flexible tools that are capable of rapidly

[49] OLG Düsseldorf [2017] VI-Kart 13/15 (V).

reacting to unforeseen events, contingent developments or technical application problems. In general, the technical quality of EU soft law instruments was considered to be very high. On the contrary, assessments of the legitimacy and a legal status of soft law instruments were more divergent. Actors further away from legislative work and closer to practical implementation, ie, agencies and subnational layers of the administration, were typically less concerned about a potential lack of legitimacy and emphasised instead pragmatic concerns. One interview partner surmised that a pragmatic attitude is entrenched among practitioners. In contrast, concerns about a lack of legitimacy were voiced primarily by actors closer to the legislative process. Judges also explicitly pointed out the non-binding nature of soft law, whilst simultaneously acknowledging its efficiency-enhancing potential. Thus, questions of legitimacy and accountability will be answered very differently depending on the respondent's relative position in the policy process. We expect that the opposing dynamics between the legal and practical relevance of EU soft law will persist in Germany for some time.

10

The Approach of Hungarian Authorities to Soft Law

On the Road to Where?

PETRA LEA LÁNCOS*

I. INTRODUCTION

THE PRESENT CHAPTER analyses the application of EU soft law in Hungary, with a particular focus on the fields of competition law and environmental law.[1] The analysis of the reception of EU soft law in Hungary shows a mixed picture. The application of EU competition soft law in Hungary may be considered a success, owing chiefly to the system of EU competition law enforcement and the proactive stance of the Hungarian Competition Authority (Gazdasági Versenyhivatal).[2] Meanwhile, the application of EU environmental soft law is problematic, and the gathering of reliable data is hampered by the dismantling and fragmentation of environmental authorities in Hungary.

Apart from the specific policy contexts of soft law application, it is necessary to recall the dualist traditions of the post-socialist State to understand the status of EU soft law in the national legal order and the approach of Hungarian courts and authorities to these norms. This tradition, coupled with text-positivism, continues to exert its influence on the use of what are considered 'external' legal sources. Besides considering such lingering traditions, the system governing the transposition of EU soft law is also examined. The finding is that the transposition of EU soft law is non-systematic, a situation that is complicated further by the fact that implementing legal acts do not necessarily refer to their EU origin through a 'harmonisation clause'. This lack of transparency conceals the EU

* I am indebted to the judges and public officials participating in the research for their invaluable help.

[1] Due to space constraints, financial regulation and social policy are not covered.

[2] Gazdasági Versenyhivatal, the competition authority of Hungary entrusted with enforcing antitrust and consumer protection rules, as well as the prohibition of unfair market practices.

origins of implementing domestic norms. An awareness about soft norms is also low: judges in general have little knowledge of the existence and applicability of EU soft law, while there are huge differences in the awareness and application of soft norms among national authorities.

The hypothesis is that all of the above factors influence the status of EU soft law and its reception by national courts and authorities. To test the hypothesis, a mixed research methodology was used. To gauge the attitude of Hungarian courts and public authorities towards EU soft law, I conducted a survey among the National Office for the Judiciary,[3] the Hungarian Constitutional Court and individual judges among my personal contacts, as well as the Deputy Commissioner Responsible for Future Generations (hereinafter 'the Green Ombudsman'), the regional authorities responsible for environmental protection and the Hungarian Competition Authority. Besides the survey, a total of six expert interviews were also conducted with different public authorities. The survey and the interview questions were based on the European Network of Soft Law Research (SoLaR) template. Finally, a keyword search analysis was conducted using the two different public databases containing Hungarian court judgments. On the basis of the data, I tried to determine the status of EU soft law in the Hungarian legal order, their overall perception by domestic courts and authorities, as well as their possible contribution to legal certainty and transparency.

This chapter also illustrates the difficulties in conducting research into judicial attitudes and case law, and, in particular, into the practice of administrative authorities. These difficulties are in part related to the organisational changes that have taken place in the past few years, but also the searchability of, or even lack of, relevant electronic databases.

In what follows, I describe the general approach to soft norms in Hungary, based on legal traditions and the implementation of EU law. Next, I describe the research methodology I applied to gathering the data on the application of EU soft law in Hungary. Then I turn to the sectoral analysis of EU soft law application, investigating the use of guidelines, communications, guidance documents etc in the context of competition law (excluding State aid law) and the protection of the environment. Finally, I draw some tentative conclusions on the role of EU soft law in Hungary.

II. FACTORS INFLUENCING THE PERCEPTION AND AWARENESS OF SOFT LAW IN HUNGARY

Before delving into the actual application of EU soft law, it is worth looking into the domestic soft law and the research concerning the perception of soft

[3] Országos Bírósági Hivatal, entrusted with the administration of the Hungarian judicial system. Oversight over the National Office for the Judiciary is exercised by the National Judicial Council.

law norms by Hungarian courts and authorities.[4] Two important factors are at play: the tradition of State-centred text-positivism and the system of EU law implementation, which both strongly influence the perception and awareness of soft norms in Hungary.

A. Perception of International and EU Soft Law Norms in Hungary

While domestic soft law exists in the Hungarian legal system, issued primarily by authorities, courts and rarely and more recently by ministries, these recommendations, opinions, protocols and ethical codes are not part of university curricula, nor are there scholarly works detailing their taxonomy or application. Where soft norms are issued by national authorities, the courts are quick to underline the non-binding nature of these norms.[5] Meanwhile, where soft law, usually in the form of recommendations, stems from the Curia (the Supreme Court of Hungary), lower courts refer to it and comply with its substance.[6]

The story is more complex for 'external' soft law. Hungary follows a dualistic system requiring the transposition of 'external sources' before they become part of Hungarian law (with the exception of *ius cogens*).[7] This dualist mindset significantly impacts legal practice because norms not transposed into Hungarian law are rarely considered by national courts and authorities. Among other things, commentators trace this judicial approach back to text-positivism,[8] according to which referring to external sources of jurisprudence is uncustomary.[9] Text-positivism is a characteristic of socialist legal practice, where legal interpretation was to be merely declaratory, reflecting the exact will of the legislator, but it also reflects strong State-centredness: 'sovereignty was perceived as international independence which also applied against international human rights treaties' and international sources in general.[10] In addition, judges in the socialist legal order felt it was safe for them to stick to the letter of the national positive law enacted by the single-party legislature.[11]

[4] Supreme Court Kfv.IV.37.138/2010/4. E Csatlós (n 113), 480.

[5] eg Decision No Kf.VI.38.198/2018/6 of the Curia; Decision No 19.Gf.40.284/2019/9 of the Metropolitan Regional Court.

[6] Decision Nos 10.Gf.40.601/2019/16, 19.Gf.40.236/2019/19 and Gf.III.30.025/2020/5 of the Metropolitan Regional Court; Gf.III.30.025/2020/5.

[7] *cf* art Q, para 3 of the Fundamental Law; T Molnár, 'A nemzetközi jog és a magyar jog viszonya', ijoten.hu/szocikk/a-nemzetkozi-jog-es-a-magyar-jog-viszonya (Online Legal Encyclopaedia).

[8] *cf* A Jakab, 'A közigazgatási jog tudománya és oktatása Magyarországon' in A Jakab and A Menyhárd (eds), *A jog tudománya* (Budapest, Hvg Orac, 2015) 193 ff.

[9] T Bán, '(Fórum) Strasbourg és a magyar joggyakorlat' (2005) 1 *Fundamentum* 47, 47.

[10] A Jakab and J Fröhlich, 'The Constitutional Court of Hungary' in A Jakab, A Dyevre and G Itzcovich (eds), *Comparative Constitutional Reasoning* (Cambridge, Cambridge University Press, 2017) 395, 397.

[11] As Csaba Varga observed, Central and Eastern European legal practice were pervaded by 'legal positivism, a mainstream organising idea that once transfigured from continental pre-WWII textual or rule-positivism into so-called Socialist normativism in the entire region. It is a syndrome called "textocentrism" that originates from it. This resulted in "perverted forms of mechanical

A survey of domestic court judgments conducted by Csatlós arrives at the conclusion that courts only 'exceptionally refer to a non-binding decision of an international organization in their reasoning'.[12] Where they do, Hungarian courts usually refer to a relevant decision of the Constitutional Court citing international soft law. Moreover, there seems to be a persistent conviction amongst judges of ordinary courts that they are only bound by 'national law',[13] which has not entirely subsided. Meanwhile, some good practices are emerging at the level of higher courts: judges of the Curia (ie, the Hungarian Supreme Court)[14] reported that in the event of legal gaps or problems of interpretation, they will consciously search for documents, legal practices or model laws for guidance.[15] In fact, EU law may require the application of international soft norms. An example would be the EU insolvency regulation,[16] which refers to international soft law, helping national judges to expand the scope of the applicable measures in the case before them. Owing to the position of Curia judgments in the legal order, lower court judges will pick up references in areas covered by Curia decisions, with the result that in certain narrow areas of the law, references to international non-binding sources may gradually become routine.

While in general, one may conclude that references in Hungarian court judgments to what were once considered 'external sources' are increasing,[17] the same cannot be said of EU soft norms. One reason for this seems to be the low awareness of EU soft law owing to the non-systematic implementation of non-binding EU measures in Hungary.[18]

jurisprudence: applying law according to its letter"'; see C Varga, 'Inertia or Pattern Following? Phase Lag of and Defiance by the Judiciary: A Central and Eastern European Overview' (international conference on Europeanization and Judicial Culture in Contemporary Democracies, Lucian Blaga University Faculty of Law, Sibiu, 10–12 October 2013) 11–12. See also A Sajó, 'New Legalism in East Central Europe: Law as an Instrument of Social Transformation' (1990) 17 *Journal of Law and Society* 331 ff.

[12] E Csatlós, 'A Kúria (Legfelsőbb Bíróság) gyakorlata és a nemzetközi jog' in L Blutman, E Csatlós and I Schiffner (eds), *A nemzetközi jog hatása a magyar joggyakorlatra* (Budapest, HVG Orac, 2014) 480.

[13] M Weller, '(Fórum) Strasbourg és a magyar joggyakorlat' (2005) 1 *Fundamentum* 59, 59.

[14] *Kúria* is the highest court in the judicial system with the task to ensure the uniformity of the application of law by lower courts and to make uniformity decisions which shall be binding on them.

[15] An example mentioned was the IBA Guidelines on Conflicts of Interest in International Arbitration 2014 in the ambit of arbitration rules.

[16] See Regulation (EU) 2015/848 of the European Parliament and of the Council of 20 May 2015 on insolvency proceedings [2015] OJ L141/19, preamble recital (48). Such best practices include the European Communication and Cooperation Guidelines for Cross-border Insolvency Developed under the aegis of the Academic Wing of INSOL Europe ('CoCo principles') and the EU Cross-Border Insolvency Court-to-Court Cooperation Principles ('EU JudgeCo Principles').

[17] On the reception of 'Strasbourg case law' in Hungary, see PL Láncos, 'The Innocuous Impact of Pan-European General Principles of Good Administration on Hungarian Law and Legal Practice' in U Stelkens (ed), *Pan-European General Principles of Good Administration* (Oxford, Oxford University Press, forthcoming).

[18] The symptomatic non-consideration of soft law norms in Hungary stands in stark contrast to the fact that one of the very first scholars to identify and describe international soft law was the Hungarian László Buza, who termed them 'program-like norms', which are legal commitments without giving rise to enforceable rights. See L Búza, *A törvényesség és az igazságosság elve a nemzetközi jogban* (Acta Universitatis Szegediensis, Acta Juridica et Politica, Tomus III Fasc 1 Szeged, 1957) 19.

B. The (Non-systematic) Implementation of EU Soft Law in Hungary

To map the practice of implementing EU norms in Hungary, I interviewed two officials of the Legal Harmonization Department and the EU Legal Compliance Department of the Hungarian Ministry of Justice, the latter being responsible for coordinating the national implementation of EU law.[19] I compared the data obtained with the statutory rules on harmonisation and the information available in the so-called Harmonization Database.

In Hungary, the responsibility for coordinating the national implementation of EU law lies with the Ministry of Justice. The central piece of legislation guiding implementation is the Harmonization Decree setting out the procedure to be followed and the tasks of the different government bodies.[20] While the Decree does not differentiate between hard and soft EU measures, the system described in the Decree is not necessarily followed when implementing EU soft law. According to the system of the Decree, the Legal Harmonization Department of the Ministry of Justice monitors EU legislation to identify possible legislative tasks of implementation. Apart from directives and other binding norms requiring implementation, it is up to the Department's staff to decide whether or not they consider a particular soft norm to give rise to 'legislative tasks'. This means that it is up to the Department whether or not to specifically call the ministries' attention to soft norms. The Legal Harmonization Department transfers the norm to the competent ministry, and the latter may put forward a harmonisation proposal,[21] which is entered into the so-called Harmonization Database,[22] where implementing norms can be tracked. Departing from the system foreseen under the Decree, ministries monitoring EU legislation may also come to the conclusion that they wish to initiate implementing legislation concerning an EU soft norm. In this case, they either submit a harmonisation proposal to the legislator or they simply implement the norm without arranging for it to be entered into the Harmonization Database. Finally, where corresponding Hungarian legislation already exists and no implementation is necessary, a reference to the

[19] The interviews were conducted on 9 March 2018 and 8 October 2018.

[20] Government Decree No 302/2010 (XII 23) on the fulfilment of legislative preparatory tasks necessary for compliance with European Union law (Harmonization Decree).

[21] Article 3, para 1 of Government Decree No 302/2010 (XII 23).

[22] *Jogharmonizációs Adatbázis*, jogharmonizacio.im.gov.hu. The Hungarian Ministry of Justice operates a database offering insight into the progress made in implementing EU legislation since November 2005. The operation of the Harmonization Database is now governed by the Harmonization Decree. Article 7 provides that the Minister of Justice is to record and publish in the database tasks pertaining to implementation as well as data relating to draft legislation and final acts. In the open-access version of the database, search queries may be made, with results including the full data of the EU act referred to and the status of the related national implementing tasks. In essence, the Harmonization Database is not a notification tool, but rather a national instrument facilitating the coordination of harmonisation tasks as well as ensuring the (restricted) transparency of the national legal system. See PL Láncos, 'The Phenomenon of "Directive-Like Recommendations" and Their Implementation: Lessons from Hungarian Legislative Practice' in P Popelier et al (eds), *Lawmaking in Multi-level Settings* (Baden-Baden, Nomos, 2019).

EU norm must always be entered into the Harmonization Database. Hence, there is no single solution for managing the implementation of EU soft norms in Hungary.[23]

The harmonisation clause is an important indicator of the EU origins of a norm and a tool for guaranteeing transparency within the national legal order. The Decree on the drafting of legal acts[24] foresees a range of exceptional cases where the implementing measure does not have to carry a harmonisation clause, such as implementation by means of a fundamental principle laid down in a comprehensive legal code or where the legislative duty emanates from a decision of the Court of Justice of the European Union (CJEU). While this means that national measures implementing soft law are not exempted from including the harmonisation clause, in practice, the majority of soft law implementation occurs without indication to its EU origins. This is a departure from the system laid down by the Decree on the drafting of laws,[25] making it difficult to identify EU origins of national implementing measures, thereby reducing transparency for those applying the law.[26]

In sum, apart from regulations, EU law is rarely considered by Hungarian courts and authorities if it is not transposed into national law. However, while EU directives are routinely transposed, the transposition of norms other than directives (ie, soft law) follows no apparent pattern. If soft law is transposed, the national implementing provisions often lack the so-called harmonisation clause that would indicate the EU norm behind the national implementing provision. This is problematic, since even where the courts and authorities are in fact applying norms of EU origin, they rarely recognise this, thereby missing the chance of consulting and referring to the original norm as well.

Owing to the uncertainties surrounding EU soft law implementation, an awareness of EU soft norms, even when they have been implemented, is low. This may be one of the reasons why the courts and authorities have the impression that they are simply applying domestic law and, due to the lack of a harmonisation clause, fail to recognise, consult and refer to the EU soft law measure.

III. ORGANISATION OF THE RESEARCH AND GENERAL FINDINGS

In what follows, I will first present some general results regarding the application and perception of EU soft law by judges and public officials, without refining these results for the specific policy fields of competition law and environmental

[23] The only authority from among the authorities active in State aid, competition law and environmental law that feature applicable EU soft norms on their website is the Office for Controlling State Aid (an area I am not analysing here).

[24] Article 90 of Decree No 61/2009 (XII 14) on the drafting of legal acts.

[25] Articles 88–90 of Decree No 61/2009 (XII 14).

[26] See also O Ştefan, ch 19 in this volume.

law. I will discuss these policy fields in section IV. As a whole, the data seems to confirm the hypothesis that the perception of EU soft law as an 'external' source and the low awareness of these norms contribute to the non-application of EU soft law in Hungary.

The mixed research methodology relied on a survey and interviews to gather empirical data, as well as database research to collect data on the application of EU soft law by the courts and authorities. For the purposes of the survey, I translated the SoLaR questionnaire into Hungarian and sent it to the Office for the National Judiciary. I also sent out the same SoLaR questionnaire to individuals working at different levels of the Hungarian judiciary to whom I had access. In light of the fact that my focus was on the application of EU soft law in competition matters and environmental protection, I also sent out the SoLaR questionnaire to the Hungarian Competition Authority and the 'Green Ombudsman', as well as individuals in the Hungarian ministries working in the field of environmental law. In total, out of 40 questionnaires I sent out, I received 18 filled-in questionnaires: three questionnaires having been sent back by the National Office for the Judiciary, one by the Hungarian Competition Authority, three by the 'Green Ombudsman', one by a ministerial official, and the rest by judges and Constitutional Court *référendaires*. Finally, I conducted interviews with the Hungarian Competition Authority and the 'Green Ombudsman'.

The ongoing centralisation and fragmentation processes in the Hungarian judicial system and the administrative organisation complicated the empirical research. For example, I was compelled to turn to the National Office for the Judiciary[27] with my questionnaire instead of contacting the individual courts themselves. While this mainstreaming of requests and dataflow may be beneficial in reducing the workload of those trying to receive empirical data from the courts, I only received three filled-in questionnaires from the National Office for the Judiciary. To resolve this problem, I contacted individuals through my personal contacts on different levels of the judiciary. These included judges and their *référendaires* from the Constitutional Court, the Curia and regional as well as district courts. A similar problem arose with the Departments for Environmental Protection and Nature Preservation located at the different regional Government Offices. These departments are responsible for environmental administration at the regional level. In contrast with the centralisation of the Hungarian court system, these authorities experienced incremental fragmentation.[28] None of these Departments answered my inquiries or returned filled-in questionnaires.

[27] The National Office for the Judiciary is responsible for the administration of the Hungarian courts. It can issue recommendations, decisions and codes governing the judiciary.

[28] The reluctance of subjects to fill in the questionnaire claiming that they were never faced with the task of applying soft law was also an issue. To obtain empirical evidence that gave a realistic picture of EU soft law application in Hungary, I had to convince them that no experience with soft law application was relevant data for my research.

A. Empirical Evidence from the Survey

Based on a total of 18 responses received, the general finding is that, with the exception of the field of competition law, Hungarian judges and public officials rarely, if ever, deal with soft law instruments. In particular, respondents working in the field of constitutional law, civil law and criminal law reported a lack of contact with EU soft norms. Judges pointed out that due to their excessive workload, they do not have the time to research EU soft norms that might possibly be relevant to their cases. If EU soft law is used at all, it is invoked by parties and considered an interpretative aid to facilitate the application of hard law. While accepting that soft law may be the appropriate device to fill in legal gaps and clarify problems of interpretation, soft law will generally only be applied to reinforce an argument. If the judge does not agree with the thrust of the soft norm, he or she will not refer to it or will underline the measure's non-binding nature. The respondents agreed that, save for competition cases, there is absolutely no culture of EU soft law application in domestic courts or public authorities.

Finally, the perception of soft law with all its possible advantages and disadvantages varied widely from one respondent to the other, with opinions ranging from a total rejection of soft law as non-legitimate to calls for more an extensive consideration and application of these norms.

Figure 10.1 Pie chart depicting the proportion of motivating factors reported for the usage of soft law by Hungarian courts and public authorities

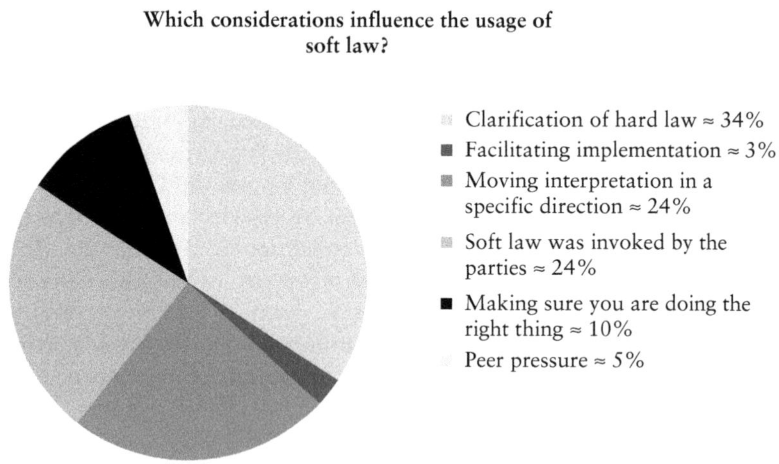

B. Evidence from Electronic Databases

To glean data on the application of EU soft law by national courts and public authorities, I relied on various publicly available electronic databases. As a preliminary remark, it is worth noting that the gathering of data was not without its difficulties. As far as searches in databases are concerned, the lack of open access databases in the case of administrative authorities, the non-systematic referencing used by courts and the Competition Authority, and the poor search functions made data collection tedious or simply impractical.

In Hungary, judicial practice may be traced with the help of the electronic database called the Compendium of Court Decisions, which is operated by the National Office for the Judiciary.[29] To measure the number of references to EU soft law in general, and EU competition and environmental soft law in particular, I conducted a keyword search in the Compendium focusing on the list of specific SoLaR instruments in the field of competition law and environmental law. With certain exceptions, the Compendium includes anonymised judgments, decisions and opinions of the Hungarian courts, including the Curia, since 1 July 2007. With the database now spanning a decade's worth of judgments, changes in the judicial frequency of referencing EU soft law may also be traced.

The Compendium does not allow for refined searches of multiple keywords. The fact that there are no standard rules for citing EU law in Hungarian court judgments and orders further complicates the use of keyword search. In order to overcome difficulties, I devised different strategies. I first carried out specific searches for the title of the soft law act included in the SoLaR list for environmental law and competition law. These searches yielded no results because Hungarian court decisions rarely give a full citation of the EU act they refer to. I then conducted another search combining document numbers and more general terms such as 'Commission communication'. These searches returned a total of 13 hits, including all kinds of EU soft law measures, not only SoLaR soft law. The results from the Compendium included 11 references to competition cases and two decisions citing environmental soft law. These judgments either made an incomplete reference to the soft law measure concerned or completely lacked the title and document number. In the latter cases, I had to infer the specific soft law measure by considering the context and substance of the judgment.

In order to triangulate the findings, I also conducted a keyword search in another database, operated by the Hungarian Competition Authority. This database[30] only comprises court decisions rendered in competition law matters between 1994 and 2017. Based on the hits generated through this database, the Curia and the Budapest Court of Appeal referred 13 times to various EU guidelines and communications in the context of competition law. As the search in the Compendium returned only 11 hits in the competition law, the database search in the Compendium missed at least two court decisions referring to soft law.

The keyword searches confirm that the Hungarian courts only sporadically refer to EU soft law measures. The fact that a decade's worth of judgments yielded a rough average of only one reference to EU soft law per year means that

[29] *Bírósági Határozatok Gyűjteménye*, birosag.hu/birosagi-hatarozatok-gyujtemenye.
[30] https://www.gvh.hu/dontesek/birosagi_dontesek.

even though there is a possibility that due to the non-systematic referencing of such measures in court judgments, some references may have been missed, there is no tradition of referring to EU soft law by the Hungarian courts.

Looking more closely at the judgments, the courts refer to EU soft law for various reasons. The grounds for citing EU soft law range from references made by parties, but left unconsidered by the court,[31] through bolstering the court's findings with further arguments,[32] using them as interpretative aids,[33] to applying them directly to the case.[34] In the rare cases where courts refer to these sources to bolster findings, aid interpretation or solve the case, the non-binding nature of these norms is not emphasised.

Figure 10.2 Pie chart depicting the purpose of referencing soft law in Hungarian courts

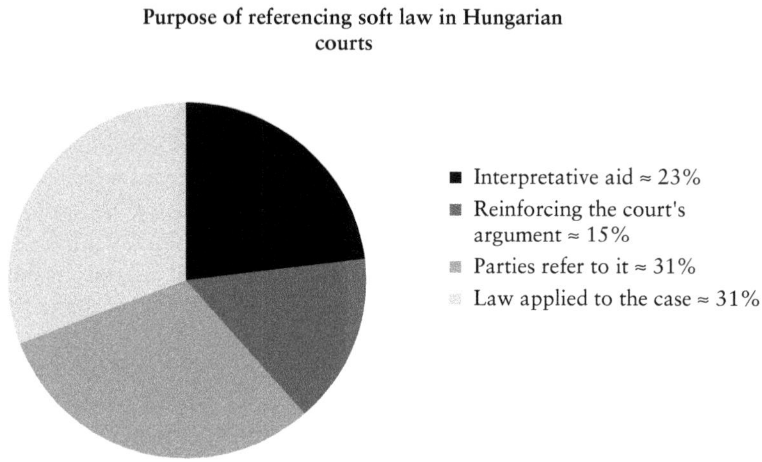

IV. SECTORAL ANALYSIS OF SOFT LAW APPLICATION IN HUNGARY

In what follows, I focus my analysis on the application of EU soft law measures in the field of competition law and environmental law by the courts and authorities in Hungary. These two policy fields perfectly illustrate the contradictoriness

[31] eg, Judgment of the Budapest Municipal Court, Judgment No 15.G.40.806/2010/24, citing European Commission, 'Guidelines on Vertical Restraints' [2010] OJ C130/01.

[32] eg, Judgment of the Debrecen Court of Appeal, Judgment No Gf.II.30.106/2015/7, citing European Commission, 'Communication from the Commission to the European Parliament, the Council and the European Economic and Social Committee on the on the European Union Strategy for the Protection and Welfare of Animals 2012–2015' COM (2012) 6.

[33] eg, Judgment of the Tatabánya Regional Court, Judgment No 9.G.40.083/2011/20, citing European Commission, 'Communication from the Commission – Notice – Guidelines on the Application of Article 81(3) of the Treaty' [2004] OJ C101/08.

[34] eg, Judgment of the Budapest Capital Regional Court, Judgment No 23. G. 41.739/2013/125, citing European Commission, 'Communication from the Commission – Community guidelines on State aid for rescuing and restructuring firms in difficulty' [2004] OJ C244/02.

of soft law application in Hungary: while the field of competition law enforcement may be considered a relative success story of EU soft law application, the area of environmental protection shows a more diverse picture.

Besides the searches conducted in the judicial Compendium, I collected data on the application of EU soft law in the decisions of Hungarian public authorities with a special focus on competition law enforcement and environmental protection. Using the SoLaR template, I also surveyed the stance of public officials in the fields of competition law enforcement and environmental protection towards soft law (supplemented with an in-person interview with two members of the Competition Authority). The survey and the interviewers help in understanding the historical accounts regarding the development and transformation of the organisational background of, and the institutional approach to, these policy areas.

A. The Application of EU Soft Law in the Area of Competition Law: A Relative Success Story

i. Historical and Organisational Aspects

Competition policy, law and enforcement is highly integrated throughout the Member States, including Hungary, owing to the system of competition law enforcement introduced by Regulation 1/2003.[35] This system relies on national competition authorities to proceed in both national and EU-level cases of competition law infringements, compelling Member State authorities to apply EU soft norms adopted by the Commission to facilitate competition law enforcement.

Due to their double-hatted nature and in a bid to increase predictability for undertakings, national competition authorities apply EU soft law not only in EU-level cases, but also in domestic cases. Thus, while EU competition law still leaves some leeway for Member States to pursue their own policy – for example, in leniency and until recently, in fining – the Hungarian Competition Authority chose to harmonise its rules with the soft law of the EU.[36] In fact, in the case of fining rules,[37] the Hungarian Competition Authority chose the path of so-called spontaneous approximation, converging its rules[38] to an EU soft norm

[35] Council Regulation (EC) No 1/2003 of 16 December 2002 on the implementation of the rules on competition laid down in Articles 81 and 82 of the Treaty [2003] OJ L1/1.

[36] On Member States' voluntary convergence in the field of competition enforcement, see 'Commission staff working paper accompanying the Communication from the Commission to the European Parliament and Council – Report on the Functioning of Regulation 1/2003 {COM(2009)206 final}, 61–62.

[37] See in detail PL Láncos, 'The Power of Soft Law: Spontaneous Approximation of Fining Policies for Anti-competitive Conduct' (2019) 40 *European Competition Law Review* 541.

[38] Communication No 11/2017 of the President of the Competition Authority and the Chair of the Competition Council of the Hungarian Competition Authority on the setting of the amount of fines in case of anti-competitive agreements and concerted practices, the abuse of dominant position and the abuse of significant market power.

that was not designed to induce voluntary harmonisation, but was of a merely informative nature.[39]

The openness of Hungarian competition policy towards European competition law dates back to the transition of the country to democracy[40] and its association agreement with the European Communities concluded in the early 1990s.[41] In fact, Act No LVII of 1996 on the prohibition of unfair and restrictive market practices (Tpvt), the law governing competition rules and enforcement in force today, reproduced in essence the substantive rules of EU competition law. This sameness of Hungarian and EU competition rules has consequences for the interpretation and application of the Tpvt. As the CJEU observed in the *Allianz* case, 'the Tpvt must in fact be interpreted in the same way as the equivalent concepts in Article 101(1) TFEU and that it is bound in that regard by the interpretation of those concepts provided by the Court'.[42]

ii. The Hungarian Competition Authority's Approach

Describing the institutional approach of Hungarian competition policy, Tihamér Tóth noted that '[the] sovereign approach emphasizing the distinctness of competition policy and enforcement in Hungary has never materialized'.[43] Instead, the Hungarian Competition Authority 'has always been open to following EU case law and the practice of the EU Commission. Even when it had no legal obligation to do so, it often relied upon the relevant judgments of the EU courts and the relevant guidelines of the Commission'.[44] Apart from the apparent reflex to follow EU competition law, reasons for spontaneous harmonisation included regulatory economy: as András Tóth, Vice-President of the Hungarian Competition Authority, observed, it is important to look for workable solutions to avoid unnecessary duplication of regulatory efforts. Since the Commission guidelines on fines or the communication on mergers were tried-and-tested

[39] Guidelines on the method of setting fines imposed pursuant to Article 23(2)(a) of Regulation No 1/2003 [2006] OJ C210/2. Guidelines are informal soft law measures, ie, non-binding acts of the Commission not mentioned in art 288 TFEU enumerating secondary sources of EU law. The CJEU underlined that 'in the absence of binding regulation under European Union law on the subject, [it was up to the] Member States to establish and apply national rules' on issues governed by guidelines. Although guidelines merely bind the author, they are in fact important informative measures. Such is the case with the Commission's guideline on fines, which enables undertakings to estimate possible sanctions to be imposed on them for anti-competitive behaviour.

[40] Cited by T Tóth, 'The Reception and Application of EU Competition Rules in Hungary: An Organic Evolution', Pázmány Law Working Papers, 2013/17, 1.

[41] 'Europe Agreement establishing an association between the European Communities and their Member States, of the one part, and the Republic of Hungary, of the other part' [1993] OJ L347/1.

[42] Case C-32/11 *Allianz Hungaria Biztosító Zrt. and Others v Gazdasági Versenyhivatal* [2013] EU:C:2013:160, paras 21–22.

[43] Tóth (n 40) 1.

[44] ibid 4.

measures, there was no need to come up with a very different national solution for these in domestic cases.[45]

This approach to EU competition law and EU soft law in general was confirmed by the Competition Authority. In its response to the SoLaR questionnaire, the Authority noted that in the event of 'the textual sameness and the identical interpretation of the concepts',[46] it also follows and refers to EU law, including EU soft law norms, for the enforcement of competition law in domestic cases.[47] The interview conducted with Competition Authority staff further substantiated that the use of EU competition soft law was routine practice at the Authority, resulting in an awareness of and openness towards EU soft law unprecedented in courts and other authorities in Hungary. Competition Authority officials stated in the interview that in the majority of cases, they apply EU soft law to interpret hard rules of competition law or to give additional weight to an argument. As such, these norms help increase the transparency of rights and obligations of undertakings, and enhance the predictability of legal consequences in cases of infringement. The Competition Authority's staff also underlined the important role played by EU competition soft law in ensuring the uniformity of competition law application, including the effective enforcement of EU law. Finally, the Competition Authority's staff reported that they perceived EU soft law as a means for avoiding overregulation and to ensure *effet utile*, yet they acknowledged that the lack of legitimacy behind soft sources and the apparent flexibility they ensure may lead to diverging interpretations causing uncertainty.[48]

iii. Court Practice

Based on the search for EU soft law in general in the Compendium of Court Decisions and the results of the survey, on the whole, Hungarian courts rarely refer to such norms. By contrast, in the narrower field of competition law, and as a consequence of the consistent application of soft norms by the Competition Authority,[49] undertakings are well aware of these norms, making frequent

[45] Communication No 11/2017 follows the Commission's guidelines on fines, while Communication No 6/2017 of the President of the Competition Authority and the Chair of the Competition Council of the Hungarian Competition Authority discusses, among other things, the application of Commission Consolidated Jurisdictional Notice under Council Regulation (EC) No 139/2004 on the control of concentrations between undertakings in domestic merger cases. 'Even in areas where there was no formal law harmonization obligation, the Hungarian legislator, relying on the proposals elaborated by the GVH, imported certain procedural instruments which worked well on the European level. T Tóth, 'The reception and application of EU competition rules in Hungary: an organic evolution'; Pázmány Law Working Papers 2013/7, 4.

[46] Decision Vj/055/2013.

[47] On file with the author.

[48] Interview conducted with staff members of the Hungarian Competition Authority, 2 July 2019.

[49] The application of soft law by the Authority is also discernible from its database containing the Authority's decisions.

references to them in domestic court cases. Consequently, they will then appear in the decisions of the national courts. All of the 11 cases where a reference is made to soft law are competition law cases.[50]

This proliferation of the application of EU competition soft norms in domestic competition law cases prompted the Curia to make an effort to rein in what was considered a perfunctory referencing of soft measures of the EU, such as guidelines. The Curia declared that the 'judicial practice placing a Commission guideline that is not even a legal act of the Union, into the centre of the judgment's reasoning' is mistaken.[51] In a subsequent judgment, it clarified that the courts were compelled to carry out a full judicial review of decisions rendered by the Competition Authority and, in this respect, it does not suffice for the courts to refer to the leeway enjoyed by the Authority and restrict themselves to a formal review of legality.[52]

Based on the interview conducted with two members of the Authority in the field of Hungarian competition policy, law and enforcement, there is a willingness both to borrow EU soft law solutions for domestic implementation, but also to directly apply EU soft law in antitrust or merger decisions. This openness towards EU soft law seems to be the outcome of a number of contributing factors, such as the organisational background of EU competition enforcement resulting in double-hatted national competition authorities, the strive for regulatory economy and transparency as well as the undertakings' awareness and references to EU soft law in their respective cases. The function of EU competition soft law as an interpretative aid is perceived to enhance transparency and predictability and, as such, legal certainty in competition cases.

B. Application of EU Soft Law in the Ambit of Environmental Law: A Mixed Picture

i. Organisational and Historical Aspects

While the Hungarian judicial system is experiencing strong centralisation, the institutional system of environmental protection seems to be suffering centrifugal tendencies with an ongoing fragmentation of institutions and responsibilities. To elucidate the organisational backdrop of environmental protection in Hungary, I will first briefly summarise the progressive institutional decline that

[50] Competition law-related hits in the Compendium: judgments of the Budapest Municipal Court: 7.K.31.116/2007/44, 15.G.40.806/2010/24, 19.K.33/718/2009/42; judgment of the Budapest-Capital Administrative and Labour Court: 5.K.33.512/2014/53; judgments of the Kúria: Kfv.III.37.441/2016/7, Kfv.II.37/110/2017/13, Kfv.VI.38.108/2016/26; judgment of the Budapest Court of Appeal: 2-Lf-27-042/2011/5; judgments of the Budapest-Capital Regional Court: 3.G.40.722/2014/946, 23.G.41.739/2013/125; and judgment of the Tatabánya Regional Court: 9.G.40.083/2011/20.

[51] Kfv.III.37.441.2016/7, para 31.

[52] Kfv.11.37.110/2017/13, para 29.

is currently taking place and will then turn to the practice of the courts and the 'Green Ombudsman' in invoking EU environmental soft law.

The past decade of environmental protection in Hungary has been characterised by a gradual dismantling of the institutional system, which seems to have left its mark on both the awareness and the use of European environmental law sources in Hungary. In 2010, the Ministry for Environmental Protection was abolished and its responsibilities were distributed between other ministries. The re-election of the government in 2014 did not bring about the establishment of a Ministry for Environmental Protection. Instead, the different branches of environmental policy were further dispersed between the different ministries representing conflicting or very different policy issues: water policy was integrated into the Ministry of Internal Affairs, the environmental and nature conservation authorities were put under the supervision of the Ministry for Administration, waste management was allocated to the Ministry for National Development, while the Ministry for Rural Development became responsible for the management of national parks. The year 2018 saw layoffs in the different departments of the Ministry for Agriculture responsible for environmental protection of between 40 and 47.5 per cent, jeopardising the fulfilment of environmental obligations under national and EU law.[53] Hopes for an independent and single governmental representation of environmental affairs also subsided, with Hungary becoming the only EU Member State without a ministry dedicated to the protection of the environment. At a lower level, departments for environmental protection and nature preservation are assigned to the regional government offices, which are responsible for environmental administration at the regional level.

In contrast with the Hungarian court system, the environmental authorities did not experience centralisation, but rather gradual fragmentation. While I sent the questionnaire to these departments, I received no answer, save for one department, which indicated that it is awaiting permission to answer the questions. To gain insight into the practice of public authorities active in the field of environmental law, I relied on my personal contacts at different public authorities involved in managing different aspects of the broad topic of environmental protection.

ii. Assessment of the Ombudsman's Practice and Relevant Court Judgments

The Office of the Commissioner for Fundamental Rights was established in 1993 as a body responsible to the Hungarian Parliament, with the task of protecting citizens against maladministration and promoting fundamental rights protection. Besides the Commissioner for Fundamental Rights, special

[53] greenfo.hu/hir/akik-maradtak-szivnak-a-kornyezetvedelmi-apparatust-megsemmisitettek.

ombudspersons, such as the 'Green Ombudsman', were appointed.[54] The Green Ombudsman, as the institution is referred to in general parlance, investigates issues related to the right to a healthy environment, the right to the preservation of physical and mental health, and the protection of natural values.[55] One of the most important powers of the Green Ombudsman is the power to initiate the constitutional review procedure of the Constitutional Court in relation to legislation that is potentially harmful to the environment.[56]

Based on the interviews conducted with three members of the Office of the Green Ombudsman,[57] the environmental soft law of the EU is considered highly important in their work, in particular for its role in clarifying hard law rules, but also as an inspiration for national environmental protection legislation. As far as the most relevant soft environmental measures of the EU are concerned, the staff of the Green Ombudsman were unanimous in saying that EU documents relating to the Environmental Liability Directive were particularly relevant in designing proposals for improving national legislation. Other instruments cited include the 7th Environment Action Programme[58] and the Council's conclusions on the implementation of the UN's Agenda for Sustainable Development.[59] The interviews highlighted the advantage of soft law in accommodating existing diversity within the Member States, while offering them ambitious commitments to voluntarily undertake.

As far as judicial references to environmental soft law of the EU are concerned, as noted above, the search in the Compendium of Court Decisions yielded only two hits, neither of which referenced the measures enumerated in the SoLaR list.

[54] The General Ombudsman worked alongside the Ombudsman Responsible for National and Ethnic Minorities and the Data Protection Ombudsman before the position of the Ombudsman for the Protection of Future Generations was established in 2007. See in detail L Csink, 'Az Ombudsman' in A Jakab and G Gajduschek (eds), *A magyar jogrendszer állapota* (Budapest, MTA TK JTI, 2016) 600 ff.

[55] According to art P) of the Hungarian Fundamental Law (Constitution): 'Natural resources, in particular arable land, forests and the reserves of water, biodiversity, in particular native plant and animal species, as well as cultural assets shall form the common heritage of the nation; it shall be the obligation of the State and everyone to protect and maintain them, and to preserve them for future generations.' Article XX, para (1) of the Fundamental Law stipulates: 'Everyone shall have the right to physical and mental health.' Finally, art XXI, para (1) guarantees that: 'Hungary shall recognise and give effect to the right of everyone to a healthy environment.'

[56] Such initiatives include the initiative for the constitutional review of the Joint Decree No 27/2008 (XII 3) of the Ministry for Environmental Protection and Rural Development and the Ministry of Health on setting the thresholds for environmental noise and vibration pollution (Case No II/00902/2012); the constitutional review of Governmental Decree No 358/2008. (XII 31) on licensing activities for businesses (Case No II/00782/2012) and the initiative for the constitutional review of Act No XXXVII of 2009 on forests, the protection of forests and forest management (II/00201/2019).

[57] 11 June 2019, 20 July 2019 and 3 August 2019.

[58] Decision No 1386/2013/EU of the European Parliament and of the Council of 20 November 2013 on a General Union Environment Action Programme to 2020 'Living well, within the limits of our planet' [2013] OJ L354/171.

[59] Council of the European Union, 'Towards an ever more sustainable Union by 2030. Council Conclusions' (9 April 2019) 8286/19.

Instead, the Pest County Court referred to the Commission's Communication on waste and by-products,[60] using the communication as an interpretative aid, while the Debrecen Court of Appeal referred to the Commission's Communication on animal welfare[61] to bolster its own argumentation for an interpretation of the national law.

The application and consideration of EU soft norms in the sphere of environmental protection is markedly different from what we have seen in the ambit of competition enforcement. While I received no input from the regional departments responsible for environmental administration, and no access to such administrative decisions was available, there is no evidence that EU environmental soft law is taken into account by authorities, and even the courts only exceptionally refer to such norms. The reason for the lack of references to EU environmental soft law could be, as mentioned earlier, the pervasive conviction that courts are only bound by domestic law. The excessive caseload and the strong language barrier most probably exacerbate the disregard for EU soft law. Meanwhile, when it comes to the office of the Green Ombudsman, the relevant EU soft law is considered thoroughly and is often proposed as a model to be followed by the legislator.

V. CONCLUSION

Based on the findings gleaned from a general assessment of soft law application by the Hungarian courts and authorities, and a more specific analysis of the areas of competition law enforcement and environmental protection, the relevance of EU soft law in the Hungarian legal order is negligible. Save for the isolated field of competition law enforcement and the Office of the Green Ombudsman, there is no culture of, or incentives for, soft law application. This is confirmed by both the results of searches conducted in the Compendium of Court Decisions and the survey responses by judges and public officials.

The majority of respondents considered soft law to be an important source for interpreting hard law rules and reinforcing arguments preferred by the court or the authority. Nevertheless, while only a few respondents emphasised the disadvantages of EU soft law, citing its lack of legitimacy and its possible contribution to uncertainty, most judges and officials do not apply EU soft law routinely in the cases before them. In fact, they are rarely if ever faced with such norms and will generally only engage with soft EU law in cases where it

[60] European Commission, 'Communication from the Commission to the Council and the European Parliament on the Interpretative Communication on waste and by-products' COM (2007) 59; Judgment of the Pest County Court, 2.K.26.424/2009/20.

[61] European Commission, 'Communication from the Commission to the European Parliament, the Council and the European Economic and Social Committee on the European Union Strategy for the Protection and Welfare of Animals 2012–2015' COM (2012) 6; Judgment of the Debrecen Court of Appeal, Gf.II.30.106/2015/7.

has been referred to by the parties to the (competition law) case.[62] Besides the excessive caseload of courts or the workload of public officials, this is due to the low awareness of EU soft law and its implementation in national law. Owing to the State-centred disregard for 'external sources', judges and public officials will only refer to measures that had been brought into focus by higher courts applying EU soft law to fill in legal gaps. Overall, the potential of EU soft law to contribute to the uniform application of law and to promote legal certainty through transparency and predictability appears to be restricted to competition law enforcement in Hungary.

[62] *cf* E Polgári, 'The European Convention on Human Rights and the Case law of the European Court of Human Rights in Hungarian Judicial Practice' (2008) 5 *Fundamentum* 74 and 78.

11

Judges, Public Authorities and EU Soft Law in Italy

How You Cannot Tell a Book by its Cover

JACOPO ALBERTI AND MARIOLINA ELIANTONIO*

I. INTRODUCTION

THIS CHAPTER FOCUSES on the use of EU soft law by national courts and public authorities in Italy. Our point of departure is that the Italian legal system rests on a traditional – pyramidal – understanding of the sources of law, where non-binding measures do not have a place. As a consequence, one might expect to find little evidence of the use of EU soft law in the administrative and judicial practice, and even less evidence of EU soft law producing legal effects. This chapter partially contradicts this view by showing that, at least in some policy fields, national administrations and courts make frequent use of EU soft law and endow it with binding effects.

By studying a selected sample of EU soft law measures and carrying out interviews as well as a case law analysis, this chapter demonstrates that Italian civil servants and judges use EU soft law regularly, at least in the fields of competition and State aid, financial regulation and environmental policy.

In particular, we have conducted 17 interviews with Italian judges, administrative officials and representatives of the private sector (so as to also include the perspective of addressees of the soft law instruments) acting across three of the four European Network of Soft Law Research (SoLaR) policy fields.[1]

* Even though this chapter is the result of common reflections by the authors, sections I and II can be attributed to M Eliantonio, and sections III, IV and V to J Alberti.

[1] These 17 interviews were completed in the period from November 2017 to October 2019 in the following way: three interviews in the context of environmental policy, five in relation to financial

We have furthermore examined case law from both first instance and appeal courts, namely tribunals, Courts of Appeal and the Court of Cassation with regard to civil litigation, and Regional Administrative Tribunals and the Council of State for administrative justice. When required, other courts' case law also has been analysed; in particular, the Constitutional Court's judgments in the competition policy field, as well and the decisions of the Arbitrator for Financial Litigation *(Arbitro per le controversie finanziarie*: a peculiar arbitrator with competences in the field of financial regulation in Italy) have been analysed. Drawing on these interviews as well as on case law research, we describe when and how Italian authorities and courts use EU non-binding norms and to what end.

This chapter proceeds as follows. Section II briefly describes the sources of law in the Italian legal system, focusing on the most common 'domestic' soft law measure, namely the *circolare*, and discusses the more recent developments in this field of soft law in Italy and the impact of these developments on the advancement of the debate on soft law in general. We will show that while there is a rich literature on domestic soft law, research on EU soft law has remained in the shadows in the Italian academic debate. In fact, EU soft law does not seem to have been conceived as a specific conceptual category in the Italian legal system and, crucially, no doctrinal links are generally made between the functionally similar domestic and EU soft law measures. Section II also discusses the various and very diverse transposition practices of EU soft law with respect to the measures selected for the SoLaR project.

Section III discusses the findings from the interviews and the case law research with respect to the use of EU soft law by national courts and civil servants in three of the four SoLaR focus areas, namely financial regulation, competition and State aid law, and environmental policy. Section IV then further analyses the data, focusing on how EU soft law is affecting the principle of transparency and democratic legitimacy. Even though EU soft law generally has a very good press at least in those policy fields where it is used the most (competition and financial regulation), some problematic issues still arise with regard to the general amount of both soft and hard rules (ie, overregulation) and the legitimacy of the procedures through which soft law is adopted, in particular because of the lack of transparency on how public consultation is conducted. By way of a conclusion, this chapter argues that the Italian approach to EU soft law seems to be rather pragmatic and 'utilitarian', in that soft law seems to be used somewhat 'at random', without a clear dogmatic or theoretical underpinning, and largely because of its perceived concrete benefits in solving cases and deciding on applications.

policy and nine in the context of competition and State aid. No interviews were carried out for the social policy field. Out of 17 respondents, eight were judges, seven worked in administration and two were employees (a top manager and a medium-level officer) of different private banks, who have been interviewed in the fields of competition and financial regulation. For the methodology, see M Hartlapp and E Korkea-aho, ch 4 in this volume.

II. THE STATUS AND EFFECTS OF DOMESTIC AND EUROPEAN SOFT LAW IN ITALY

A. Kelsen is Dead, Long Live Kelsen? Italian Soft Law in the Hierarchy of Sources

The Italian legal system is anchored in a Kelsenian positivistic understanding of the sources of law, which sees at the apex the Constitution and laws which either have constitutional relevance or contain amendments to the Constitution. Below the constitutional sources are laws adopted by the Parliament, laws adopted by the Regions within their constitutionally attributed competences, and other acts which, by virtue of the Constitution, have the same normative force as law, namely acts adopted by the government under conditions which are clearly regulated in the Constitution itself.[2] Under this group are the normative acts issued by competent administrative authorities, namely governmental regulations (by ministers or the government as a whole), and regulations issued by local authorities. At the bottom of the pyramid are unwritten sources of law, such as customary law.

From this picture, one might be tempted[3] to conclude that soft law does not exist in the Italian legal environment. However, this would be very far from the truth.

Since time immemorial, and with a tradition going back to Roman law[4] and the military context, the Italian legal system recognises formally non-binding norms and, in particular, the so-called *circolari*. These have traditionally been considered as purely internal measures, through which administrative authorities gave instructions to hierarchically subordinated authorities. Their use has only increased throughout the years, and the Italian doctrine has come to distinguish a number of types of circulars according to their – interpretational, decisional, explicative – content.[5] However, what has remained clear and has consistently been repeated in case law is that circulars do not constitute sources of law and ought only to be regarded internal measures through which

[2] There are the so-called law-decrees (*decreti legge*), which, pursuant to art 77 of the Constitution, can only be issued in cases of urgency and need to be converted into law by the Parliament within 60 days of their adoption, and the so-called legislative-decrees (*decreti legislativi*), which can only be issued upon delegation by the Parliament.

[3] It is worth noting that in 1961, Bobbio argued somehow prophetically and provocatively that the dichotomy between binding and non-binding rules would soon be treated as a novelty, despite its long-standing roots in the Italian legal tradition: see N Bobbio, 'Comandi e consigli' (1961) *Rivista trimestrale di diritto e procedura civile* 369 ff.

[4] T Gziaro, 'Dal soft law moderno al soft law antico' in A Somma (ed), *Soft law e hard law nelle società postmoderne* (Turin, Giappichelli, 2009) 83.

[5] See further MS Giannini, 'Circolare' in *Enciclopedia Giuridica*, vol VII (Milan, Giuffrè Editore, 1960); MP Chiti, 'Circolare – I) Circolare amministrativa' in *Enciclopedia Giuridica*, vol VI (Rome, Treccani, 1988).

public authorities organise their activities.[6] As a consequence, circulars do not possess any external relevance vis-a-vis individuals, and even lower authorities, according to the Italian Council of State, are not bound by circulars issued by higher authorities, since in the Italian legal system, the only parameter of legality for the administrative action is the law; hence, it is perfectly possible for a lower authority to refuse to apply a circular which it deems to be in violation of the law.[7] Furthermore, it has been considered that circulars do not have any self-binding effect for the issuing authority: an opposite conclusion would lead to the paradoxical conclusion that the administration is entrusted with normative powers that it does in fact not have.[8] Finally, it has been consistently held that circulars do not bind the judiciary, as the illegality of an administrative measure only arises in cases of the violation of national or EU sources of binding law.[9]

B. The 'Soft Law Turn' in the Italian Legal System and How it Did (Not) Affect EU Soft Law

While Italian soft law in the form of *circolari* has been an important part of the Italian administrative law, a new soft law phenomenon has emerged in the last few years, which has shaken the foundations of the Italian understanding of binding and non-binding norms. Specifically, in 2016, the so-called Public Procurement Code (*codice dei contratti pubblici*)[10] has conferred upon the National Anti-Corruption Authority (Autorità nazionale anticorruzione (ANAC)) the power to adopt so-called 'guidelines' (*linee guida*).[11] Those guidelines which do not have binding force[12] have been qualified by the Council of

[6] See, eg, Regional Administrative Court of Milan, 20 September 1996, no 1383; Regional Administrative Court of Basilicata – Potenza, 28 March 2000, no 197.

[7] Council of State, chamber IV, 27 November 2000, no 6299; Council of State, chamber IV, 29 January 1998, no 112.

[8] Consiglio di Stato, chamber VI, 13 September 2012, no 4859, citing Consiglio di Stato, chamber IV, 15 October 2010 no 7521: 'It is undisputed in the case law that the administrative circulars, as interpretative measures, are not binding for the subjects outside the administration, while for the authorities which are the addressees, they are binding only if they are lawful, so that they may be set aside if they are unlawful.'

[9] Regional Administrative Court of Lazio, 30 August 2012, no 7395, para 10.

[10] Enacted through the Legislative Decree 18 April 2016 no 50.

[11] According to art 213 of the Legislative Decree 18 April 2016 no 50, ANAC is tasked with the regulation, monitoring and control of public contracts, and may, for this purpose, adopt, amongst other things, guidelines and other instruments of 'flexible regulation'. See on this MP Chiti, 'Il nuovo codice dei contratti pubblici – Il sistema delle fonti nella nuova disciplina dei contratti pubblici' (2016) 4 *Giornale di diritto amministrativo* 436; M Delle Foglie, 'Verso un "nuovo" sistema delle fonti? Il caso delle linee guida ANAC in materia di contratti pubblici', 5 July 2017, https://www.giustamm.it/ga/id/2016/6/5253/d; G Morbidelli, 'Linee guida dell'Anac: comandi o consigli?' (2016) 3 *Diritto amministrativo* 273.

[12] It should be noted that ANAC can issue three types of 'guidelines': those that are later incorporated into Ministerial Decrees, those that remain guidelines but have been granted binding force and, finally, non-binding guidelines.

State as so-called 'general administrative acts' (*atti amministrativi generali*),[13] which, according to the Italian conceptualisation of this dogmatic category, imply that administrative authorities may decide not to apply them when adopting an individual administrative act. However, if they do so, they have to provide an adequate reason.[14] It is with the introduction of this new instrument that the Italian doctrine expressed an interest for the topic and terminology of 'soft law'.[15]

This recent development is significant both from the perspective of the legislator who used the – unusual for Italy– terminology of 'flexible regulation' and that of the Italian doctrine that had to engage with soft forms of regulation beyond the traditional circulars. However, it is too early to conclude that a true 'soft law turn' is taking place in Italy. It is even less straightforward to conclude that these new developments had any influence on raising the profile of EU soft law in Italy. Indeed, while there has been a rich and old doctrinal debate on Italian soft law,[16] the discussion of EU soft law has remained relatively limited.[17]

[13] MC Romano, 'Atti amministrativi generali' in S Cassese (ed), *Dizionario di diritto pubblico* (Milan, Giuffrè Editore, 2006) 491 ff.

[14] Consiglio di Stato opinion no 1767 of 2016; and repeated in opinion no 1257 of 29 May 2017.

[15] N Mari, 'Linee Guida ANAC: la soft law e la gerarchia delle fonti', 4 April 2017, www.italiappalti.it/leggiarticolo.php?id=3392; M Chiarelli 'La soft regulation e il caso delle nuove linee guida ANAC', 6 February 2009, www.federalismi.it/nv14/articolo-documento.cfm?Artid=38024; P Mantini, 'Autorità nazionale anticorruzione e soft law nel sistema delle fonti e dei contratti pubblici', 2017, www.giustamm.it/print/dottrina/5516.

[16] A Catelani, *Le circolari della pubblica amministrazione*, 2nd edn (Milan, Giuffrè Editore, 1984); A Amorth, *Efficacia esterna delle circolari amministrative* (Milan, Giuffrè Editore, 1941); R Lucifredi, *Osservazioni sull'efficacia delle circolari amministrative* (Naples, CEM, 1947); G Salemi, *Le circolari amministrative* (Palermo, A Reber, 1913); F Garri, 'Le circolari amministrative' (1972) *L' amministrazione italiana* 481; A Catelani, 'Aspetti e attualità delle circolari normative della pubblica amministrazione' (1993) *Rivista trimestrale di diritto pubblico* 999; F Saitta, 'Sulle circolari amministrative e sul loro trattamento processuale' (2012) XXI *Nuove autonomie* 487; Giannini (n 5); Chiti (n 5); more recently, see Somma (n 4).

[17] For the very few early examples, see M Antonioli, 'Le comunicazioni della Commissione fra diritto comunitario e diritto interno' (1995) *Rivista italiana di diritto pubblico comunitario* 41; A d'Atena, 'L'anomalo assetto delle fonti comunitarie' (2001) *Il Diritto dell'Unione Europea* 591. More recently, one can find more interest in the topic of EU soft law; see, eg, E Mostacci, *La soft law nel sistema delle fonti: uno studio comparato* (Padua, Cedam, 2008); A Poggi, 'Soft law nell'ordinamento comunitario' in Associazione italiana dei costituzionalisti, *L'integrazione dei sistemi costituzionali europeo e nazionali. Atti del XX Convegno Annuale dell'Aic, Catania, 14–15 Ottobre 2005* (Padua, Cedam, 2007) 372; G de Minico, 'La soft law: nostalgie e anticipazioni' in F Bassanini and G Tiberi (eds), *Le nuove istituzioni europee. Commento al Trattato di Lisbona* (Bologna, Il Mulino, 2008) 327; P Costanzo, 'Hard law e soft law: il senso di una distinzione' in P Costanzo, L Mezzetti and A Ruggeri (eds), *Lineamenti di diritto costituzionale dell'Unione europea* (Turin, Giappichelli, 2014) 261; B Pastore, 'Soft law, gradi di normatività, teoria delle fonti' (2003) 1 *Lavoro e diritto* 5; B Pastore, 'Il soft law nella teoria delle fonti' in Somma (n 4) 123; A Algostino, 'La soft law comunitaria e il diritto statale: conflitto fra ordinamenti o fine del conflitto democratico?', 29 January 2017, www.costituzionalismo.it/la-soft-law-comunitaria-e-il-diritto-statale-conflitto-fra-ordinamenti-o-fine-del-conflitto-democratico; G Fiengo, *Gli atti 'atipici' della Comunità europea* (Naples, Editoriale Scientifica, 2008); P de Luca, *Gli atti atipici nel diritto dell'Unione Europea* (Turin, Giappichelli, 2012); F Ferraro, 'Natura ed effetti degli atti atipici della Comunità europea' in G Guzzetta (ed), *Le forme dell'azione comunitaria nella prospettiva della Costituzione europea* (Padua, Cedam, 2005) 64; D Strazzari, 'Tra soft e hard law: prime riflessioni in favore della giustiziabilità degli atti emanati

Those who have – especially more recently – engaged with EU soft law agree that there is no clear place for it in the Italian legal system and, as reported by other chapters in this collection, there does not even seem to be an Italian translation for the term (and the English phrase 'soft law' is commonly used in Italian-language publications). In general, the Italian academic debate seems to be struggling to doctrinally place EU soft law in the Italian hierarchy of norms and sees opposing camps: those who see EU soft law as non-binding law, and therefore as being unable to produce any legal effects whatsoever (albeit ascribing to soft law an important interpretational function),[18] and those who subscribe to a view of gradual normativity where soft law may find a place as a source of law.[19]

Second, no dogmatic link has traditionally been made between the doctrine and case law on Italian soft law with the – relatively new for the Italian system– phenomenon of EU soft law. Instead, it seems that the discussions have continued in 'silo mode', with administrative lawyers discussing the nature and legal effects of circulars, and EU lawyers interrogating themselves on the very same questions with respect to functionally equivalent – yet EU-born – soft law measures, with the debate on the ANAC guidelines only recently beginning to timidly and partially shake this landscape.

C. EU Soft Law in Italy: Uneven Status and Transposition Practices

This blurred picture in terms of the place of EU soft law in the Italian hierarchy of sources does not become clearer once the transposition practices are examined. Even though limited to a small sample of instruments within an equally small sample of EU policy areas, it is clear that there are many variations on the theme. In the environmental field alone, it has been found that some of the relevant EU soft law is transposed into 'domestic' non-binding manuals,[20] while other measures are simply translated into Italian and published on the

nell'ambito del metodo aperto di coordinamento' in M Barbera (ed), *Nuove forme di regolazione: Il Metodo Aperto di Coordinamento delle Politiche Sociali* (Milan, Giuffrè Editore, 2006) 317; A Gardella, 'L'EBA e i rapporti con la BCE e con le altre autorità di supervisione e regolamentazione' in MP Chiti and V Santoro (eds), *L'Unione bancaria europea* (Pisa, Pacini Editore, 2016) 115; C Figliolia, 'Il Meccanismo di vigilanza unico e i rapporti con le banche centrali nazionali' in Chiti and Santoro, above, 225; V Ferraro, 'Il rapporto tra il "Comitato unico di risoluzione" e le pubbliche amministrazioni nazionali' in Chiti and Santoro, above, 341.

[18] R Bin, 'Soft Law, No Law' in Somma (n 4) 35 (in particular, the author argues that 'deviating from the orthodox way of rule-making entails the loss of one of the strongholds of the rule of law').

[19] Pastore uses the concept of 'sources of law' in a broad sense ('there are sources that provide immediately a valid norm and sources that provide only ideas, inspiration, guidance, directions'). See B Pastore, 'Soft law, gradi di normatività, teoria delle fonti' (n 17) 12–14.

[20] See, eg, 'Manuali per il monitoraggio di specie e habitat di interesse comunitario (Direttiva 92/43/CEE) in Italia: specie animali' no 141 (2016), www.isprambiente.gov.it/public_files/direttiva-habitat/Manuale-141-2016.pdf, which transposed the 'Guidance Document on the strict protection of animal species of Community interest under the 'Habitats' Directive 92/43/EEC'.

website of the national competent authority.[21] Other soft law measures are instead transposed into hard law, either at the central[22] or the regional[23] level. Finally, for other measures, only a link to the EU soft law is offered on the website of the competent authority.[24]

In a similar yet distinct way, in the field of financial regulation, the soft law measures under scrutiny (ie, European Securities and Markets Authority (ESMA) guidelines) are usually transposed into Italian law mainly through guidelines (*orientamenti*) or communications (*comunicazioni*). These acts are formally non-binding and they are adopted only after all the interested parties have been heard through a public consultation. Recently, and particularly for transposing the guidelines related to the so-called second 'Markets in Financial Instruments Directive' (MiFID II),[25] the Italian competent authority has been experimenting with a new method of implementation, namely transposing EU soft law through national binding regulations. Therefore, at least in this case, ESMA guidelines become 'hard' through their national implementation.[26]

In the field of social policy, it is remarkable that out of the three selected soft law measures, one – the Buying Social guide – has been transposed into hard law,[27] another – the Recommendation 'Investing in children: breaking the cycle of disadvantage' – into a number of policy documents,[28] while the third – the Recommendation on strengthening the principle of equal pay between men and women through transparency – does not seem to have been transposed at all.[29]

[21] See the 'Documento di orientamento sull'articolo 6, paragrafo 4 della direttiva "Habitat" (92/43/CEE)' (2007), https://www.minambiente.it/sites/default/files/archivio/allegati/rete_natura_2000/Documento_di_orientamento_sullxarticolo_6x_paragrafo_4x_della_direttiva_xHabitatx_92-43-CEE_-_Gennaio_2007.PDF, which is a translation of the 'Guidance Document on Article 6(4) of the Habitats Directive 92/43/EEC'.

[22] This is the case for the 'Guidance document on Managing Natura 2000 sites', which was implemented through the Decree of the Ministry of Environment of 3 September 2002 (Decreto del Ministero dell'Ambiente e della Tutela del Territorio 3 September 2002, GU no 224 of 24 September 2002).

[23] 'Guidance document on the Assessment of Plans and Projects significantly affecting Natura 2000 sites (November 2001)', which has been transposed through the Decree of the President of the Regional Council of Campania no 9 of 29 January 2010 (Decreto del Presidente della Giunta Regionale della Campania 29 January 2010, no 9, Bollettino Ufficiale della Regione Campania no 10 of 1 February 2010).

[24] https://va.minambiente.it/it-IT/Comunicazione/DettaglioNotizia/230.

[25] Directive 2014/65/EU of the European Parliament and of the Council of 15 May 2014 on markets in financial instruments and amending Directive 2002/92/EC and Directive 2011/61/EU (MiFID II) [2014] OJ L173/349.

[26] For an in-depth discussion on the implementation of ESMA guidelines into Italian law, see J Alberti, 'The Unbearable Lightness of ESMA's Soft Law: An Italian Perspective' in M Buscemi, N Lazzerini, L Magi and D Russo (eds), *Legal Sources in Business and Human Rights: Evolving Dynamics in International and European Law* (Leiden, Brill, 2020) 307 ff.

[27] Interministerial Decree of 11 April 2008.

[28] See F Spera and M Eliantonio, 'National Report on Italy: The Use of EU Soft Law by National Courts and Administration in the Field of EU Social Policy' in M Hartlapp (ed), 'Studying Soft Law Effects in Social Policy' (2020) SoLaR Working Paper, https://papers.ssrn.com/sol3/papers.cfm?abstract_id=3668981.

[29] ibid.

Finally, EU competition soft law is applied directly without any implementation at the national level. However, in the field of competition, EU soft law may well be taken as a model by the national authorities to develop their own soft law measures to rule on situations that fall outside the scope of application of EU soft law: the most remarkable example in the Italian legal order is provided by the guidelines of the Italian Competition Authority on setting fines.[30]

III. EU SOFT LAW IN THE HANDS OF THE ITALIAN COURTS

A. The Judges' Voices: The 'Official View' on Soft Law

Against this fragmented and unclear framework, it does not come as a surprise that what emerges from interviews is that both judges and national administrations have felt compelled to stick to the 'official view' on soft law: namely, its inability to produce legal binding effects vis-a-vis third parties.

In the field of competition law, neither civil nor administrative judges have come so far to admit that the Commission's soft law creates rights and obligations for private parties, but they did confirm that legal effects can be produced vis-a-vis the enacting authority.[31] For instance, once the Commission adopts 'procedural' guidelines (eg, those on setting fines or on cooperation within the Network of Competition Authorities), then judges have to follow those provisions in order to respect the legitimate expectations of private parties.[32]

In the environmental sector, the interviewed judges were unanimous in maintaining that in their view, soft law does not constitute a benchmark of legality of the administrative action and is therefore incapable of creating rights and imposing obligations on national authorities and individuals. They do not feel bound by soft law, but they have all recognised that it can be useful for the interpretation of hard law.[33]

[30] See Italian Competition Authority (Autorità Garante della Concorrenza e del Mercato), 'AGCM Resolution no. 25152 of October 22th, 2014 – Guidelines on the method of setting pecuniary administrative fines pursuant to Article 15, paragraph 1, of Law no 287/90', 22 October 2014, no 25152.

[31] J Alberti and F Croci, 'National Report on Italy: The Use of Soft Law by National Courts and Administration in the Field of EU Competition and State Aid Law' in O Ştefan (ed), 'EU Competition and State Aid Soft Law in the Member States: Finland, France, Germany, Italy, the Netherlands, Slovenia and the UK', (2020) SoLaR Working Paper, https://papers.ssrn.com/sol3/papers.cfm?abstract_id=3667387, 95.

[32] It is worth noting that such an approach can be deemed to be coherent with the recent case law of the Court of Justice affirming that, at least in the field of State aid, the Commission cannot act in contrast with the provision that the same Commission has stated within a Communication. See Case C-431/14P *Greece v Commission* [2016] EU:C:2016:145, paras 69–70.

[33] G Lisi and M Eliantonio, 'National Report on Italy: The Use of EU Soft Law by National Courts and Administration in the field of EU Environmental Law', in M Eliantonio and G Lisi (eds), 'EU Environmental Soft Law in the Member States: A Comparative Overview of Finland, France, Germany, Italy, the Netherlands, Slovenia and the UK', (2020) SoLaR Working Paper, https://papers.ssrn.com/sol3/papers.cfm?abstract_id=3656418.

Only with regard to the financial sector, some contrast appears. ESMA guidelines are deemed as being fully binding, mainly because hard law is made up of general principles, which are too broad to be applied without guidelines. However, it is worth noting that in this case, the respondent was not a judge, but a member of the Arbitrator for Financial Litigation. It is an important and influential alternative dispute resolution (ADR)-like body that has much more technical knowledge than a normal court.[34]

B. The Case Law Analysis: Some Common Features in the Use of EU Soft Law …

While the interviews have brought to the fore a rather formalistic approach to EU soft law, in our case law analysis, a different scenario has unfolded. Indeed, despite the Kelsenian approach in Italy and the 'mainstream' answers received in all but the financial policy interviews, national judges seem quite confident in using soft law.

Four elements should be highlighted in this regard.

From a quantitative perspective, in the field of competition and State aid, the use of soft law is particularly intense. The Italian database counts up to 175 judgments,[35] a figure that is four to five times higher than in other Member States analysed in the SoLaR research project.[36] Financial litigation (ie, cases involving ESMA guidelines) is also more extensive in Italy than in other Member States of the SoLaR project, thanks to the case law of the already-mentioned Arbitrator for Financial Litigation, which often uses ESMA guidelines.[37] An intense use of EU soft law has also been noted with respect to the environmental policy field,[38] a result that stands in contrast to the situation in France, another legal system examined in the SoLaR project, which has a similar tradition in administrative law.[39]

Moreover, in all the examined policy fields, the use of EU soft law is usually not subject to any justification. This is something that deserves to be highlighted; for instance, French judges use EU competition soft law, usually adding some caveats such as 'without taking away its judicial discretion, the

[34] J Alberti (n 26) 314.

[35] For further details on the time framework, the acts under scrutiny, the keywords and the databases used for the research, see Alberti and Croci (n 31) 98.

[36] See the other chapters in this part.

[37] J Alberti, 'The Implementation of ESMA's Guidelines at National Level – Italian Report' in M Avbelj (ed), 'EU Financial Regulation Soft Law in the Member States: Finland, France, Germany, Italy, the Netherlands, Slovenia and the UK' (2020) SoLaR Working Paper, https://papers.ssrn.com/sol3/papers.cfm?abstract_id=3668793.

[38] Lisi and Eliantonio (n 33).

[39] G Lisi, M Eliantonio, S Maljean-Dubois and Eve Truilhé-Marengo, 'National Report on France: The Use of EU Soft Law by National Courts and Administration in the field of EU Environmental Law' in Eliantonio and Lisi (n 33).

court observes that the recommendations of the European Commission [may be relevant for the present purposes] …'.[40] Given the affinity between the Italian and the French legal orders concerning the use of soft law and the sources of law, it seems remarkable that Italian judges appear to be much more free in terms of mentioning and using EU soft acts, since only in a minority of cases do they provide reasons for doing so.

Furthermore, civil judges in the field of competition and arbitrators in financial regulation have reported that if they want to argue against a soft law act (be it a Commission's Communication or ESMA guidelines), they always provide reasons for this.[41] The case law of the Court of Justice of the European Union (CJEU) is a primary source of 'justification' for this purpose. For the sake of clarity, there is no evidence in the case law of such an approach: indeed, in both policy fields, there are only few cases of explicit rejection of soft law.[42] However, this 'duty of providing reasons' seems paradoxical and serves to emphasise that the value of soft law goes far beyond the simple self-commitment of the enacting authority.

A variation of the duty to provide reasons can also be found in the field of environmental law, where one of the interviewed judges stated that if a piece of (EU or national) soft law were relevant to decide on an application, and the competent administrative authority decided in a way that is not in line with the relevant soft law without giving reasons for this in the decision, the administrative judge would be capable of annulling this decision on grounds of *détournement de pouvoir* (*eccesso di potere*), that is, on the grounds of a lack of adequate reasons-giving.[43] Interestingly, this bears some resemblance to the approach adopted with respect to the ANAC guidelines mentioned above in section II.

[40] M Lamoureux and N Rubio, 'National Report for France: The Use of EU Soft Law by National Courts and Administration in the Field of EU Competition Law and State Aid' in Ştefan (n 31).

[41] It is worth noting that this approach is certainly 'inspired' by the case law of the Court of Justice, according to which an institution should provide motivations when acting against a soft act that it has adopted. See Case 148/73 *Louwage v Commission* [1974] EU:C:1974:7, para 12; Case C-520/09 P *Arkema v Commission* [2011] EU:C:2011:619, para 88; Joined Cases C-189/02 P, C-202/02 P, C-205/02 P to C-208/02 P and C-213/02 P *Dansk Rørindustri et al v Commission* [2005] EU:C:2005:408, paras 209–11; Case C-667/13 *Banco Privado Portugues* [2015] EU:C:2015:151, para 69.

[42] For the concept of 'explicit rejection' in the field of competition law, see Z Georgieva, 'The Judicial Reception of Competition Soft Law in the Netherlands and the UK' (2016) 12 *European Competition Journal* 54; Z Georgieva, 'Soft Law in EU Competition Law and its Judicial Reception in the Member States: A Theoretical Perspective' (2015) 16(2) *German Law Journal* 223; Z Georgieva, 'Competition Soft Law in French and German Courts: A Challenge for Online Sales Bans Only?' (2017) 24(2) *Maastricht Journal of European and Comparative Law* 175. For its application in the Italian context, see Alberti and Croci (n 31) 98–110. For a deeper discussion on Italian financial case law, see Alberti (n 26) 312 ff. Please note that in this latter field, there are some cases of explicit (albeit unmotivated) rejection of soft law, but only looking at the (scant) judgments delivered by courts; in the decisions of the Arbitrator for Financial Litigation, there are none.

[43] Lisi and Eliantonio (n 33).

Finally, the case law analysis reveals that, besides interpretative purposes, EU soft law is also endowed with hard legal effects in the decisional practice. In all three policy fields where there is case law on EU soft law, the interpretative function of soft law is prominent and EU soft law is routinely used by the courts to give flesh to the underlying national or EU hard law.[44] What is even more striking that in some cases, Italian judges use EU soft law acts exactly as if they were hard law.

For example, soft law is regularly used as hard law in the litigation concerning financial matters, even if only by the Arbitrator for Financial Litigation. Here ESMA guidelines are used as hard law in nearly 60 per cent of cases.[45] It should be noted that this outcome might (also) be generated by the fact that the Arbitrator is an ADR-like body, of a very technical nature, also composed of civil servants having a financial and not purely legal background. Less frequently but still remarkably often, in the field of antitrust, the Commission soft law is treated as binding in around 30 per cent of cases, all of them decided in normal courts, by judges having a purely legal background.[46] Moreover, similar examples stand out with regard to the EU environmental soft law, where the national administrative courts have considered that the relevant soft law actually imposed a certain interpretation of the underlying hard law provision.[47]

C. … and Some Difficulties in Finding a Common Rationale for its Use

Even though some common features in the use of EU soft law by Italian judges can definitely be highlighted, it is nevertheless hard to identify general patterns for predicting how EU soft law is used in the Italian courts and the extent to which it has an impact on litigation.

This chapter argues that, at least for the time being, the main divide is still to be found in each policy field. In particular, each policy sector has its own practices and habits concerning soft law: the more the field is used to soft law, the more the judges are open to overlooking the ambiguous nature of soft acts and, consequently, to go over the very well-known hard/soft law divide.

Indeed, according to our research, the use of EU soft law in Italian courts does not depend on its characteristics and taxonomy. For instance, there are cases in which soft law has a strong legal basis in hard law, which states that a certain issue will be regulated through soft law. However, the existence of the

[44] ibid; Alberti and Croci (n 31); Alberti (n 37).

[45] Alberti (n 26) 314 ff.

[46] For a deeper discussion on this, see J Alberti and F Croci, 'L'impatto del soft law dell'Unione europea nei giudizi interni: un'analisi sul campo' in G Palmisano (ed), *Il diritto internazionale e dell'Unione europea nei giudizi interni – atti del Convengno annuale della Società Italiana di Diritto Internazionale e di Diritto dell'Unione Europea,* Naples, 2020, 323 ff.

[47] Lisi and Eliantonio (n 33).

legal basis does not necessarily mean that soft law will be used as hard law by judges. Indeed, both the ESMA guidelines and Commission Communications are sometimes used as hard law in Italian case law, although only the former enjoy (in certain cases) a strong connection to hard law.[48]

Moreover, paradoxically enough, the use of EU soft law by Italian judges seems impromptu. What emerges both from the interviews and the case law analysis is that there is no reasoning on how to use soft law and on the relationship between soft and hard law. EU soft law is used because it is handy and practical. In the field of State aid, during an interview a judge stated that he/she uses Commission's Communication because 'there's everything you need there! A collection of the relevant case law and the interpretation given by the European Authority in charge of the regulation of that sector'.[49]

Finally, the instinctive (and, in our view, sometimes rather naive) way in which Italian judges use EU soft law is also shown by the fact that there seems to be no consensus among judges or in the case law on two crucial issues for the use of EU soft law in court, namely the two principles of *iura novit curia* (can soft law be used by judges even if the parties have not mentioned it?) and *tempus regit actum* (can soft law be used even if it was not existing at the time when the challenged act was enacted?).[50]

IV. THE IMPACT OF EU SOFT LAW ON THE PRINCIPLES OF TRANSPARENCY AND DEMOCRATIC LEGITIMACY: THE ITALIAN AUTHORITIES' PERSPECTIVE

In the fields of competition law and financial regulation, where the interviewees agreed to provide their 'evaluation' on the phenomenon, soft law has generally been assessed in a positive light. Almost no interviewee acknowledged it forming a threat to the legislative prerogatives of the Parliament. When direct questions on this were posed to the interviewees, virtually every respondent answered that the possible erosion of democratic legitimacy was offset by the possibility offered by soft law to take swift decisions on detailed issues on which no law-maker no longer has the necessary expertise.[51]

[48] On this point, see A Hofmann, ch 3 in this volume.

[49] Alberti and Croci (n 31).

[50] This point stands out in particular in the field of competition law, which is also the one where judges mostly engage with EU soft law. For a deeper discussion, see Alberti and Croci (n 31) 102–03.

[51] Such an approach raises some doubts: several soft instruments in the field of competition are actually dated and they have not been amended. Therefore, the argument for the necessity of swift decision-making process does not always seem to be well founded. Furthermore, the lack of expertise in the Parliament – and the fact that the main actors involved in those policy fields explicitly recognise such a shortage – may well imply some problems for law-makers attempting to hold to account the independent authorities that enact soft measures in these policy fields (ie, the European Commission and ESMA, together with their national counterparts). However, this debate is very well known in the academic literature and cannot be dealt in detail here; the interviews conducted with SoLaR hope to bring some new insights to this discussion.

In the field of financial regulation, the reason for the positive approach towards soft law can also be found in the fact that the conferral of soft powers to ESMA has certainly contributed to ensuring financial stability within the EU. Soft law-making has fostered a common culture of supervision and has laid the foundations for creating a level playing field among market operators. The utmost importance of these goals has certainly played a role in making accepted and appreciated the means through which the objectives have been achieved.

Furthermore, the fact that ESMA guidelines are drafted together with national authorities and are 'implemented' by the latter has also fostered their legitimacy and popularity at the national level. According to our interviews, the Italian Securities and Markets Authority trusts EU-level decision-making processes, since whatever comes from ESMA is the outcome of several compromises among the 27 Member States. Therefore, in order to refuse the national implementation of ESMA soft law acts, 'the most relevant national interests have to be at stake'.[52] From another perspective, such a positive approach (it is worth noting that Italy has implemented all the guidelines issued so far) also seems to demonstrate the warm reception of the same guidelines within the national financial industry. Indeed, Italian banks are very much in favour of the adoption of guidelines for the harmonisation of EU financial law and therefore push the Italian regulator as much as possible to implement them faithfully.[53]

However, it has to be highlighted that the multi-level nature of soft financial law also seems to have some shortcomings, in particular since it creates a complex and burdensome regulatory structure with too many legal texts at different levels.

Indeed, both the private sector and the public sector expressed concerns about overregulation, arguing that regulatory complexity increases uncertainty about obligations to which actors are subject. Thus, a single rulebook has been indicated as a more efficient solution; interestingly enough, both the respondents from the private sector and those from the Italian Securities and Markets Authority argued that the power to draft such a single legal text should be given to ESMA.[54] Therefore, also from this perspective, the cooperation between ESMA and the Italian Securities and Markets Authority seems remarkable.

As regards the field of competition, our research has shown that soft law performs some peculiar functions that are able to affect – sometimes positively, sometimes negatively – the principles of transparency and democratic legitimacy.

On the positive side is the use of soft law as a tool to increase transparency, through a 'crystallisation' of the outcome of a political negotiation process and/or of specific policy choices.

[52] Alberti (n 37).
[53] ibid.
[54] ibid.

A noticeable example arose in an interview with a civil servant of the Department of European Affairs – State Aid Office, who made a reference to a 'non-paper' issued by the Commission with regard to State aid to the tourism sector, to which they could not give any specific reference because the decision on the matter had not yet been made. According to the Commission, such a 'non-paper' was allegedly a purely internal document; however, surprisingly enough, it was notified to the national administrations of all the Member States. The Member States have therefore ended up taking this document into consideration, even though it was not made public and allegedly has no legal value. In this context, as reported by the interviewee, some national administrations asked the Commission to adopt the 'non-paper' at issue *as a soft law measure*, thus making the position of the institution on the matter explicit and clearly recognisable. However, the Commission, responded in the negative.

Although this might appear paradoxical, the above-mentioned case shows that soft law-making – traditionally regarded as an ambiguous process and open to criticism – is likely to be more respectful of basic principles than some other regulatory practices. In other words, soft law should be considered not only as a form of intervention that is less structured (and accountable) than hard law, but also as an instrument that – paradoxically enough – offers greater protection and transparency than other institutional practices or behaviour, such as the adoption of non-papers and other even more ambiguous acts.

On the other hand, some criticism has also been voiced against soft law, deeming it a regulatory tool that can be more easily captured by influential interest groups/Member States than hard law.

This argument was put forward in particular with regard to public consultations. For instance, some respondents both from the private and public sectors highlighted the fact that, very often, the text of a draft Communication of the Commission submitted to public consultation already represented a locked-in compromise between different interests. In this way, the Commission substantially transforms the consultation into a de facto formality, which is not really capable of influencing the content of the measure at issue, since it had been previously defined in its essential aspects.[55]

V. CONCLUSION

This chapter has shown that despite a pyramidal view of the hierarchy of sources, where non-binding norms do not have an official place, at least in some of the SoLaR policy fields, national administrations and courts make frequent use of EU soft law and endow it with binding legal effects. However, this research argues that – despite a growing and unpredicted use of EU soft law by Italian

[55] Alberti and Croci (n 31) 110.

courts and the increasing attention given to the phenomenon in the doctrine – no real 'mentality shift' has occurred. Italian judges and authorities do engage with soft law, albeit cautiously, and they use EU soft law when it is considered useful and as long as it provides relevant arguments for solving the legal disputes in question. However, there is still no legal reasoning about (and legal acceptance of) its new and hybrid nature. There is an elephant in the room, but no one seems willing to point it out and tackle the legal consequences that it implies.

12

Soft Law and Guidance in the Netherlands

At Odds with Legal Principles?

BARBARA BEIJEN

I. INTRODUCTION

THIS CHAPTER EXAMINES how the Dutch courts and authorities use soft law, with a special focus on EU soft law. It takes as its starting point van Dam's research on the alleged positive effects of EU guidance documents on the principles of legal certainty, equal treatment, transparency and legality in the Netherlands.[1] While van Dam's research concerns guidance documents connected to the Habitats Directive,[2] the Citizenship Directive[3] and the Common Agricultural Policy,[4] the European Network of Soft Law Research (SoLaR) project looked at a wider category of soft law instruments in financial regulation, competition and State aid law, environmental policy and social policy. Drawing on the empirical work conducted within SoLaR, this chapter asks whether van Dam's findings apply to other types of soft law measures in different policy fields and, more broadly, if there is a particularly Dutch approach to soft law.

[1] JCA van Dam, *Guidance Documents of the European Commission in the Dutch Legal Order* (Leiden, M Meijers Instituut voor Rechtswetenschappelijk onderzoek van de Faculteit Rechtsgeleerdheid van de Universiteit Leiden, 2020).

[2] Council Directive 92/43/EEC of 21 May 1992 on the conservation of natural habitats and of wild fauna and flora (Habitats Directive) [1992] OJ L206/7.

[3] Directive 2004/38/EC of the European Parliament and of the Council of 29 April 2004 on the right of citizens of the Union and their family members to move and reside freely within the territory of the Member States amending Regulation (EEC) No 1612/68 and repealing Directives 64/221/EEC, 68/360/EEC, 72/194/EEC, 73/148/EEC, 75/34/EEC, 75/35/EEC, 90/364/EEC, 90/365/EEC and 93/96/EEC (Citizenship Directive) [2004] OJ L158/77.

[4] Regulation (EU) 1306/2013 of the European Parliament and of the Council of 17 December 2013 on the financing, management and monitoring of the common agricultural policy [2013] OJ L347/549; Regulation (EU) 1307/2013 of 17 December 2013 establishing rules for direct payments to farmers under support schemes within the framework of the common agricultural policy [2013] OJ L347/608.

This chapter proceeds as follows. Section II briefly describes the role of soft law in the Dutch legal system and discusses the research conducted by Dutch academics on soft law, both domestic and EU. Section II also examines the ways in which EU soft law instruments are received and 'transposed' at the national level. Section III describes the findings from the interviews and the case law research.[5] Section IV further reflects on the empirical material, asking how the usage by the domestic actors of EU soft law affects the principles of transparency and legality comparing the results of the SoLaR research with van Dam's findings. By way of a conclusion, this chapter argues, first, that the Dutch approach to EU soft law is earnest and sincere, as long as actors are aware of its existence. However, the fact that EU soft law is often difficult to find weakens the promise of transparency at the national level. Second, although there is no doubt about the non-bindingness of EU soft law among the Dutch judges and authorities, the tendency to routinely apply it seems to give rise to binding effects in practice.

II. SOFT LAW IN THE DUTCH LEGAL SYSTEM

A brief introduction to the Dutch legal system and the role of national soft law is necessary to better understand the peculiarities in the reception and use of EU soft law in the Dutch context.

A. Domestic Soft Law

Historically, there is a strong tradition of, and preference for, written legislation in the Dutch legal system. Besides legislation, other important sources of law are explanatory memoranda from the legislative process and case law.[6]

Legislation is often intentionally written in a way that leaves significant discretion to administrative authorities. This aspect relates to the need to allow the balancing of (conflicting) interests in specific situations: is something necessary to protect the public order? Should the permit be granted or not? In order to have something tangible to guide administrative discretion when interpreting and applying the law, administrative authorities can lay down so-called 'policy rules' (*beleidsregels*) in which they describe how they intend to exercise the discretion conferred upon them by the legislation.[7] The legal basis for drafting such policy rules can be found in Article 4:81 of the General Administrative Law Act (GALA; Algemene wet bestuursrecht (AWB)), according to which an

[5] The members of the Dutch team conducted a total of 19 interviews across the four policy fields.

[6] SE Zijlstra et al (eds), *Wetgeven. Handboek voor de centrale en decentrale overheid* (Deventer, Kluwer, 2012) 585.

[7] For more information, see, eg, H Bröring, 'Bestuursrechtelijke soft law: tien opmerkingen' in T Barkhuysen et al (eds), *25 jaar Awb. In eenheid en verscheidenheid* (Deventer, Wolters Kluwer, 2019); and van Dam (n 1) 95.

administrative authority can draft policy rules for every discretionary power conferred upon it. Article 4:82 further states that administrative authorities can substantiate their decisions by referring to policy rules. An important characteristic of policy rules is that they are not legally binding in individual cases, although they do have a 'self-binding effect' for the administration.[8] The administrative authority is, according to Article 4:84 GALA, supposed to act in conformity with the policy rules, unless adherence to the policy rules would lead to an unjust result, given the specific circumstances of the case.

Policy rules help ensure that the administration applies the law in a consistent and predictable way, thus contributing to the consistency of policy-making and the protection of legitimate expectations. Policy rules have to be published in the Government Gazette (*Staatscourant*) or at the decentralised level (Article 3:42 GALA). As policy rules are usually binding on the authority that has issued them (Article 4:84 GALA), the publication of policy rules assists individuals and businesses in estimating their chances to obtain a permit, subsidy or other public law instrument and planning future conduct. The authority must take the individual circumstances of the case into account, but the publication of policy rules allows an applicant to identify and put forward arguments why the policy rules should not be applied in their case.[9] Policy rules are prevalent in the Netherlands. A search for policy rules from the municipality of Nijmegen alone gives 48 results, ranging from social support to assistance for people with problematic debts, rules on parking cars, night shops and so on.[10]

Another form of national soft law are guides (often called *richtsnoeren*) drafted by various organisations and designed to be used by administrative authorities.[11] Examples are guides drafted by the Association of Dutch Municipalities (which is not an official authority itself, but an overarching umbrella organisation through which the municipalities cooperate), which are intended as guidance for local authorities when applying national legislation.[12] Some of these documents concern environmental law, while others deal with issues as diverse as municipal support structures concerning youth or people with special needs. There are also guides issued by PIANOO (the expertise centre on public procurement)[13] or by the National Institute for Public Health and the Environment (RIVM).[14] Their main purpose is to streamline the activities of decentralised public authorities, because it does not make sense for every municipality to figure out on its own how to assess the impact of environmental noise on health or how to organise the integration of immigrants. It is thus considered more efficient for an expert

[8] Van Dam (n 1) 95.
[9] eg, ECLI:NL:RVS:2016:2840, para 4.3.
[10] www.overheid.nl/zoekresultaat/5/1/10/lijst/postcode%5B0%5D%3D6525%26titel%5B0%5D%3Dbeleidsregel%26geldend_op%5B0%5D%3Dnow%26organisatietype%3DGemeente.
[11] Van Dam (n 1) 96.
[12] www.vng.nl/onderwerpenindex/ruimte-en-wonen/omgevingswet/publicaties/handreiking-bedrijven-en-milieuzonering.
[13] www.pianoo.nl/nl/document/17635/handreiking-van-beleid-naar-inkoop-de-inburgering.
[14] www.rivm.nl/nieuws/handreiking-gezondheidseffecten-omgevingsgeluid.

organisation to draft a guide on an issue that has relevance for multiple municipalities, harmonising local practices. Such guides do not have a specific legal basis in the law, but they are commonly applied by authorities and accepted by the reviewing judges.[15]

The Dutch way of using domestic soft law rules resembles the EU's 'comply-or-explain' approach. Policy rules are not formally binding and actors can depart from them, but such departure should always be duly motivated and explained. In the absence of special circumstances, authorities are supposed to apply soft law rules.[16]

B. Judicial Review

In the Netherlands, it is possible to bring a claim against most administrative acts (*besluiten*) in individual cases.[17] After review by the administrative authority itself, an applicant can bring an action before an administrative judge (Articles 8:1 and 7:1 GALA). The court will base its ruling on the grounds put forward by the applicant. There is only a limited possibility for the judge to add or examine other grounds *ex officio*, with the permitted *ex officio* grounds including arguments relating to the jurisdiction of the court, the power of the administrative authority or formal limitations in the right to appeal (Article 8:69 GALA). However, in practice, the grounds are interpreted broadly. If the applicant puts forward an argument that a specific project is too noisy, without referring to specific legislation on noise nuisance, the court will proceed to verify whether or not the project is in breach of the applicable noise legislation. Further, if the applicant refers to a specific piece of legislation, the court will take the relevant national soft law into account as well. Yet, as the SoLaR interviews illustrate, EU soft law relating to national legislation upon which the decision is based will in most cases only be taken into account if referred to by the parties or if the court is aware of its existence and relevance for the case in hand.[18]

Domestic policy rules are excluded from judicial review (Article 8:3(1-a) GALA), but in a case challenging a specific decision (eg, an environmental permit), an applicant can claim that the policy rules applied by the authority in his or her case are invalid or erroneously applied, or that the policy rules cannot

[15] eg, ECLI:NL:RVS:2016:854.

[16] van Dam (n 1) 95.

[17] ibid 99.

[18] C Cauffman, 'Financial Soft Law in the Netherlands' in M Avbelj (ed), 'EU Financial Regulation Soft Law in the Member States: Finland, France, Germany, Italy, the Netherlands, Slovenia and the UK' (2020) SoLaR Working Paper, https://papers.ssrn.com/sol3/papers.cfm?abstract_id=3668793, 93; BA Beijen, 'National Report on the Netherlands: The Use of EU Soft Law by National Courts and Administration in the Field of EU Environmental Law' in M Eliantonio and G Lisi (eds), 'EU Environmental Soft Law in the Member States: A Comparative Overview of Finland, France, Germany, Italy, the Netherlands, Slovenia and the UK' (2020) SoLaR Working Paper, https://papers.ssrn.com/sol3/papers.cfm?abstract_id=3656418, 107–08.

be applied because of some exceptional circumstances. In this indirect way, it is then possible to have policy rules judicially reviewed. Other forms of domestic soft law such as the guides are usually not considered 'decisions' (*besluiten*) for the purposes of judicial review, which means that no direct judicial action against these documents is available. But just as with policy rules, it is possible to indirectly control them in a case brought against a specific decision in the context of which soft law rules were invoked.

It is not up to a national court to decide on the validity of EU soft law, just as it is with EU hard law.[19] But because national judges, especially administrative law judges, are used to applying and *indirectly* reviewing domestic soft law, there are neither formal nor practical obstacles to doing the same with EU soft law. Moreover, parties could also – in theory at least – draw attention to EU soft law. Especially in the judgments in the context of environmental law and competition law and State aid, there are references to EU soft law (see section III below). Yet, as explained below, the judgments often fail to clarify what role soft law played in the decision, making it difficult to evaluate its usage. Judicial silence is evident in SoLaR case law, but has also been noted in earlier research.[20] Silence takes many forms. Sometimes a party invokes an EU soft law document, but the national court does not explicitly say anything about the status or nature of the document, or simply remarks that it is not applicable in the case under review. Sometimes the court applies EU soft law without any remarks on its status. There are further cases in which the court considers that a piece of EU soft law is important for the interpretation of the law or uses a similar wording to justify the use of soft law.[21] No cases in which the court explicitly sets aside a soft law document have been identified in the context of the SoLaR research.

C. Dutch Research on National and EU Soft Law

The use of soft law, especially in the form of *beleidsregels*, is a long-standing practice in the Netherlands. Handbooks on general administrative law cover this subject,[22] but there is also literature focusing specifically on different types of national soft law.[23]

[19] Case 314/85 *Foto-Frost* [1987] EU:C:1987:452.

[20] JE van den Brink and JCA van Dam, 'Nederlandse bestuursrechters en unierechtelijke "beleidsregels"' (2014) *JBplus* 3, 26.

[21] C Cauffman and NJ Philipsen, 'National Report on the Netherlands: The Use of EU Soft Law by National Courts and Administration in the Field of EU Competition Law and State Aid' in O Ştefan (ed), 'EU Competition and State Aid Soft Law in the Member States: Finland, France, Germany, Italy, the Netherlands, Slovenia and the UK' (2020) SoLaR Working Paper, https://papers.ssrn.com/sol3/papers.cfm?abstract_id=3667387, 121; Beijen (n 18) 104.

[22] See, eg, RJN Schlössels and SE Zijlstra, *Onderwijseditie Bestuursrecht in de sociale rechtsstaat* (Deventer, Kluwer, 2017) 224.

[23] See, eg, JH van Kreveld, *Beleidsregels in het recht* (Deventer, Kluwer, 1983); A Tollenaar, *Gemeentelijk beleid en beleidsregels* (The Hague/Groningen, BJu, 2008). For a less exhaustive but more recent account, see H Bröring (n 7).

The Dutch academic literature on EU soft law is not vast but is relatively influential, also beyond the Netherlands. Senden was among the first EU law scholars to systematically study EU soft law as an instrument of integration.[24] Together with Luijendijk, she has also examined the way in which the Dutch legislator and the courts deal with EU soft law.[25] In their view, EU soft law is relevant for the interpretation of hard law in the Dutch legal order. The national effects of EU soft law depend on the framework within which it is drafted, but soft law often appears to have binding effects in practice, possibly because national actors are usually quite pragmatic about its lawfulness and legitimacy.[26] Also looking at the role of EU soft law in the national decision-making process, Klap points out the differences in the possible effects of soft law, ranging from non-committal to binding. In his view, EU soft law has an indirect effect nationally. Only if it is transposed into national soft law does EU soft law become binding and capable of limiting the discretion of national authorities.[27]

Comparatively speaking, an appreciable interest of Dutch scholars in EU soft law can be explained by the fact that the importance of EU law for national legislation is generally accepted in the Netherlands and that soft law is often seen pragmatically as a relevant source to help understand EU hard law. However, the accepted role of EU soft law in the national legal order raises significant questions about its legal value and the ways in which national authorities apply it.

D. Transposition of EU Soft Law in the Dutch Legal Order

The Dutch implementation of soft law takes multiple forms. In the environmental law field, the selected SoLaR measures are not formally 'transposed', and governmental websites simply contain links to the relevant pieces of EU environmental soft law.[28] The selected financial soft law is also referred to on the website of the competent authority (Autoriteit financiële markten (AFM)).[29] The AFM mentions that it does not apply one specific form of guideline on reporting obligations from the Joint Guidelines on complaints-handling for the securities (ESMA) and banking (EBA) sectors (JC 2014 43).[30] In State aid

[24] LAJ Senden, *Soft Law in European Community Law* (Oxford, Hart Publishing, 2004).

[25] J Luijendijk and LAJ Senden, 'De gelaagde doorwerking van Europese administratieve soft law in de nationale rechtsorde' (2011) 7 *SEW Tijdschrift voor Europees en economisch recht* 312.

[26] ibid 349, 350–51.

[27] AP Klap, 'Bestuur in de tang? Over de toepassing van Europese soft law door Nederlandse bestuursorganen' in B Schueler and R Widdershoven (eds), *Europeanisering van het algemeen bestuursrecht* (The Hague/Groningen, BJu, 2014) 169–79.

[28] Beijen (n 18) 95–97; www.helpdeskwater.nl/onderwerpen/wetgeving-beleid/kaderrichtlijnwater/uitvoering/europees (Water Framework Directive); and www.synbiosys.alterra.nl/natura2000/gebiedendatabase.aspx?subj=achtergronddocumenten (Habitats Directive).

[29] www.afm.nl/nl-nl/professionals/onderwerpen/esa-richtsnoeren-bu.

[30] Cauffman (n 18) 92, www.afm.nl/nl-nl/professionals/onderwerpen/esa-richtsnoeren-bu/klachtenbehandeling.

and competition law, soft law references can be found in the policy documents of the Autoriteit Consument en Markt (ACM, the Dutch competition authority), but there is no actual 'transposition' of EU soft law into national (hard or soft) law.[31] Yet the ACM relies on Commission competition and State aid soft law, and published, for instance, an announcement that it will act in line with the Commission Guidelines on Article 81 of the Treaty on the Functioning of the European Union (TFEU) in national competition cases.[32] The SoLaR social policy soft law is referred to in national policy documents, but only in a passing manner.[33]

The most typical way to 'transpose' EU soft law in the Dutch legal order is thus to refer to it in policy documents or on official websites, but not to formally transpose it or adapt it to local circumstances. These findings resonate with those of Luijendijk and Senden, who have demonstrated that EU soft law can take multiple effects nationally, ranging from direct transposition in national legislation to references in national legislation or national soft law in different degrees of bindingness.[34] All of these forms of reception are used in the Dutch practice, so the option of a formal transposition also exists, although it appears to be rarely used and was not found with respect to the SoLaR measures. The choice between the different forms of implementation depends on a multiplicity of factors, such as the type of soft law, the existence of a specific obligation to cooperate with the Commission, whether the Netherlands agrees to the content of the piece of soft law, and whether there is a tension between soft and hard law.[35]

III. SOLAR RESULTS: CASE LAW AND INTERVIEWS

This section discusses the findings from the interviews and the case law research with respect to the use of EU soft law by national courts and civil servants in the four SoLaR areas.

A. Financial Regulation

Eight interviews were conducted with judges and their staff and civil servants in the field of financial regulation.[36] These interviews revealed that EU financial

[31] Cauffman and Philipsen (n 21) 116–18.

[32] https://wetten.overheid.nl/BWBR0033029/2013-04-01.

[33] BA Beijen, 'National Report on the Netherlands: The Use of EU Soft Law by National Courts and Administration in the Field of EU Social Policy' in M Hartlapp (ed), 'Studying EU Soft Law Effects in Social Policy' (2020), SoLaR Working Paper, https://papers.ssrn.com/sol3/papers.cfm?abstract_id=3668981, 79–80; www.rijksoverheid.nl/documenten/brochures/2013/04/23/informatiebladmaatschappelijk-aanbesteden.

[34] Luijendijk and Senden (n 25) 339–40.

[35] ibid 341.

[36] Cauffman (n 18) 90–91.

soft law is applied on a regular basis by the competent administrative authority, the Dutch Financial Markets Authority (Autoriteit Financiële Markten (AFM)). Judges indicated familiarity with soft law, but there were discernible differences between courts. In civil courts, the ESMA soft law was hardly ever used. This is logical because civil courts deal with conflicts between private parties, and ESMA soft law is not, primarily at least, intended to guide private party relationships. Decisions of the AFM can be contested before the administrative courts, which means, as a consequence, that administrative judges are more familiar with EU soft law, as evidenced by 16 cases with references to ESMA soft law. These references were not simply cursory mentions. In a judgment by the District Court of Rotterdam, the Court, for instance, engaged with ESMA soft law, holding that the interpretation of the AFM of ESMA Guidance 17 was in contrast with AIFM Directive 2011/61 and could not therefore be applied.[37] However, this appears not to be a statement about the validity of the guidance, but only of the AFM interpretation.

In general, the respondents in this policy area are positive about the clarificatory function of EU soft law, which in their view increases overall transparency. At the same time, they express reservations about the lack of democratic legitimacy, the non-transparent drafting process and the fact that soft law is at odds with the separation of powers.[38]

B. Environmental Law

In the field of environmental law, guidance documents with respect to the Habitats Directive, the Water Framework Directive (WFD) and the Environmental Impact Assessment Directive (hereinafter the 'EIA Directive') were analysed.[39] National environmental jurisprudence did not include references to WFD soft law, that is, documents given in the context of the Common Implementation Strategy. A search for the EIA Directive returned two cases.[40] As in other Member States, the Habitats Directive soft law was more regularly referred to, in particular the Guidance document on the strict protection of species with 10 cases.[41]

EU environmental guidance documents are seen as a relevant source of information by the applicants, administrative authorities and judges themselves.[42]

[37] ECLI:NL:RBROT:2017:3150, para 3.4.

[38] Cauffman (n 18) 95.

[39] Beijen (n 18) 98. This search followed the general SoLaR template for case law research and was confined to the case law of the highest administrative court in environmental cases, the administrative law division of the Council of State.

[40] ECLI:NL:RVS:2011:BR3209 and ECLI:NL:RVS:2012:BW5239.

[41] ECLI:NL:RVS:2007:AZ6380, ECLI:NL:RVS:2009:BH3985, ECLI:NL:RVS:2010:BL0689, ECLI:NL:RVS:2012:BV3215, ECLI:NL:RVS:2012:BV5086, ECLI:NL:RVS:2012:BV8041, ECLI:NL:RVS:2012:BW4561, ECLI:NL:RVS:2012:BY2464, ECLI:NL:RVS:2014:281 and ECLI:NL:RVS:2014:4024.

[42] Beijen (n 18) 106–07.

There are examples of the applicant relying on a guidance document,[43] but also of the administrative authority referring to it.[44] The judgments make clear that guidance documents are not binding, regularly adding caveats to that effect.[45] However, if a party relies on a guidance document, the reference is taken seriously and judged on its merits.[46] The cases concerning the EIA guidance documents demonstrate that guidance documents can influence the interpretation of Dutch legislation.[47] Further, it is remarkable that in a number of cases, the applicant refers to an EU guidance document to support the claim, but the national court dismisses the claim because it does not share the way in which the applicant interprets the document. This shows that although EU soft law documents are meant only as a clarification, they can be of determining value for litigation.[48] The fact that applicants refer to soft law also demonstrates that national actors are aware of, and knowledgeable about, EU soft law.

A total of six interviews were conducted with civil servants and judges.[49] The interviewed judges and the civil servants all agreed on the fact that soft law is an important source of information and knowledge, although they also all liked to emphasise its non-bindingness. The interviews suggest that civil servants tend to closely follow EU soft law in a bid to avoid conflicts with the Commission. They would probably only deviate from soft law if there are strong reasons for doing so. The judges also follow EU soft law, unless they have reasons to doubt its substantive correctness. One of the judges remarked that soft law helps prevent delays, as there is less need to refer cases to the European Court of Justice for a preliminary ruling.[50]

C. Competition and State Aid Law

In competition law, there are nearly 30 published court cases with references to the SoLaR competition soft law.[51] In these cases, EU soft law is mainly used as a source of interpretation. Sometimes EU soft law measures are called 'an *important* source of interpretation',[52] whereas in other cases they only contain

[43] ECLI:NL:RVS:2007:AZ6380, ECLI:NL:RVS:2009:BH3985, ECLI:NL:RVS:2012:BV5086, ECLI:NL:RVS:2012:BV8041, ECLI:NL:RVS:2012:BY2464 and ECLI:NL:RVS:2014:4024.

[44] ECLI:NL:RVS:2010:BL0689 and ECLI:NL:RVS:2012:BV3215.

[45] See, eg, ECLI:NL:RVS:2012:BV3215, para 2.33.5.

[46] See, eg, ECLI:NL:RVS:2014:4024, para 14.

[47] ECLI:NL:RVS:2011:BR3209, para 2.5 and ECLI:NL:RVS:2012:BW5239, para 2.4.2. See also Beijen (n 18) 106.

[48] Beijen (n 18) 104.

[49] ibid 105–06.

[50] ibid 108. For the same role of CIS guidance documents in WFD litigation, see also E Korkea-aho, *Adjudicating New Governance. Deliberative Democracy in the European Union* (Abingdon, Routledge, 2015) 209–10.

[51] Cauffman and Philipsen (n 21) 120.

[52] ECLI:NL:GHLEE:2009:BJ9567, emphasis added.

'*indications* for interpretation'.[53] In some cases, they are mentioned as part of the overall legislative framework, without any attention to their non-binding nature.[54] Parties also proactively invoke and refer to EU soft law in this area. However, parties' proactiveness does not automatically lead to the court applying EU soft law: courts sometimes consider EU soft law irrelevant for the case at hand[55] or not applicable for procedural reasons.[56] In one case, the undertaking accused of abusing its dominant position invoked the Article 82 Guidance Paper and stated that not only was it binding for the Commission, but also that the ACM considered itself bound by it.[57] However, the ACM disputed the undertaking's interpretation. As the court did not need to address this argument in its judgment, it never considered the legal value of the Commission Guidance Paper and whether the national authority is or can be bound by Commission soft law. The way in which soft law is used in competition cases resembles the approach in environmental cases: soft law is used by parties as well as courts as an aid for interpretation, but it is not decisive and often only mentioned without clarifying the function it plays in the case.[58]

In relation to State aid, there are not many cases to be found. EU soft law was taken into account in the 12 cases found, but without an explicit motivation for its use or an explanation of its legal status.[59] The legal status of soft law was not questioned by the parties either.[60]

The interviews show that the Dutch Competition Authority frequently uses soft law.[61] Then again, the interviewed administrative judge did not recall applying soft law at all and had not formed strong opinions about its use in court. The interviewed civil court judge had more experience with soft law as a former member of an advisory board on administrative appeal against decisions of the Competition Authority. The observations of both interviewed judges are in line with the general SoLaR findings: soft law can be of help, but it cannot extend competences or increase powers of the government, and the absence of democratic legitimation in its adoption must lead to a careful use of soft law documents by both governments and courts.[62] In the context of State aid, the interviewed administrative judge confirmed that soft law is used as a source of information, but that it is not always explicitly mentioned in judgments and that it is important to keep in mind that soft law is not legally binding.[63]

[53] ECLI:NL:RBUTR:2007:BA5375, emphasis added.
[54] ECLI:NL:GHSGR:2011:BQ2091.
[55] ECLI:NL:GHSHE:2012:BX3346.
[56] ECLI:NL:RBDHA:2015:10095.
[57] ECLI:NL:CBB:2010:BN9947.
[58] Cauffman and Philipsen (n 21) 120.
[59] See, eg, ECLI:NL:CBB:2010:BN0344, ECLI:NL:CBB:2016:282 and ECLI:NL:RBALK:2010:BO5112.
[60] Cauffman and Philipsen (n 21) 134.
[61] There were four interviews in total; see ibid 140–42.
[62] ibid 142.
[63] ibid 143.

In conclusion, EU competition and State aid soft law is generally accepted in the Netherlands. The pragmatic attitude of practitioners can be explained by the fact that most of State aid and competition soft law is interpretative and de facto codifies the case law by the CoJ.[64] National judges feel safe to use Commission soft law without explicitly justifying its use.

D. Social Policy

The SoLaR social policy soft law does not seem to have much impact on the Dutch legal system, a finding that resonates with all SoLaR countries. For instance, equal pay between men and women is a relevant and high-level policy issue in the Netherlands, with several pending policy initiatives to oblige companies to be more transparent about pay.[65] However, there are no references to the Recommendation on Equal Pay 2014/124/EU, not even in initiatives for new legislative acts on this matter.[66] It seems that as a topic, equal pay is regarded important, but no connection is made to EU-level policy discussions or to concrete measures such as the Commission Recommendation. The same holds true for the two other SoLaR instruments. There is a national-level awareness about poverty among children and socially sustainable public procurement practices, but there is no (or only very limited) attention to the EU instruments in these fields.[67]

Unsurprisingly then, a search for national case law did not generate a single reference to the SoLaR soft law – a finding replicated in other national jurisdictions.[68] For various reasons, it was also difficult to find interview partners, so in the end, only one interview was carried out with an official from the College for Human Rights, which is a semi-judicial body with the power to give authoritative advice in conflicts involving human rights.[69] The College does not actively use EU soft law when formulating and delivering its advice.[70]

E. EU Soft Law in the Netherlands: Is it Possible to Discern a Common Pattern?

The SoLaR research reveals that EU soft law is taken seriously in the Netherlands. As demonstrated above, it is common to find references to EU soft law in judgments, and soft law is seen as an authoritative, although not a legally binding,

[64] Luijendijk and Senden (n 25) 348.
[65] Beijen (n 33) 81–82.
[66] Kamerstukken II 2013/14, 33 922, nr 2.
[67] Beijen (n 33) 80–81.
[68] ibid 83–84.
[69] ibid 84.
[70] Published on mensenrechten.nl.

source of law. Given the complexity of EU hard law, both judges and civil servants are positive about the guidance offered in the form of EU soft law. As the interpretation of hard law may raise thorny questions, guidance on the correct interpretation of the law is a welcome aid for administrative authorities and judges.[71] This means that in practice, soft law can have rather hard effects, as it is likely to be followed unless there are convincing arguments against its use. At the same time, courts do not consistently make clear how they treat EU soft law and what function it plays in the legal reasoning of the judges.

Furthermore, differences can be observed between different types of soft law measures. Interpretative guidance is used more often by judges than other forms of soft law such as recommendations. This finding is clear on the basis of the case law research for the SoLaR project, but is also confirmed by other available research in this field.[72] Interpretative guidance is typically given in connection with hard law, and when, for instance, a directive must be applied in a case, it is logical for the judge or the authority to use the interpretative guidance specifically adopted to clarify the interpretation of the directive. It is more difficult to justify the use of a recommendation, which is not connected to a piece of EU hard law.[73] Indeed, there were no references in the Dutch case law to recommendations in the field of social policy.[74] In the other policy fields, it is more common to also find references to other forms of EU soft law. However, courts are not always transparent about or consistent in the way in which they use soft law, and they may use it without mentioning it.[75] For example, although the 'Guidance document on Species Protection (Habitats Directive)' is referred to much more frequently than the 'Managing Natura 2000 Guidance Document', judges claim to use both documents just as often.[76] Indeed, the number of references does not say everything about how often a document is used in the background.

The unclear status of soft law in the Dutch legal order is demonstrated by the *Koninklijke KPN et al v ACM*, in which the question was raised about the relationship between an EU directive and a recommendation in the field of electronic communication networks. The case originated from the Netherlands and is interesting for our purposes because the national regulator adopted a certain interpretation of the soft law at stake, which was disputed by the operators. Confronted with this issue and having to decide which interpretation of the soft law measure had to be adopted, the Dutch asked the CoJ how much weight had to be attached to the soft law measure and whether it would be possible to depart from it.[77] The CoJ held that the recommendation is not binding, but

[71] Beijen (n 18) 107–08; Cauffman (n 18) 92.
[72] Van Dam (n 1) 269.
[73] See A Hofmann, ch 3 in this volume.
[74] Beijen (n 33) 83–84.
[75] Cauffman (n 18); Cauffman and Philipsen (n 21) 142.
[76] Van Dam (n 1) 186.
[77] ECLI:NL:CBB:2015:4.

emphasised that the directive requires national authorities to 'take the utmost account of the Commission recommendations' and, consequently, the recommendation can only be departed from when reasons are stated.[78] In the final ruling, the national court decided that there was no pressing reason to depart from the recommendation, siding with the national regulator.[79]

From this perspective, it seems that the national experience with the Dutch *beleidsregels* is quite different from EU soft law, as the latter are – uncontroversially – binding on the national authority bar in the case of special circumstances. At the same time, it should not be forgotten that *beleidsregels* are meant to bind the author itself, while EU soft law is drafted at the EU level, but is applied by national actors.

IV. THE EFFECTS OF EU SOFT LAW ON LEGAL PRINCIPLES

This section further analyses the data, focusing on the effects of EU soft law on the principle of transparency and legality, comparing in particular how the SoLaR findings relate to van Dam's findings with respect to guidance documents.

A. Transparency

The SoLaR interviews reveal that judges and civil servants think that the transparency of soft law should be increased.[80] However, they do not see the (lack of) transparency of the drafting process at the EU level as a key problem, but rather they worry about the lack of transparency in the sense of accessibility of EU soft law.[81] These documents cannot always be found in EUR-Lex, and there is no one single place where all EU soft law acts are published and deposited. Further, the respondents would like to have references to these documents in the underlying (hard) law to improve accessibility.[82] In most cases, administrative authorities think that they know where to find these documents, but this does not necessarily mean that all civil servants for whom soft law documents may be relevant know of the documents or know where they can be found. Judges, on the other hand, are dependent on the parties to refer to the documents.[83] They will not always have the time to thoroughly research, for instance, the context and background of a directive to locate relevant soft law. If the parties do not explicitly

[78] Case C-28/15 *Koninklijke KPN et al* [2016] EU:C:2016:692, paras 34–38.
[79] ECLI:NL:CBB:2017:213.
[80] Beijen (n 18) 107; Cauffman (n 18) 95.
[81] See O Ştefan, ch 19 in this volume.
[82] Beijen (n 18) 107.
[83] Cauffman (n 18) 93.

refer to soft law and the judges are not already familiar with a particular piece of soft law, the chances that soft law will be used in the judgment are small.[84] Especially in environmental law and competition law, applicants are nevertheless well informed about EU soft law and invoke it, which then increases the relevance of soft law nationally.[85]

Tellingly, the interviewed administrative judge in the context of financial regulation said that despite several cases dealing with aspects of EU financial regulation, they are not aware of EU soft law in this area. However, the same judge did apply soft law instruments in competition cases without any reservations about their legal nature.[86] This finding points to a problem of accessibility of soft law, not to general reluctance towards non-binding instruments. In environmental law, some of the interviewees indeed remarked that they would be willing to apply soft law, but that this will only be possible if one knows it exists in the first place.[87]

A related issue is that while some EU soft law is available in all official languages, other documents are only available in English. Especially when a soft law document is long, complex and technical, the lack of different-language versions makes it difficult for national actors to properly understand and engage with such a document in a deep enough manner.[88] Finally, the interviews revealed that soft law is considered to contribute to transparency to the extent that it helps clarify EU hard law.[89] However, it may also lead to unpredictable policy changes to the detriment of transparency.[90]

Van Dam's hypothesis was that EU guidance documents enhance the transparency of the national implementation process of the underlying directive,[91] but she eventually concluded that the contrary is true and that the use of EU guidance documents remains highly invisible at the national level.[92] Guidance documents may be important during the implementation process, but the problem is that they are not explicitly referred to. Such invisible use of guidance documents has, instead of the expected positive effects, a highly negative effect on transparency.[93]

The use of soft law by courts can contribute to transparency to the extent that the judgment explicitly mentions the soft law document and is clear about its legal status. However, as noted above, the use of soft law by courts is

[84] Beijen (n 18) 107–08.
[85] See, eg, ECLI:NL:RVS:2007:AZ6380, para 2.2 and ECLI:NL:RVS:2009:BH3985, paras 2.4 and 2.5.
[86] Cauffman (n 18) 91.
[87] Beijen (n 18) 107.
[88] ibid 110.
[89] Cauffman (n 18) 95.
[90] ibid.
[91] Van Dam (n 1) 51.
[92] ibid 250.
[93] ibid 251. Some of the guidance documents in van Dam's research were not even published, which limits the possibilities for their transparent use.

unarticulated, with negative consequences for overall transparency.[94] Van Dam also points to an interesting replicative pattern in the judicial use of soft law: once a certain soft law document has been used in a judgment, it is more likely to be used again.[95] At the same time, a document that has never been invoked in court may remain unknown, even though substantially it might be even more relevant than the cited piece of soft law. Luijendijk and Senden also argue that judges are extremely succinct and sparse in terms of words when it comes to the use of soft law.[96] The justification for its use is often lacking altogether or is very limited.

Although soft law potentially increases transparency, in practice its potential is not realised. Soft law is not either used at all due to problems with the accessibility of soft law or its use is invisible and inaccessible to the observer. The potential merits of soft law are thus not fully exploited.

B. Legality

A second principle which plays a role in van Dam's research is the principle of legality pursuant to which government must act on the basis of a legislative empowerment and in accordance with the law. At the EU level, this means that the EU institutions 'shall only act within the limits of the competences conferred upon it by the Member States in the Treaties'.[97] To illustrate what this means in the context of soft law, consider, for instance, the SoLaR social policy soft law, which includes two recommendations. Recommendations are recognised as a legal instrument in Article 288 TFEU with due respect to its non-bindingness. Due to legislative empowerment, recommendations do not pose particular problems as regards legality. There is a legal basis for their adoption, and the legal status of recommendations is clear. However, for others forms of soft law, there is no legal basis in the Treaties. This means that soft law cannot in principle be used to create new obligations for the Member States.[98] In the national context, the principle of legality as applied to soft law means that national authorities can only use soft law as an aid for implementation, but must remain vigilant about its non-binding nature. National courts need to respect this non-bindingness as well.[99]

The SoLaR research shows that administrative authorities and judges are well aware of the non-bindingness of EU soft law.[100] At the same time, they are

[94] ibid 258; Cauffman (n 18) 95; Cauffman and Philipsen (n 21) 142.

[95] Van Dam (n 1) 275; Beijen (n 18) 108.

[96] Luijendijk and Senden (n 25) 348. For the same point with regard to the French jurisprudential style, see N Rubio and O Ştefan, ch 8 in this volume.

[97] Article 5(2) of the Treaty on European Union (TEU). See also van Dam (n 1) 53–54.

[98] Van Dam (n 1) 56.

[99] ibid 57.

[100] Cauffman (n 18) 94; Beijen (n 18) 107.

inclined to use soft law, unless there are serious doubts about its factual correctness. If soft law appears to go beyond the boundaries of hard law, it would be a good enough reason for the national judge to disregard soft law.[101] However, none of the respondents could think of an example in which this would have been the case.[102] As noted above in terms of environmental soft law, national courts may use EU guidance documents as an interpretation aid instead of referring the case to the CoJ for a preliminary ruling.[103] This arguably increases the power of the Commission and at the same time decreases the role of the CoJ as a final arbiter on the interpretation of EU law.[104] One may well argue that the non-bindingness of soft law is exactly the reason why it would be good to refer cases to the CoJ.[105]

Van Dam argues that the normative relevance of soft law is taken for granted and soft law is applied as if it were binding.[106] One interesting sign of such attitudes is that rather than referring cases to the CoJ, judges turn to (interpretative) soft law for guidance and inspiration.[107] This is despite the judges emphatically acknowledging the non-bindingness of soft law and mentioning it in judgments.[108] This judicial behaviour challenges the argument about the non-bindingness of soft law and may end up eroding the prerogative of the CoJ to give the final interpretation on EU law.[109] Although soft law seems to remain within the limits of EU hard law and is generally tagged and described as non-binding, it does have binding effects in practice, potentially leading to an erosion of the interpretative authority of the CoJ.

V. CONCLUSION

Overall, EU soft law is well received and accepted in the Netherlands, both by judges and the administration. At the same time, most actors stress the fact that soft law is not binding. They do not feel obliged to use soft law and see it merely as a (welcome) aid in the interpretation of EU law, using it when convenient and apt, given the particularities of the case in hand. This does not speak for coherence and predictability. Furthermore, soft law is not always explicitly mentioned in judgments and, if it is mentioned, the legal status typically remains unaddressed and unclear. Emblematic in this sense is the *Koninlijke* case. This shows that the placement of EU soft law amongst the legal sources in the Netherlands

[101] Beijen (n 18) 107; Cauffman (n 18) 96.
[102] Beijen (n 18) 107.
[103] ibid 108–09.
[104] Van den Brink and van Dam (n 20) 26.
[105] Luijendijk and Senden (n 25) 351.
[106] Van Dam (n 1) 252.
[107] ibid 260.
[108] ibid 259–60.
[109] Van Dam (n 1) 261.

is perhaps at a less 'mature' stage than the Dutch soft law correspondent, the *beleidsregels*, for which a mandatory comply-or-explain paradigm is in force.

The accessibility of soft law is perceived as a major issue – the finding that came through both in SoLaR interviews and van Dam's research. It can be difficult to find relevant soft law, because the Commission as an institution that issues most EU soft law does not follow any pattern in publishing it, nor is there a search engine like EUR-Lex for soft law in particular. If soft law is hard to find, it is likely that national judges or the administration do not apply it in cases for which it might be relevant. This is a waste of a good effort to provide clarity through soft law. From this point of view, a lesson could be learned from the *beleidsregels*, which are published and easily accessible.

Finally, questions are raised in the Netherlands about the legality of soft law. For most cases of EU soft law, there is no explicit legal basis in the law for its adoption, which means that soft law cannot be used to impose new obligations on the Member States. Usually this does not cause particular problems because, and with due respect for the principle of legality, (interpretative) soft law stays within the boundaries provided by underlying hard law. However, soft law has in practice more normative force than its non-binding character gives away and might even end up trumping the role of the Court of Justice as the ultimate interpreter of EU law in the minds of the Dutch judges and authorities.

13

The Uneasy Reception of EU Soft Law in the Slovenian Legal Order

MATEJ AVBELJ AND KATARINA VATOVEC*

I. INTRODUCTION

As this volume attests, soft law mechanisms have been on the rise over the last decades in the legal order of the EU. Consequently, the legal orders of the Member States could not have escaped unaffected from this phenomenon either. However, the reception of soft law across the EU has varied. This chapter concentrates on the status and role of EU soft law in the legal order of the Republic of Slovenia. Slovenia joined the EU during the big bang enlargement in May 2004. At the time, it was portrayed as the best disciple and a role model for all other acceding (and yet to accede) Central and Eastern European States. While this portrait, as has been argued in greater detail elsewhere,[1] did not do full justice to the actual state of affairs in Slovenia, this chapter queries whether Slovenia could be considered a role model in the field of reception of soft law too.

The response, as we shall see, is a mixed one. This is, above all, due to the legacy of the legal systems to which Slovenia has been historically wedded. A combination of Kelsenian pure theory of law in practice and five decades of totalitarian communism have left an indelible mark on the legal culture (mind-set) of institutional actors in Slovenia, with more than significant consequences for the status and role of EU law in general, as well as its soft law in particular. While the overall nature of EU law is certainly specific and continues to be contested in many corners of political and academic life,[2] the specificity of EU

* The research for this chapter has also benefited from the support of the Slovenian Research Agency within the framework of the research project No J5-1791, 'An Integral Theory on the Future of the European Union'.

[1] M Avbelj and J Letnar Černič, *The Impact of European Institutions on the Rule of Law and Democracy, Slovenia and Beyond* (Oxford, Hart Publishing, 2020).

[2] M Avbelj, 'The Perplexing Novelty of European Integration' (2007) *University College Dublin Law Review, Symposium Edition* 65.

soft law instruments is accentuated even more. In the EU institutions themselves, the jury is still out on the advantages and disadvantages of soft law.[3] On the one hand, there are those who stress the strengths of soft law, citing its flexibility and efficiency.[4] On the other hand, there are others who insist that these strengths are offset by the concerns for soft law's democratic legitimacy, by the transparency of soft law-making procedures and even by the risks for 'detrimental effects on Community legislation and institutional balance',[5] which eventually speak in favour of approaching EU soft law with caution.[6]

Against this backdrop, the present chapter will analyse the use of EU soft law instruments in Slovenia by paying specific attention to four regulatory fields: competition law and State aid, financial regulation, environmental protection, and social policy. The analysis derives from a threefold methodology that was used in the European Network of Soft Law Research (SoLaR) project. First, the relevant literature on soft law in Slovenia, albeit scarce, was looked into. Second, the research consulted the website of the Legal Information System of the Republic of Slovenia (LIS) and in particular the official judiciary database 'sodnapraksa.si' using a variety of relevant keywords. The LIS provides free and comprehensive access to the regulations constituting the legal order of the Republic of Slovenia. For example, it consists of the online version of the Official Gazette of the Republic of Slovenia, official and unofficial consolidated texts of regulations, but also decisions of the Constitutional Court and case law of the Supreme Court, higher courts and the Administrative Court. However, the database does not contain the first instance courts' decisions and sometimes the online publication of judgments might be slightly delayed. For the case law of the Constitutional Court, its web portal was used as well.[7] Third, interviews were conducted with judges as well as with the officials or public servants at the relevant administrative authorities and/or independent regulatory agencies.[8]

The chapter aims to show how the existence and relatively widespread use of soft law instruments in the EU influence the Slovenian legal order and how these instruments are used by Slovenian courts and administrative authorities in the researched areas. The national reception of EU soft law is therefore observed through the prism of judiciary and administrative authorities as well as their case law or the lack of it. In what follows, the chapter is, accordingly, divided

[3] G Shaffer and MA Pollack, 'Hard vs Soft Law: Alternatives, Complements and Antagonists in International Governance' (2010) 94 *Minnesota Law Review* 717.

[4] L Senden, *Soft Law in European Community Law* (Oxford, Hart Publishing, 2004).

[5] European Parliament, 'European Parliament resolution on 4 September 2007 on institutional and legal implications of the use of 'soft law' instruments (2007/2028/(INI))' statement AA 1 [2008] OJ C187E/75.

[6] ibid.

[7] See www.us-rs.si.

[8] In total, 18 interviews were conducted with Slovenian judges and administrative officials and public servants acting across four researched policy fields.

into five sections. The essential traits of the Slovenian legal order are presented first. Sections III–V discuss the legislative, judicial and administrative reception of EU soft law in Slovenia. The sixth and final section concludes.

II. THE SLOVENIAN LEGAL ORDER IN CONTEXT

To understand the reception of EU soft law in the Slovenian legal order, the latter must be contextualised first. The Slovenian legal order forms part of a broader Central European legal family. Its legal culture has long combined the negative legacy of Kelsen's pure theory of law[9] – manifesting as excessive legal formalism – with the practice of totalitarian communist regimes. As a result, law in Central Europe is still considered a pure science of its own. Legal acts and decisions are perceived to be exclusively generated in a hierarchical manner, almost automatically cascading down from the *Grundnorm* to statutes, by-laws and individual judicial and administrative acts. This creates a sealed-off hierarchical legal system, which must be strictly separated both from politics and morals – eg, from non-legal norms – hence leaving no or very little theoretical and practical room for soft law.[10] Consequently, the attitude of the Slovenian legal community towards the use of soft law has traditionally been reserved or at least indifferent.

This has been gradually changing since the country's accession to the EU in 2004. At the time, Slovenia successfully adopted the *acquis communautaire* as the 'genetic inheritance' of the EU,[11] a comprehensive body of EU law,[12] including its soft law instruments such as communications, resolutions, guidance notes, rules of conduct and practice, and action plans.[13] The accession of Slovenia to the EU required amendments to the Slovenian Constitution. The most important amendment was Article 3a, which regulates the relationship between domestic law and the EU legal system. This provision – although providing no textual recognition of the EU – lays down the conditions under which Slovenia became part of the EU, essentially stating that EU law is valid and shall be applied in Slovenia in accordance with the EU's own fundamental principles. As a result, on a theoretical level at least, EU law influences widely and intensively the domestic legal system. The reception of EU law has namely

[9] H Kelsen, *Pure Theory of Law* (Clark, NJ, Law Book Exchange Ltd, 2002).

[10] See M Avbelj, 'Central Europe as a Legal Phenomenon' (2015) 7 *Journal on European Perspectives of the Western Balkans* 53. See also M Bobek (ed), *Central European Judges under the European Influence: The Transformative Power of the EU Revisited* (Oxford, Hart Publishing, 2015).

[11] C Delcourt, 'The *Acquis Communautaire*: Has the Concept Had its Day?' (2001) 38 *CML Rev* 829, 869–70.

[12] ibid 853.

[13] See also K Engelbrekt, 'The Impact of Enlargement on Institutional Integrity in Central and Eastern Europe' in C Chiva and D Phinnemore (eds), *The European Union's 2007 Enlargement* (New York, Routledge, 2012) 19, 21.

been slow, and it has taken, in particular on the part of the judiciary, almost a decade to ensure that EU law is used not just more frequently, but also correctly.[14] Initially, not just EU soft law, but EU law as such, was almost absent from the practices of public authorities, and the academic discussions of EU law were also scarce, almost non-existent.[15] Even at present, no critical overview of the literature discussing the ways in which EU soft law is being used by judiciary and by national authorities exists.

III. LEGISLATIVE RECEPTION OF EU SOFT LAW

Legislative acts in Slovenia, unlike in the case of transposition of EU hard law, generally do not mention that they are transposing a certain soft law instrument.[16] But there are several unconnected exceptions that challenge this rule of thumb. The Electronic Communications Act,[17] for example, makes a direct reference to guidelines and recommendations of the European Commission, although not pointing to a specific soft law instrument.[18] It is therefore difficult to ascertain whether EU soft law is in fact incorporated into national binding law, since a legislative reference to an EU soft law instrument is indirect or tacit and can be established mainly by considering the explanatory notes of a legislative proposal.

[14] M Avbelj, 'Slovensko ustavno pravo v odnosu do prava EU' in I Kaučič (ed), *Dvajset let Ustave Republike Slovenije: pomen ustavnosti in ustavna demokracija* (Ljubljana, Pravna fakulteta, Ustavno sodišče Republike Slovenije, 2012) 341.

[15] To an extent, this has recently changed. See, eg, M Repas, 'Soft Law Instruments and Their Use in Slovenian Local Self-Government' (2015) 13 *Lex Localis – Journal of Local Self Government Annual Conference: Special Issue* 681; V Rošic Feguš, 'The Growing Importance of Soft Law in the EU' (2014) 1 *InterEU Law East: Journal for the International and European Law, Economics and Market Integrations* 145; V Rošic Feguš, *Hibridnost pravnega normiranja v Evropski uniji (Pravni in institucionalni vidiki uporabe mehkega prava in pojav hibridnih pravnih področij)* (Maribor, Maribor University Press, Pravna fakulteta, 2016); R Knez and V Rošic, 'Slovenia' in JH Jans, R Macrory and A-M Moreno Molina (eds), *National Courts and EU Environmental Law* (Amsterdam, Europa Law Publishing, 2013) 355; M Avbelj, 'Pravno varstvo posameznika v upravnem pravu EU' (2014) 14 *Hrvatska i komparativna javna uprava* 851; M Damjan, K Podobnik and A Vlahek (eds), *Izbris kvalificiranih obveznosti bank: pravna analiza primera Kotnik* (Ljubljana, Inštitut za primerjalno pravo pri Pravni fakulteti, 2019).

[16] V Rošic Feguš, 'National Report of the Republic of Slovenia: The Use of EU Soft Law by National Courts and Administration in the Field of EU Competition Law and State Aid' in O Ştefan (ed), 'EU Competition and State Aid Soft Law in the Member States: Finland, France, Germany, Italy, the Netherlands, Slovenia and the UK', (2020) SoLaR Working Paper, https://papers.ssrn.com/sol3/papers.cfm?abstract_id=3667387. See also K Vatovec, 'National Report on Slovenia: The Use of EU Soft Law by National Courts and Administration in the Field of EU Environmental Law' in M Eliantonio and G Lisi (eds), 'EU Environmental Soft Law in the Member States: A Comparative Overview of Finland, France, Germany, Italy, the Netherlands, Slovenia and the UK', (2020) SoLaR Working Paper, https://papers.ssrn.com/sol3/papers.cfm?abstract_id=3656418.

[17] Official Gazette of the Republic of Slovenia Nos 109/12, 110/13, 81/15 and 40/17.

[18] Articles 98–100 of the Electronic Communications Act provide that when assessing significant market power and establishing the relevant market, the Slovenian Agency for Communication Networks and Services shall take into account guidelines and recommendations of the European Commission adopted in this regard. See Rošic Feguš (n 16) 150.

The Agriculture Act[19] partly transposes a number of EU soft law instruments, for example, the 'European Union Guidelines for state aid in the agriculture and forestry sectors and in rural areas 2014 to 2020'.[20]

The Banking Communication[21] was also tacitly transposed into the Slovenian legal order through amendment L to the Banking Act that included writing off equity capital, as well as hybrid capital and subordinated debt.[22] The Commission Recommendation of 7 March 2014 on strengthening the principle of equal pay between men and women through transparency (2014/124/EU)[23] is another example of an EU soft law instrument that is to an important extent incorporated into the binding national legislation and no longer considered as (EU) soft law.[24]

IV. THE JUDICIAL RECEPTION OF EU SOFT LAW

As in most civil law systems, the Slovenian judicial system is composed of ordinary courts and two specialised courts: administrative and labour-social courts, topped by a Supreme Court. The latter's role is to rule as a last instance in criminal and civil cases, commercial lawsuits, administrative review, and labour and social security disputes. Thus, it decides on ordinary and extraordinary legal remedies. It might also perform other functions provided for by law.[25] Slovenia also has a Constitutional Court, although this is not part of the ordinary judiciary. The Constitutional Court Act defines it as 'the highest body of the judicial power for the protection of constitutionality, legality, human rights, and fundamental freedoms'.[26]

The analysis of the available legal databases demonstrates that for a long time, soft law has not played any (meaningful) role before the Slovenian administrative and judicial authorities. The trigger for a real change was the Constitutional

[19] Official Gazette of the Republic of Slovenia Nos 45/08, 57/12, 26/14, 32/15, 27/17 and 22/18.

[20] European Commission, 'European Union Guidelines for State aid in the agriculture and forestry sectors and in rural areas 2014 to 2020' [2014] OJ C204/1.

[21] European Commission, 'Communication from the Commission on the application, from 1 August 2013, of State aid rules to support measures in favour of banks in the context of the financial crisis ("Banking Communication")' [2013] OJ C216/1.

[22] ZBan-1L (Official Gazette of the Republic of Slovenia No 96/13). See also Rošic Feguš (n 16) 152.

[23] European Commission, 'Commission Recommendation of 7 March 2014 on strengthening the principle of equal pay between men and women through transparency (2014/124/EU)' [2014] OJ L69/112.

[24] G Justinek, 'National Report on Slovenia: The Use of EU Soft Law by National Courts and Administration in the Field of EU Social Policy' in M Hartlapp (ed), 'Studying Soft Law Effects in Social Policy' (2020) SoLaR Working Paper, https://papers.ssrn.com/sol3/papers.cfm?abstract_id=3668981.

[25] See Courts Act (Official Gazette of the Republic of Slovenia Nos 94/07 – official consolidated text, 45/08, 96/09, 33/11, 63/13, 17/15).

[26] Official Gazette of the Republic of Slovenia No 64/07, art 1.

Court's decision,[27] including the preliminary reference to the Court of Justice of the European Union (CJEU), in the *Kotnik* case.[28] This case concerned the constitutionality of the Slovenian Banking Act,[29] which implemented EU crisis-management mechanisms, including the Banking Communication instructions (soft law) of the European Commission providing burden-sharing (ie, bail-in) measures and the criteria for the compatibility of State aid granted to the financial institutions with the EU internal market rules.[30] By way of the constitutional challenge to the Banking Act, the Banking Communication was indirectly challenged too, which raised the awareness of the existence of EU soft law in Slovenia. Nevertheless, the EU's Banking Communication was escorted by a critique that emphasised faithfulness to the traditional legal understanding, stressed the strict hierarchy of legal norms and warned against the deficiencies of EU soft law, which lacks the properties of the law properly so called.[31] The application of EU soft law by Slovenian courts has thus generally increased over the years, but in the specific policy fields that this research has been concerned with, the number of cases remains small.

In the area of financial regulation, the Administrative Court, for example, adopted two judgments analytically referring to the Joint Guidelines on the prudential assessment of acquisitions and increases of qualifying holdings in the banking, insurance and securities sectors.[32] In other cases, the Joint Guidelines on the prudential assessment of acquisitions and increases of qualifying holdings in the financial sector was frequently relied upon.[33]

In the field of EU environmental law, a judgment was found where the Administrative Court relied, to an important extent, on a European Commission's guidance document stemming from the Habitats Directive, ie, the Guidance document on the strict protection of animal species of Community interest under the Habitats Directive 92/43/EEC.[34] It relied on the guidance document as its source of interpretation of the provision of the Habitats Directive, without awarding it with binding legal effects.

A very limited reliance on EU soft law instruments has been identified in the field of State aid.[35] The Banking Communication was echoed in the decisions

[27] USRS Decision U-I-295/13 of 19.10.2016, ECLI:SI:USRS:2014:U.I.295.13.

[28] Case C-526/14 *Tadej Kotnik and Others v Državni zbor Republike Slovenije* [2016] EU:C:2016:570.

[29] Official Gazette of the Republic of Slovenia No 99/10.

[30] Court of Justice of the European Union, 'The Communication from the Commission on Aid to the Banking Sector is Valid', press release, 19 July 2016, No 80/2016.

[31] J Sladič, 'Ali se lahko soft law EU obravnava kot hard law' (2014) 33 *Pravna praksa* ii.

[32] UPRS Judgment I U 1568/2018-25 of 12.2.2019, ECLI:SI:UPRS:2019:I.U.1568.2018.25; UPRS Judgment I U 1316/2018-26 of 26.3.2019, ECLI:SI:UPRS:2019:I.U.1316.2018.26.

[33] UPRS Order and Judgment I U 2370/2018 of 24.4.2019, ECLI:SI:UPRS:2019:I.U.2370.2018.10, paras 2, 3 and 5; UPRS Judgment I U 1542/2018 of 24.4.2019, ECLI:SI:UPRS:2019:I.U.1542.2018.9, paras 3 and 13.

[34] UPRS Judgment I U 1522/2015, ECLI:SI:UPRS:2016:I.U.1522.2015, 7 July 2016. See in detail Vatovec (n 16) 116–17.

[35] Rošic Feguš (n 16) 155.

of the Supreme Court,[36] whilst its legality was (indirectly) challenged before the Constitutional Court in the above-mentioned *Kotnik* case.[37] There the Constitutional Court, following the CJEU preliminary ruling, recognised that the EU Banking Communication had certain normative effects, which were made part and parcel of a constitutionality review of the disputed Slovenian Banking Act. The Constitutional Court explicitly stated that 'it is impossible to deny the indirect legal effect of the Banking Communication on Member States, as the Communication represents important information for the states as to how the Commission will carry out its competences in the field of the assessment of the admissibility of state aid'.[38] Moreover, 'the content of the Banking Communication is not irrelevant to the Constitutional Court [and] must be taken into account [as] the actual substantive basis [of the national legislation]'.[39]

The reliance on EU soft law instruments has been more frequent in the field of competition law. The Administrative Court used the Guidelines on the applicability of Article 101 of the Treaty on the Functioning of the European Union (TFEU) to horizontal co-operation agreements[40] as a source of interpretation.[41] In the same manner, the Commission Notice on cooperation within Network of Competition Authorities[42] was applied by the Supreme Court.[43] The Guidance on the Commission's enforcement priorities in applying Article 82 of the EC Treaty to abusive exclusionary conduct by dominant undertakings (now the Guidance Paper on Article 102)[44] was used in administrative disputes as an additional confirmation of interpretations arising from national legislation.[45] In addition, a judgment of the Supreme Court applies the Guidelines on horizontal agreements as an additional argument for the interpretation otherwise given on the basis on national case law.[46] The Commission Notice on the handling of

[36] VSRS Judgment II Ips 173/2017 of 28.3.2018, ECLI:SI:VSRS:2018:II.IPS.173.2017.

[37] USRS Decision U-I-295/13 of 19.10.2016, ECLI:SI:USRS:2014:U.I.295.13.

[38] ibid para 75.

[39] ibid para 76.

[40] European Commission, 'Communication from the Commission – Guidelines on the applicability of Article 101 of the Treaty on the Functioning of the European Union to horizontal co-operation agreements' [2011] OJ C11/1.

[41] UPRS Judgment I U 1819/2014 of 15.9.2015, ECLI:SI:UPRS:2015:I.U.1819.2014; UPRS Judgment I U 881/2015-23 of 30.5.2017, ECLI:SI:UPRS:2017:I.U.881.2015.23; UPRS Judgment and Decision I U 903/2015 of 13.12.2016, ECLI:SI:UPRS:2016:I.U.903.2015; UPRS Judgment I U 1815/2014 of 27.10.2015, ECLI:SI:UPRS:2015:I.U.1815.2014.

[42] European Commission, 'Commission Notice on cooperation within the Network of Competition Authorities' [2004] OJ C101/43.

[43] VSRS Judgment G 25/2011 of 27.9.2011, ECLI:SI:VSRS:2011:G.25.2011, para 8.

[44] European Commission, 'Communication from the Commission – Guidance on the Commission's enforcement priorities in applying Article 82 of the EC Treaty to abusive exclusionary conduct by dominant undertakings' [2009] OJ C45/7.

[45] UPRS Judgment I U 412/2015-50 of 14.11.2017, ECLI:SI:UPRS:2017:I.U.412.2015.50 para 33. See also UPRS Judgment I U 1871/2013 of 9.12.2014, ECLI:SI:UPRS:2014:I.U.1871.2013.

[46] VSRS Judgment X Ips 70/2010, ECLI:SI:VSRS:2010:X.IPS.70.2010.

complaints by the Commission under Articles 81 and 82 of the EC Treaty[47] was also relied upon.[48]

There are also cases where EU soft law was invoked by the parties, but it was ignored by the court. For example, the Guidelines on vertical restraints were invoked by the parties, but the Administrative Court based its judgment solely on national competition rules, simply ignoring the existence of guidelines.[49] In two cases, the defendant invoked the Commission Guidelines on the application of Article 101 TFEU for horizontal agreements, but the Administrative Court based its argumentation on national competition law provisions, Article 101 TFEU and the case law of the CJEU, disregarding soft law.[50]

Comparing the outcome of the case law research exclusively in the four policy fields, it can be concluded that EU soft law instruments are much more frequently applied in the field of competition law and State aid than in the other fields under research. This can be explained by the fact that soft law by its very nature plays a much more important role in the field of competition law. The lack of references to EU soft law mechanisms by Slovenian courts can, to some extent, be explained by the fact that there is no need for such references, because soft law mechanisms are already incorporated into the binding national legal acts.[51] For example, the Joint Guidelines on the prudential assessment of acquisitions and increases of qualifying holdings in the financial sector; the Guide to Taking Account of Social Considerations in Public Procurement (Buying Social); the Commission Recommendation of 20 February 2013 'Investing in children: breaking the cycle of disadvantage' (2013/112/EU);[52] and the Commission Recommendation of 7 March 2014 on strengthening the principle of equal pay between men and women through transparency (2014/124/EU)[53] are to an important extent incorporated into the binding national legislation and no longer considered as (EU) soft law.[54]

As indicated above, the Slovenian legal culture in general is less inclined to use soft law instruments.[55] The doubts relating to the validity and application of EU soft law are sometimes even explicitly raised by the courts. The High

[47] European Commission, 'Commission Notice on the handling of complaints by the Commission under Articles 81 and 82 of the EC Treaty' [2004] OJ C101/65.

[48] UPRS Judgment I U 1871/2013 of 9.12.2014, ECLI:SI:UPRS:2014:I.U.1871.2013.

[49] UPRS Judgment I U 306/2015 of 5.1.2016, ECLI:SI:UPRS:2016:I.U.306.2015, para 25.

[50] UPRS Judgment and Order I U 1800/2013 of 10.4.2014, ECLI:SI:UPRS:2014:I.U.1800.2013; UPRS Judgment I U 786/2013 of 22.4.2014, ECLI:SI:UPRS:2014:I.U.1786.2013.

[51] M Avbelj, 'The Implementation of ESMA's guidelines in Slovenia' in M Avbelj (ed), 'EU Financial Regulation Soft Law in the Member States: Finland, France, Germany, Italy, the Netherlands, Slovenia and the UK' (2020) SoLaR Working Paper, https://papers.ssrn.com/sol3/papers.cfm?abstract_id=3668793.

[52] European Commission, 'Commission Recommendation of 20 February 2013 Investing in children: breaking the cycle of disadvantage (2013/112/EU)' [2013] OJ L59/5.

[53] OJ L69/112 (n 23).

[54] Justinek (n 24) 91.

[55] Vatovec (n 16) 118.

Court in Ljubljana, for example, concurred with the first instance court, in that that it did not have to respond to defendants' statement regarding the recommendation of the European Commission because this act 'is not of a binding nature and thus the defendant cannot refer to it'.[56] The Supreme Court similarly refrained from using consultation documents,[57] draft guidelines on quantifying harm in actions for damages based on breaches of Article 101 or 102 TFEU, and the draft directive[58] arguing that 'the legal order of the EU does not determine that national courts must be bound by consultation documents, their drafts and draft directives'.[59] Indeed, 'national courts of EU member states are not bound by these and similar documents even when deciding in a case in which EU law should be applied next to the national law'.[60]

Nonetheless, there are also judicial statements recognising and attaching some importance to EU soft law instruments. An example of this is a decision of the Slovenian Supreme Court, in which it stated that while '[it] does not deny the legal importance to the Commission Notice, it nevertheless stresses that in the examination of substantive law it is bound solely by legally binding EU acts and the relevant case law of the CJEU'.[61] This view, as we have seen above in the discussion of the *Kotnik* case, is shared by the Constitutional Court that regarded the Banking Communication as having an indirect legal effect, conveying important information as to how the European Commission would exercise its competences in the field of State aid.[62]

All in all, it is clear that the use of EU soft law instruments in the case law of Slovenian courts is inconsistent, which certainly does not facilitate research. At times, judgments explicitly mention the specific EU soft law instrument only in the Slovenian language (seldom in abbreviation or more often in its official name).[63] Sometimes, but much rarely, judgments address the particular

[56] VSL Judgment II Cp 1317/2012 of 21.11.2012. ECLI:SI:VSLJ:2012:II.Cp.1317.2012, para 9.

[57] European Commission, 'Green Paper – Damages actions for breach of the EC antitrust rules' COM (2005) 672 final; European Commission, 'White Paper on Damages actions for breach of the EU antitrust rules' COM (2008) 165 final.

[58] European Commission, 'Proposal for a Directive of the European Parliament and of the Council on certain rules governing actions for damages under national law for infringements of the competition law provisions of the Member States and of the European Union' COM/2013/0404 final – 2013/0185 (COD).

[59] VSRS Judgment III Ips 101/2015 of 29.3.2016, ECLI:SI:VSRS:2016:III.IPS.101.2015, para 35.

[60] ibid.

[61] VSRS Judgment G 7/2013 of 3.12.2013, ECLI:SI:VSRS:2013:G.7.2013, para 33.

[62] USRS Decision U-I-295/13 of 19.10.2016, ECLI:SI:USRS:2014:U.I.295.13, para 75.

[63] eg, UPRS Judgment I U 1542/2018 of 24.4.2019, ECLI:SI:UPRS:2019:I.U.1542.2018.9, para 3; UPRS Judgment II U 431/2009 of 2.10.2019. ECLI:SI:UPRS:2019:II.U.431.2019.6; UPRS Judgment I U 648/2014 of 21.5.2014, ECLI:SI:UPRS:2014:I.U.648.2014; VSRS Judgment II Ips 173/2017 of 28.3.2018, ECLI:SI:VSRS:2018:II.IPS.173.2017; UPRS Judgment I U 630/2011 of 18.1.2012, ECLI:SI:UPRS:2012:I.U.630.2011; UPRS Judgment I U 1819/2014 of 15.9.2015, ECLI:SI:UPRS:2015:I.U.1819.2014; VSRS Judgment G 25/2011 of 27.9.2011, ECLI:SI:VSRS:2011:G.25.2011; UPRS Judgment I U 423/2015-48 of 9.1.2018, ECLI:SI:UPRS:2018:I.U.423.2015.48.

instrument in its Slovenian and English versions.[64] There are cases where judgments include a link to the webpage where the instrument was published.[65] Very rarely, they explicitly name the authority adopting the particular instrument.[66] Soft law instruments are sometimes cited in the footnote,[67] but more often in the reasoning of the court.[68]

For all these reasons, and to determine the real effect of EU soft law in Slovenia, our research benefited from the interviews with judges. These have demonstrated that judges are well aware of EU soft law instruments, but in principle and typically base their decisions exclusively on the binding law.[69] As one respondent explained: 'A judge, who is instructed to work on the basis of Constitution and Law, can hardly refer to a non-binding soft law instrument.'[70] Nevertheless, and in particular taking the authority of an issuing institution into account, EU soft law may be considered too.[71] Interviews confirmed that even where the cases do not exhibit the use of EU soft law, the judges do consult or consider it in their *in camera* deliberations, typically using it as a source of inspiration or as one of the many arguments for their decisions.[72]

On the basis of the researched case law and the interviews conducted, it can be concluded that the judicial use of EU soft law instruments in Slovenia has many faces. It stretches from the straightforward refusal to apply it, over ignorance of EU soft law, to the cases in which the latter is used as an inspiration, a tool of interpretation or a direct source of law through reliance on national or EU case law. Whereas the interviewees, judges of the Administrative Court, noted that the parties very rarely, if at all, invoke soft law, the researched case law proves that EU soft law instruments are mainly explicitly mentioned in judgments when they are invoked by parties to the procedure.[73] The cases mentioning soft law show that EU soft law is typically mentioned in passing. The case law also demonstrates that Slovenian courts never perceive soft law as an autonomous source of rights and obligations, and that the judiciary often does not provide reasoning or argumentation for relying on or not referring to EU soft law instruments. There are, however, some cases which show that EU

[64] UPRS Judgment I U 1568/2018-25 of 12.2.2019, ECLI:SI:UPRS:2019:I.U.1568.2018.25, para 6; UPRS Judgment I U 1522/2015, ECLI:SI:UPRS:2016:I.U.1522.2015 of 7.7.2016, para 12; UPRS Judgment I U 1871/2013 of 9.12.2014, ECLI:SI:UPRS:2014:I.U.1871.2013.

[65] UPRS Judgment I U 1568/2018-25 of 12.2.2019, ECLI:SI:UPRS:2019:I.U.1568.2018.25, para 6.

[66] UPRS Judgment I U 1568/2018-25 of 12.2.2019, ECLI:SI:UPRS:2019:I.U.1568.2018.25, para 6; UPRS Judgment I U 1542/2018 of 24.4.2019, ECLI:SI:UPRS:2019:I.U.1542.2018.9.

[67] VSRS Judgment X Ips 70/2010, ECLI:SI:VSRS:2010:X.IPS.70.2010.

[68] eg, UPRS Judgment I U 1542/2018 of 24.4.2019, ECLI:SI:UPRS:2019:I.U.1542.2018.9; USRS Decision No U-I-295/13 of 19.10.2016, ECLI:SI:USRS:2014:U.I.295.13.

[69] Avbelj (n 51) 100; Vatovec (n 16) 119.

[70] Justinek (n 24) 94.

[71] Avbelj (n 51) 101.

[72] Vatovec (n 16) 119, 121.

[73] See, eg, UPRS Judgment I U 1568/2018-25 of 12.2.2019, ECLI:SI:UPRS:2019:I.U.1568.2018.25; UPRS Judgment I U 1316/2018-26 of 26.3.2019, ECLI:SI:UPRS:2019:I.U.1316.2018.26; UPRS Judgment I U 648/2014 of 21.5.2014, ECLI:SI:UPRS:2014:I.U.648.2014.

soft law is applied in the same manner as hard law, serving as a legal source for the definition of a certain term (for example, for the definition of 'relevant market') or serving as a back-up for the argumentation otherwise adopted on the basis of national law, national case law, case law of the CJEU or decisions of the European Commission.[74] This means that, to a significant extent, EU soft law functions as an extra argument in legal reasoning, which is mainly or exclusively based on hard law. The role of EU soft law instruments in Slovenia is thus essentially ancillary and instrumental,[75] but it keeps growing.

Therefore, it does not come as a surprise that the advantages of the use of soft law, such as limiting discretion and offering additional arguments for a more compelling use of a particular binding legal act,[76] have frequently been quoted by the interviewed judges. It has also been argued that soft law contributes to a greater degree of harmonisation inside the EU.[77] The application of EU soft law instruments hinges on, first, its persuasiveness and, second, its contribution to the reasoning in a concrete case.[78] The argumentative strength of a soft law instrument also determines its practical relevance.[79] Judges of the Administrative Court, for example, did find many positive consequences of applying soft law instruments. For them, soft law has been increasingly relevant when constructing legislative acts that are highly technical and complex; they have allowed for soft law's procedural impact, changing a course of a procedure in a given case.[80] They have, for example, even noted that EU soft law can shift the substantive course of action by offering an improved definition of some contested legal concepts.[81] It also turned out that the openness of judges towards soft law depends on their exposure to good practices abroad or to the peer pressure by the international judicial colleagues.[82] Several judges thus identified soft law as a catalyst for successful international cooperation, finding it well suited to deal with the complexity of European affairs and their diversity, but not in regulating sensitive sectors and in situations requiring swift action.[83]

V. ADMINISTRATIVE RECEPTION OF EU SOFT LAW

If Slovenian judges are thus relatively reserved towards the use of EU soft law, their peers in the national administration have been much more open to it.[84]

[74] Rošic Feguš (n 16) 160.
[75] Avbelj (n 51) 101.
[76] ibid; Vatovec (n 16) 119.
[77] Avbelj (n 51) 101.
[78] ibid.
[79] ibid.
[80] ibid; Vatovec (n 16) 119.
[81] Avbelj (n 51) 101.
[82] ibid.
[83] ibid 102.
[84] Vatovec (n 16) 118.

This is the main general finding stemming from the interviews conducted with public officials.[85] Nevertheless, the research across different fields of law has revealed quite a significant variation in the administration's attitude to EU soft law.

In the field of financial regulation, the main administrative authority is the Slovenian Securities Market Agency. This Agency is the competent authority in terms of paragraph 3 of Article 16 of Regulation No 1095/2010[86] to confirm whether it complies or intends to comply with an issued guideline or recommendation. The Agency decides on the application of individual guidelines and recommendations of ESMA and accepts them or rejects them in whole or in part. This decision is published in the Official Gazette of the Republic of Slovenia. The applicable guidelines are then published in the Slovenian language and are thus accessible on the webpage of the Agency.[87] However, the Agency declined to participate in the research project.[88]

The competent national authority in the field of environmental law is the Ministry of the Environment and Spatial Planning. Certain guidance documents stemming from the selected directives in the field of EU environmental law are published on the webpage of the Ministry. As a rule, it is possible to access them in its original (English) language or, in some cases, their translations.[89] The interviews confirmed that the Ministry and its public servants consider the guidance documents and discuss their contents, pointing out that they do so also at the European Commission's suggestion.[90] The interviewees at the Ministry cited many advantages of EU soft law, stressing in particular that it facilitates the interpretation and application of increasingly broad and complex EU environmental regulation.[91] They also indicated that they use soft law instruments rather pragmatically, especially when the European Commission refers to them.[92] None of the interviewees considered soft law instruments to be a valid source of law. The deficiencies of EU soft law, such as the lack of transparency, accountability and democratic legitimacy, were pointed out.[93] The fact

[85] Interviews were conducted with the senior legal adviser of the Slovenian Central Bank (financial regulation); senior public officials from the Ministry of the Environment and Spatial Planning, and the Office of the Government for Legislation (environmental protection); an official working at the Administrative Court, an Officer at the Slovenian Competition Protection Agency and an Officer at the Ministry of Finance (competition law and State aid); the President of the National Review Commission for Reviewing Public Procurement Award Procedures, the Director of Public Procurement Directorate at the Ministry of Public Administration, and a senior public official at the Ministry of Labour, Family, Social Affairs and Equal Opportunities (social policy).

[86] Regulation (EU) No 1095/2010 of the European Parliament and of the Council of 24 November 2010 establishing a European Supervisory Authority [2010] OJ L331/84.

[87] See www.a-tvp.si/smernice-esma/veljavne-smernice-esma.

[88] Avbelj (n 51) 100.

[89] Vatovec (n 16) 115.

[90] ibid 118.

[91] ibid 119, 120.

[92] ibid 120.

[93] ibid 121.

that many EU soft law instruments are available only in English and that they are adopted only after the deadline for the transposition of EU measures has expired was also criticised.[94]

The adoption of the administrative decisions in the field of competition and State aid lies within the competence of the Slovenian Competition Protection Agency (for competition) and the Ministry of Finance (for State aid). The research of the decisions of the Competition Protection Agency published online shows that EU soft law instruments are frequently mentioned in their decisions.[95] The same is true of the Ministry of Finance, which confirms a regular use of EU soft law mechanisms in the field of State aid, typically as a legal basis for the explanation of specific terms, criteria and elements of State aid.[96] Soft law is used alone or together with hard law, without discussing its binding character or the lack thereof. In many instances in the field of competition and State aid, soft law is used in the same way as a statute or other binding legislation either simply by applying the relevant soft law provision (which is normally the case) or with additional explanation that these are EU rules in the field of State aid.[97]

The Slovenian Competition Protection Agency regularly recognises legal and practical effects of soft law and it uses such instruments in two different ways.[98] First, in the majority of decisions, soft law is used together with the primary and secondary EU law and the national competition rules as a source of interpretation of certain terms or prohibitions; soft law in these situations is used for the purposes of interpretation.[99] Second, soft law can be used as a supplementary aid to confirm interpretation or argumentation given on the basis of hard law (EU or national), decisions of the European Commission or case law of the CJEU.[100] In these cases, the Agency first defines concepts and uses arguments as they transpire from hard law or court case law, and then it backs up such interpretation by relying on EU soft law. This was the case, for example, in a decision[101] where a definition of the relevant market was first given on the basis of the decisions of the European Commission and then such interpretation was confirmed with reference to soft law.[102] The research of the

[94] ibid.

[95] Rošic Feguš (n 16) 160.

[96] ibid 152.

[97] ibid 153.

[98] ibid 156–57.

[99] ibid 157.

[100] ibid 158.

[101] Decision of the Slovenian Competition Protection Agency No 306-35/2005-98, dated 28 May 2008.

[102] European Commission, 'Commission Recommendation of 9 October 2014 on relevant product and service markets within the electronic communications sector susceptible to ex ante regulation in accordance with Directive 2002/21/EC of the European Parliament and of the Council on a common regulatory framework for electronic communications networks and services (2014/710/EU)' [2014] OJ L295/79. See also Rošic Feguš (n 16) 162.

administrative practice further showed that 'there are no decisions in which the use of soft law would be denied or not recognised if referred to by the parties, and there are no decisions where administrative authorities would claim not to be bound by soft law due to its non-binding effect'.[103] The attitude of national authorities towards soft law in the field of competition and State aid is hence positive, confirming the advantages of soft law, such as its flexibility and fast adoption.[104] It is believed that soft law is appropriate for administrative use, it acts as a catalyst for successful international cooperation, and is well suited to deal with the complexity of EU affairs and partly to regulate sensitive sectors.[105] Among the disadvantages of EU soft law in this field, the widening of discretion at the expense of the institutional and constitutional balance within the EU was pointed out.[106]

Finally, in the field of social policy, administrative authorities have also exhibited a high level of awareness and good knowledge of the relevant EU soft law mechanisms, and they have also reported a frequent use of EU soft law.[107] The public officials stressed both the importance and utility of various EU soft law mechanisms, especially those drafted by the European Commission, whose work is therefore closely followed.[108] Soft law has been positively perceived as a means of facilitating interpretation and application (of the too-rigid) EU law.[109] On the other hand, the growing scope of soft law might also increase the complexity of the legal regulation and hence detract from its clarity and predictability.[110]

VI. CONCLUSION

The research and conducted interviews demonstrate that EU soft law is mostly welcome in administrative practice, whereas Slovenian courts show a much more cautious approach due to the embedded strict positivist legal system. Dealing with EU soft law instruments also seems dependent on the official position each interviewee holds and their academic background. The use of EU soft law instruments is steadily increasing in importance in the Slovenian legal system. There was no case law in the researched areas a few years ago, but the situation is now gradually changing. EU soft law is gaining momentum in the Slovenian legal order. However, it can be expected that with its more frequent use, more deficiencies would be noticed.

[103] Rošic Feguš (n 16) 167.
[104] ibid 173.
[105] ibid.
[106] ibid.
[107] Justinek (n 24) 94.
[108] ibid 95.
[109] ibid 100.
[110] ibid.

14

In Search of Symmetry Lost
European and Spanish Soft Law before the Spanish Authorities

LUIS ARROYO JIMÉNEZ AND JOSÉ MARÍA RODRÍGUEZ DE SANTIAGO*

I. INTRODUCTION

ONE OF THE defining roles of EU soft law is to enhance the effectiveness and homogeneity of EU law's enforcement.[1] Soft law measures serve, amongst other things, to provide guidance to domestic authorities in charge of enforcing EU law, thereby reconciling the application of legally binding instruments throughout the EU.[2] However, there are various factors that can lessen soft law's homogenising effect,[3] one of them being that Member States can award soft law provisions a different nature, effects and scope. The purpose of this chapter is to describe how the Spanish administrative and judicial authorities implement and apply EU soft law, so that the final results can be compared to those of other Member States. The chapter is structured as follows: first, there is an overview of the methodology and a description of the empirical findings (section II). We then focus on the position of EU and domestic soft law within the Spanish legal order (section III), as well as on its judicial control before national courts (section IV). The subsequent sections address the legal effects of soft law (sections V and VI) and its implications regarding certain general legal principles (section VII). The final section concludes (section VIII).

* This chapter has been written with the support of a grant of the Spanish National Research Plan (PGC2018-101476-B-I00).

[1] L Senden and T van den Brink, *Checks and Balances of EU Soft Law Rule-Making* (Strasbourg, European Parliament, 2012) 14.

[2] See O Ştefan, ch 19 in this volume.

[3] Senden and van den Brink (n 1) 17.

II. METHODOLOGY

The methodology followed in this chapter is twofold. First, a doctrinal analysis of the position of soft law within Spanish law will be provided, along with an empirical analysis of the application of EU soft law by the administrative and judicial authorities. The first step entails examining Spanish legal provisions as well as scholarly and case law doctrine on soft law measures. It should be noted that the status of soft law within the Spanish legal order has not been established exclusively by reference to EU law. Indeed, long before Spain joined the European Communities, administrative law in Spain already had non-binding administrative instruments or measures with the most diverse forms, names and legal effects. Second, empirical analysis including a case law review and a series of interviews with Spanish officials and judges was carried out.[4] The case law study assesses the impact of selected EU soft law measures in the four European Network of Soft Law Research (SoLaR) policy areas on the case law of Spanish last instance courts.[5] The interviews reveal additional information on how administrative bodies and courts construe and apply soft law.

From a quantitative standpoint, we have found only very few Supreme Court rulings referring to the selected EU soft law measures, and none from the Constitutional Court. Moreover, the results of the case law review are somewhat divergent regarding the four sector-specific areas under analysis. There is a significant inconsistency in Spanish case law between the presence of the selected soft law measures within competition law and in the other policy areas.[6] The Spanish Supreme Court has recognised an interpretative value to several EU soft competition law acts.[7] In particular, we have found explicit references to them in five rulings of the Supreme Court. In turn, there is no mention of the soft law measures within the other three policy areas studied by SoLaR. However, we did find references to other soft law measures in some of these areas.[8] Moreover, Spanish courts often apply the relevant hard law instruments and the case law of the Court of Justice of the European Union (CJEU)

[4] See M Hartlapp and E Korkea-aho, ch 4 in this volume. Interviews were conducted between March 2019 and January 2020. The 11 interviewees have heterogeneous profiles: officials acting as high-level government legal advisors (three), Supreme Court (three) and Constitutional Court law clerks (four) and Justices from the Administrative law Chamber of the Supreme Court (one).

[5] The case law review has focused on Constitutional Court and Supreme Court judgments. We have used the official databases of the Supreme Court (www.poderjudicial.es) and the Constitutional Court (www.tribunalconstitucional.es), as well as the most commonly used private database of Spanish courts case law (www.aranzadidigital.es). The selected areas are environmental protection, social policy, competition law and financial regulation. Within each of them, for the sake of comparability, we have focused on the list of instruments selected for the SoLaR project, searching for their titles and references.

[6] This has been attested to by those interviewees serving as law clerks at the Supreme and Constitutional Courts.

[7] See section V below.

[8] One example of this, relating to the Guidelines on sound remuneration policy issued by the European Banking Authority, will be discussed in section V below.

interpreting them, without explicitly referring to soft law measures taken by EU authorities in these areas.[9]

The interviews we have conducted suggest that this divergence is due to several circumstances. The first relates to how difficult it has become for certain cases to reach higher courts, since the latter are now entitled to pick and choose the cases they hear.[10] The second circumstance concerns the potential incorporation of EU soft law content into binding domestic provisions. In Spain, there is no general policy of EU soft law transposition or incorporation into national law. Nor is dissemination via a website a visible trend throughout the four SoLaR policy areas. However, when EU soft law and domestic hard law overlap, the national hard law provision will subsequently be raised and applied by administrative and judicial authorities, to the detriment of the EU soft law measure.[11] Finally, as some of these soft law instruments embody the Court of Justice case law, it is plausible that courts and parties refer to case law instead of soft law.

III. THE LEGAL NATURE OF SOFT LAW UNDER SPANISH LAW

The position of soft law within Spanish law is similar to its status within the EU legal order.[12] Under Spanish law, soft law measures are conceived of as measures adopted by public authorities that are intended to drive the behaviour of their addressees, yet without laying down legally binding obligations or prohibitions.[13] This definition is rooted in three elements. First, soft law measures are not single-case decisions, but rather contain abstract criteria that will be used for future decision-making. The second defining feature is their steering or directing purpose. There is also a tremendous diversity in this regard.[14] Administrative bodies sometimes impose guidelines for action on other bodies with whom they engage in hierarchical relationships. This has been the underlying rationale of the so-called 'instructions' under Spanish law ever since 1958 (*instrucciones* or *circulares* in Spanish).[15] Article 6(1) of the Act on the Legal Regime of Public

[9] Examples of this will be described in section VI below.

[10] This was stressed by several Supreme and Constitutional Court law clerks, who play a central role in the operation of these selection systems.

[11] One example of this, which will be discussed in section VI below, was offered by one Constitutional Court law clerk.

[12] R Alonso García, 'El soft law comunitario' (2001) 154 *Revista de Administración Pública* 63; L Senden, *Soft Law in European Community Law* (Oxford, Hart Publishing, 2004); HCH Hofmann, GC Rowe and AH Türk, *Administrative Law and Policy of the European Union* (Oxford, Oxford University Press, 2011) 536–86; O Ştefan, *Soft Law in Court. Competition law, State Aid and the Court of Justice of the European Union* (Alphen aan den Rijn, Kluwer Law, 2012).

[13] D Sarmiento, *El soft law administrativo* (Madrid, Civitas, 2008) 89–106.

[14] JA Santamaría Pastor, *Principios de Derecho administrativo español*, vol I (Madrid, Iustel, 2015) 263–65; M Sánchez Morón, *Derecho administrativo. Parte general* (Madrid, Tecnos, 2016) 189–90.

[15] M Moreno Rebato, 'Circulares, instrucciones y órdenes de servicio' (1998) 147 *Revista de Administración Pública* 159; Sarmiento (n 13) 108–11.

Authorities (LRJSP)[16] provides that 'higher bodies will generally be entitled to guide lower bodies' activities by means of instructions and circular notices'. Sometimes, they will jointly lay down action criteria and standards resulting from the cooperation between public authorities.[17] Soft law measures can also be aimed at guiding the future behaviour of the very authorities adopting them, or even at (indirectly) guiding the conduct of private entities or persons within a sector-specific area.[18] In sum, hierarchy, cooperation, self-guidance and sectoral regulation are the four rationales for adopting soft law measures.

The third defining element of soft law is its non-binding nature. As shown below, this does not entail that soft law measures have no legal effects. Rather, it simply means that they lack a legally binding nature.[19] Article 6(2) LRJSP accurately illustrates this defining aspect: 'Failure to comply with instructions … does not by itself affect the validity of acts issued by administrative bodies.' Soft law measures cannot directly invalidate another act or provision, since they do not comprise autonomous validity requirements.[20] This is the standard applied by Spanish courts in order to decide whether certain contested measures amount to soft law provisions or otherwise to administrative rules, both regarding unilateral measures[21] and agreements between various administrative authorities.[22]

A different issue altogether is how to apply this general standard. Concerning its content, both an administrative rule – ie, a regulation passed by the government or by an administrative authority (*reglamento*) – and a soft law instrument provide rules of conduct addressed to the future decision-making body. However, they differ in their formal dimension; if the measure is incorporated into a formal instrument acknowledged as a source of law, it will have a binding effect. Otherwise, such a measure will have no binding force. The authority should assess the advantages and disadvantages of both approaches to guiding administrative action. As a matter of principle, judicial bodies should respect the scope of discretion awarded to the authority to decide how to guide administrative action, therefore simply applying the relevant legal framework for hard or soft law.[23]

[16] Act No 40/2015 on the Legal Regime of Public Authorities, Official Journal No 236, of 2 October 2015 (Ley de Régimen Jurídico del Sector Público).

[17] JM Rodríguez de Santiago, *Los convenios entre Administraciones públicas* (Madrid, Marcial Pons, 1994) *passim*; Sarmiento (n 13) 117–20.

[18] Sarmiento (n 13) 120–33.

[19] See N Xanthoulis, ch 18 in this volume.

[20] Sarmiento (n 13) 164–167. Nevertheless, non-compliance with a given soft law measure can trigger the application of other provisions with such invalidating effects or other legal consequences. See Sarmiento (n 13) 212–13; and section VI below.

[21] Judgments of the Supreme Court of 19 December 2018 (cassation appeal no 31/2018); and of 26 November 2015 (cassation appeal no 31/2018).

[22] Supreme Court Judgment of 2 December 2 2013 (cassation appeal no 4479/2010).

[23] JM Rodríguez de Santiago, *Metodología del Derecho administrativo. Reglas de racionalidad para la adopción y el control de la decisión administrativa* (Madrid, Marcial Pons, 2016) 113–20.

This is also the stance of domestic authorities with regard to EU soft law. They are not entitled to correct the formal designation or the decision-making procedure of measures adopted by EU institutions. Nevertheless, it is not the approach followed by Spanish courts regarding measures stemming from domestic authorities. Indeed, Spanish case law and academic scholarship, far from acritically accepting the form chosen by the authors of the soft law at stake, have due regard to their contents, purpose and effects on the legal framework, rather than to the procedure or the *nomen iuris*.[24] Accordingly, if they think that the measure, despite being passed as a soft law instrument, actually hides a binding norm, they would treat it as such. Spanish case law offers examples of this in cases of measures passed as both unilateral soft law instruments[25] and soft law agreements.[26] This approach resembles that of the Court of Justice regarding soft law measures adopted within the EU.[27]

Spanish scholarship and case law have traditionally approached soft law from the perspective of the system of sources of law. As in EU law, in Spain there has been an attempt to shed light on the legal regime of soft law instruments within the formal classification of acts and provisions of public law.[28] However, Rodríguez de Santiago has recently come up with an alternative proposal inspired by German administrative law. In spite of their major differences, all soft law measures have one thing in common: their main purpose is to lay down additional criteria to further specify the undefined regulatory boundaries of administrative discretion.[29] Soft law measures help anticipate the exercise of administrative discretion by putting forward abstract provisions.[30] While the former approach favours a more rigid and binary account of soft law instruments – law being either hard or soft – the latter facilitates a more nuanced approach to the various kinds of legal effects produced by soft law measures.

IV. JUDICIAL REVIEW

Under Spanish law, administrative rules passed either by the government or by an administrative authority can be challenged before courts specialised in administrative law by public and private parties alike. Articles 25 and 27 of the

[24] Santamaría Pastor (n 14) 264–65.

[25] Supreme Court Judgment of 26 November 2015 (cassation appeal no 3405/2014) para 1; and of 19 December 2018 (cassation appeal no 31/2018) para 4.

[26] Supreme Court Judgment of 2 December 2013 (cassation appeal no 4479/2010) para 4.

[27] Case C-16/16 P *Belgium v Commission* [2018] EU:C:2018:79, para 32; Case C-16/16 P *Belgium v Commission* [2018] EU:C:2017:959, Opinion of AG Bobek, para 63.

[28] Sánchez Morón (n 14); Santamaría Pastor (n 14) 264–65; Sarmiento (n 13).

[29] Rodríguez de Santiago (n 23) 115.

[30] See also H-P Nehl, 'Judicial Review of Complex Socio-economic, Technical, and Scientific Assessments in the European Union' in J Mendes (ed), *EU Administrative Discretion and the Limits of Law* (Oxford, Oxford University Press, 2019) 157, 172.

Act on Administrative Law Courts (LJCA)[31] provide for both direct and indirect actions of annulment. However, soft law measures are not administrative rules in the sense of Article 25 LJCA. The lack of legally binding force impedes direct actions of annulment against them. Yet, precluding the measure from being directly challenged does not prevent courts from indirectly reviewing the criteria and standards laid down in soft law provisions, following an appeal against the implementing acts that produce legal effects vis-a-vis their addressees. Thus, those criteria 'may be challenged by their addressees in the appeal that they raise against the single-case decisions that apply them'.[32] Likewise, the legality of a soft law measure 'should be examined, where appropriate, on the occasion of their implementing acts, which, obviously, would be subject to challenge and, therefore, control'.[33]

As a general rule, indirect judicial review provides for sufficiently effective judicial protection against soft law. Nevertheless, there are some cases where soft law, albeit lacking legally binding force, produces significant legal effects vis-a-vis its addressees. In these situations, Spanish courts exceptionally grant admissibility to direct actions of annulment. The way in which this exception is construed differs between the Supreme Court and the Constitutional Court. As for the former, we have already seen how qualifying a given measure as a soft law provision or as a binding rule revolves around pragmatism and flexibility. When the Supreme Court wants to admit a direct action of annulment lodged against a measure that was originally passed as soft law, it first declares that in view of its content, scope and effects, the measure actually hides an administrative binding rule. In turn, if the Supreme Court formally defines a contested measure as soft law, it will not admit a direct challenge. Thus, as opposed to what the Court of Justice does with EU law, in the case law of the Spanish Supreme Court, flexibility is not achieved by allowing for direct appeals against soft law measures,[34] but rather correcting the nature of the soft law measure in question.

Conversely, the Constitutional Court has granted leave to proceed to appeal for constitutional protection (*recursos de amparo*) directly challenging non-binding hierarchical instructions, in view of the fundamental right to an effective judicial protection (Article 24(1) of the Spanish Constitution (SC)).[35]The outcome remains the same – admitting direct judicial review when the court sees it as necessary in terms of judicial control effectiveness – but the avenue followed by the Constitutional Court is different: it accepts that the

[31] Act No 29/1998 on Administrative Law Courts, Official Journal No 167, of 14 July 1998 (Ley de la Jurisdicción Contencioso-Administativa).

[32] Supreme Court Judgment of 3 November 2003 (cassation appeal no 232/2001) para 2.

[33] Supreme Court Judgment of 19 December 2018 (cassation appeal no 31/2018) para 4.

[34] M Eliantonio, 'Soft Law in Environmental Matters and the Role of the European Courts: Too Much or Too Little of it?' (2018) 37 *Yearbook of European Law* 496, 504–08.

[35] Constitutional Court Judgment 47/1990 of 20 March 1990, para 4; M Bacigalupo, 'Sobre la impugnabilidad "directa" de las instrucciones administrativas' (2005) 26 *UNED. Boletín de la Facultad de Derecho* 563, 565–71.

instruction lacks binding force and thus belongs to the category of soft law, but admits a direct action of annulment.

It is now time to turn to EU soft law before Spanish courts. Under the *Foto-Frost* doctrine, challenging soft law measures drafted by EU institutions, bodies and agencies before domestic courts is precluded in any event.[36] However, an implementing act adopted by domestic administrative authorities might be challenged on the grounds of the invalidity of the underlying EU soft law instrument. National courts would definitely be entitled to request preliminary rulings of both interpretation and validity.[37] Nevertheless, this has not been the case in either the sector-specific areas selected in this research or in any other.

V. INTERPRETATIVE EFFECTS

Although they lack direct invalidating effects, soft law measures can have other legal effects. Next, we will focus on two of them: interpretative effects and indirect invalidating effects. As regards the former, soft law can have varying effects on the interpretation of legal provisions. Three types of interpretative effects will be discussed here: the ordinary interpretative effects of soft law measures, the duty to take them into consideration and the duty to interpret hard law in conformity with soft law.

First, soft law instruments can provide arguments and lines of reasoning (eg, teleological ones) when interpreting binding provisions to which they relate, in order to clarify vagueness, settle contradictions or fill gaps.[38] Most rulings handed down by Spanish courts applying the investigated soft law instruments (or similar soft law measures) award them this ordinary interpretative effect.[39] The Spanish Supreme Court has conferred such an effect with regard to Articles 101 and 107 of the Treaty on the Functioning of the European Union (TFEU) on the EU Guidelines on Vertical Restraints,[40] the Guidelines on Horizontal Cooperation Agreements,[41] the Commission Notice on the enforcement of State

[36] Case 314/85 *Foto-Frost* [1987] ECR I-4199, para 17.

[37] *Belgium v Commission* (n 27) Opinion of AG Bobek, para 108; J Scott, 'In Legal Limbo: Post-legislative Guidance as a Challenge for European Administrative Law' (2011) 48 *Common Market Law Review* 329; M Eliantonio, 'Soft Law in Environmental Matters' (n 34) 507; E Korkea-aho, 'National Courts and European Soft Law: Is *Grimaldi* Still Good Law?' (2018) 37 *Yearbook of European Law* 470.

[38] *Belgium v Commission* (n 27), Opinion of AG Bobek, paras 91; Eliantonio (n 34) 508–11.

[39] In the interviews conducted in this research, this ordinary interepretative effect has been stressed by legal advisors, law clerks and judges alike. Some of them have specifically underlined the importance of EU soft law in order to interpret EU binding provisions.

[40] European Commission, 'Guidelines on Vertical Restraints' [2010] OJ C130/1. Judgment of the Supreme Court of 2 June 2 2015 (cassation appeal no 4502/2012) paras 1 and 4.

[41] European Commission, 'Communication from the Commission – Guidelines on the applicability of Article 101 of the Treaty on the Functioning of the European Union to horizontal co-operation agreements' [2011] OJ C11/1; Orders of the Supreme Court of 18 September 2017 (cassation appeal no 1396/2017); and of 15 March 2018 (cassation appeal no 4323/2017).

aid law by national courts[42] and the *De Minimis* Notice.[43] Another example of this is the Supreme Court Judgment of 19 December 2018, where the court had to interpret Article 34 of Act No 10/2014 of 26 June on credit institutions[44] in a case relating to an early termination of an employment contract. This provision regulates the ratio between fixed and variable remuneration of bank staff. In order to interpret this last concept, the Supreme Court used the Guidelines on sound remuneration policy issued by the European Banking Authority, which states that severance payments should be considered variable remuneration.[45]

Second, a different issue altogether is if the criteria laid down in soft law provisions must somehow be taken into account in the interpretation of the relevant binding rules. In the *Grimaldi* case, the Court of Justice stated that national courts 'are bound to take ... into consideration' EU soft law measures.[46] Both judicial and administrative authorities in Spain are bound by this requirement. Nonetheless, where soft law arises from Spanish authorities, and thus the *Grimaldi* doctrine is not applicable, such a general obligation fades away. In particular, Spanish courts are not bound to take into consideration *ex officio* soft law measures passed by national political and administrative authorities. However, the fundamental right to effective judicial protection (Article 24(1) SC) does require courts to give reasons that fully address the parties' claims.[47] Under Article 24(1) SC, the fact that the norms to be interpreted fall under the scope of EU law does not affect this duty.[48] If the parties invoke a soft law measure as the basis to plead a given legal interpretation, the deciding court will thus be required to give reasons as to whether it upholds or rejects the interpretative criteria arising from such a measure. However, this duty does not result from the nature and effects of soft law, but from the fact that its content has become part of the parties' pleadings. If the party has not invoked national soft law measures in its pleading, the relevant court is not bound to take them into account.

[42] European Commission, 'Commission notice on the enforcement of State aid law by national courts' [2009] OJ C85/1; Order of the Supreme Court of 1 March 2019 (cassation appeal no 7010/2018).

[43] European Commission, 'Communication from the Commission – Notice on agreements of minor importance which do not appreciably restrict competition under Article 101(1) of the Treaty on the Functioning of the European Union (*De Minimis* Notice)' [2014] OJ C291/1; Supreme Court Judgments of 17 March 2016 (cassation appeal no 446/2011) para 2; of 17 December 2015 (cassation appeal no 108/2012) para 2; of 16 April 16 2012 (cassation appeal no 436/2009) para 2; and of 15 February 2012 (cassation appeal no 1560/2008) para 7.

[44] Supreme Court Judgment of 19 December 2018 (cassation appeal no 31/2018).

[45] European Banking Authority, 'Guidelines on sound remuneration policies under Articles 74(3) and 75(2) of Directive 2013/36/EU and disclosures under Article 450 of Regulation (EU) No 575/2013' [2016] (EBA/GL/2015/22) para 155. The Executive Board of the Bank of Spain endorsed these on 27 July 2016.

[46] Case C-322/88 *Grimaldi* [1989] ECR I-4407, para 18.

[47] See, eg, Constitutional Court Judgment no 214/1999, 29 November, para 4.

[48] L Arroyo Jiménez, *Empatía constitucional. Derecho de la Unión Europea y Constitución Española* (Madrid, Marcial Pons, 2016) 77–84.

As a consequence, there is a major discrepancy between: (i) those cases subject to binding secondary law and covered by EU soft law instruments, where domestic courts are required under *Grimaldi* to take soft law instruments into consideration *ex officio*; and (ii) those other cases exclusively covered by national soft law measures, wherein the courts are only bound to take them into account if they are pleaded by the parties. The scarce presence of the selected EU soft law instruments within the case law doctrine of higher courts can also be due, at least partially, to the confusion between these two groups of cases: Spanish courts are used to dealing with soft law provisions drafted by Spanish authorities, wherein they have never been required to take them into consideration unless they are expressly invoked by the parties to support their claims. Apparently, they extend this to cases where soft law measures taken by European authorities are at stake, incorrectly disregarding the *Grimaldi* doctrine. The interviews conducted within this research seem to confirm the validity of this hypothesis: the main reason given by judges and law clerks to explain the lack of case law references to soft law instruments is that it is not pleaded by the parties.[49] But this view seems to rest on the wrong assumption that the *Grimaldi* obligation is somewhat qualified by the principle according to which the parties delimit the scope of the case (*principio dispositivo*).

Finally, Spanish administrative and judicial authorities do not have a duty to interpret hard law in conformity with soft law. On the one hand, *Grimaldi* merely imposes a duty to take EU soft law into account. On the other hand, since Spanish courts are not required to take into consideration and examine the criteria laid down by national soft law unless they are referred to in the pleadings of the parties, they will not be bound by a duty to interpret domestic legislation in conformity with soft law provisions drafted by the Spanish authorities.[50] Such a conforming interpretation requirement is not in line with soft law's non-binding nature, and it breaches the constitutional principle under which judges are independent and solely subject to the rule of law (Article 19 of the Treaty on European Union (TEU), Article 47 of the Charter of Fundamental Rights of the European Union (CFREU) and Articles 24 and 117 SC).

VI. INDIRECT INVALIDATING EFFECTS

Given their non-binding nature, the breach of soft law measures by a rule or act does not in and of itself affect the validity of the latter. Nevertheless, there are two cases where non-compliance with soft law can have indirect invalidating

[49] This point was made by one Constitutional Court clerk, two Supreme Court law clerks and one Supreme Court Justice. One Supreme Court law clerk stressed that in competition law cases, the parties usually plead European Commission guidelines and notices in order to explain why in this area, the Court takes EU soft law measures into consideration.

[50] *Contra* Sarmiento (n 13) 167–77.

effects. Such effects are 'indirect' because the grounds for annulment are not the infringement of soft law as such, but rather breaches of other hard law rules or principles. The first case relates to binding rules incorporating soft law measures, so that any subsequent acts in breach thereof will be invalid.[51] This is exemplified by provisions referring to or incorporating soft law content in their articles or annexes, or making a project's authorisation dependent on the fulfilment of best practice requirements. In these cases, any invalidating effects are not directly triggered by the breach of this soft law instrument, but rather by the violation of the relevant rule or act which incorporated soft law content. EU soft law can also be incorporated into domestic hard law. This partly explains why there are no references to EU soft law in the case law examined herein, for example, regarding water-related matters. There are rulings by Spanish courts repealing river basin plans for breaching the relevant domestic legislation on water planning and ecological flows.[52] Despite the fact that these rulings do not make references to European Commission's guidance documents on the matter, the content of EU soft law and national legislation partially overlap.[53]

Second, non-compliance with soft law can be one of the conditions triggering invalidating effects under a general principle of law. For instance, a failure to decide on the basis of standards laid down in EU or national soft law requires administrative authorities and courts to give due reasons if such standards had been consistently followed in previous cases. Non-compliance with this duty can violate the right to an equal application of the law both by the courts and administrative bodies (Article 14 SC and Article 35(1)(c) of the Administrative Procedure Act).[54] Concerning EU soft law, there is another case of indirect invalidating effects: a violation of the requirement to take into consideration provisions of EU soft law set forth by the *Grimaldi* doctrine. In these two situations, any subsequent acts will not be invalidated solely on grounds of soft law breaches; rather, the invalidating effects would directly arise from the violation of those other norms that require a duly reasoned decision to be made or the relevant soft law provisions to be taken into consideration: the principle of equality and the *Grimaldi* doctrine. However, within Spanish case law, there are no signs that such indirect invalidating effects have been found with regard to EU soft law.

[51] ibid 142–50.

[52] Amongst many others, see Supreme Court Judgment of 11 April 2019 (cassation appeal no 4351/2016).

[53] See, eg, the Regulation on Water Planning (Royal Decree No 907/2007, of 6 July) and the Technical Instruction on Water Planning (Ministerial Order ARM/2656/2008, of 10 September), on the one hand; and the Guidance Document No 11 on Planning Processes, issued within the framework of the Common Implementation System, on the other.

[54] Act No 39/2015 on Administrative Procedure, Official Journal No 236, of 2 October 2015 (Ley de Procedimiento Administrativo Común); S Díez Sastre, *El precedente administrativo* (Madrid, Marcial Pons, 2008) 298–304; Nehl (n 30) 173.

VII. SOFT LAW AND CONSTITUTIONAL PRINCIPLES

When deciding cases, administrative law courts rarely need to elucidate the constitutional foundations of soft law measures. Rather, they apply soft law measures to guide administrative behaviour, to interpret hard law provisions or to annul administrative action by virtue of what above have been called the indirect invalidating effects of soft law. However, the impact of soft law on the constitutional principles of administrative law, both European and Spanish, is explored by academic scholarship. The outcome of this theoretical work contributes to form a common understanding in the Spanish legal community of the constitutional foundations of soft law. As will be demonstrated, the interviews that we have conducted show that such a common understanding is widely shared by Spanish lawyers serving at both courts and administrative bodies. It is reasonable to assume that this shared view of soft law's implications on constitutional principles affects how soft law is implemented and dealt with by the institutions served by these professionals. The interviews also show that the relationship between soft law and constitutional principles is seen as being manifold and contradictory. The interviews display another interesting aspect relating to the professional background of the interviewees. In Spain, top legal advisors of public bodies, judicial clerks and justices of superior courts can have either an academic or a professional background. Those with the former seemed to be more ready to answer this part of the questionnaire, while the interviewees with a civil service background were less prone to give detailed views on the various impacts of soft law on constitutional principles. In turn, whether the interviewees served in administrative authorities or in courts did not play any role in this respect. We now describe this relationship in view of both secondary sources and the conducted interviews.

First, soft law instruments certainly enhance some elements of the rule of law (Article 2 TEU and Article 1(1) SC). Anticipating and disclosing how public bodies will exercise their discretionary powers and construe the rules to which they are bound increases legal certainty (Article 9(3) SC). As public authorities discipline their own future actions, they reduce the risk of breaching the principles of equality (Article 2 TEU and Articles 1(1) and 14 SC) and impartiality (Article 41 CFREU and Article 103(1) SC).[55] Finally, increasing the density of regulation of administrative action (even if through soft law) makes it possible to indirectly increase the effectiveness of judicial review (Article 47 CFREU and Article 24(1) SC). Nonetheless, resorting to soft law instruments can also conceal the drafter's true intention to bypass the limits (mostly procedural ones) applicable to rule-making powers.[56] Similarly, restrictions on the right to challenge

[55] These two points were made by many interviewees.

[56] Senden and van den Brink (n 1) 16–17. One interviewed person stressed the risk of circumventing the principle of legality in the area of administrative sanctions by using soft law measures.

soft law measures (eg, exclusion of direct action) may reduce the effectiveness of judicial review.

Second, soft law can also increase the effectiveness of administrative action,[57] which is a principle enshrined in the Spanish Constitution (Article 103(1)),[58] as well as in EU administrative law.[59] From this perspective, it might be advisable for public authorities to adopt as soft law instruments the standards they will apply when assessing facts or the impact of their decisions. This increases the effectiveness of administrative action, thereby also making it more legitimate.[60]

Soft law can also support the democratic principle (Article 2 TEU and Articles 1(1) and 1(2) SC). However, from this perspective, the consideration of these non-binding instruments can be as diverse and heterogeneous as the types of soft law measures in place or the actual mechanisms through which public bodies gain democratic legitimacy. On the one hand, democratic legitimacy of administrative action within continental European public law rests, among other aspects, on its ties to government and, where appropriate, on the latter's connection with Parliament.[61] Internal and unilateral soft law measures – such as the instructions set forth in Article 61(i) LRJSP – provide for top-down, hierarchical driving impulses throughout the administrative structure and, by so doing, they facilitate political guidance and control over administrative action. Consequently, this type of soft law measure can improve the public administration's democratic legitimacy. In turn, unpublished domestic soft law measures may reduce the transparency of administrative action, thereby making it less likely for citizens to hold the public administration accountable.[62] On the other hand, creating fora and spheres for stakeholders and parties concerned by administrative action to engage and participate within the context of administrative organisation and procedures, as well as the drafting of soft law instruments enshrining the results of such participation mechanisms, may boost democratic legitimacy (Article 10(3) TEU and Article 23 SC).[63]

[57] Two interviewees pointed out that international and EU soft law measures are used in order to justify the opportunity of new rules, as well as the urgency in their adoption in emergency situations. This last consideration might be seen as related to the principle of effectiveness.

[58] L Parejo Alfonso, *Eficacia y Administración. Tres estudios* (Madrid, MAP, 1995); Santamaría Pastor (n 14) 74–80.

[59] P Craig, *EU Administrative Law* (Oxford, Oxford University Press, 2018) 275–76.

[60] P Craig, 'Legitimacy in Administrative Law: European Union' in M Ruffert (ed), *Legitimacy in European Administrative Law: Reform and Reconstruction* (Groningen, Europa Law Publishing, 2011) 197–216; F Velasco, 'The Legitimacy of the Administration in Spain' in M Ruffert (ed), *Legitimacy in European Administrative Law: Reform and Reconstruction* (Groningen, Europa Law Publishing, 2011) 102–106.

[61] HH Trute, 'Das demokratische Legitimation der Verwaltungs' in W Hoffmann-Riem, E Schmidt-Aßmann and A Voßkuhle (eds), *Grundlagen desVerwaltungsrechts*, vol I (Munich, CH Beck, 2006) 334–36; Velasco (n 60) 101–02.

[62] This was a concern expressed by many of the interviewees regarding internal hierarchical instructions.

[63] Sarmiento (n 13) 160–62.

Finally, soft law can also help fulfil the constitutional principles governing the relationships between the various territorial levels of government, such as sincere cooperation (Article 4(3) TEU and Articles 2 and 103(1) SC). On the one hand, in areas of shared legislative powers, soft law measures agreed amongst the various competent levels can lead to a harmonious or uniform regulation of the relevant matter.[64] On the other hand, experience shows that the EU can resort to soft law instruments precisely within those areas where it has no sufficient competences to act.[65] Under Spanish law, this does not apply to the relationship between the State and the Autonomous Regions. The general rule is that the latter's autonomy (Article 2 SC) precludes the former from directing its action through soft law, where there is no room for State hard law. In other words, the State cannot do via soft law what it could not do via hard law.[66]

VIII. CONCLUSIONS

We shall now draw four key conclusions. First, from an empirical point of view, we found a significant inconsistency in Spanish case law between the presence of soft law measures within competition law and the other policy areas.[67] This is due to various factors, such as certain specificities of Spanish administrative and procedural law relating to the admissibility of appeals before higher courts;[68] the incorporation of certain EU soft law measures into domestic hard law, although clearly this is not a general practice;[69] and, above all, the scant attention paid to the *Grimaldi* doctrine by Spanish courts, which appear to be inclined to take EU soft law into consideration only when it is invoked by the parties.[70]

Second, from a theoretical standpoint, we have not found significant procedural gaps in soft law's judicial review, as long as indirect actions are always available.[71] However, the reluctance of Spanish courts to openly discuss EU soft law measures hinders the requests for preliminary rulings on interpretation and validity, thereby questioning how complete the system of legal remedies provided for by EU law actually is.[72]

Third, although it lacks binding force and thus direct invalidating effects,[73] EU soft law can have various legal effects under Spanish administrative law. Two of them have been explored here. On the one hand, domestic courts have awarded

[64] ibid 50–55, 153–57. The contribution of EU soft law to the uniformity of EU law enforcement was pointed out during some interviews.

[65] *Grimaldi* (n 46) para 143; *Belgium v Commission* (n 27) Opinion of AG Bobek, paras 92–93.

[66] This was stressed by several interviewees.

[67] This finding is in line with other Member States. See G Gentile, ch 5 in this volume.

[68] See section II above.

[69] See section VI above.

[70] See section V above.

[71] See section IV above.

[72] Case 294/83 *Parti écologiste 'Les Verts' v European Parliament* [1986] ECR I-01339, para 23.

[73] See section III above.

interpretative effects to EU soft law measures regarding EU and national hard law provisions in the areas of competition and banking law.[74] On the other hand, soft law measures can have indirect invalidating effects under certain conditions. This has been a long-standing interpretation regarding domestic measures. Yet, although it would be at least theoretically possible, Spanish courts have never explicitly awarded them to EU soft law measures.[75] This leads to an excessive discrepancy between the legal effects conferred by national courts to European and internal soft law, which can also be seen in other Member States.[76]

Lastly, the interviews show that soft law's impact on the constitutional principles of administrative law is manifold, making it impossible to draw an unambiguous conclusion.[77] Constitutional principles lay down various requirements so that their impact on soft law can be inconsistent. Soft law measures are also heterogeneous and they can lead to varying consequences from the perspective of the same constitutional principle.

[74] See section V above.
[75] See section VI above.
[76] See Gentile, ch 5 in this volume.
[77] See section VII above.

15

EU Soft Law in the UK on the Eve of Brexit

(Not) Much Ado about Nothing?

MARY DOBBS AND OANA ŞTEFAN*

I. INTRODUCTION

THIS CHAPTER INVESTIGATES the role of EU soft law instruments within the UK legal order. It considers the legal effects of these instruments through examining case law and administrative practice in selected fields. The European Network of Soft Law Research (SoLaR) methodology was employed to gather data. The main challenge was obtaining interviews,[1] increasing the significance of other sources of data. With regard to the documentary analysis, materials were mostly accessible online in official databases or through the Westlaw portal. For case law we used the database of the British and Irish Legal Information Institute.[2]

The chapter investigates whether the nature of the UK's legal system impacts upon the role of EU soft law. As we will see, one would expect that soft

* Our thanks to Conor McCormick, Steffen Post, Ewan McGaughey, Andrea Biondi, Takis Tridimas, Alexander Türk, Napoleon Xanthoulis, Giulia Gentile, Mariolina Eliantonio, Emilia Korkea-aho and the SoLaR-UK interviewees for their contribution to the project and/or comments on an earlier version of this chapter. Any errors or omissions are the authors'.

[1] Some of the rejections we received were linked to Brexit, both as a sensitive topic and as a reason for increased workload and lack of time. Furthermore, we could not use some of the material as the consent form was not signed by some of the interviewees, even though they were open to very frank conversations. The reason given was the high political salience of topics connected to the EU. With regard to judges, while in principle some expressed informally their willingness to take part, we could not undertake any interviews as, to date, we have not received any answer to our official application for the participation of judiciary to the SoLaR project. Our team interviewed eight public servants in financial regulation and competition. Out of these, one of the interviewees responded in a personal capacity only and was not included in this chapter. Unfortunately, we have not received any positive reply for the environmental and social policy sectors.

[2] www.bailii.org.

law would be utilised wherever relevant and useful, and that its effects would increase through use. However, whilst the data indicates that where these instruments are utilised they have a strong interpretative role, it also indicates that the initial use of such instruments is haphazard and there is no guarantee that all instruments will be utilised where relevant. The chapter concludes with very brief consideration on the future of EU soft law in the UK in light of Brexit.

II. THE SIGNIFICANCE OF THE UK LEGAL SYSTEM'S NATURE

Before considering the approach to EU soft law within the UK, it is first necessary to briefly sketch out two contextual elements: first, the complex nature of the UK's legal system itself together with its approach to EU law more generally; and, second, their likely impact on the reception of EU soft law.

A. The UK Legal System: The Rule of (Hard) Law?

i. The Formal Status of Soft Law Instruments

The UK is a constitutional monarchy, based on the rule of law, parliamentary sovereignty and predominately common law traditions.[3] This seeming bundle of contradictions leads to a hierarchy of norms, with Acts of Parliament and particularly 'constitutional statutes' at the pinnacle.[4] Crucial from our perspective is that while the law encompasses legislation, statutory instruments, judicial precedents, incorporated international treaties and so on,[5] the UK and its courts clearly distinguish between binding law and all other non-binding elements.[6] Unless incorporated via binding law, policy instruments, circulars, guidance documents etc are only 'quasi-legislation'[7] – they remain outside the hierarchy of (hard) norms.

The consequence of such a statement is significant. If even the lowliest of local by-laws conflict directly, then the soft law instruments must be disregarded. They have no binding, legal force and indeed are not justiciable[8] – as they are not 'law', they are not appropriate for adjudication by the courts. Consequently, one might expect them not to play a significant role within the UK – whether before

[3] Scotland proves to be the exception, as it comprises a mixed tradition.

[4] M Elliott and R Thomas, *Public Law* (Oxford, Oxford University Press, 2011) 46.

[5] ibid ch 2.

[6] ibid 147–48.

[7] G Ganz, *Quasi-legislation: Recent Developments in Secondary Legislation* (London, Sweet & Maxwell, 1987).

[8] On justiciability, see PG Ingram, 'Justiciability' (1994) 39 *American Journal of Jurisprudence* 353; or D McGoldrick, 'The Boundaries of Justiciability' (2010) 59 *ICLQ* 981.

the courts or in executive or administrative decision-making. However, that is not the end of the story.[9]

ii. The Use of Soft Law Instruments

First, it is possible for the soft law instruments to be incorporated by reference, even into Acts of Parliament – for example, legislation may impose obligations to 'have regard' to national planning policy frameworks or to national policy statements, as proposed in the 2019 Environment (Principles and Governance) Bill regarding a policy statement on environmental principles. The soft law instrument would effectively be part of the law until the legislation is amended. Of concern, however, is the ease with which the soft law instrument itself may be amended or replaced, thereby bypassing ordinary scrutiny and accountability measures.[10]

Second, even without incorporation, this does not stop soft law instruments being used – either expressly or implicitly, to a greater or lesser extent. Provided that there was no conflict with binding norms, decision-makers could avail of them daily – something that raises considerable concerns about democracy, legal certainty and the rule of law, especially if the soft law documents are not publicly available. Decision-makers generally ought to take account of any appropriate 'relevant considerations'[11] and disregard any irrelevant ones, which begs the question as to whether the soft law instrument in question is a relevant consideration.

Third, courts in a common law system must adjudicate on legal debates where the law is clear, but also where it is opaque or where there are effectively gaps. In contrast to a civil law system, the law is not codified to the same extent, judges are not restricted to stating what the law is, and binding judicial precedent is an essential component of the law. Therefore, the courts are both experienced in and must undertake the interpretation of law, including where this is highly challenging. In doing so, courts may turn to whatever seems useful, and soft law instruments are an obvious source – as potentially directly relevant to the issue at hand and, for instance, providing insight into the objectives behind legislation or guidance on its implementation.[12]

Therefore, where incorporated by reference, there is a heightened expectation that the soft law instruments referred to will be utilised by the decision-makers

[9] For more on this, see G Weeks, *Soft Law and Public Authorities: Remedies and Reform* (Oxford, Bloomsbury, 2016).

[10] OW Pedersen, 'Post-Brexit Environmental Accountability and Enforcement: Who is Afraid of the Courts?' (2018) 20 *Environmental Law Review* 133. Further issues arise, as noted in C Brennan et al, 'Out of the Frying Pan, into the Fire? Environmental Governance Vulnerabilities in Post-Brexit Northern Ireland' (2019) 21 *Environmental Law Review* 84.

[11] H Woolf, J Jowell, C Donnelly and I Hare, *De Smith's Judicial Review*, 8th edn (London, Sweet & Maxwell, 2018) 305–12.

[12] See, eg, www.hse.gov.uk/research/rrpdf/rr010.pdf; or B Hurwitz, 'Clinical Guidelines and the Law: Advice, Guidance or Regulation?' (1995) 1 *Journal of Evaluation in Clinical Practice* 49.

and raised before the courts – indeed, the decision-maker may be obliged to utilise it. However, even without incorporation by reference, one might expect due to sheer convenience to see soft law instruments being utilised where useful and where not in conflict with the law.

iii. Burgeoning Legal Force

The regular use of soft law instruments by decision-makers or the courts may give them credence and potentially not merely legal effects but also legal force. This can occur via judicial precedent and also via the doctrine of legitimate expectations.

Within the common law system, a considerable source of binding law is in the form of case law whereby judicial precedent is developed over the centuries by the courts under the doctrine of *stare decisis*.[13] *Stare decisis* (let the decision stand) means that the decisions of the superior courts (the High Court, the Court of Appeal and the Supreme Court) are binding on lower courts and also usually courts of the same level. Not only are broad legal principles and doctrines developed by the courts, but the specific reasoning (the *ratio*) must be applied in similar cases. If a superior court refers positively to a soft law instrument in a case and relies on it in its reasoning – for example, to help justify the outcome or in noting that the decision-maker must consider the soft law instrument – then this can become interwoven into the precedent. Thereby, the soft law instrument can both help develop binding precedent, even if not referred to in later cases, and even be given force for the future due to the precedent.

Another way through which soft law can be endowed with legal force is through the operation of the principle of legitimate expectations. Legitimate expectations arise in the context of UK public law. Where there is a legitimate expectation due to the prior actions, inactions or representations of decision-maker that they will behave in a certain way, the courts may intervene to prevent them going against that expectation if it were unfair or inconsistent with the principles of good governance to allow the decision-maker to depart from that practice.[14] Thus, if a decision-maker is known to use specific soft law instruments in their decision-making, then it might be possible to establish a legitimate expectation that they would continue to do so.[15]

However, a significant issue remains due to the decision-makers being organs of the State. It is not at all clear whether legitimate expectation can be used effectively due to a combination of parliamentary sovereignty and a reasonably strict separation of powers. First, an Act of Parliament is sacrosanct. Second,

[13] R Cross and JW Harris, *Precedent in English Law*, 4th edn (Oxford, Clarendon Law, 1991).

[14] D Feldman, *English Public Law*, 2nd edn (Oxford, Oxford University Press, 2009) 681–84 and 730 ff. Obviously, limitations and exceptions can arise, eg, where the decision-maker provides advance warning of a change in practice or where the legislation has since been amended.

[15] ibid 254–55.

within the judicial review system, whilst there are reasonably tight controls of procedural elements, ie, whether specific steps were taken, including having regard to guidance documents where required, there is considerable deference when it comes to the substantive decision[16] – something that is the focus of an Aarhus complaint currently.[17] Consequently, even if soft law instruments were to be considered justiciable and used as a decisive, independent factor before the courts, this would not necessarily enable decision-makers to be held to account over the substantive decision.[18]

B. Relationship with EU Law?

The second contextual element is the UK's legal relationship to date with the EU. For, despite the EU claiming supremacy of EU law over domestic law and developing doctrines such as direct effect, the UK has been less enthusiastic on this front, which is linked to the UK's dualist system and parliamentary sovereignty. Nonetheless, eventually the UK relied on Parliament's decision (under the European Communities Act 1972) to abide by EU law and concluded that any domestic legislation that directly conflicted with EU law would simply be disapplied in that instance.[19]

Two points regarding EU soft law need to be highlighted. First, as EU soft law remains 'soft', an obligation to transpose, implement and enforce EU law does not extend to EU soft law. Any adherence will depend on ancillary obligations created at the EU or the domestic level, or just on what is useful nationally (see, for instance, the obligation to comply or explain with financial regulation soft law issued by the European Supervisory Authorities). Second, EU soft law may prove especially useful. EU law is influenced by its mixed origins – both common and civil law. It also remains relatively new, is growing continuously and is frequently technical. The creation of hard law becomes more politically challenging with increased numbers of Member States and the principle of subsidiarity also especially impacts on the level of detail of EU law in areas of shared competence. Consequently, soft law documents abound and may be very helpful (if also questionable democratically), increasing the likelihood of their use.

[16] *Associated Provincial Picture Houses Ltd v Wednesbury Corporation* [1948] 1 KB 223; M Lee, 'Brexit and Environmental Protection in the United Kingdom: Governance, Accountability and Law Making' (2018) 36 *Journal of Energy & Natural Resources Law* 351.

[17] UNECE, 'ACCC/C/2017/156', www.unece.org/environmental-policy/conventions/public-participation/aarhus-convention/tfwg/envppcc/envppcccom/acccc2017156-united-kingdom.html.

[18] Environmental Audit Committee, 'The Government's 25 Year Plan for the Environment. Eighth Report of Session 2017–19' (HC 803, 24 July 2018), publications.parliament.uk/pa/cm201719/cmselect/cmenvaud/803/803.pdf.

[19] *R v Secretary of State for Transport ex p Factortame Ltd* [1990] UKHL 7, with caveats noted later in *R HS2 Action Alliance Ltd* [2014] UKSC 3. This is further supported by s 18 of the European Union Act 2011.

Overall, therefore, whilst neither domestic nor EU soft law is, in principle, binding on decision-makers or the courts in the UK, one would expect to see the instruments being used wherever useful by decision-makers or the courts to help interpret the hard law or develop policies, although this does not guarantee that they will be expressly referred to. Where they are referred to expressly by decision-makers, courts or in legislation, then their influence and strength grow, to the point that they may end up with de facto binding force in the long run. Thus, their role and weight will not be uniform, but will instead depend on how helpful they are and their use to date. However, the limitation remains that the legal system does not provide for effective substantive judicial review and thereby curtails the role of any hard or soft law instruments.

III. FINDINGS REGARDING THE IMPACT OF EU SOFT LAW ON SPECIFIC FIELDS

This section is based on empirical research undertaken within the European Network of Soft Law Research (SoLaR) project regarding the role of sample EU soft law instruments in the UK in the fields of competition, the environment, financial regulation and social policy. The choice of fields is particularly interesting and provides for varying contexts. For instance, due to the extraordinary experience in regulating the biggest financial market in the EU, UK experts have played a leading role in drafting the soft law issued by the European Securities and Markets Authority (ESMA). For competition law, a blanket stipulation in the legislation provides that statutory interpretation should pay due regard to statements issued by the European Commission. Environmental law is an area of devolved (decentralised) power in the UK, while, in terms of social policy, the British exceptionalism is widely known. The data is gathered from interviews to a limited extent, but in particular from documentary analysis of official websites, laws and cases. The results suggest a number of interesting trends, which can be grouped into three categories relating to the transposition of EU soft law in the UK, the use made of soft law by administrations and courts, and finally the effects of EU soft law in the UK legal order.

A. The Status of EU Soft Law in the UK Legal Order

i. The Transposition of EU Soft Law in the UK

Judging from their official websites and published documents, the UK authorities consider that all types of EU soft law instruments are relevant, including everything from official guidance to even Q&As,[20] preventing a ranking/

[20] For instance, ESMA Q&As as referred to in FCA, 'The Perimeter Guidance Manual: PERG' (Handbook, June 2018) 8.30B.4.

taxonomy of EU soft law. However, EU soft law is not systematically or officially transposed into the UK legal order and the approach appears in part sector-dependent; indeed, in relation to social policy, our team could not retrieve any form of transposition of the targeted EU soft law.

The most popular way of 'transposing' EU soft law is by way of reference within national guidance on various websites or in handbooks. Thus, Dobbs[21] notes that when EU and national environmental protection systems overlap, the domestic guidance might make brief references to EU guidance.[22] The key mechanism to transpose EU environmental soft law is through circulars,[23] which should be considered by the decision-makers,[24] but the reception across the UK varies. Similarly, national competition law guidance frequently refers to soft law. In terms of State aid, the Manual published by the Department for Business, Energy, and Industrial Strategy (BEIS)[25] includes reference to both hard and soft law. A civil servant stated in an interview that the Manual is a translation of formal EU documentation into a more practical guide to the rules. This is because EU guidance is written in a very continental, civil law fashion, which does not always translate well into common law terms.[26] In terms of financial regulation, EU guidance is mostly included in the interactive handbook[27] of the Financial Conduct Authority (FCA). Such non-binding guidance is influential, as the FCA treats compliance thereto as compliance with the binding rule to which the guidance relates.[28] However, as noted by Post in the UK financial regulation report, the targeted guidelines of the European Supervisory Authorities (ESAs) are 'normally only added into the handbook by way of reference at the beginning of a section'.[29]

[21] M Dobbs, 'National Report on the United Kingdom' in M Eliantonio and G Lisi (eds), 'EU Environmental Soft Law in the Member States' (2020) SoLaR Working Paper, https://papers.ssrn.com/sol3/papers.cfm?abstract_id=3656418, 130.

[22] The English National Planning Policy Framework (NPPF) is mainly inward-looking, but does include reference to the EU regimes; see www.gov.uk/government/uploads/system/uploads/attachment_data/file/6077/2116950.pdf.

[23] Circular 02/99 previously provided general guidance on the implementation of the EIA Directive, with a specific focus on England/Wales; see also www.gov.uk/government/uploads/system/uploads/attachment_data/file/7676/155958.pdf.

[24] As stated in (Scottish) 'Planning Circular 1/2017: Environmental Impact Assessment Regulations', 16 May 2017, www.gov.scot/publications/planning-circular-1-2017-environmental-impact-assessment-regulations-2017.

[25] BEIS, 'Guidance. State Aid Manual', 10 July 2015, www.gov.uk/government/publications/state-aid-manual.

[26] O Ştefan and A Biondi, 'National Report on the United Kingdom' in O Ştefan (ed), 'EU Competition and State Aid Soft Law in the Member States' (2020) SoLaR Working Paper, https://papers.ssrn.com/sol3/papers.cfm?abstract_id=2356227, 178.

[27] FCA, 'FCA Handbook', www.handbook.fca.org.uk/handbook.

[28] FCA, 'Reader's Guide: An Introduction to the Handbook', January 2019, www.handbook.fca.org.uk/handbook-readers-guide, 11.

[29] S Post, 'EU Soft Law Effects in Financial Regulation: Insights from the United Kingdom' in M Avbelj (ed), 'EU Financial Regulation Soft Law in the Member States' (2020) SoLaR Working Paper, https://papers.ssrn.com/sol3/papers.cfm?abstract_id=3668793, 122.

Such unsystematic, selective presence of EU guidance documents in the UK regulatory landscape makes it difficult to track a certain pattern of soft law transposition. It also might negatively impact stakeholders, for instance, by obscuring planning or licensing processes regarding environmental protection – despite non-transposition, soft law instruments may be relevant and used by decision-makers.

ii. The Place of EU Soft Law in the Hierarchy of Legal Sources

One serious consideration for transposition concerns the weight to be attached to EU soft law. In some sectors, such as financial regulation, authorities occasionally make clear that EU guidance is superior to the national guidance in the hierarchy of legal sources.[30] This might be explained by the fact that the UK financial authorities are quite influential in drafting EU guidance themselves.[31] However, as noted by Dobbs,[32] EU soft law, in contrast to EU hard law, will never directly trump national *legislation*.[33] The interviews for competition and State aid confirmed that soft law is placed at the bottom of the hierarchy of legal sources. Hard law instruments (that are further explained by soft law) as well as case law rank higher. One interviewee mentioned that it is the duty of the administration to keep track of such clashes, as businesses (especially small and medium-sized enterprises (SMEs)) will find it difficult to scrutinise everything.[34]

iii. Mutual Learning through Soft Law

Soft law shows once again that the EU and the UK legal systems co-exist in an environment of dialogue and mutual exchange. On the one hand, EU soft law writing techniques might inspire UK authorities. For example, the FCA makes recourse to Q&As in its handbook in order to shed further light on the rules.[35] Furthermore, some EU environmental guidance documents have heavily influenced the content of national or regional guidance in the UK.[36] On the other

[30] ibid 137.

[31] M van Rijsbergen, 'EU Agencies' Soft Rule-Making: Lessons Learnt from the European Securities and Markets Authority' (dissertation, Utrecht University Repository, 2018).

[32] Dobbs (n 21) 147.

[33] *Edwards v Rhondda Cynon Taff County Borough Council* [2014] UKUT 435 (LC).

[34] Ştefan and Biondi (n 26) 189.

[35] Post (n 29) 136.

[36] Natural England, 'Guidance. Great Crested Newts: Protection and Licences', 9 October 2014, www.gov.uk/guidance/great-crested-newts-protection-surveys-and-licences; Forestry Commission and Natural England, 'Guidance. Manage and Protect Woodland Wildlife', 9 July 2018, https://www.gov.uk/guidance/manage-and-protect-woodland-wildlife; 'Guidance on Managing Woodlands with Great Crested Newts in England', version 3, 5 April 2016, https://assets.publishing.service.gov.uk/government/uploads/system/uploads/attachment_data/file/697602/england-protected-species-newt.pdf; European Commission, 'Guidance document on the strict protection of animal species of Community interest under the Habitats Directive 92/43/EEC' final version (February 2007),

hand, EU soft law is sometimes either UK-inspired or drafted in collaboration with UK authorities. Some of the most interesting recent developments in the compatibility of State aid for energy and environmental objectives have been modelled on UK cases[37] approving the various forms of support foreseen by the Electricity Market Reform.[38] These developments were later codified in the 2014 Energy and Environmental Aid guidelines.[39]

With regard to social policy, McGaughey considers that the EU soft law studied by the SoLaR team has been influenced by policies developed in the UK under its most actively pro-EU government, namely the Tony Blair and Gordon Brown administrations.[40] Finally, regarding financial regulation, the weight that the UK representatives have on the board of the ESAs has been documented in the literature.[41]

B. Is EU Soft Law Referred to in Case Law and Administrative Practice?

Our empirical research shows that soft law does feature in the UK's administrative practice and case law. One interviewee identified UK courts as generally 'open minded when it comes to soft law',[42] while the Court of Appeal has noted that '[a]lthough the Guidance is not binding, it is nonetheless instructive and compelling'.[43] Overall, interviewees agreed that the EU legal order is better off with soft law than without soft law. In the words of one interviewee, soft law is 'not only a question of regulating, but a question of transparency, consistency, and certainty'.[44] However, the references vary greatly.

Thus, in competition law, as already noted by Devine and Eliantonio,[45] our empirical research shows that the Competition and Markets Authority (CMA)

ec.europa.eu/environment/nature/conservation/species/guidance/pdf/guidance_en.pdf; European Commission, 'Guidance document. Wind energy developments and Natura 2000' (2011) section 2.4.2, ec.europa.eu/environment/nature/natura2000/management/docs/Wind_farms.pdf, to be compared to Natural England and DEFRA, 'Guidance. Bats: Surveys and Mitigation for Development Projects', 28 March 2015, www.gov.uk/guidance/bats-surveys-and-mitigation-for-development-projects.

[37] Commission Decisions on contract for differences and on capacity mechanism. See European Commission, 'State Aid: Commission Authorises UK Aid Package for Renewable Electricity Production', press release, 23 July 2014, europa.eu/rapid/press-release_IP-14-866_en.htm.

[38] Department of Energy and Climate Change, 'Electricity Market Reform: Policy Overview', November 2012, assets.publishing.service.gov.uk/government/uploads/system/uploads/attachment_data/file/65634/7090-electricity-market-reform-policy-overview-.pdf.

[39] European Commission, 'Communication from the Commission – Guidelines on State aid for environmental protection and energy 2014–2020' [2014] OJ C200/1.

[40] E McGaughey, 'Soft Social Law in the United Kingdom' in M Hartlapp (ed), 'Studying EU Soft Law Effects in Social Policy' (2020) SoLaR Working Paper, https://papers.ssrn.com/sol3/papers.cfm?abstract_id=3668981, 107.

[41] Van Rijsbergen (n 31) 108.

[42] Ştefan and Biondi (n 26) 188.

[43] *Morge, R (on the Application of) v Hampshire County Council* [2010] EWCA Civ 608, para 24.

[44] Ştefan and Biondi (n 26) 190.

[45] T Devine and M Eliantonio, 'EU Soft Law in the Hands of National Authorities: The Case Study of the UK Competition and Markets Authority' (2018) 11 *Review of European Administrative Law* 71.

relies on EU guidance when deciding on cases.[46] Soft law is either referred to on its own or in conjunction with case law. As observed by Post, the FCA relies on ESMA guidelines and Q&As in its enforcement actions in the UK; in fact, the FCA seems to consider such guidance to enforce the duties of the firms to be within the remit of ESMA.[47] However, a complete vacuum arose in the context of social policy instruments.

This variation in use begs the following question: why are some instruments never referred to? In part, the answer may be sector-specific – in the social policy sector, McGaughey noted a complete lack of awareness towards EU soft law. The team contacted multiple sources from the Crown Commercial Service, the Child Poverty Unit of the Department of Work and Pensions, and the Government Equalities Office's Gender Pay Gap Reporting staff. Unfortunately, there appeared to be *nobody* with sufficient knowledge or awareness of *any* EU soft law measure.[48] However, this does not account for all variations.

A further cause could be the high degree of generality of EU guidance, as confirmed by an interviewee in relation to the Technology Transfer Guidelines.[49] Interviews reveal that most people in the public sector recognise that a framework is needed in order to facilitate competition within the market and to limit financial expenses. However, this does not mean that they will use any framework – the uptake of soft law by decision-makers clearly depends on awareness, clarity and relevance.

These variations are accentuated when it comes to the results of the case law searches. In social policy and financial regulation, the searches for the EU guidance documents chosen by the SoLaR team yielded no results. The former could be explained by the same reasons as for the uptake by decision-makers or, indeed, as a knock-on effect of that vacuum. Regarding financial regulation, this might be related to the narrow scope of the research, but after expanding the searches to other EU soft law, only one financial regulation court case was found which dealt with one national guidance document that appeared to be drafted in identical terms to the corresponding EU guidance.[50] In terms of State aid, three cases referred to soft law, mostly outside the SoLaR sample, yet the situation is slightly different than for financial regulation and social policy, as UK courts rarely deal with State aid cases.[51]

By contrast, numerous references were found in the fields of competition and the environment. Substantial references to soft law are not rare, with some cases quoting them extensively.[52] However, the UK courts seldom refer to EU

[46] Ştefan and Biondi (n 26) 185–86.
[47] Post (n 29) 138.
[48] McGaughey (n 40) 113.
[49] Ştefan and Biondi (n 26) 189.
[50] Post (n 29) 140.
[51] Ştefan and Biondi (n 26) 186–88.
[52] See, for instance, on State aid: *R (Sky Blue Sports & Leisure Ltd) v Coventry City Council* [2014] EWHC 2089 (Admin), confirmed in *R (Sky Blue Sports and Leisure Ltd) v Coventry City Council*

guidance on its own and always link it either with corresponding hard law or the case law of the Court of Justice of the European Union (CJEU). For example, in the *An Taisce* environment case, the High Court pointed out that the 'definitive interpretation of Union law is the sole prerogative of the European Court'.[53] At the same time, a Scottish court considered the interpretation of the EU soft law document, then considered the jurisprudence briefly as confirming this approach and consequently interpreted a binding obligation upon the relevant parties.[54] Guidance which is perceived as particularly helpful might even be used in draft form (for instance, the Notice on the Notion of Aid),[55] while other guidance might not be used at all.

Without clear insight into the courts' reasoning via judicial interviews, it is not possible to determine precisely why the courts do not always refer to soft law instruments. This could be because the instruments are unnecessary, as the hard law is sufficiently clear or precise, the instruments are controversial, or simply the instruments are not useful. According to one of our interviewees, sometimes soft law is simply not relevant in a case.[56] A good example is the Guidance Paper on Article 102 of the Treaty on the Functioning of the European Union (TFEU).[57] As noted by Georgieva in 2016, this instrument was not very popular with UK courts, even though it was mentioned by the claimants, and this was explained on the ground that it was highly controversial.[58] The interviewee expressed a different view with regard to the *Purple Parking* case, noting that the rejection of the Guidance Paper was not a reflection of the quality of the instrument, but simply an illustration of its limits.[59] Moreover, our searches show that the attitude towards the Guidance Paper might have changed. The Guidance was referred to in the recent *Socrates Training* case to explain the subtle differences between tying and bundling.[60] Most interestingly, in *British Telecommunications*, the Competition Appeal Tribunal (CAT) appears to be persuaded by the case law of the CJEU (in particular, the *TeliaSonera* opinion)[61] to use the Guidance Paper on Article 102 as a 'point of reference' in assessing

[2016] EWCA Civ 453; and on the environment, *Loader, R (on the Application of) v Secretary of State for Communities and Local Government and Others* [2012] EWCA Civ 869.

[53] *An Taisce (National Trust for Ireland), R (on the Application of) v Secretary of State for Energy and Climate Change and Another* [2014] EWCA Civ 1111, para 144.

[54] *Royal Society for the Protection of Birds, Re Judicial Review* [2016] ScotCS CSOH_103, 250.

[55] *R (Sky Blue Sports & Leisure Ltd) v Coventry City Council* (n 52), confirmed in *R (Sky Blue Sports and Leisure Ltd) v Coventry City Council* (n 52).

[56] Ştefan and Biondi (n 26) 189.

[57] European Commission, 'Communication from the Commission – Guidance on the Commission's enforcement priorities in applying Article 82 of the EC Treaty to abusive exclusionary conduct by dominant undertakings' [2009] OJ C45/7.

[58] Z Georgieva, 'The Judicial Reception of Competition Soft Law in the Netherlands and the UK' (2016) 12 *European Competition Journal* 54.

[59] Ştefan and Biondi (n 26) 189.

[60] *Socrates Training Ltd v Law Society of England and Wales* [2017] CAT 10.

[61] Case C-52/09 *Telia Sonera* [2011] ECR I-527, Opinion of AG Mazak.

margin squeezes. The judgment notes that the Guidance is not binding on CAT or on Ofcom, and proceeds to assess it in conjunction with the case law of the CJEU.[62] Finally, in *Streetmap v Google*, Justice Roth relied on the *Guidance Paper on Article 102* in order to determine the issue of objective justification in an abuse of dominance case. The Guidance was used in support of the argument that technical improvements in the quality of the goods are part of relevant efficiencies, and also in order to lay down the requirements of the proportionality test.[63] This example shows that the attitude towards a certain soft law instrument might change over time, and we can hypothesise that this is a result of the evolution of the EU case law itself, the socialisation of national judges to soft law or, simply, the relevance of an instrument for certain cases.

Overall, it appears that there is an openness to the use of soft law where the decision-makers and judges consider it useful or appropriate. That can be linked to clarity, precision or acceptability, or simply awareness of the documents. There is no guarantee they will be used unless an obligation arises.

C. Legal Effects and Mechanisms of Compliance

As expected, soft law is mostly used as an interpretation aid,[64] with the administration and courts not considering themselves *bound* by EU soft law. However, as noted by Dobbs in the environmental report, there is evidence within the cases that UK courts may be willing to go quite far in this respect.[65] For example, in the environmental case of *Loader*, EU guidance was referred to as part of European and national authority. However, it is difficult to infer that UK courts consider soft law binding in and of itself, as also noted in a UK Supreme Court case: 'It is important to emphasise that the legal requirements must be found in the legislation, as interpreted by the CJEU itself, not (with respect) in the opinions of the Advocates General nor in guidance issued by the Commission (however useful it may be as an indication of good practice).'[66]

[62] *British Telecommunications plc v Office of Communications (VULA) (Judgment (Non-specified Price Control Matters)* [2016] CAT 3, paras 90–92.

[63] *Streetmap EU Ltd v Google Inc* [2016] EWHC 253 (Ch), paras 145–46.

[64] On the environment, see the High Court judge in *Alternative A5 Alliance, Judicial Review* [2013] NIQB 30, para 81, who stated that: 'In relation to these submissions I consider that assistance can be obtained in relation to the meaning of "integrity" from the Commission's guidance on Article 6 of the Directive, "Managing Natura (2000)".' This is also seen in the Supreme Court judgment of *Champion, R (on the Application of) v North Norfolk District Council and Another* [2015] UKSC 52.

[65] Dobbs (n 21) 145.

[66] *Champion, R (on the Application of) v North Norfolk District Council and* Another (n 64) para 39. This is also reflected in the Court of Appeal stating that the EU guidance in question was not binding and that '[o]f much greater importance than the Guidance are, of course, the decisions of the ECJ which bind us' in *Morge, R (on the Application of) v Hampshire County Council* (n 43) paras 24–25; and the High Court, which has stated that 'the guidance is not the law. The law is to be found in the relevant provisions of the Habitats Directive and the 2010 regulations, and in

There are various reasons for which soft law is relied on by the UK courts and administration. The first relates to national statutory obligations. In the field of competition, section 60(3) of the UK Competition Act 1998 (CA 1998)[67] advises authorities to 'have regard to any relevant decision or statement of the [European] Commission'.[68] Indeed, Georgieva finds that the existence of such consistency obligation in the national legal order might make the application of soft law in court more likely.[69] The point is made in relation with a CAT judgment in *Cityhook*,[70] where, in the absence of relevant case law in the matter, the Court used section 60(3) of the CA 1998 in order to support its reliance on Commission guidance as an interpretation aid. As observed by Devine and Eliantonio, the administration also feels somewhat bound by soft law as a result of this statutory provision.[71] In *MasterCard*, the Office for Fair Trading (OFT; the predecessor of the CMA) interpreted the duty of section 60(3) as having 'to give serious consideration' to the Commission's statements.[72] Most interestingly, this approach appears to have been relaxed 10 years later, following the *Expedia* judgment of the CJEU in 2011.[73] In that case, the CJEU expressly stated that national authorities are not bound by EU's *De Minimis* Notice. In its 2013 decision in *Mobility Scooters*, the OFT noted that, 'notwithstanding the potential application of the Commission's *De Minimis* Notice, the OFT will also consider a number of factors in determining whether the infringements are appreciable by reference to the actual circumstances of the agreement'.[74]

Compliance might not only be the result of national statutory provisions, but also of EU statutory provisions. Article 16(4) of the ESMA Regulation, which introduces a 'comply-or-explain' mechanism with regard to ESMA guidance, is one such example. While this does not provide, strictly speaking, for a binding enforcement mechanism, ESMA can use other soft enforcement tools to foster compliance of national authorities, such as 'naming and shaming' through compliance tables, or peer reviews according to Article 30 of the ESMA Regulation.[75]

The high margin of discretion of the Commission also appears to be a factor that would influence administrative compliance with EU guidance. With regard to State aid, an area of exclusive competence of the Commission, an interviewee confirms that compliance with guidelines is triggered by the need to comply

any jurisprudence that sheds light on their meaning' in *Prideaux, R (on the Application of) v FCC Environment UK Ltd* [2013] EWHC 1054 (Admin), para 112.

[67] The UK Competition Act was first published in 1998: www.legislation.gov.uk/ukpga/1998/41/contents.

[68] *Independent Media Support Ltd v Office of Communications* [2008] CAT 13.

[69] Georgieva (n 58).

[70] *Cityhook Ltd v Office of Fair Trading* [2007] CAT 18, para 255.

[71] Devine and Eliantonio (n 45) 57.

[72] OFT Decision *MasterCard UK Members Forum Limited* [2005] CA98/05/05, paras 107–16.

[73] Case C-226/11 *Expedia* [2011] EU:C:2012:795.

[74] *Mobility Scooters (Pride Mobility)* CE/9578-12, A.76.

[75] Post (n 29) 133–34.

with EU State aid rules.[76] Interestingly, in relation to the Guidelines on fines, the OFT clearly states that they do not feel bound by Commission guidelines, 'particularly where the Commission has itself a wide margin of discretion'.[77] While both State aid and competition are areas of exclusive competence, this diverging approach can be explained by the fact that competition enforcement is nowadays decentralised and the UK authorities have *already* adopted a different methodology on fines, for example.

Some instances show that the reliance on soft law is connected in UK courts to general principles of EU law, such as consistency or the duty of sincere cooperation. With regard to consistency, the Court of Appeal noted in *MasterCard*, in relation to the Article 101(3) Guidelines,[78] that 'although … they are not legally binding and therefore some flexibility in whether they should be applied and followed is permissible, we consider that, as with the nature of evidence required to satisfy the first condition, consistency of approach across Member States is important'.[79] The judgment also refers to the fact that counsels for the parties did not suggest that 'national courts in other Member States have departed from the Guidelines in considering the issue of exemption under article 101(3)'.[80] Therefore, comparative approaches seem to be of relevance in the case law. In relation to the environment, Dobbs did not find any clear evidence that the principle of consistency would play a role,[81] although in one case, it was considered that the court's use of the EU soft law, alongside references to ECJ judgments, leads to coherency and consistency.[82] With regard to the duty of sincere cooperation, the early case of *Intreprenneur v Crehan* needs to be mentioned. Already in paragraph 5, Lord Bingham of Cornhill underlined the 'particular importance of wholehearted cooperation between national courts and the Commission in the field of competition' as 'reflected in the Commission's 1993 Notice on Cooperation between National Courts and the Commission in Applying Articles 81 and 82 of the EC Treaty … and in the Commission's Notice on cooperation within the Network of Competition Authorities'.[83] The contribution that soft law can have towards clarifying certain aspects of the law, thus also fostering transparency, appears to be acknowledged as well by UK judges. Indeed, in *Wye Valley*, in relation to the Commission's guidance on the interpretation of certain project categories in Annexes I and II to the EIA Directive, the Court of Appeal has stated that: 'The objective of the guidance is twofold: first, the document aims to improve understanding of what

[76] Ştefan and Biondi (n 26) 188.
[77] OFT Decision *Dairy Retail Price Initiatives* CE/3094-03.
[78] European Commission, 'Communication from the Commission – Notice – Guidelines on the Application of Article 81(3) of the Treaty' [2004] OJ C101/97.
[79] *Sainsbury's Supermarkets Ltd v MasterCard and Others* [2018] EWCA 1536 (Civ), para 106.
[80] ibid.
[81] Dobbs (n 21) 148–50.
[82] *Royal Society for the Protection of Birds, Re Judicial Review* (n 54) para 250.
[83] *Inntrepreneur Pub Company (CPC) and Others v Crehan* [2006] UKHL 38, para 5.

can be reasonably considered to be covered by certain project categories that have proved particularly difficult to interpret in practice; secondly, it is intended to provide an overview of existing useful sources of information at EU level.'[84]

IV. CONCLUSION

Overall, the research indicates a significant willingness to avail themselves of relevant soft law documents where the decision-makers or courts consider it useful and appropriate. When it comes to the role played by soft law in practice, sometimes the mentions are relatively tokenistic or in passing, but often the more frequent the mentions, the more the role increases and strengthens before the courts. However, the extent to which they are used varies across and even within the sectors, with a greater presence in the context of competition and environmental law than in social policy, for instance.

One solution for a more systematic reception of EU soft law might be to either transpose all relevant guidance into UK law or to create new domestic guidance. However, there has been a reluctance to transpose the targeted EU soft law into statute or as new national soft law, as noted by Dobbs in the environmental report.[85] This has arguably been done in the name of simplification and as transposition has been considered unnecessary, with courts noting that an informed decision-maker would know which guidance to take into account and where to find it.[86] According to one of our interviewees, inserting only brief references to EU financial guidance in the FCA handbook was done in order to keep the volume of the rules at a manageable level.[87] It appears that incorporating soft law by reference is an appropriate alternative solution: not only does it keep the core documents briefer, but it might even increase the weight of EU soft law more generally by demonstrating that the instruments are relevant and applicable internationally, without the need for full transposition.

While these recommendations might work well for an EU Member State, in our case the elephant in the room is Brexit. The UK has undertaken significant preparatory work for Brexit, especially the EU Withdrawal Act.[88] The objective of the Act is largely to plug the holes posed by Brexit through enabling statutory instruments to amend existing legislation now and in the future. The Withdrawal Act even provides for the continued application of existing CJEU judgments, as part of 'retained EU law', but with caveats. A major gap that

[84] *Wye Valley Action Association Ltd, R (on the Application of) v Herefordshire Council* [2011] EWCA Civ 20, para 18.

[85] Dobbs (n 21) 128–40.

[86] *Morge v Hampshire County Council* [2009] EWHC 2940 (Admin), para 60, states that 'it might be confidently expected that Natural England were aware of the terms of the Habitats Directive, the Commission Guidance and the Habitats Regulations, given that they were the authority responsible'.

[87] Post (n 29) 135.

[88] European Union (Withdrawal) Act 2018.

has not been addressed at all is the future of EU soft law. A significant question is whether to transpose it domestically into either hard or soft law or just let it lie. A factor in this debate is that current and future EU soft law would remain persuasive whether incorporated or not and decision-makers or courts could still avail themselves of it where relevant if they so wished. The question remains: how politic would it be for UK courts or administrators to still consider and apply EU soft law? Our crystal-ball prediction is that the application of EU soft law will remain at best haphazard in the UK in the following years. While judges and administrators might, in their work, find EU soft law instruments useful, express references to such instruments might indeed be fewer and fewer.

16

Three Worlds of Chinese Soft Law

FRANCIS SNYDER

I. INTRODUCTION*

THIS CHAPTER IS an exercise in understanding soft law in China. It is inspired first by an observation by Carlo Ancelotti, a celebrated football coach, that rules are important, but culture is even more important.[1] This statement from the world of sport may appear to be exotic in a legal academic setting, but in fact it is a useful introduction to our subject. It reminds us that rules are embedded in culture and society. It opens the possibility that such rules include both hard law and soft law, whether adopted by the State or other social organisations. It also insists that State hard law may be less important than other types of rules, such as the multiple varieties of soft law.

A second source of inspiration is Advocate General Bobek's Opinion in the recent EU case *Belgium v Commission*. It suggested that the Court of Justice of the European Union (CJEU) should recognise 'the changing legislative landscape of (not only) EU law, which is marked by a proliferation of various soft law instruments', such that 'there are norms generating significant legal effects that find themselves beyond the binary logic of binding/non-binding legal rules'.[2] This proposal, promoting substantive justice over formal justice, goes to the heart of the current debates about the rule of law. Though not accepted by

* Preliminary drafts of this chapter were presented at the Fourth SoLaR Workshop, Ljubljana, 11–12 October 2018, the SoLaR Final Event, Aix-en-Provence, 17–18 October 2019, and the STL Faculty Scholarship Workshop, Peking University School of Transnational Law, Shenzhen, 4 December 2019. I am grateful for the helpful comments received on these occasions. I also wish to thank Hu Zhouke, Liu Chenying, Phil McConnaughay, Ni Lili, Anne-Lise Strahtmann, Tian He, Wang Jiayi, Yang Wenbo, Zheng Xinjia and Zhou Xuan for their contributions to the chapter. I am especially grateful to Susan Finder for her invaluable comments and help. Wu Yanbin provided excellent research assistance. I thank Peking University School of Transnational Law and Peking University Shenzhen Graduate School for their support.

[1] See C Ancelotti (with C Brady and M Forde), *Quiet Leadership: Winning Hearts, Minds and Matches* (London, Portfolio Penguin, 2016) 157–65.

[2] Case C-16/16P *Kingdom of Belgium v European Commission*, Opinion of Advocate General Bobek, delivered on 12 December 2017.

the CJEU, it should stimulate serious comparative reflection on contemporary legal and normative systems.

A third source of inspiration is Luo Haocai and Song Gongde's *Soft Law Governance: Towards an Integrated Approach*.[3] This was the first major work on soft law in China that was written for Western scholars. Its purposes were, first, to integrate hard law and soft law into a single conception of law, and, second, to revise and replace the traditional state-centred conception of law with a new model of public governance in the transition to the rule of law in China.

China is a society that is very different from Europe. For the present purposes, we may bear in mind several salient features. China is a big, complex country (or 'civilisation')[4] with a long history and a large population of about 1.4 billion. In terms of GDP per capita, it ranks as an upper middle-income, developing country.[5] It is a party-state,[6] in which the basic principles of governmental organisation, including the Communist Party of China (CPC), differ fundamentally from Western, Weberian conceptions.[7] It has a civil law system, particularly influenced by Germany via Japanese law, with a significant legacy of Confucian thought, borrowings from the former Soviet Union and an increasing number of elements received from other legal systems, including the EU and the US, as well as a long-standing practice of using flexible rules, provisional measures, legal experimentation and personal relations as ways of governing society.[8]

This chapter introduces aspects of soft law in China, not only to inform but also to stimulate comparative reflection about what, if anything, is distinctive about soft law in China and also in European (and perhaps other Western) legal systems. The following section sketches the normative framework, authors and acts of Chinese soft law. The remainder of the chapter identifies three overlapping worlds or semi-autonomous social fields of soft law in China: the evolution of Chinese government policy from soft law to social governance to social management (World 1); soft law in legal scholarship (World 2); and soft law

[3] Luo Haocai and Song Gongde, *Soft Law Governance: Towards an Integrated Approach*, B Armour and Tang Hailong (trans) (Buffalo, NY, William S Heiner & Co, 2012).

[4] LW Pye, *The Spirit of Chinese Politics* (Cambrige, MA, Harvard University Press, 1992) 235.

[5] data.worldbank.org/country/china.

[6] Constitution of the People's Republic of China, art 3, www.wipo.int/edocs/lexdocs/laws/en/cn/cn147en.pdf; Constitution of the Communist Party of China (Chinese–English), amended and adopted at the 16th National Congress of the Communist Party of China on 14 November 2002 (Beijing, Foreign Languages Press, 2001).

[7] See, eg, F Snyder, *Food Safety Law in China: Making Transnational Law* (Leiden, EJ Brill, for the Xiamen Academy of International Law, 2016) 65–78.

[8] See, eg, J Needham, *Science and Civilisation in China, Volume 2, History of Scientific Thought* (Cambridge, Cambridge University Press, 1954, reprinted 2005) 544–47; S Heilman, EJ Perry and PM Thornton (eds), *Mao's Invisible Hand: The Political Foundations of Adaptive Governance in China* (Cambridge, MA, Harvard University Asia Center, 2011).

in Chinese courts (World 3). The conclusion draws these strands together and summarises the discussion.

II. RULE-MAKING AND SOFT LAW

A. The Framework

The framework in China for making governmental norms consists of the Legislation Law (2015 Amendment, hereinafter 'LL'),[9] the State Council Regulations on Procedures for the Formulation of Rules,[10] the State Council Regulations for the Formulation of Administrative Regulations,[11] the 2018 State Council Circular on administrative normative documents,[12] and Supreme People's Court (SPC) Interpretations.[13] The LL provides for the delegation of

[9] Legislation Law of the People's Republic of China (2015 Amendment) (Zhonghua Renming Gongheguo Lifafa), 《中华人民共和国立法法》（2015年修正）www.chinalawtranslate.com/2015lawlaw/?lang=en, adopted at the Third Session of the Ninth National People's Congress, 15 March 2000, amended by the Ninth Session of the Twelfth National People's Congress, 15 March 2015 (Order No 20 of the President, effective date 1 July 2000). The NPC recently authorised the National Supervisory Commission (NSC) to 'formulate supervisory regulations in accordance with the Constitution and laws', but at the time of writing, the LL has not yet been amended to take this authorisation into account: Stanford Law School and China Guiding Cases Project, 'New Source of Chinese Law and China's Anti-corruption Commissions'' 7 *China Law Connect* | 《中国法律连接》 第7期, cgc.law.stanford.edu.

[10] Regulations on Procedures for the Formulation of Rules [Effective] (规章制定程序条例 [现行有效]), issued on 16 November 2001 by the State Council, Decree No 322 of the State Council of the People's Republic of China, promulgated and effective as of 1 January 2002, revised on 22 December 2017 as the Regulations on Procedures for the Formulation of Rules, www.gov.cn/zhengce/content/2018-01/16/content_5257080.htm.

[11] Regulations on Procedures for the Formulation of Administrative Regulations (Xingzheng Fagui Zhingding Chengxu Tiaoli) [行政法规制定程序条例] (State Council Order [2001] No 321, promulgated 16 November 2001, effective 1 January 2002), art 4 (in Chinese), www.gov.cn/zhengce/content/2018-01/16/content_5257039.htm (in Chinese), revised by Decision of the State Council on Amending the Regulation on the Procedures for the Development of Administrative Regulations, 22 December 2017; Ordinance concerning the Procedures for the Formulation of Administrative Regulations (2017 Revision, (Xingzheng Fagui Zhiding Chengxu Tiaoli) 《行政法规制定程序条例》 2017修订'.

[12] Guowuyuan Bangongting Guanyu Jiaqiang Xingzheng Guifanxing Wenjian Zhiding he Jiandu Guanli Gongzuo de Tongzhi (State Council General Office Circular on Strengthening the Formulation and Supervision of the Management of Administrative Normative Documents) (Guo Ban Fa [2018] No 37, 31 May 2018), State Council website (in Chinese); Laney Zhang, 'China: State Council Issues Rules on Administrative Normative Documents', *Global Legal Monitor*, Library of Congress (US), 28 August 2018, www.loc.gov/law/foreign-news/article/china-state-council-issues-rules-on-normative-documents.

[13] eg, Interpretation of the Supreme People's Court on Application of the Administrative Litigation Law of the People's Republic of China, No 1 [2018] of the Supreme People's Court, adopted at the 1726th meeting of the Judicial Committee of the Supreme People's Court on 13 November 2018, issued 6 February 2018, entry into force 8 February 2018. For thorough studies of SPC interpretations, see S Finder, 'The Supreme People's Court of the People's Republic of China' (1993) 7 *Journal of Chinese Law* 145, 164–90; S Finder, 'China's Translucent Judicial Transparency' in *Transparency Challenges Facing China* (2018) Peking University School of Transnational Law Research Paper 141, 162–72, 173, ssrn.com/abstract=3344466.

norm-making power from the National People's Congress (NPC) to the State Council and its departments (ministries) (Article 9). It also provides for the specification of norms by subordinate governmental units to adapt national norms to local conditions or to adopt new norms appropriate for local conditions (Article 72), and also for analogous powers by provincial or other local administrative authorities (Article 82), Such norms must not be contrary to the PRC or CPC Constitutions or to CPC policy. The LL does not apply to non-legally binding acts.

The Regulations on Procedures for the Formulation of Rules seek 'to standardise the procedures for the formulation of rules and to ensure the quality of rules' (Article 1). They apply to all governmental organisations which have the power to formulate rules according to legislation or administrative regulations. They also apply to '[d]ecisions or orders with general binding force to be made or issued by the local people's governments at or above county level that do not have the power to formulate rules according to law' (Article 36). '[R]ules formulated in violation of these Regulations are null and void' (Article 2). In 2017, these Regulations were revised to provide that:

> Without laws or the basis of administrative regulations, decisions, orders of the State Council, departmental rules may not set norms that derogate from citizens, legal persons, and other organisations' rights or increase their obligations, and may not increase the power of the department or reduce the statutory duties of the department.[14]

These Regulations concern only legally binding rules and only those rules made by governmental authorities at or above county level. They do not apply to governmental measures which are not legally binding, regardless of their author, or to non-governmental rules, such as norms of self-regulation by social organisations. Nor do they seem to apply to interpretations issued by the SPC or the Supreme People's Procuratorate (SPP).

The Regulations on Procedures for the Formulation of Administrative Regulations, as revised in 2017, apply to 'proposing, drafting, reviewing, adopting, publishing, and interpreting of administrative regulations' (Article 2). They provide, inter alia, that: 'The lawful rights and interests of citizens, legal persons and other organisations shall be effectively protected, and the corresponding rights and the ways of guaranteeing the realisation of the rights shall be prescribed while the obligations to be performed are prescribed' (Article 12(4)).[15] They do not apply to acts that are not legally binding.

[14] Ordinance Concerning the Procedures for the Formulation of Administrative Regulations (2017 Revision) (XingzhengFagui ZhidingChengxu Tiaoli) 《行政法规制定程序条例》（2017修订）; Decision of the State Council on Amending the Regulations on the Formulation of Procedures, State Council Order No 695, promulgated 22 December 2017 and entered into force on 1 May 2018.

[15] Decision of the State Council on Amending the Regulation on the Procedures for the Development of Administrative Regulations, Order of the State Council (No 694), issued and to come

The 2018 State Council Circular set out definitions and procedures governing the issue of administrative normative documents, which accounts for much government agency soft law. The Circular requires public consultation when such documents are drafted and availability to the public once approved; unpublished documents should not be used as a basis for administrative practice.[16] In one specialist's words, the Circular 'reflects the continuing struggle to manage regulatory documents'.[17]

SPC and SPP Interpretations both have independent normative force. With regard to transparency, the 2018 SPC Interpretation on Application of the Administrative Litigation Law requires people's courts that judge administrative cases to cite any SPS interpretation which they apply and provides that such courts may cite lawful rules and 'other regulatory documents in force'.[18] However, it is not clear whether 'in force' refers only to legally binding acts.

B. Authors and Acts

Numerous authorities,[19] in addition to central government institutions, the SPC and the SPP, may adopt norms. China's 34 provincial-level administrative units have the power to adopt legislative and administrative acts, and so too do certain cities. In an earlier article, I and my co-authors found that they included:

> NPC legislation (jiben falu) and State Council regulations (xingzheng fagui)/(guizhang), decisions (jueding) and orders (mingling), which may be either definitive or provisional (zanxing). State Council departments (ministries) and commissions may issue regulations (guizhang), directives (zhishi), orders (mingling), provisions (guiding), rules (shishi xize), circulars (tongzhi) and other normative documents (guifanzing wenjian), which may be known as orders (mingling), decrees (ling), directives (zhiling), resolutions (jueyi), decisions (jueding), instructions (zhishi) or announcements (gong gao). Provincial and lower levels of government may issue local regulations (difangxing fagui), resolutions (jueyi), decisions (jueding), local administrative rules (difangxing xingzheng guizhang) or other normative documents (guifanxing wenjian).[20]

into force on 1 May 2018, VI (4), renumbered art 11 as art 12 and amending the article to read as quoted.

[16] Laney Zhang (n 13).

[17] JP Horsley, 'China's Central Government Seeks to Rein in Regulatory Documents', *Regulatory Review*, 7 May 2019, www.brookings.edu/opinions/chinas-central-government-seeks-to-rein-in-regulatory-documents.

[18] SPC Interpretation (n 13) art 100.

[19] This section relies heavily on F Snyder, Hu Zhouke and Ni Lili, 'Transnational Law in the Pacific Century: Mapping Pesticide Regulation in China' in P Zumbansen (ed), *The Many Lives of Transnational Law: Critical Engagements with Jessup's Bold Proposal* (Cambridge, MA, Cambridge University Press, 2020).

[20] ibid 168–69.

Soft law is widely used in Chinese domestic law,[21] as well as in China's international relations, for example, in policy dialogues with the EU,[22] and food safety cooperation with the Association of Southeast Asian Nations (ASEAN).[23]

One example is the Made in China 2025 (MIC 2025) 10-year strategic plan that was announced in May 2015, building on previous industrial policy and inspired by Germany's Industry 4.0 strategy.[24] It focuses on high-tech industries: 'automotive, aviation, machinery, robotics, high-tech maritime and railway equipment, energy-saving vehicles, medical devices and information technology [including 3D printing] to name only a few' of the areas of smart manufacturing.[25] It is designed to upgrade Chinese industry in line with the Fourth Industrial Revolution of automation and data exchange in manufacturing and high technology[26] – in other words, 'essentially to build an economic structure and capabilities similar to that of Germany and Japan'.[27] It has a domestic industrial development component and a foreign investment component, as well as the promotion of Chinese standards as international standards, partly through the Belt and Road Initiative (BRI) (One Belt, One Road (OBOR)), which likely will have a major impact on European countries.

Made in China 2015 involves different types of normative instruments, starting with China's 13th Five-Year Plan (FYP) (2016–20), the MIC 2025 itself, the 'Made in China 2025 Major Technical Roadmap' (the Green Book),[28]

[21] Shen Kui, 'Administrative "Self-Regulation" and the Rule of Administrative Law in China' (2018) 13 *University of Pennsylvania Asian Law Review* 72; Wei Cui, 'When Do Chinese Ministries Make Law?', papers.ssrn.com/sol3/papers.cfm?abstract_id=3469312. See also He Zhi-peng and Shang Jie, 'Soft Law Study in China: Achievement and Problems' (2014) 12 *Hebei Legal Science*, en.cnki.com.cn/Article_en/CJFDTOTAL-HBFX201412001.htm (in Chinese); Huang Maoqin, 'On the Soft Law Measure in the Economic Field: Analysis Based on Empirical and Normative Research Methods' (2011) 2 *Economic Law Review*, en.cnki.com.cn/Article_en/CJFDTOTAL-ZDXB201503012.htm (in Chinese); Zhai Xiaobo, 'Soft Law and Public Governance' (2007) 2 *Science of Law* (in Chinese).

[22] F Snyder, *The European Union and China, 1949–2008: Basic Documents and Commentary* (Oxford, Hart Publishing, 2009), Chinese translation by Institute of European Studies, Chinese Academy of Social Sciences, Beijing, published as *欧洲联盟与中国(1949–2008):基本文件与评注/平装]* (Beijing, Social Sciences Academic Press China, 2013).

[23] Lu Yi, 'Challenges in China-ASEAN Food Safety Cooperation Governance through Soft Law' (2015) 3 *Peking University Transnational Law Review* 141.

[24] European Commission, 'Digital Single Market: Implementation of an Industry 4.0 Strategy – The German Plattform Industrie 4.0', guest blog post by Henning Banthien, ec.europa.eu/digital-single-market/en/blog/implementation-industry-40-strategy-german-plattform-industrie-40; Germany Trade and Invest (GTAI), 'Industrie 4.0 – What is it', https://www.gtai.de/gtai-en/invest/industries/industrie-4-0. For overviews, J Wübbeke, M Meissner, MJ Zenglein, J Ives and B Conrad, 'Made in China 2025: The Making of a High-Tech Superpower and Consequences for Industrial Countries', Mercator Institute for Chinese Studies (MERICS), No 2 (December 2016), www.merics.org/sites/default/files/2017-09/MPOC_No.2_MadeinChina2025.pdf; United States Chamber of Commerce, 'Made in China 2015: Global Ambitions Built on Local Projections' (2017) 9–17, www.uschamber.com/sites/default/files/final_made_in_china_2025_report_full.pdf.

[25] Wübbeke et al (n 24) 6.

[26] ibid 12.

[27] ibid 16.

[28] On updates, see Eng.Gov.Cn, State Council and People's Republic of China, 'Made in China 2025 Roadmap Updated', english.gov.cn/news/top_news/2018/01/27/content_281476027458050.htm.

explanations and development plans, policies, industry outlines, legislation, administrative regulations, and standards. Several examples will suffice. The Green Book targets are not legally binding.[29] In addition to the 2016 State Council 'Guiding Opinions for Promoting SOE Restructuring and Reorganizing',[30] there are plans or explanations for several sectors: for example, the MIC 2025 Explanation: Strengthening Quality and Brand Construction, the Robotic Industry Development Plan (2016–20), the Guangdong Province Plan for the Development of Smart Manufacturing (2015–25)[31] and the 2014 State Council 'Guidelines to Promote National Integrated Circuit Industry Development'.[32] In May 2016, the CPC Central Committee and the State Council issued the National Innovation-Driven Development Strategy Outline.[33] In the same year, seven ministries and the People's Bank of China issued the 'Several Opinions on Finance to Support Industry Stable Growth, Restructuring, and Improving Profit'.[34] In 2016, the Ministry of Industry and Information Technology (MIIT) issued a draft 'Notice on Regulating Business Behavior in the Cloud Service Market'.[35] All are soft law measures.

A second example concerns the regulation of toxic pesticides. In the Chinese legal system today, there are more than 135 different acts currently in force about pesticides; this does not include either international or regional measures or general policy documents, which in China are often recognised to have legal force.[36] More than one-third of all the norms identified above (47 out of 135) were soft law.[37] This number itself is a severe underestimate, because it includes acts of only two provinces and one municipality.[38] The term for the act does not always indicate the norm-making authority; sometimes the same term may be used for norms made by different authorities.

[29] Wübbeke et al (n 24) 12.
[30] ibid 24.
[31] ibid 14–15.
[32] ibid 19.
[33] ibid 16.
[34] ibid 18.
[35] ibid 28.
[36] See Snyder et al (n 19).
[37] I define soft law as 'rules of conduct which, in principle, have not legally binding force but which, nevertheless, may have practical [and even] legal effects'. See F Snyder, 'The Effectiveness of European Community Law' (1993) 56 *MLR* 19, 32, further developed in F Snyder, 'Soft Law and Institutional Practice in the European Community' in SD Martin (ed), *The Construction of Europe: Essays in Honour of Emile Noël* (Deventer, Kluwer, 1994) 197–225.
[38] This normative complex includes the following types and numbers of acts, *ji ben fa lu* (laws) (three), *guo ji tiao ye* international treaties (two), *xing zheng fa gui* (administrative regulations) (five), *tong zhi* (circulars) (41), *fa gui jie shi* (interpretations) (two), *jue ding* (decisions) (one), *zhi dao yi jian* (guidance opinions) (three), *ming ling* (orders) (11), *xing zheng gui zhang* (provisions) (seven), *gong gao* (announcements) (32), *shi shi xi ze* (rules) (two), *gui hua* (proposals) (one), *zheng ce jie xian* (department regulatory documents) (one), *gui ding* (provisions) (five), *di fang xing fa gui* (local regulations) (one), *gui fan xing wen jian* (normative documents) (five) and *di fang xing xing zheng gui* (local administrative rules) (12).

Soft law is exemplified by measures from two of the most important agricultural provinces, Shandong and Shaanxi. Shandong Province promulgates many more local regulations to respond to and specify administrative rules from the central government. For example, Shandong Province has adopted a Notice to require improvement of ploughed land, such as to reduce the use of toxic pesticides.[39] In contrast, Shaanxi Province mainly relies on national measures. However, it has also adopted a trial governmental policy document, which is not binding on citizens but is binding on the government, to guide governmental action and encourage structural adjustment through differentiated pesticide registration policy. It is intended to facilitate registration by high-tech pesticide companies and to eliminate the use of highly toxic pesticides.[40] The two provinces differ in terms of the extent to which they adopt soft law measures, with the number being correlated roughly with population density, wealth and complexity of economic activity.

III. FROM SOFT LAW TO SOCIAL GOVERNANCE TO SOCIAL MANAGEMENT

The world of government policy has informed and conditioned the worlds of academic scholarship and of judicial practice. Three phases can be distinguished: soft law (*ruanfa*（软)), social governance (*shehui zhili*（社会中治理)) and social management (*shehui guangkong* (社会管控)). However, these phases are not unilinear, and the terms are ambiguous and 'may have different meanings depending on the context, the time, and the actor using them'.[41] In 2004, the 16th CPC Central Committee proposed to promote a 'social management system' featuring Party committee leadership, government responsibility, social coordination and public participation.[42] In its 2010 Rule of Law Opinion, the State Council stated that 'administration according to law is a key component

[39] Notice of the General Office of the People's Government of Shandong Province on Printing and Distributing the Planning of Cultivated Land Quality in Shandong Province (2014~2020) (Geng Di Zhi Liang Ti Sheng Gui Hua Tong Zhi (2014~2020))《山东省人民政府办公厅关于印发山东省耕地质量提升规划的通知（2014~2020）》, www.shandong.gov.cn/art/2014/12/23/art_285_6753.html. It sets forth four principles: overall planning with step-by-step implementation, adjustment of measures to local conditions, give priority to prevention and combine prevention and treatment, and governmental guidance with popular participation. It also identifies specific districts for special treatment regarding pesticide residues.

[40] Opinions of the General Office of the People's Government of Shaanxi Province on Promoting the Reduction of Use of Chemical Fertilizers and Pesticides (*Shaanxi Ren Min Zheng Fu Ban Gong Ting Guan Yu Tui Jin Geng Di Lun Zuo Xiu Geng Shi Xing Hua Fei Nong Yao Shi Yong Jian Liang Hua Yijian*)《陕西省人民政府办公厅关于推进耕地轮作休耕实行化肥农药使用减量化的意见》, knews.shaanxi.gov.cn/0/sxzb/8963.htm.

[41] H Snape, 'Social Management or Social Governance: A Review of Party and Government Discourse and Why it Matters in Understanding Chinese Politics' (2019) 24 *Journal of Chinese Political Science* 685.

[42] Decision of the CPC Central Committee on strengthening the construction of the party's governing capacity (adopted at the Fourth Plenary Session of the 16th CPC Central Committee on September 19, 2004), www.sina.com.cn.

of rule of law'.[43] The reference to social coordination and public participation stimulated considerable legal research focused on soft law.[44]

The phase of 'social governance' (*shehui zhili*) began on 12 November 2013. At the Third Plenary Session of the 18th Central Committee, the CPC Central Committee announced a series of major reforms in its Decision on Several Major Issues of Comprehensively Deepening Reform ('comprehensive deepening reforms' (全面深化改革; *quánmiàn shēnhuà gǎigé*)).[45] The reforms included 'uphold[ing] the unity of the rule of law, law-based government and law-based administration, and the integral development of a law-based country, government and society as a whole'.[46] Section XIII was devoted to making innovations in the social governance system. It stated that:

> To make innovations in social governance, we must direct our primary attention to safeguarding the fundamental interests of the broadest masses of the people, increase the factors of harmony to the maximum, invigorate social development and improve the social governance level, comprehensively promote the building of 'China of law and order', safeguard national security, ensure that the people live and work in peace and contentment, and that the society is stable and orderly.

In order to improve social governance, the Decision announced that:

> We will persist in implementing system governance, strengthen leadership by the Party committee, give full play to the leading role of the government and encourage and support the participation of all sectors of the society, so as to achieve positive interaction between the government management on the one hand and social self-management and residents' self-management on the other.

It thus officially adopted the concept of 'social governance'.[47] The first legislation to embrace 'social governance', as far as I am aware, was the 2015 Food Safety Law, which provided as follows: 'In the food safety work, priority shall be given to prevention, risk management and full process control shall be implemented, *the whole society shall participate*, and a scientific and rigid regulatory system shall be established' (emphasis added).[48]

[43] State Council Opinions concerning Strengthening Rule of Law Government Construction, posted on 10 October 2010, updated 7 May 2013, (GF No (2010)33), chinacopyrightandmedia.wordpress.com/2010/10/10/state-council-opinions-concerning-strengthening-rule-of-law-government-construction and www.gov.cn/zwgk/2010-11/08/content_1740765.htm, translation by N Howson, 'Enforcement without Foundation? Insider Trading and China's Administrative Law Crisis' (2012) 60 *American Journal of Comparative Law* 955, 986.

[44] Zhang Wenxian, 'Forty Themes on the Innovation and Development of Chinese Legal Research in the Reform and Opening up Era' (2019) 14 *Frontiers of Law in China* 2, 15.

[45] Decision of the Central Committee of the Communist Party of China on Some Major Issues Concerning Comprehensively Deepening the Reform (original English version), www.china.org.cn/china/third_plenary_session/2014-01/16/content_31212601.htm.

[46] On means, see ibid ss 30–35.

[47] Shen Kui沈岿(2018):《为了权利与权力的平衡 — 评罗豪才教授的法律思想》(Professor Luo Haocai's legal thoughts for the balance of rights and powers) [J], 行政法学研究2018(4):46.

[48] FSL 2015 Art 3. See Food Safety Law of the People's Republic of China (2018 Amendment) [Effective], Order No 22 of the President of the People's Republic of China, Art 3. See also

A third phase refers to 'social management' (*shehui guangkong*). After the 18th National Congress of the CPC, the CPC Central Committee replaced the concept of 'social governance' with that of 'social management'.[49] This resulted from a severe critique of the shortcomings of social governance, including hard law and soft law.[50] Following the 18th National Congress, the social management system comprised 'the leadership of Party committees, government responsibility, social coordination, public participation, and rule-of-law safeguard'.[51] The expression 'social management' thus emphasised increased state control over all aspects of society, in contrast to 'social governance' or 'public governance', which suggested limits on the power of the state, and encouragement and support for market actors and social subjects, such as self-regulatory organisations, to participate in the governance of public affairs.

From the policy perspective, President Xi Jinping drew many of these academic strands together at the CPC Central and Legal Work Conference on 15–16 January 2019. He emphasised the importance of adhering to the Party's absolute leadership of political and legal work and accelerating the modernisation of social governance. Returning to the policy of the mass line, he stressed that the social governance system 'is composed by CPC committee leadership, government responsibility, social coordination, public participation, and the rule of law guarantee, so as to create a social governance pattern of co-governance and sharing':[52] a cooperative governance.[53] Subsequently, these conclusions were summarised by legal scholars, who especially emphasised the importance of taking account of the different schools of thought about soft law in China, of carrying out empirical research on Chinese soft law, and of considering Chinese history and culture in order to build the legal system of the future.[54]

M Roberts and Ching-Fu Lin, 'China Food Law Update: The 2015 Food Safety Law and Social Governance on Food Safety' (2016) 12 *Journal of Food Law and Policy* 238; 涂永前 (Tu Yongqian), '关于当前我国食品安全治理若干问题的思考' ('Reflections on China's Current Food Safety Governance') (2017) 34 *Journal of Jianghan University (Social Science Edition)*; F Snyder and Yi Seul Kim, 'China's 2015 Food Safety Law: Crossing the River But Feeling the Stones and Avoiding Law Branches?' (2018) 6 *Chinese Journal of Comparative Law* 1, 38–39.

[49] Zhang Wenxian (n 44) 15–16.

[50] Zhang Wenxian, 'The Modernization of Social Governance and the Construction of the Social Governance Jurisprudence' (2019) 7 *China Legal Science* 4, 6.

[51] Zhang Wenxian (n 45) 15.

[52] Xi Jinping, Speech at the Central Political and Legal Work Conference, 15–16 January 2019, Beijing; verbatim translation by Wu Yanbin from original Chinese version, 11 November 2019.

[53] Zhang Shufen (张淑芬), 'Shehui Zhili Xuyao Ruanfa Baozhang' ('Social Governance Needs Soft law Guarantee') (2017) 89 *Journal of People's Rule of Law – Famous Column, The Way of Soft Law (China)*.

[54] Xu Kai and Xu Hanming, 'Accelerating the Establishment of "Three Major Systems" in Social Governance Jurisprudence and Promoting the Modernization of Social Governance' (2019) 7 *China Legal Science* 12; E Clark, 'China's Soft Law a Major Factor for Success in Future', 17 October 2013, www.china.org.cn/opinion/2013-10/17/content_30321578.htm. On different schools of thought, see also Xu Kai and Hu Hanming (ibid) 18; He Zhi-peng and Shang Jie, 'Soft Law Study in China: Achievement and Problems' (2014) 12 *Hebei Legal Science*, en.cnki.com.cn/Article_en/CJFDTOTAL-HBFX201412001.htm (in Chinese).

IV. SOFT LAW IN LEGAL SCHOLARSHIP

The intellectual founder of Chinese soft law scholarship was Professor Luo Haocai (1934–2018), who had a distinguished career as Peking University Professor, Dean and Vice-President, Vice-President and Judge of the Supreme People's Court, Vice-Chair and Chairman of the Central Committee of the China Zhi Gong Party (Public Interest Party), and Vice-Chair of the Chinese People's Political Consultative Conference (CPPCC). He also served as the first President of the academic organisation China Society for Human Rights Studies (CSHRS).[55] After 1999, he served as Advisor to the Chinese Association for International Understanding (CAIU, now CAFIU), a non-governmental organisation (NGO) that has consultative status with the UN Economic and Social Council (ECOSOC), and as President of the China Council for the Promotion of Peaceful National Reunification, focused on Taiwan.[56] Influenced by his theory of 'balance' in administrative law, Luo Haocai's work on soft law contributed to the birth and development of a perspective on law and governance that has been and remains very influential in China, partly as a point of departure for thinking about law today, but more often perhaps as an invisible backcloth or implicit foil in current debates.[57]

Starting in 2006, Luo Haocai and colleagues published a series of influential articles on soft law. They first urged the government to take soft law seriously, because both hard law and soft law had been used in Chinese practice since the end of the planned economy.[58] Globalisation, democratisation and marketisation entailed an irreversible trend from central government management (hard law) to public governance (*gongzhong zhili* (公众治理)), including soft law.[59] Exclusive reliance on state hard law was an important reason for governmental failure. Soft law was essential to increase innovation, enhance public participation, open up new areas such as the internet, improve the capacity of norms to catch up with social development, allow the use of industry norms and self-discipline created by social communities and autonomous organisations to fill gaps in hard laws, and improve implementation of rules because of greater public participation, wider consultation and improved responsiveness to diverse

[55] www.chinahumanrights.org/html/2014/BRIEFINGS_0801/126.html; www.chinahumanrights.org/html/2014/TRENDS_0725/57.html.

[56] www.zhongguotongcuhui.org.cn. For its constitution, see www.zhongguotongcuhui.org.cn/zt/hwhzh/tchjs/201308/t20130806_4555535.html; www.hoover.org/sites/default/files/research/docs/06_diamond-schell_sec03_2ndprinting_web.pdf.

[57] On the evolution of mainly constitutional law scholarship in China generally during this period, see S Seppänen, *Ideological Conflict and the Rule of Law in Contemporary China: Useful Paradoxes* (Cambridge, Cambridge University Press, 2016).

[58] Luo Haocai and Song Gongde (2006) 罗豪才，宋功德:《认真对待软法——公域软法的一般理论及其中国实践》('Take Soft Law Seriously – The Theory of Soft Law and its Chinese Practice')[J]，中国法学2006(2):4.

[59] ibid 10.

interests, thus reducing conflicts and costs.[60] Luo Haocai and colleagues considered that hard law and soft law had different social roles: the former concerned national management by mandatory rules, while the latter emphasised flexibility, guidance and incentives.[61] A transition from omnipotent government to more limited government was necessary to allow social organisations and people to innovate and manage their own affairs.[62]

In their 2013 book, Luo Haocai and Song Gongde defined soft law to mean:

- those legal norms embodied within those laws, regulations and rules that describe legal facts, or which are demonstrative, hortative, enticing, promotional, consultative or guiding in nature;[63]
- those reams of documents incorporating normative standards (normative documents), such as those legitimately created by national agencies as guidelines, instructions, standards, plans, discretionary bases and measures;
- those self-regulatory norms devised by various political organisations seeking to determine such political issues as exercise of power, participatory government and public political discourse;
- the extensive array of self-regulatory norms created by various societal communities – the systematisation, standardisation and procedur[al]isation of social self-regulation are important component parts of democratic politics.[64]

This inclusive conception embraced not only state law but also rules emanating from political organisations and societal communities engaged in self-regulation. It may appear to be a version of legal pluralism, but such was not the authors' objective, which instead was to go beyond the idea that the state was the sole source of 'law' and to propose a new way of thinking about the sources, characteristics and types of rules by integrating hard law and soft law.

To replace the traditional legalist, Kelsenian-flavoured state-administration paradigm, the book proposed a model of public governance: a 'diversified mixed law mode',[65] or hybrid legal regime, using both hard law and soft law, from a multiplicity of sources, in which different types of rules were tailored as appropriate to different objectives. The ambitious, central argument was revealed in the titles of successive chapters: (1) 'Out of the Predicament Inherent in the "State Control Paradigm" in the Transition to the Rule of Law'; (2) 'Reflections on a Revision of the Definition of "Law"'; (3) 'Rational Choice of a Rule of Law Mechanism According to Legal Objectives'; (4) 'Differentiation between Hard and Soft Law'; (5) Characteristics, Functions and Boundaries of Soft Law'; and

[60] Luo Haocai and Miao Zhijiang (2011)罗豪才，苗志江:《社会管理创新中的软法之治》('Soft Law in Social Management Innovation') [J]，法学杂志2011:3.

[61] ibid.

[62] ibid 4.

[63] Luo Haocai and Song Gongde (n 4) xvii.

[64] ibid xviii.

[65] Luo Haocai (2009) 罗豪才:《公共治理的崛起呼唤软法之治》('The Rise of Public Governance Calls for the Rule of Soft Law') [J]，政府法制 2009:12.

(6) 'The Integration of Hard and Soft Law'. The book also included a survey of foreign and Chinese studies of soft law. This argument embodied a specific legal strategy, which was that China was a large, diverse country in the midst of social transformation, so it 'must fully deploy the comparative advantages of its various institutional resources, rather than rigidly adhering to a statist view of law'.[66] Understood in its context, the argument could be viewed as a partial critique of the then-existing state-based legal system, as a convincing justification for a new way of thinking about law or as a clear and detailed theoretical blueprint for the future.

For Luo Haocai and colleagues, law meant more than hard law, because soft law, like hard law, was also an 'important governance tool'.[67] Their 'multidimensional view' sought to resolve a controversial practical and theoretical question by including CPC norms as soft law:

> The inner-party regulations issued by the Communist Party of China play a very important role in the national social governance, which involves the positioning of the inner-party laws and regulations in the construction of a country under the rule of law, the relationship between the inner-party regulations and the national legal documents, and so on. There is no ready-made answer to these questions. In this case, there is no precedent in the world to build a country under the rule of law. For a long time, 'inner-party regulations issued by the CPC play a very important role in the national social governance' which has been regarded as a phenomenon of illegal governance or even anti rule of law, and as an obstacle to the realization of the rule of law. The emergence of soft law theory can bring these unique political systems and phenomena into the orbit of rule of law. On the one hand, it bridges the gap between the concept of rule of law and the actual system, on the other hand, it provides the standard of rule of law to eliminate and regulate the existing norms.[68]

From their perspective, soft law governance was an essential part of the rule of law.[69] In their view, soft law could even more effective: '[it] does not rely on the state's coercive force, but relies on the public opinion, media, morality and other social influences, as well as the use of self-discipline and mutual law mechanisms to achieve its effect'.[70]

Other academic research focused on soft law as a form of 'modern social public governance', in the words of Peking University Professor Jiang Mingan.[71] He has argued that '[t]oday's rule of law is to a large extent the rule of soft

[66] Luo Haocai and Song Gongde (n 4) 43.

[67] Luo Haocai and Zhou Qiang罗豪才，周强(2013):《软法研究的多维思考》('Multidimensional Thinking of Soft Law Research') [J], 中国法学2013(5):106.

[68] ibid 109.

[69] Luo Haocai and Zhou Qiang罗豪才，周强(2016):《法治建设中的软法治理》('Soft Law Governance in the Construction of Rule of Law') [J], 江海学刊2016(1):126.

[70] ibid 127.

[71] Jiang Mingan姜明安 (2010):《完善软法机制，推进社会公共治理创新》('Improve the Soft Law Mechanism and Promote the Innovation of Social Public Governance') [J], 中国法学2010(5):17.

law'. Using hard law, the government has to sacrifice substantial justice for formal justice, to strictly enforce the law and to mechanically enforce the law at the expense of human dignity, thus causing the sharp opposition between the law enforcer and the governed.[72] Soft law could help to modernise national governance, regulate administrative discretion,[73] promote participatory and consultative democracy, and 'balance the relationship between reform, development, innovation and the rule of law'.[74] In his view:

> The rule of law includes formal rule of law and substantive rule of law. The formal rule of law mainly requires that there are laws to abide by, law enforcement to be strict, and violations to be prosecuted. The substantive rule of law not only requires the state governance to strictly abide by the law and enforce the law, but also requires that the law it abides by is 'good law'; not only requires the state governance to follow the specific provisions and rules of the law, but also the principles, spirit and the concept of the rule of law; not only requires the state governance to follow the hard law, but also consciously follow the soft law (the law not guaranteed by the state force, such as constitutional convention, basic principles of law, articles of association and self-discipline rules of social public power organization, laws and regulations within the ruling party, policy outline and guidelines issued by state organs, and agreements on public affairs signed between public power subjects, etc.) and consciously subject to soft law.[75]

Soft law thus proposed a diversity of norms,[76] embracing diverse levels of government, fields of activity[77] and sanctions, such as 'the punishment pressure brought by the soft law responsibility mechanism, such as the derogation of personal social evaluation and criticism from the public'.[78] Its aims included to promote the common governance of state public power and social public power,[79] in which 'the leader of the construction of the rule of law, namely the ruling party, has recognised the dual authority structure of the state public power and the social public power',[80] thus reflecting the evolution of government policy from soft law to social governance to social management.

[72] ibid 19.

[73] Jiang Mingan姜明安 (2014):《软法在推进国家治理现代化中的作用》('The Role of Soft Law in Promoting the Modernisation of National Governance') [J], 求是学刊2014(9):79.

[74] ibid 86.

[75] Jiang Mingan姜明安 (2014):《改革法治与国家治理现代化》('Reform of the Rule of Law and Modernisation of National Hovernance') [J], 中共中央党校学报2014(8):50.

[76] ibid. See also Bi Honghai毕洪海 (2016):《从丑小鸭到白天鹅—软法研究十年侧记》('From Ugly Ducklings to White Swans, Ten Years of Soft Law Research') [J], 人民日报2016(3); Chen Guang陈光 (2019):《论法治社会建设中的多元规范及其结构》('On Multiple Norms and Their Structures in the Construction of a Society Ruled by Law') [J], 时代法学2019(6):15.

[77] Chen Guang (n 76) 16–17.

[78] ibid 22.

[79] Jiang Mingan (n 75) 53.

[80] Chen Guang (n 76) 15; see also Zheng Yi(郑毅), 'Quanmian Tuijin Yifu Zhiguo Zhongde Ruanfa Juese' ('The Role of Soft Law in the Comprehensive Promotion of the Rule of Law') (2017) 87 *Journal of People's Rule of Law – Famous Column, The Way of Soft Law (China)*.

V. SOFT LAW IN CHINESE COURTS

Soft law is often used in Chinese courts,[81] although, of course, litigation does not reflect the extent of the actual use of non-legally binding measures by Chinese governmental authorities.[82] In general, a court applies soft law, usually in the form of an administrative normative document (*guifanxing wenjian*),[83] in three ways. First, a court may apply soft law as an auxiliary of hard law, even though the court could have reached a conclusion according to the relevant provisions of laws or regulations, in order to enhance the persuasiveness of judicial reasoning, but without examining the normative validity of the documents. For example, in *Meitong*,[84] a case on administrative punishment, the appeal court pointed out that the non-legally-binding Opinions (*yijian*) of the General Administration of Quality Supervision (AQSIQ) Concerning the Implementation of the Food Safety Law stated that the Regulations on the Administration of Industrial Product Production License (*tiaoli*) and the Rules for the Implementation of Quality and Safety Supervision (*xize*) are State Council administrative regulations, which should not conflict with the Food Safety Law (*falu*) enacted by the NPC. Second, a court may request an opinion from an administrative authority about how to interpret a legal document. In a 2004 case, the SPC requested an opinion from the People's Bank of China (PBOC) about how to interpret the term 'external reasons' in a marine cargo transportation insurance contract. The power of interpretation belonged in theory to the SPC, and the PBOC reply was not legally binding. Nevertheless, the SPC accepted the PBOC reply as a valid interpretation of the insurance contract.

Third, a court may apply soft law separately as the basis for judging the legality of a challenged administrative act, without reviewing the legality of the normative documents or quoting the normative basis of other superior norms. The normative status of governmental and departmental rules (*guizhang* (规章)) and other normative documents (*guizhang wenjian*) has been the subject of considerable legal debate.[85] Judicial review of other normative documents was considered in the preparation of the revision of the 2015 Administrative Litigation Law (ALL),[86] which had excluded informal rule-making from

[81] See S Finder's articles on SSRN: https://www.ssrn.com/index.cfm/en/.

[82] See Shen Kui (n 21). On the use of soft law by governmental authorities and 'the calculus of lawmaking', see Wei Cui and Jian Wan, 'When Do Chinese Subnational Governments Make Law?', ssrn.com./abstract-3467703; Wei Cui, 'When Do Chinese National Ministries Make Law ?', 10 October 2019, ssrn.com/abstract=3469312 or dx.doi.org/10.2139/ssrn.3469312; Howson (n 43).

[83] 'Informal policy directive' (IPD) is the translation used by Wei Cui, Jie Cheng and D Wiesner, 'Judicial Review of Government Actions in China', 31 May 2018, ssrn.com/abstract=3228175 or dx.doi.org/10.2139/ssrn.3228175, published as Wei Cui, Jie Cheng and D Weiser, 'Judicial Review of Government Actions' (2019) 1 *China Perspectives* 29.

[84] *Wuxi Meitong Food Technology Co Ltd v Wuxi Quality and Technology Supervision Bureau Zone Branch*, Bulletin of the Supreme People's Court, No 7, 2013.

[85] See Jianfu Chen, *Chinese Law: Context and Transformation*, revised and expanded edn (Leiden and Boston, Brill and Nijhoff, 2016) 254–55.

[86] Wei Cui et al (n 83).

judicial review. A 2018 SPC Interpretation excluded administrative guidance, administrative actions without external effect, internal supervisory acts to the list of exclusions and 'actions having no actual impact on the rights and obligations of citizens, legal persons or other organizations'.[87] However, courts do review and give legal effect to such acts. Before 2018, courts could not invalidate these informal policy documents; they could only decide to apply them or not.[88]

The 2018 SPC Interpretation drew on the ALL provision that:

> Citizens, legal persons or other organizations feeling that a state council department's or local people's government or its departments' normative document on which an administrative act was based is unlawful, they … [request] a review of the normative document when they raise a lawsuit over the administrative act. Normative documents … do not include rules.[89]

When a citizen, a legal person or any other organisation filed a complaint against an administrative action and concurrently requested a review of the regulatory document as the basis thereof, the court having jurisdiction over the administrative action case was required to conduct a concurrent review.[90] If the court concluded that the normative document was possibly illegal, it was required to hear the opinion of the issuing authority, but failure to obtain such an opinion could not prevent the court from reviewing the document.[91]

A court may review the document to ascertain whether it exceeded the powers of the issuing authority, violated statutory procedures or breached any provisions of ALL Article 64, namely that it:

> (1) [Was o]utside the statutory remit of the developing authority, or beyond the authorization by the law, regulations or rules.
> (2) Contraven[ed] the provisions of any law, regulations, rules, or any other superordinate law.
> (3) [W]ithout a basis in any law, regulations or rules, illegally increase[d] any obligation, or derogating from the lawful rights and interests, of any citizen, legal person, or any other organization.
> (4) Fail[ed] … to comply with the statutory approval procedure or the public issuance procedure, or seriously violating the development procedure.
> (5) Otherwise violat[ed] … the law, regulations or rules.[92]

If the court determined that the document was illegal, it could provide the issuing authority with judicial proposals for amendment or repeal. Some observers describe this power as 'extraordinary',[93] apparently because it transgresses the

[87] SPC Interpretation (n 13) arts 1(3), (5), (6), (10).
[88] Wei Cui et al (n 83) 12.
[89] Administrative Litigation Law 2015, art 53.
[90] SPC Interpretation (n 13) art 145.
[91] ibid art 147.
[92] ibid art 148.
[93] Wei Cui et al (n 83) 19. This is based on art 64 of the 2015 ALL, as interpreted by the SPC in 2018.

classic Western liberal constitutional conception of the separation of powers, which does not exist in China. Provision was also made for the recording of the judgment by higher administrative and judicial authorities and for retrial.[94] If the court concluded that the regulatory document was legal, the document could serve as the basis for determining the legality of the administrative action. From one perspective, other normative documents that are legal 'are now binding on courts' and must be given legal effects.[95] Seen from another perspective, this 'incidental review' substantially enhances the power of the judiciary and may promote the judicial review of other government documents.[96]

VI. CONCLUSION

The Chinese legal system makes extensive use of soft law. The profile of soft law in China has been informed by a long history, the co-existence of various philosophical traditions, borrowings from a variety of other legal systems, the co-existence of the CPC and the government in a system of dual rule since 1949, and a centuries-old tradition of apparently highly centralised government combined with great normative diversity in an extensive territory with a large population. The range and variety of soft law used in China are much greater than those used in Europe. This is accentuated by the legal and institutional features of Chinese government, the relative weakness and limited role of Chinese courts until recently, or the legal principle that an act can only be interpreted by the author of the act, not by the judiciary (except the SPC), which might otherwise play a unifying or harmonising role.

In many ways, Chinese soft law is similar to soft law in many Western legal systems. However, there are significant differences between the use of soft law in China and its use in Europe. The histories, cultures, and economic and political systems in Europe are different from those of China. In Europe, the debate about soft law has always been informed by its contrast with hard law, in the context of a sharp distinction between law and politics, features which are often ascribed to post-Westphalian states. The EU of course is not a state, but rather a regional integration scheme of sovereign states, and is hence a divided-power system, based on the principle of attributed competences and powers. Its use of soft law mainly derives from these features, its institutional structure, its recent enlargement and consequent diversity.[97] In China, however, the profile,

[94] SPC Interpretation (n 13) arts 149–51.

[95] Wei Cui et al (n 83) 19. However, compare Case 22/70 *Commission v Council (ERTA)* [1971] ECR 263.

[96] Horsley (n 17).

[97] F Snyder, 'Soft Law and Governance: Aspects of the European Union Experience', based on a presentation at the Workshop on Soft Law, Peking University Law School Soft Law Research Centre, Beijing, 4 November 2007.

theory and practice of soft law do not depend on these elements. China is a unitary state, so the contraposition of central soft law and the courts of smaller (sovereign) units does not exist. Instead, Chinese soft law confronts a historical distinction between legalism and Confucianism[98] and a revolutionary period of adaptive governance,[99] is contraposed to a long tradition of centralised government and now strong administration, is concerned with gradually transforming a centrally planned economy and its related state law, and is often oriented to building a multi-centred normative system, with the state at the centre. Soft law, social governance and social management appear as means and ideologies of recalibrating, rebalancing and re-orienting a strongly administrative, state-centred legal system and gradually transforming a centrally planned economy while maintaining social stability.

This chapter has sought to explore soft law in China by considering three worlds or semi-autonomous social fields. Clearly, these worlds are interconnected and sometimes overlapping. The world of government policy supplied a rough chronological framework, key themes and intellectual focus for the world of soft law scholarship, creating 'a restrictive political participatory channel',[100] though academic research was often oriented to legal theory or prescriptions for the future, and remained to some extent a partly autonomous academic realm. The world of government policy also provided a chronological framework for the world of soft law in legal practice, not for everyday court judgments directly, but rather in terms of an occasional emphasis on substantive justice and of key developments emanating from central state institutions, such as the 2018 SPC ALL Interpretation and the 2018 Circular regulating administrative normative documents. Soft law, like so-called 'hard law', is embedded in society, and Chinese soft law is no exception. As this chapter has shown, soft law is alive and well in different parts of the world. However, first impressions of great similarity may be misleading and it is necessary to bear in mind the importance of culture and society in shaping the social meanings of rules.

[98] See also Howson (n 43) 993.

[99] BL Liebman, 'A Return to Populist Legality? Historical Legacies and Legal Reform' in Heilman et al (n 8).

[100] Snape (n 41) 689.

Part III

Evaluation

17

Judicial Review of Soft Law before the European and the National Courts

A Wind of Change Blowing from the Member States?

MARIOLINA ELIANTONIO

I. INTRODUCTION

WHAT ARE THE legal effects of EU soft law? To what extent is EU soft law 'binding' upon its addressees, be it the Member States or the European institutions? These are thorny issues that have been addressed by earlier research,[1] as well as by many chapters in this volume.[2] While there is no unequivocal answer to these questions, there is a consensus in the literature (and the findings of this volume confirm this) on the fact that EU soft law generates some legal effects for the Commission and the national

[1] The literature on this subject is vast. Without any attempt at completeness, see, eg, O Ştefan, *Soft Law in Court: Competition Law, State Aid and the Court of Justice of the European Union* (Deventer, Kluwer Law International, 2012); L Senden, *Soft Law in European Community Law* (Oxford, Hart Publishing, 2004); Z Georgieva, 'Competition Soft Law in French and German Courts: A Challenge for Online Sales Bans Only?' (2017) 24 *Maastricht Journal of European and Comparative Law* 175; Z Georgieva, 'The Judicial Reception of Competition Soft Law in the Netherlands and the UK' (2016) 12 *European Competition Journal* 54; T Devine and M Eliantonio, 'EU Soft Law in the Hands of National Authorities: The Case Study of the UK Competition and Markets Authority' (2018) 11 *Review of European Administrative Law* 49. A comprehensive account of the literature can be found in O Ştefan et al, 'EU Soft Law in the EU Legal Order: A Literature Review', https://papers.ssrn.com/sol3/papers.cfm?abstract_id=3346629.

[2] See all the national contributions in this volume, as well as the chapters by G Gentile and N Xanthoulis (chs 5 and 18 in this volume, respectively).

competent authorities, and guides the administrative discretion at the EU and national levels.[3]

Taking this observation as a starting point and keeping in line with one of the overarching questions of the European Network of Soft Law Research (SoLaR) project, this chapter investigates the possibilities of judicially controlling the validity of EU soft law. If EU soft law is capable of producing legal effects in a 'Community based on the rule of law',[4] it should then be possible to bring judicial review claims to control its validity.

The judicial review of EU soft law was the focus of the 2018 *Belgium v Commission* ruling by the Court of Justice of the European Union (CJEU),[5] in which the Court did not follow the opinion of the Advocate General (AG) Bobek pleading for a relaxation of the admissibility requirements applicable in annulment actions at the EU level, which have traditionally excluded judicial review of soft law measures in most cases. Remarkably, AG Bobek relied on comparative law to show that at the Member State level, a growing trend can be observed towards the relaxation of the rules applicable to direct challenges of *domestic* soft law measures. Judicial review of national soft law and the emergence of less strict admissibility rules have therefore been used as a benchmark to assess the extent to which the CJEU is upholding an overly restrictive approach to the control of EU soft law.

In December 2019, the question of judicial review of EU soft law came again before the CJEU through a preliminary question by the French Council of State, with the relaxation of rules concerning the judicial control of domestic soft law again taking centre stage. In particular, the French highest administrative court asked the CJEU whether a set of guidelines issued by the European Banking Authority (EBA) could be subject to an annulment action under Article 263 of the Treaty on the Functioning of the European Union (TFEU).[6] The case concerns a claim against the act through which the French Prudential Control and Resolution Authority (Autorité de contrôle prudentiel et de resolution) has declared to comply with the EBA's guidelines. Having concluded that in light of the recent jurisprudential developments, the opinion of the French authority – albeit a soft law measure – can be subject to judicial review, the Council of State asked whether the EU soft law in question can be reviewable in an annulment action. In order to justify the need to have an answer to this question, the French court used the 'ploy' of the *Textilwerke Deggendorf* case law,[7] on the

[3] O Ştefan, 'Helping Loose Ends Meet? The Judicial Acknowledgement of Soft Law as a Tool of Multi-level Governance' (2014) 21 *Maastricht Journal of European and Comparative Law* 359, 367–68.

[4] Case C-294/83 *Parti écologiste 'Les Verts' v European Parliament* [1986] EU:C:1986:166, para 23.

[5] Case C-16/16 P *Belgium v Commission* [2018] EU:C:2018:79.

[6] Conseil d'État, 9ème–10ème chambres réunies, 4 December 2019, no 415550, ECLI:FR:CECHR:2019:415550.20191204, registered as Case C-911/19 *Fédération bancaire française (FBF) v Autorité de contrôle prudentiel et de résolution (ACPR)* (pending).

[7] Case C-188/92 *TWD Textilwerke Deggendorf GmbH v Bundesrepublik Deutschland* [1994] EU:C:1994:90.

basis of which an act which can 'without any doubt' be challenged directly in a direct action cannot subsequently be challenged indirectly through a preliminary question of validity. Considering that it needs to have an answer in relation to the possibility of directly challenging the EBA guidelines in order to make a determination as to whether an indirect challenge is available to the applicant, the Council of State 'cornered' the CJEU into giving an answer on the question of the judicial review of EU soft law.

The opinion of AG Bobek in *Belgium v Commission* and the pending preliminary ruling question show, on the one hand, that the discussion concerning the admissibility requirements is far from settled and, on the other hand, that this discussion is inextricably linked to that concerning the judicial review of domestic soft law. In light of this, this chapter provides a comparative law perspective to the criteria applicable to the judicial review of domestic soft law measures, and applies those findings to the measures covered by the SoLaR research, with the aim of evaluating the CJEU's approach vis-a-vis its national counterparts. Although EU soft law can also be reviewed indirectly through the preliminary question of validity under Article 267 TFEU and – in the case of domestic soft law – through a direct challenge of an administrative measure based on that soft law instrument, this chapter is exclusively focused on the *direct* judicial control of EU soft law. The system of indirect review of EU soft provides an additional avenue for litigants; however, as highlighted by AG Jacobs in the *UPA* ruling,[8] it is not an adequate substitute for the lack of direct actions. Because of the present focus on the direct judicial control of EU soft law, the analysis at the national level will be limited to the rules on direct actions against domestic soft law measures.

This chapter proceeds as follows. After introducing the case law of the CJEU on direct actions against soft law measures, it considers the SoLaR soft law measures and investigates whether, on the basis of the case law, they would be reviewable by the CJEU. The analysis shows that none of the selected measures would be readily reviewed by the Court of Justice in an annulment action, although some (especially in the financial regulation field) may stand a higher chance of passing the threshold than others. The chapter then moves on to discuss the rules applicable to the review of domestic soft law in four of the SoLaR jurisdictions: France, England, Germany and Italy. It examines whether national courts are more generous than the European courts in terms of admitting direct claims against soft law measures, and the extent to which the selected SoLaR measures would be reviewable by national courts. Apart from being part of the SoLaR jurisdictions, this sample of legal systems reflects the various 'families' (Romanic, Germanic and common law) of administrative law – and of judicial review – in Europe. Furthermore, France and Germany are interesting

[8] Case C-50/00 P *Unión de Pequeños Agricultores v Council of the European Union* [2002] EU:C:2002:197, Opinion of AG Jacobs.

because they have been included by AG Bobek in his comparative overview as legal systems which have witnessed an evolution in terms of openness towards the judicial control of soft law measures.[9]

On the basis of these findings, the chapter will conclude that the a wind of change is blowing from several Member States in respect to the judicial control of soft law. Moreover, the pending preliminary question from the French Council of State may well be the golden opportunity for transforming the 'wind of change' into a 'perfect storm' which will force the Court of Justice to revisit its restrictive approach.

II. SOFT LAW BEFORE THE EUROPEAN COURTS

A. The CJEU's Case Law on Judicial Review of EU Soft Law: 'Still Confused, But on a Higher Level'[10]

The notion of 'reviewable act' is key to determining the possibilities to judicially review soft law. Pursuant to Article 263 TFEU, 'the Court of Justice of the European Union shall review the legality of legislative acts, of acts of the Council, of the Commission and of the European Central Bank, other than recommendations and opinions, and of acts of the European Parliament and of the European Council intended to produce legal effects vis-à-vis third parties. It shall also review the legality of acts of bodies, offices or agencies of the Union intended to produce legal effects vis-à-vis third parties'.

At first sight, this provision seems to exclude the review of soft measures. However, the Court in the *ERTA* case expanded the scope of application of judicial review to all acts intended to produce legal effects. According to the Court, 'an action for annulment must be available in the case of all measures adopted by the institutions, whatever their nature or form, which are intended to have legal effects'.[11] In the *IBM* case, the Court explained that legal effects are deemed to exist where the measure is 'binding on, and capable of affecting the interests of the applicant by bringing about a distinct change in his legal position'.[12] Furthermore, according to the Court, 'the form in which such acts or decisions are cast is, in principle, immaterial as regards the question whether they are open to challenge under that article'.[13]

On the basis of this case law, the *ERTA/IBM* threshold – that is, the capacity to produce legal effects, which is the 'gateway' to reviewability in actions for annulment – has been held to be met, as far as soft law is concerned, when

[9] Case C-16/16 P *Kingdom of Belgium v European Commission* [2017] EU:C:2017:959, Opinion of AG Bobek, para 84.

[10] This quote is commonly attributed to Enrico Fermi.

[11] Case C-22/70 *Commission v Council* [1971] EU:C:1971:32, para 42.

[12] Case C-60/81 *IBM v Commission* [1981] EU:C:1981:264, para 9.

[13] ibid.

guidance is construed as introducing a new obligation,[14] where a soft law measure determines the way in which an EU institution intends to exercise its discretion[15] or where the measure at stake has been produced in cooperation with the Member States.[16]

Because of the limited circumstances in which these criteria are met, there has been a call from academics for 'more stringent control',[17] arguing that such limited access to court with respect to soft law measures 'fails to acknowledge important consequences that soft law can have on the rights and obligations of individuals'.[18] Matters are further complicated by the vagueness of the *ERTA/IBM* case law, because the notions contained therein (such as 'capable of affecting the interests of a person', 'bringing about a distinct change' in a person's 'legal position') are not consistently applied by the Court, so that it is not easy to foresee when a soft law measure will be considered reviewable.[19]

An additional layer of uncertainty is added by the Court's criteria to assess whether an act produces legal effects, namely 'the wording, the context, the substance of the act, as well as the intention of its author'.[20] These terms are in themselves unclear and the relative weight of each of these factors has never been fully clarified by the Court. Furthermore, in the analysis of the wording and context of the act, more attention is increasingly given to the perception of the addressees of a soft law measure.[21]

Yet another source of uncertainty is generated by the inconsistent approach of the Court with respect to the use of the phrase 'legal effects'. As observed by AG Bobek,[22] there has been a shift in the case law with respect to this point. In the earlier case law, the requirement for reviewability was that the act in question was intended to produce 'legal effects', whereas in the more recent case law, the requirement has become that of an act intended to have 'binding legal effects'.[23]

[14] Case C-366/88 *France v Commission* [1990] EU:C:1990:348. Along the same lines, see Case C-325/91 *France v Commission* [1993] EU:C:1993:245.

[15] Joined Cases C-189/02 P, C-202/02 P, C-205/02 P, C-208/02 P and C-213/02 P *Dansk Rørindustri and Others v Commission* EU:C:2005:408, para 211.

[16] Case C-311/94 *Ijssel-Vliet Combinatie BV v Minister van Economische Zaken* [1996] EU:C:1996:383.

[17] L Senden, 'Soft Post-legislative Rulemaking: A Time for More Stringent Control' (2013) 19 *European Law Journal* 57. See also J Scott, 'In Legal Limbo: Post-legislative Guidance as a Challenge for European Administrative Law' (2011) 48 *Common Market Law Review* 329; Ştefan (n 3); M Eliantonio and O Ştefan, 'Soft Law before the European Courts: Discovering a "Common Pattern"?' (2018) 37 *Yearbook of European Law* 457; J Alberti, 'Challenging the Evolution of the EMU: The Justiciability of Soft Law Measures Enacted by the ECB against the Financial Crisis before the European Courts' (2018) 37 *Yearbook of European Law* 626; AH Türk and N Xanthoulis, 'Legal Accountability of European Central Bank in Bank Supervision: A Case Study in Conceptualizing the Legal Effects of Union Acts' (2019) 26 *Maastricht Journal of European and Comparative Law* 151.

[18] Ştefan (n 3) 369.

[19] See Xanthoulis, ch 18 in this volume.

[20] *Commission v Council* (n 11).

[21] Eliantonio and Ştefan (n 17).

[22] Joined Cases C-463/10 P and C-475/10 P *Deutsche Post AG and Germany v Commission* [2011] EU:C:2011:656.

[23] This is noted in the Opinion of AG Bobek in *Kingdom of Belgium v European Commission* (n 9) paras 69–70. He notes that in *ERTA*, the court stated that 'an action for annulment must … be

This has led commentators to conclude that 'it has been difficult to predict with certainty when Union acts can be subject to judicial control and in which judicial forum'.[24]

B. Through the Looking Glass: SoLaR Soft Law before the CJEU

The above section has shown that the approach of the CJEU has been restrictive and highly unpredictable with respect to the possibility of judicial control of soft law measures. This conclusion is now tested with regard to the SoLaR soft law measures.[25]

In the field of financial regulation, all four soft law instruments studied were guidelines authored by the European Securities and Markets Authority (ESMA) and addressed to national supervisory bodies as well as directly to financial market participants. These soft law measures, while not being formally binding, have an in-built comply-or-explain mechanism, on the basis of which national authorities are required to notify ESMA and justify their action in case they decide not to follow them.

While ESMA guidelines have never been the object of a direct action before the CJEU, a case could be made in favour of their justiciability before the CJEU. Ştefan and Petri have argued, with respect to guidelines issued by the Agency for the Cooperation of Energy Regulators, that market operators may well feel that they have essentially no choice but to comply with the soft law instruments.[26] These guidelines, because of their aim, wording and addressees, might well be compared to the ESMA guidelines at stake. Also, the ESMA instruments are written in a 'prescriptive' language[27] and the perception of prescriptiveness is further reinforced by the 'comply-or-explain' mechanism enshrined therein. If the perception of the addressees is to play a role in the equation, this mechanism certainly strengthens the bindingness of the measure in the eyes of competent authorities, which have to take an additional step if they want to disregard the guidelines. A fortiori, this perception of bindingness is confirmed when considering the perspective of market operators that see compliance with the guidelines as their only realistic option. Therefore, it is not out of the question that the Court of Justice would admit a claim against these measures, based

available in the case of all measures adopted by the institutions, whatever their nature or form, which are intended to have *legal effects*' (para 60). On the other hand, in *Deutsche Post AG and Germany v Commission* (n 22), the Court referred to the fact that 'any measures adopted by the institutions, whatever their form, which are intended to have *binding legal effects* are regarded as acts open to challenge, within the meaning of Article 263 TFEU' (para 36), emphasis added).

[24] Türk and Xanthoulis (n 17).

[25] See Annex I to the Introduction for a list of the measures selected for the SoLaR project.

[26] O Ştefan and Marina Petri, 'Too Weak to Be Controlled: Judicial Review of ACER Soft Law' (2018) 37 *Yearbook of European Law* 525, 534–39.

[27] See, eg, the many 'Competent authorities should ensure that …' in the 'Guidelines on complaints-handling for the securities (ESMA) and banking (EBA) sectors' (2018).

on the case law according to which a soft law measure is considered as producing legal effects if it contains a new obligation vis-a-vis the hard law measure it is considered to concretise. This conclusion seems to be supported by the *Clearing Houses* case, in which the General Court (GC) admitted a claim against a 'policy' by the European Central Bank. In this case, the Court emphasised the very specific language used in the instrument – comparable to that used by the ESMA guidelines under examination – as well as 'the way in which the parties concerned could reasonably have perceived' it.[28]

In the field of competition and State aid law, the SoLaR project comprised 13 Commission-authored instruments, in which the Commission explains how it will enforce EU law. At first sight, these measures seem to be less prescriptive than the SoLaR financial regulation instruments. However, the Court in the *Dansk Rørindutri* case construed a 'comply-or-explain' mechanism for competition and State aid measures, which resembles the mechanism contained in the above-mentioned ESMA guidelines. On the basis of this case, soft law in this field has a 'self-binding' effect on the institution issuing the measures and can only be departed from if the authority duly provides reasons for doing so.[29] Nevertheless, this mechanism only applies to the issuing EU institution and not to the national authorities. In the *Expedia* ruling, the Court of Justice – departing from the AG's position[30] – stated that national competition authorities 'may take into account [Commission Notices,] but [are] not required to do so'.[31] On the basis of this case law, and applying the *ERTA* case law (possibly even 'corrected' by the increased attention towards the 'perception of the addressees' to establish whether a measure is intended to produce legal effects), it seems unlikely that any of those measures will be considered reviewable by the Court of Justice.

This conclusion seems to be corroborated by two rulings brought against one of the SoLaR State aid measures, ie, the 'Guidelines on State aid for environmental protection and energy 2014–2020'.[32] In these cases, the Court did not admit a claim brought against this soft law instrument, but rather than pointing out a lack of a 'reviewable act', it denied the claim on the basis of lack of 'direct concern' for the purposes of Article 263(4) TFEU. The Court did not discuss whether the guidelines constituted a reviewable act under Article 263(4) TFEU and proceeded to determine whether the measure was of 'direct concern' to the application, ie, whether it was liable to directly affect the legal situation of the

[28] Case T-496/11 *United Kingdom of Great Britain and Northern Ireland v European Central Bank (ECB)* [2015] EU:T:2015:133.

[29] *Dansk Rørindustri* (n 15).

[30] Opinion of AG Kokott in Case C-226/11 *Expedia Inc v Autorité de la concurrence and Others* [2012] EU:C:2012:544.

[31] Case C-226/11 *Expedia Inc. v Autorité de la concurrence and Others* [2012] EU:C:2012:795, para 53.

[32] Case T-694/14 *EREF v Commission* [2015] EU:T:2015:915; Case T-670/14 *Milchindustrie-Verband and Deutscher Raiffeisenverband v Commission* [2015] EU:T:2015:906.

individual. This judicial attitude supports the literature which has observed the conceptual confusion in the Court's case law[33] between the notions of 'reviewable act' and that of 'direct concern', as they are both linked to the idea of a measure being able to produce 'legal effects'.[34]

For the environmental law field, the SoLaR sample included a number of interpretative soft law measures stemming from three environmental directives. These measures, coming with various names, publication and translation statuses, all aim at 'giving practical guidance in the implementation of technically complex pieces of legislation, including the interpretation of ambiguous legal terms'.[35] Because of their interpretative nature and despite the criticism expressed in earlier writings,[36] and more recently by AG Bobek,[37] it is unlikely that these soft law measures will be considered as producing 'binding legal effects' and thereby pass the 'reviewability act' test. This is because, first of all, these soft law measures constitute interpretative aid addressed to Member States. They do not contain statements of how the Commission is going to exercise its discretion. Furthermore, they have not been adopted in the framework of a *specific* cooperation obligation between the Member States and the Commission.[38] Finally, the environmental guidance documents contain disclaimers as to their non-binding nature and lack of intention to create any new obligations.

Finally, in the social policy field, the SoLaR project has selected three soft law measures. The Buying Social guide provides guidance 'chiefly for public authorities' and encourages the consideration of social criteria for selecting tenders in EU public procurement law.[39] The document is non-prescriptive in its language and only suggests options for competent authorities and market players. The Commission recommendation on investing in children, much like the recommendation at stake in *Belgium v Commission*, acknowledges that 'policies addressing child poverty are primarily the competence of Member States',[40] but suggests that 'a common European framework can strengthen synergies across

[33] See, eg, *Deutsche Post AG and Federal Republic of Germany v European Commission* (n 22) para 38: 'Where ... an action for annulment is brought by a non-privileged applicant against a measure that has not been addressed to it, the requirement that the binding legal effects of the measure being challenged must be capable of affecting the interests of the applicant by bringing about a distinct change in his legal position *overlaps with* the conditions laid down in the fourth paragraph of Article 263 TFEU' (emphasis added).

[34] Türk and Xanthoulis (n 17); see also Xanthoulis, ch 18 in this volume.

[35] See A Hofmann, ch 3 in this volume.

[36] Scott (n 17); Eliantonio and Ştefan (n 17).

[37] See Opinion of AG Bobek in *Kingdom of Belgium v European Commission* (n 9) para 104: 'Could it not be expected of a Member State, when implementing the original piece of EU legislation, to which the post-legislative recommendation is in a way "attached", to implement it in the way further clarified in that recommendation? If not, what is the recommendation then for? If yes, then the considerable and real legal effects of a recommendation can hardly be disputed.'

[38] *Ijssel-Vliet Combinatie BV v Minister van Economische Zaken* (n 16) para 44.

[39] European Commission, *Buying Social: A Guide to Taking Account of Social Considerations in Public Procurement* (Luxembourg, Publications Office of the European Union, 2011), 5.

[40] European Commission, 'Commission Recommendation of 20 February 2013 Investing in children: breaking the cycle of disadvantage' [2013] OJ L59, para 16.

relevant policy areas, help Member States review their policies and learn from each other's experiences'.[41] It therefore only 'recommends that Member States organise and implement policies to address child poverty and social exclusion ... in accordance with the following guidelines'.[42]

The third social policy soft law instrument is possibly the closest to the Recommendation which AG Bobek considered in his opinion. The Commission 'Recommendation on transparency in equal pay' builds on EU hard law and 'provides guidance to Member States to assist them in a better and more effective implementation of the equal pay principle in order to combat pay discrimination and to contribute to tackling the persistent gender pay gap'.[43] It does so in a fairly prescriptive language, by suggesting a number of measures which Member States 'should' implement.

However, none of the three comes close to the degree of precision and prescriptiveness displayed by the Commission Recommendation[44] at stake in the *Belgium v Commission* case. Nevertheless, the GC in the *Belgium v Commission* case confirmed that the wording of the Recommendation only contained an 'invitation' and that there was no intention on the Commission's part to produce binding legal effects.[45] However, as has convincingly been argued, 'the detailed prescriptive provisions of the recommendations contradict the idea that only suggestions are made and mere principles are outlined without the expectancy that Member States will also comply with the proposed recommendation'.[46] Be that as it may, the conclusions reached by the GC and reiterated by the Court of Justice in *Belgium v Commission* confirm that most probably, none of the SoLaR social policy instruments will be reviewable before the Court of Justice.

In conclusion, in all likelihood, none of the SoLaR measures would be readily considered as a reviewable act by the Court of Justice in an annulment action. The most likely candidates to pass the applicable threshold are the ESMA guidelines, if and only if the Court takes the 'comply-or-explain' mechanism and the role of the perception of the addressees seriously.

[41] ibid.

[42] ibid after para 17, 'recommends that Member States ...'.

[43] European Commission, 'Commission Recommendation of 7 March 2014 on strengthening the principle of equal pay between men and women through transparency' [2014] OJ L69, after para 24, I, 1.

[44] European Commission, 'Commission Recommendation of 14 July 2014 on principles for the protection of consumers and players of online gambling services and for the prevention of minors from gambling online' [2014] OJ L 214/38. That the measure at stake has a very prescriptive and precise language is also the assessment of AG Bobek in *Kingdom of Belgium v European Commission* (n 9) para 128.

[45] The GC in Case C-16/16 P *Belgium v Commission* (n 5).

[46] F Coman-Kund and C Andone, 'European Commission's Soft Law Instruments: In-between Legally Binding and Non-binding Norms' in P Popelier, H Xanthaki, W Robinson, JT Silveira and F Uhlmann (eds), *Lawmaking in Multi-level Settings: Legislative Challenges in Federal Systems and the European Union* (Baden-Baden, Nomos, 2019) 188.

III. THE JUDICIAL CONTROL OF SOFT LAW BEFORE THE NATIONAL COURTS: VARIATIONS ON A THEME

The above section concluded that, with varying degrees of likelihood, none of the SoLaR soft law measures will be easily amenable to judicial control in an annulment action before the European courts. This section proceeds to examine the admissibility requirements for domestic soft law in order to evaluate the extent to which the selected SoLaR measures would be reviewable by the national courts. The aim of the analysis is not to provide a detailed examination of whether functionally equivalent domestic soft law measures in the national legal systems exist and have been or would be judicially reviewable, but rather to discuss the broader trends in the review of soft law at the national level in order to compare and contrast these trends with those sketched above with respect to the EU judiciary.

A. Italy: A Traditional (Yet Not Totally Deaf) Approach to the Judicial Review of Soft Law

In the Italian legal system, the main domestic soft law measures are the 'administrative circulars' (*circolari amministrative*), measures through which administrative authorities traditionally give instructions to hierarchically subordinated authorities.[47] Given their internal nature, the case law has consistently held that they cannot be challenged directly before the administrative courts, but only together with a subsequent single-case decision that is based on an allegedly unlawful circular. This is because, as internal measures, circulars are considered incapable of producing any concrete harm to an individual's legal position.[48]

However, this general rule finds an exception for those cases in which circulars display legal effects outside the administration, by concretely governing the activities of the addressees.[49] For example, a circular which explains how to submit an application to obtain funding under the Common Agricultural Policy[50] or a circular which provides for conditions on how to carry out driving examinations[51] has been considered reviewable.

In light of this, the SoLaR soft law measures in the fields of competition law, environmental law and social policy, while not reviewable by the CJEU on the basis of the applicable case law, would also not meet the required threshold under Italian law. This is because these Commission measures are addressed

[47] See further J Alberti and M Eliantonio, ch 11 in this volume.
[48] TAR Lazio, Sez II, 30 August 2012, n 7395.
[49] TAR Lazio, Sez I, 13 February 2019, n 2800.
[50] TAR Lazio, Sez II Ter, 19 January 2015, n 802.
[51] TAR Campania Napoli, Sez III, 11 September 2007, n 7481.

to national competent authorities and so, should a claim against comparable circulars be brought before an Italian administrative court, the likely conclusion would be that these measures are of purely internal relevance, as they help authorities to interpret certain legislative terms, enforce the legislation or merely suggest a certain course of action. A different conclusion could instead be reached for the ESMA guidelines. Indeed, provided that the ESMA guidelines are explicitly addressed to market participants, they would fulfil the requirement, created by the Italian case law, on the basis of which circulars are directly challengeable when they display legal effects outside the administration, by concretely governing the activities of the addressees.[52] Therefore, while not much more open than the EU legal system, the Italian system does allow the direct judicial control of at least those soft law measures that *directly* regulate the conduct of individuals.

B. France: Towards a New Dawn for the Judicial Review of Soft Law?

Like the Italian legal system, the French legal system is also familiar with the notion of 'circulars' (*circulaires*), internal administrative measures with comparable features and functions to their Italian counterparts.[53] However, the notion of 'soft law' (*droit souple*) in France is a complex, diverse and wide-ranging phenomenon, which does not end at the – albeit fundamental – notion of circulars.[54]

The French legal system has witnessed a remarkable evolution with respect to the judicial control of soft law, which, as mentioned above, has been explicitly singled out as a 'best practice' by AG Bobek.[55] Indeed, until 2002 and on the basis of a long-standing case law (which started with the 1954 *Institution Notre-Dame du Kreisker* ruling), a circular could only be subject to an action for judicial review if it 'added to the legal system'.[56] In general, this was rarely considered to be the case for circulars, as their main function is to interpret the law and not to add new rules.[57] The *Institution Notre-Dame du Kreisker* ruling was itself a result of the evolution of an earlier jurisprudence according to

[52] See, eg, para 1 of Annex I of the 'Guidelines on the exemption for market making activities and primary market operations under Regulation (EU) 236/2012 of the European Parliament and the Council on short selling and certain aspects of Credit Default Swaps', pursuant to which: 'These guidelines apply to investment firms, credit institutions, third-country entities, firms as referred to in point (l) of Article 2(1) of Directive 2004/39/EC of the European Parliament and of the Council on markets in financial instruments (MiFID).'

[53] See further N Rubio and O Ştefan, ch 8 in this volume.

[54] C Testard, 'Le droit souple, une "petite" source canalisée' (2019) 16 *Actualité Juridique de Droit Administratif* 934.

[55] *Kingdom of Belgium v European Commission* (n 9) Opinion of AG Bobek, para 85.

[56] Conseil d'État, Assemblée, 29 January 1954, n 07134 (*Notre-Dame du Kreisker*).

[57] R Chapus, *Droit du contentieux administratif* (Paris, Domat, 2008) 750.

which circulars could never be subject to judicial control. They were invariably considered 'interpretative' in nature and therefore incapable of 'adding to the legal system'. With the *Institution Notre-Dame du Kreisker* ruling, the Council of State recognised that circulars may sometimes be able to 'add to the legal system', namely that they may go beyond merely interpreting the law towards adding new rules. Those circulars were then regarded as challengeable in an action for annulment. In 2002, one further step towards a broader review of circulars was taken with the *Duvignères* ruling. In this case, the Council of State held that the main criterion to establish the reviewability of a circular is the presence of 'mandatory terms'. On this basis, a circular that merely reiterates the mandatory terms of a legislative provision, despite not 'adding to the legal system', can nevertheless be challenged.[58]

More recently, the focus of the Council of State moved from assessing wording to evaluating the perception and impact of the particular measure on the potential addressees. For example, the 2011 *Formindep* ruling evaluated the recommendations on good medical practices issued by the competent French authority.[59] The court did not examine the mandatory nature of the content of the measure, but rather looked at how the measure would be taken into account by health professionals in light of their deontological obligations. It is also noteworthy that the Council of State linked the 'weight' that the recommendation would have on its addressees to the fact that the measure was supposed to reflect the scientific state of the art.[60] Part of this 'cultural evolution' was a report issued by the Council of State in 2013 dedicated entirely to the phenomenon of soft law. The report had the twofold aim of increasing awareness on the proliferation of soft law instruments and giving public authorities conceptual tools for its appropriate use.[61]

The trend towards a broader control of soft law measures was further confirmed in 2016 with two Council of State rulings about a statement (*prise de position*) of the French Competition Authority and press releases of the French

[58] Conseil d'État, Section du Contentieux, 18 December 2002, n 233618 (*Mme Duvignères*); see also Conseil d'État, 4ème et 5ème sous-sections réunies, 8 March 2006, 275551 (*Fédération des conseils de parents d'élèves des écoles publiques*); Conseil d'État, 1ère et 6ème sous-sections réunies, 26 September 2005, n 270234 (*Conseil national de l'ordre des médecins*); Conseil d'État, 1ère et 6ème sous-sections réunies, 17 November 2010, n 332771 (*Syndicat français des ostéopathes*); Conseil d'État, 9ème et 10ème sous-sections réunies, 3 May 2011, n 331858 (*Société Voltalis*).

[59] Conseil d'État, 1ère et 6ème sous-sections réunies, 27 April 2011, n 334396 (*Association pur une formation medicale independante (FORMINDEP)*).

[60] On this point, see further M-L Moquet-Anger, 'Brevet de juridicité et contrôle de légalité des recommandations de bonne pratique de la Haute Autorité de santé (HAS)' (2011) 42 *La Semaine Juridique Administrations et Collectivités territoriales* 2321, with reference to the earlier case law on the role of science in the determination of administrative courts' decisions. A similar position was expressed with respect to the recommendations of the French Drug Safety Agency (Agence Française de Sécurité Sanitaire des Produits de Santé): Conseil d'État, 1ère et 6ème sous-sections réunies, 4 October 2013, n 356700 (*Agence française de sécurité sanitaire des produits de santé*).

[61] 'Etude annuelle 2013 du Conseil d'État – Le droit souple', https://www.vie-publique.fr/rapport/34021-etude-annuelle-2013-du-conseil-detat-le-droit-souple.

Financial Market Authority, respectively.[62] In these cases, the Council of State again departed from the imperative nature of the wording to instead look at the capacity of the measure to produce 'significant effects', especially of an economic nature, or to 'significantly influence' the behaviour of the addressees.[63]

This position has been followed in a number of later rulings concerning a statement and several press releases of the High Council for Audiovisual Communications (Conseil supérieur de l'audiovisuel),[64] an instruction for the use of a drug drawn up by the High Authority of Health (Haute autorité de santé)[65] or guidelines concerning the use of mobile networks issued by the Regulatory Authority for the electronic communications and postal services (Autorité de régulation des communications électroniques et des postes).[66]

The question that remained following these cases was whether this case law ought to be seen as specific for the regulatory agencies and therefore not generalisable to other acts of soft law. The answer to this question is also relevant for the present purposes. Indeed, on the basis of this case law, it seems likely that the ESMA guidelines would be reviewable before French courts, because of their particular weight in the regulation of the market and their capacity to influence the behaviour of the market actors on the basis of the comply-or-explain mechanism.

The question of generalisability of the case law has been debated in doctrine. Some have argued that there are elements that speak in its favour, especially because the above-mentioned 2013 Report by the Council of State concerned soft law in general and may be taken to show a general change of mentality in the French highest administrative court.[67] This suggests – as also hinted by AG Bobek in his Opinion – that all SoLaR soft law measures could in principle be subject to judicial review on the basis of this case law, because all SoLaR measures are capable of producing 'significant effects' or 'significantly influencing'

[62] Conseil d'État, Assemblée, 21 March 2016, n 368082 and Conseil d'État, Assemblée, 21 March 2016, n 390023 (*Société Fairvesta International GmBH*).

[63] See further A Sée, 'Le droit souple des autorités de régulation' (2016) 5 *Droit administratif Commentaire* 34, who relates this case law to the earlier case law on the *mesures d'ordre interieur*. The same is argued by L Benezech, 'L'affermissement de la justiciabilité des actes de droit souple devant le Conseil d'État' (2020) 2 *Droit Administratif* Commentaire 6. The case law has been confirmed, eg, with respect to a deliberation through which the High Council for the Audiovisual Sector (Conseil supérieur de l'audiovisuel) determined that a certain advertisement cannot be broadcasted: Conseil d'État, 5ème–4ème chambres réunies, 10 November 2016, n 384691 (*Mme Marcilhacy et autres*).

[64] Conseil d'État, 5ème–4ème chambres réunies, 10 November 2016, n 384691 (*Mme Marcilhacy et autres*).

[65] Conseil d'État, 1ère–6ème chambres réunies, 19 July 2017, n 399766 (*Société Menarini France et autres*).

[66] Conseil d'État, 2ème–7ème chambres réunies, 13 December 2017, n 401799 (*Société Bouygues Télécom et autres*).

[67] Sée (n 63); for a critical discussion concerning only the soft law of regulatory agencies, see L Calandri, 'La justiciabilité variable des actes de Soft Law des autorités de régulation: retour sur une jurisprudence en construction' (2020) 1 *Droit Administratif*, Étude 2; arguing for a restrictive approach, S von Coester, 'Les communiqués', *Revue Française du Droit Administratif* 2016, 497.

the behaviour of the addressees, whether in the form of the determination of the existence of environmental effects of a certain project or a violation of competition law, or the production of new policies in the workplace or in award procedures.

This conclusion has now been reaffirmed by a 2019 ruling of the Council of State, which concerned a non-binding declaration (*déliberation*) of the French High Authority for the Transparency in Public Life (Haute autorité pour la transparence de la vie publique) concerning Marine Le Pen's statement on her financial situation, as required by the applicable legislation.[68] The French court held that even if the challenged measure was not binding, it was neverthless liable to produce 'significant effects', notably in terms of reputation, for the applicant – effects which, in turn, were liable to influence the behaviour of those to whom the applicant addresses herself, ie, the voters.

Two more rulings confirm this trend. In one of these rulings, handed down in 2019, the Council of State departed from the notion of 'economic effects' that it mentioned in *Fairvesta* to consider that the determining criterion to assess if a recommendation of the French Drug Safety Agency can be subject to judicial control is whether the measure issued by an 'administrative authority'[69] is liable to 'significantly influence the behaviour of the applicants and holders of marketing authorisation, as well as of patients'.[70] This case law constitutes an extension of the earlier *Fairvesta* case law, not only because it concerns a type of soft law measure beyond the field of economic regulation and the activities of regulatory authorities, but also because it takes into account possible 'behavioural effects' which are very far removed from the measure at stake.

The difficulties surrounding the test (How can the capability of the soft law to influence or change the behaviour of the target addressees be determined? What effects should count as 'significant'? How to define the addressees?) have not gone unnoticed in French academia.[71] However, the trend described above

[68] Conseil d'État, Assemblée, 19 July 2019, n 426389 (Marine le Pen).

[69] See on this point, L Benezech, 'L'affermissement de la justiciabilité des actes' (n 63). He notes that the Council of State changed the terminology in this case from soft law issued by a 'regulatory authority' to soft law issued by an 'administrative authority'. He considers this a further signal that the Council of State is determined to open the judicial review of soft law measures broadly.

[70] Conseil d'État, 1ère–4ème chambres réunies, 21 October 2019, n 419996 (*Association française de l'industrie pharmaceutique pour une automédication responsable*). Similar considerations are made in a ruling of just a few days before: Conseil d'État, 10ème–9ème chambres réunies, 16 October 2019, n 433069 (*Quadrature du net*).

[71] F Chaltiel, 'Nouvelle extension de la justiciabilité du droit souple – À propos de l'arrêt du Conseil d'État du 19 juillet 2019' (2019) *Petites Affiches*, 30 October, 4; C Malverti and C Beaufils, 'Le Conseil d'État donne du mou au droit souple' (2019) 34 *Actualité Juridique de Droit Administratif* 1994, who argue that: 'Or, sur ce point, la jurisprudence est, semble-t-il, condamnée à entrer "dans l'ère de la casuistique pure"' ('Now, on this point, the case law seems to be entering a phase based purely on "a case-by-case approach"'; R Lanneu and A Sée, 'Recours contre un acte de droit souple – Souplesse du droit, souplesse du juge' (2017) 2 *Droit Administratif*, Commentaire 9, 5 who consider that: 'En effet, dès lors qu'une autorité agit dans le cadre de sa fonction, ne peut-on pas considérer que toutes ses actions pourront potentiellement créer des effets notables? Ou que le but de son action n'est pas d'influencer significativement le comportement des individus?' ('Indeed, when an

signifies a clear mentality shift on the part of the French highest administrative court and confirms the acceptance of soft law measures as an 'object' of judicial review in their own right.[72] Moreover, for the purposes of this chapter, it should be observed that this approach may likely lead to the possibility of judicial control of all SoLaR measures, including the 'softer' ones such as those in the field of social policy, because they all have the potential to influence the behaviour of those to whom the measures are addressed.

C. England: Much Ado about Nothing?

In the English legal system, domestic soft law measures are very common and have a variety of names such as 'guidance', 'policy', 'guideline', 'circular' and more.[73] The question *of whether* they can be judicially reviewed is not something that has been contentious or explicitly discussed in the case law. This is because the English system of judicial review is not dogmatic with respect to the doctrine of the 'forms of administrative action',[74] unlike many continental legal systems, and virtually any form of administrative action can be regarded as a 'decision' for the purposes of bringing a claim for judicial review.[75]

On this basis, for example, 'policies',[76] 'guidance',[77] 'instructions'[78] and 'circulars'[79] have all been held to be judicially reviewable.[80]

authority acts to exercise its functions, can all its actions not be considered as potentially able to create significant effects? Or can it not be considered the aim of its actions to significantly influence the individuals' behaviour?'); C Testard, 'Le droit souple, une "petite" source canalisée' (2019) 16 *Actualité Juridique de Droit Administratif* 934, who extensively unveils the unclarities and possible inconsistencies in the new test advanced by the Council of State.

[72] See also Malverti and Beaufils (n 71), who consider the implication of this new trend for the judicial review of French soft law in general; S Boda and B Pouyau, 'Actes de droit souple – Une extension majeure du domaine des actes de droit souple faisant grief: la justiciabilité des délibérations de la Haute Autorité pour la transparence de la vie publique' (2019) 12 *Droit Administratif*, Commentaire 51.

[73] See further M Dobbs and O Ştefan, ch 15 in this volume.

[74] For more on this, see M Eliantonio and F Grashof, 'Types of Administrative Action and Corresponding Review' in M Eliantonio and C Backes (eds), *Cases, Materials and Texts on Judicial Review of Administrative Action* (Oxford, Hart Publishing, 2019).

[75] According to r 54.1(2) of the Civil Procedure Rules: '(2) In this Section – (a) a "claim for judicial review" means a claim to review the lawfulness of (i) an enactment; or (ii) a decision, action or failure to act in relation to the exercise of a public function.'

[76] See, eg, *R (Medical Justice) v Secretary of State for the Home Department* [2011] EWCA Civ 1710; *R (Suppiah) v Secretary of State for the Home Department* [2001] EWHC 2 (Admin).

[77] *R (Equality and Human Rights Commission) v Prime Minister* [2011] EWHC 2401 (Admin); *R (A) v Secretary of State for Health* [2009] ECA Civ 225; *R (Axon) v Secretary of State for Health* [2006] EWHC 37 (Admin); *R (Burke) v General Medical Council* [2005] EWCA Civ 1003; *Palestine Solidarity and Another, R (on the Application of) v Secretary of State for Housing, Communities and Local Government* [2020] UKSC 16 (29 April 2020).

[78] *R. v City of Sunderland ex p Baumber* [1996] COD 211.

[79] *R v Secretary of State for the Home Department ex p Northumbira Police Authority* [1989] QB 26; *R v Secretary of State for Health ex p K* (1998) 1 CLLR 495.

[80] See further the case law mentioned in M Fordham, *Judicial Review Handbook*, 5th edn (Oxford, Hart Publishing, 2008) 2006–10.

Particularly interesting for our purposes is *Pfizer* – a case which concerned a government circular recommending that Viagra should only be prescribed by general practitioners in exceptional circumstances and on notice to the Department of Health, and advising health authorities not to support the provision of the drug out of NHS funds. In the context of the discussion of the effects of the guidance (and their justiciability), the court explicitly stated that 'advice or guidance promulgated by a public authority may be the subject of judicial review if it contains an error of law. This is particularly so *if it is likely to be acted upon by those it addresses*' (emphasis added).[81] In the rest of the judgment, the emphasis is, similarly to the French rulings discussed above, on the authoritative nature of the circular, the fact that it could reasonably be expected that doctors would conform to it, and how it was 'perceived' as having essentially binding effects by the press.

It might thus be concluded that virtually all SoLaR measures would in principle be reviewable by the English courts. However, because the English approach is open, 'pragmatic' and context-specific, it is hard to pinpoint and identify any 'lessons' for the European courts to learn with respect to the judicial review of soft law. In this sense, the lack of a dogmatic discussion on this topic renders – somewhat paradoxically – the English 'good practice' non-inspirational and difficult to export to the EU level.

D. Germany: Hardly a 'Good Practice'?

In the German legal system, domestic soft law most often takes the shape of 'administrative directions' (*verwaltungsvorschriften*), which have a similar function as the *circulaires* discussed above for the French and Italian systems. German doctrine divides administrative directions into three broad categories, namely, administrative directions guiding the exercise of administrative discretion (*ermessenslenkende Verwaltungsvorschriften*), interpretative administrative directions (*norminterpretierende Verwaltungsvorschriften*) and administrative directions 'concretising' legal provisions (*normkonkretisierende Verwaltungsvorschriften*).[82] While the first two types are considered incapable of producing effects outside the administration, the third category has been recognised as capable of producing direct legal effects as a form of 'anticipated

[81] *R Pfizer Ltd v Secretary of State for Health* [2011] EWHC Admin 504, para 26. In this same paragraph, earlier case law concerning a circular (containing advice) in the planning area is quoted, specifically *R v Worthing Borough Council and Secretary of State for the Environment ex p Burch* [1983] 11 WLUK 152. In this case, Mann J argued: 'In my judgment, it is quite unreal to suppose that a local planning authority would do otherwise then accept the opinion as decisive … So, in practice. I am quite satisfied that the procedure that is envisaged by the Circular does constrain the local authority.'

[82] See further T Sauerland, *Die Verwaltungsvorschrift im System der Rechtsquellen* (Berlin, Dunker & Humblot, 2005).

legal advice' to the administration.[83] These are, for example, measures in the environmental law field that specify certain legal provisions contained in the legislation (eg, how much noise an installation needs to produce in order for it to qualify as a nuisance for the purposes of the legislation).[84] This type of administrative directions may be challenged in the special procedure for the control of general and abstract forms of administrative rule-making.[85] However, in order to be considered as capable of producing direct legal effects and, consequently, qualifying for judicial control, a number of conditions need to be met. First, the soft law measures must be adopted on the basis of a legislative empowerment and, second, they must be published in accordance with the publication requirements foreseen for legislation.[86]

On the basis of these conditions, none of the SoLaR soft law measures would be amenable to judicial control. Indeed, several soft law measures – such as those in the social policy field – are not adopted on the basis of a legislative empowerment and are instead a 'substitute' for rather than a 'concretisation' of legislative provisions.[87] Those for which a legislative empowerment can be found – such as the ESMA guidelines or the Guidance Documents linked to the implementation of the Water Framework Directive – lack the second requirement necessary under German law to bring a claim against a soft law measure, that is, a form of publication akin to that foreseen for legislation. Both these two sets of soft measures are only published on the official website of ESMA and the Commission, respectively, and not on the Official Journal as required for EU legislation.[88] However, this conclusion should not be taken to mean that the German legal system is in itself overly restrictive in its approach to the judicial review of soft law, but as a confirmation of earlier findings of how EU soft law falls short of fundamental publicity and accessibility criteria.[89]

IV. CONCLUSIONS

> It is apparent from the case law that, as the European Community is a community based on the rule of law in which its institutions are subject to judicial review of the

[83] Bundesverwaltungsgericht, 17. February 1978, AZ 1 C 102.76, BVerwGE 55, 250; Bundesverwaltungsgericht, 28 October 1998, AZ 8 C 16.96, BVerwGE 107, 338; Bundesverwaltungsgericht, 20 December 1999, AZ 7 C 15.98, BVerwGE 110, 216.

[84] See, eg, in the field of noise, *Technische Anleitung zum Schutz gegen Lärm*, 26 August 1998, GMBl n 26/1998, 503; in the field of air quality, *Technische Anleitung zur Reinhaltung der Luft*, 24 July 2002, GMBl n 25–29/2002, 511.

[85] The procedure to control by-laws and executive regulations (*Normenkontrollverfahren*) foreseen in §47 VwGO.

[86] Bundesverwaltungsgericht, 25 September 2012, AZ 3 BN 1.12.

[87] On this point, see A Hofmann, ch 3 in this volume.

[88] Namely, art 297(1) TFEU.

[89] See O Ştefan, ch 19 in this volume with the literature contained therein; see also the recommendations made by the SoLaR project in ch 1 of this volume.

> compatibility of their acts with the EC Treaty, the procedural rules governing actions brought before the Community courts must be interpreted in such a way as to ensure, wherever possible, that these rules are implemented in such a way as to contribute to the attainment of the objective of ensuring effective judicial protection of an individual's rights under Community law.[90]

Despite principled statements such as this, the European courts have been more than reticent to admit the judicial review of soft law measures and, despite the recent efforts made by AG Bobek to encourage the Court to 'modernise' its case law and find inspiration from the several national legal systems, the jurisprudential attitude of the Luxembourg Courts has remained unchanged.

This chapter investigated, on the basis of the current state of the case law, which of the SoLaR soft law measures would be reviewable in an action for annulment under Article 263 TFEU. It has concluded that, despite the legal and practical effects that these measures are capable of producing at a national level, none of them is *certainly* going to pass the required threshold, that is, the capacity of a measure to 'produce legally binding effects'. It then investigated the requirements applicable to the judicial review of domestic soft law measures in four SoLaR legal systems in order to compare them to those applicable at the EU level.

This comparative analysis has revealed that all legal systems, to various extents, admit the judicial review of soft law measures when these measures have relevance outside the administration. Even those legal systems which apply the most restrictive test, namely Italy and Germany, allow actions against soft law measures when they are not purely internal measures, but rather acts with external relevance. On the basis of these conditions, at least the ESMA guidelines would in principle be reviewable in Italy and Germany, were it not for the lack of 'official' publication, which is required by German law. At the other end of the spectrum exists the UK, which a-dogmatically admits judicial review of soft law and which would see no specific hurdle in the control of any of the SoLaR measures. The most spectacular evolution is certainly that of the French legal system, which has witnessed a remarkable process of opening up towards the judicial review of soft law. As things stand today, a French court, taking its cue from the case law of the Council of State, would allow for the control of all of the SoLaR measures. That it would be the same French Council of State which 30 years ago stated that soft law should be considered as a 'deterioration of the law'[91] that would be regarded today as a pioneer of the theory of normativity as a continuum[92] is certainly surprising.

[90] Case C-521/06 P *Athinaïki Techniki AE v Commission* [2008] EU:C:2008:422, para 45.

[91] Conseil d'État, Étude annuelle 1991, 'De la sécurité juridique'.

[92] According to this view, law ought to be seen as a continuum with two opposite poles, ranging from legal norms to non-legal norms, with shades of grey in between, represented, amongst other things, by soft law. See, eg, F Terpan, 'Soft Law in the European Union: The Changing Nature of EU Law' (2015) 21 *European Law Journal* 68.

What is even more unexpected is that the French Council of State is trying to bring this wind of change from Paris to Luxembourg by requesting the Court of Justice to determine whether a set of guidelines issued by the European Banking Authority could be subject to an annulment action under Article 263 TFEU.[93] Time will tell whether this wind is strong enough to change the course taken by the Court of Justice.

[93] *Fédération bancaire française (FBF) v Autorité de contrôle prudentiel et de résolution (ACPR)* (n 6).

18

Legal Effects and Reviewability of EU Acts

Between Institutional Intentions and Perceptions of Concerned Parties

NAPOLEON XANTHOULIS*

I. INTRODUCTION

WHAT ENABLES EU acts to fall under the review of EU courts is a perennial problem. The case law has made it clear that priority should be given to the substance[1] rather than the form of a contested measure to determine its reviewability; yet, the authors of EU acts and potentially affected persons still face difficulties in predicting whether an EU measure can trigger judicial intervention and, if so, what judicial avenues are available. Therefore, providing clarity on this matter has not only theoretical value but also practical significance.

The aim of this chapter is to shed light on a specific aspect of the EU courts' assessment on the justiciability of EU conduct. More specifically, I will analyse two key factors influencing the EU courts' reasoning on whether a contested act can produce legal effects – the decisive criterion for determining whether an act can be subject to judicial review – namely, the so-called 'intention of the author' and the 'perceptions of persons concerned'. The former criterion is embedded in the wording of Article 263(1) of the Treaty on the Functioning of the European Union (TFEU) and has long been used in case law. Yet its precise scope, the method of ascertaining it and its role in the EU courts' reasoning have not been systematically examined. The latter criterion has entirely evaded the attention

* I am grateful to the editors of this volume for their comments on this chapter.

[1] For a recent manifestation of this approach, see Case T-671/15 *E-Control v ACER* [2016] EU:T:2016:626; Case T-63/16 *E-Control v ACER* [2017] EU:T:2017:456.

of scholarship. Acquiring a better understanding of these notions is particularly important for analysing the legal effects and reviewability of EU soft law instruments such as guidelines, policy frameworks and codes of conduct. As will be shown, the viewpoints of national authorities and private parties about the legal significance of soft law are relevant both for assessing the effects of soft law as well as determining whether it can be the subject of judicial scrutiny.

This contribution is structured as follows. In section II, I present the Court's definition of 'reviewable act' within the meaning of Article 263(1) TFEU and briefly explain why this test has failed to provide sufficient certainty. In section III, I analyse the meaning of the criterion of 'intention of the author' and explore its subjective and objective dimensions with reference to case law. In section IV, I highlight the significance of the criterion of 'perceptions of concerned persons' for determining the capacity of an EU act to be subject to judicial review. In this context, I engage with EU acts that may impose obligations on others and acts that entail self-imposed commitments, the latter typically classified as soft law in the literature. In section V, I discuss the types of conflict that may emerge from diverse viewpoints about the legal effects of EU acts and present some ideas about how these may be addressed.

II. REVIEWABLE ACTS IN EU LAW

A. The Court's Test

EU law offers two pathways for private persons[2] seeking to contest the validity of acts adopted by EU authorities: they can seek to review the legality of an EU act *directly* via an action for annulment (Articles 263 and 265 TFEU) or *indirectly* via the preliminary ruling procedure (Article 267 TFEU) and incidental review (Article 277 TFEU), respectively. Article 263(1) TFEU does not provide for a clear definition of the measures that can be subject to review. The provision stipulates that the Court shall review legislative acts and acts of the Council, the Commission and the European Central Bank 'other than recommendations and opinions'. Furthermore, it states that the Court shall review acts of the European Parliament and the European Council, as well as those of EU bodies, offices or agencies 'intended to produce legal effects vis-à-vis third parties'.

From the beginning, the Court refused to reduce the notion of a reviewable act to the forms of acts mentioned in Article 288 TFEU – namely, regulations, directives and decisions – and instead opted for a substantive approach, albeit one in which the form still remains relevant.[3] Yet, since no definition of 'legal acts' was

[2] The rights of privileged applicants and the ad hoc or exceptional judicial protection avenues provided for in EU primary and secondary law fall outside the scope of this chapter.

[3] Although the form of an EU act would not, on its own, prevent a person from contesting its legality, the form of an act may still be taken into account by the EU courts if it helps to identify

offered under the Treaties, it was for the Court to determine whether its scope included only the acts outlined in what was then Article 189 of the EEC Treaty (currently Article 288 TFEU) or also other types of acts of those EU institutions not mentioned in the Treaties.

The Court offered its first definition of 'reviewable act' in the *ERTA* case,[4] where the contested act comprised certain Council minutes relating to the negotiation and conclusion of an international agreement. The Court held that an action for annulment is available against 'all measures adopted by the institutions, whatever their nature or form, which are intended to have legal effects'.[5] According to the *ERTA* test, the EU courts must determine, first, whether an act exists and, second, whether it intends to produce legal effects. The subsequent application of this test, with respect to various types of EU acts, quickly revealed that the Court would generally give precedence to substance over form.[6] This means that the label or form of the act is not, in itself, decisive in determining its reviewability.

In *IBM*, the Court explained that the requirement of legal effects under Article 263(1) TFEU would be met when the measure is 'binding on, and capable of affecting the interests of the applicant by bringing about a distinct change in his legal position'.[7] Like the test in the *ERTA* case, the *IBM* definition clarifies that the criterion of legal effects places emphasis on the substance of an act and not its form.[8] The scope of reviewable acts is therefore considerably wider than Article 288 TFEU would suggest. In time, the scope of reviewable act came to include 'conclusions' by the Member States adopted in Council for negotiations concerning an international agreement,[9] a letter written by Commission staff,[10] a 'communication' by a European agency,[11] provisions in policy frameworks,[12]

its nature, including its capacity to produce legal effects. Consequently, whether a letter is signed, dated or contains the EU institution's header as well as the title of the instrument may still influence the reasoning of EU courts. See Case T-170/16 *Guardian Glass España, Central Vidriera v Commission* [2017] EU:T:2017:722, paras 87–92; Case C-44/81 *Germany and Bundesanstalt für Arbeit v Commission* [1982] EU:C:1982:197, para 12; Case T-456/07 *Commission v CdT* [2010] EU:T:2010:39, para 58.

[4] Case C-22/70 *Commission v Council* [1971] EU:C:1971:32.

[5] ibid para 42.

[6] See Case C-16/16 *Belgium v Commission* [2018] EU:C:2017:959, Opinion of AG Bobek, para 63, making reference to Joined Cases C-1/57 and C-14/57 *Société des usines à tubes de la Sarre v High Authority of the European Coal and Steel Community* [1957] EU:C:1957:13, para 114, where the Court proceeded to assess whether a measured labelled as an opinion was in reality a disguised decision.

[7] Case C-60/81 *IBM v Commission* [1981] EU:C:1981:264, para 9.

[8] ibid. This also means that formal defects in the act, such as the absence of its proper identification by its author as decision, the lack of legal basis and the lack of notification, are irrelevant for the determination of the act as reviewable. See Case C-322/09P *NDSHT v Commission* [2010] EU:C:2010:701, para 47.

[9] Case C-22/70 *Commission v Council* [1971] EU:C:1971:32.

[10] See Case T-84/97 *BEUC v Commission* [1998] EU:T:1998:81, para 48; Case T-113/00 *DuPont and Others v Commission* [2002] EU:T:2002:214, para 45; *NDSHT v Commission* (n 8) para 60.

[11] Case C-402/11 P *Jager & Polacek v OHIM* [2012] EU:C:2012:649, para 70.

[12] Case T-496/11 *UK v ECB* [2015] EU:T:2015:133.

codes of conduct,[13] communications,[14] guidelines[15] and even oral decisions.[16] The Court's concern is that an assessment purely based on the form of the act would allow the act's author to avoid judicial review by choosing an atypical form.[17]

B. Uncertainty and its Causes

Although the *IBM* test places emphasis on the substance of the act, it has failed to provide clarity to when EU measures fall under the scope of judicial scrutiny. This uncertainty is the result of three interrelated causes:[18] first, there are internal flaws in the *IBM* test; second, the application of the *IBM* test is problematic; and, third and perhaps more fundamentally, the notion of legal effects is characterised by conceptual obscurity within the EU law doctrine.

To begin with, the test formulated in the *IBM* case fails to offer clear definitions of its basic components. Specifically, the Court left open three questions. First, what is the definition of 'act', that is, the object of judicial review? Second, what distinguishes acts 'capable of affecting the interests of a person by bringing about a distinct change in that person's legal position' from acts producing other kinds of effects? In other words, what is the meaning of 'binding legal effect' and how does it differ from non-binding legal effects and non-legal effects (the latter sometimes referred to as factual effects or consequences of fact)?[19] Finally, if only acts with binding legal effects are reviewable under Article 263 TFEU, what justifies the Court's readiness, under certain conditions, to review non-binding acts when the question of illegality arises in the context of indirect review proceedings (Articles 267 and 277 TFEU)?[20] In other words, if direct review is

[13] Case C-303/90 *France v Commission* [1991] EU:C:1991:424.

[14] Case C-325/91 *France v Commission* [1993] EU:C:1993:245; Case C-57/95 *France v Commission* [1997] EU:C:1997:164.

[15] Case C-366/88 *France v Commission* [1990] EU:C:1990:348.

[16] See Joined Cases 316/82 and 40/83 *Kohler v Court of Auditors* [1984] EU:C:1984:49, paras 9–13; Case T-3/93 *Air France v Commission* [1984] EU:C:1984:49, paras 57–59; Case T-85/03R *Government of the Cayman Islands Commission* [2003] EU:T:2003:83, para 60.

[17] *UK v ECB* (n 12) para 30.

[18] For a more detailed discussion of this point, see N Xanthoulis, 'Legal Effects and Judicial Review in EU Law: The ECB's Conduct in Banking Supervision and Monetary Policy' (Doctoral thesis, the Dickson Poon School of Law, King's College London, June 2020).

[19] *IBM v Commission* (n 7) para 19; Case T-377/00 *Philip Morris International v Commission* [2003] EU:T:2003:6, paras 114–15; and Case C-476/14 *Citroën Commerce* [2016] EU:C:2015:814, Opinion of AG Mengozzi, para 77. In his Opinion in the *IBM* case, AG Slynn distinguished 'legal effects' from 'effects in fact' (Case 60/81 *IBM v Commission* [1981] EU:C:1981:213, para 2664). For a systematic analysis between legal effects and factual effects, see N Xanthoulis, 'Administrative Factual Conduct: Legal Effects and Judicial Control in EU Law' (2019) 12 *Review of European Administrative Law* 39.

[20] In the Court's own words: 'Article 267 TFEU confers on the Court jurisdiction to give a preliminary ruling on the validity and interpretation of all acts of the EU institutions without exception.' See Case C-322/88 *Grimaldi* [1989] EU:C:1989:646, para 8; Case C-258/14 *Florescu and Others* [2017]

available only for acts producing binding legal effects, what legal effects, if any, must an act produce to qualify for 'indirect review'?

The design flaws of the *IBM* test are complemented by its problematic application in the Court's case law. First, the Court has faced difficulties in formulating the applicable reviewability test. Second, there is much inconsistency in the manner in which the Court uses certain criteria to carry out a substantive assessment of EU conduct. As regards the first problem, the impact of the *IBM* case on the test introduced in the *ERTA* case was not uniformly reflected in case law. Although following *IBM*, the courts were expected to change the test from a 'mere' legal effects to 'binding' legal effects, the language used in case law was not always consistent.[21] This blurred the meaning of the term 'legal effects' and the methodology for distinguishing between binding and non-binding acts.

A second layer of uncertainty is caused by the problematic use by the Court of certain criteria giving shape to its substantive approach. Even if the case law suggests that acts must be capable of producing binding legal effects to pass the reviewability test under Article 263(1) TFEU, only a substantive assessment would reveal whether a contested act qualifies for judicial review in a given case. The main criteria used by the Court in carrying out this assessment include the content, wording, context, intention of the author, perception of the parties concerned, and powers of the author.[22] The courts do not necessarily rely on all of these criteria in carrying out the reviewability assessment in concrete cases. Further, it is even less clear whether all these criteria have equal weight or whether some counterbalance the others. Moreover, there is a degree of inconsistency regarding the interplay between the different criteria; for instance, are the wording and context of an act self-standing factors or mere considerations that can determine the essence of another criterion (eg, the substance)?[23] The catalogue of criteria that may ultimately influence the Court's assessment is non-exhaustive.

And yet there appears to be one more fundamental cause underlying the Court's inability to fully articulate, interpret and consistently apply the

EU:C:2017:448, para 30; and Case C-11/05 *Friesland Coberco Dairy Foods* [2006] EU:C:2006:312, para 36.

[21] For instance, reference to 'binding' legal effects is made, inter alia, in Case C-151/88 *Italy v Commission* [1989] EU:C:1989:201, para 2; Case C-308/95 *The Netherlands v Commission* [1999] EU:C:1999:477, para 30; and Case T-673/13 *European Coalition to End Animal Experiments v ECHA* [2015] EU:T:2015:167, para 22. By contrast, the Court in Case C-294/83 *Les Verts v Parliament* [1986] EU:C:1986:16, para 24; and Case C-301/01 *Italy v Commission* [2005] EU:C:2005:727, paras 22–24 refers only to 'legal effects'.

[22] See inter alia, Joined Cases C-593/15 P and C-594/15 P *Slovakia v Commission* [2017] EU:C:2017:800, para 47; Case C-31/13 P *Hungary v Commission* [2014] EU:C:2014:70, para 55.

[23] See, eg, Joined Cases C-626/15 and C-659/16 *European Commission v Council of the European Union* [2018] EU:C:2018:362, Opinion of AG Kokott, para 53, where the 'substance' of the measure alone was considered to be the object of the Court's assessment in determining whether a contested measure produces (or is intended to produce) binding legal effects. The other objective factors – the wording, context and intention of the author – were considered to inform the Court's assessment about the substance of the contested act.

reviewability test. As I have explained elsewhere,[24] this reason can be traced back to the conceptual obscurity that characterises the notion of legal effects in EU law[25] and which manifests itself in a twofold manner. First, the concept of legal effects appears to be blended with other fundamental notions in EU law, specifically direct concern,[26] individual concern,[27] direct effect[28] and indirect effect.[29] As a result, case law has developed in a casuistic manner, which makes it difficult to predict when an EU act can be subject to judicial control. Second, the EU courts[30] have not so far offered a framework for analysing 'acts' and their 'effects' in EU law.[31] In the remaining part of this chapter, I do not expand on this problem; instead, I will shed more light on certain criteria influencing the reasoning of the EU courts in a bid to provide clarity on the issue of the reviewability of acts.

III. INTENTION OF THE AUTHOR: A SUBJECTIVE OR OBJECTIVE TEST?

In determining whether an act is capable of producing legal effects and thus be subject to review, the courts typically ask if such legal effects were 'intended'.[32]

[24] See Xanthoulis (n 18); A Türk and N Xanthoulis, 'Legal Accountability of European Central Bank in Bank Supervision: A Case Study in Conceptualizing the Legal Effects of Union Acts' (2019) 26 *Maastricht Journal of European and Comparative Law* 151.

[25] F Snyder, 'Interinstitutional Agreements: Forms and Constitutional Limitations' in G Winter (ed), *Sources and Categories of European Union Law: A Comparative and Reform Perspective* (Baden-Baden, Nomos, 1996) 453; see also L Senden, *Soft Law in European Community Law* (Oxford, Hart Publishing, 2004) 241.

[26] Joined Cases C-463/10 P and C-475/10 P *Deutsche Post and Germany v Commission* [2011] EU:C:2011:656, para 38; Case T-517/12 *Alro SA v Commission* [2014] EU:T:2014:890, para 25; Case C-25/62 *Plaumann v Commission of the EEC* [1963] EU:C:1963:7, Opinion of AG Roemer, para 114; Case C-1/64 *Glucoseries réunies v Commission of the EEC* [1964] EU:C:1964:47, Opinion of AG Roemer, para 421.

[27] *Plaumann v Commission of the EEC* (n 26) Opinion of AG Roemer, para 115.

[28] Case C-41/74 *Van Duyn v Home Office* [1974] EU:C:1974:133, para 12. See also Case C-148/78 *Ratti* [1979] EU:C:1979:110, paras 20–21; M Bobek, 'The Effects of EU Law in the National Legal Systems' in C Barnard and S Peers (eds), *European Union Law* (Oxford, Oxford University Press, 2014); M Cremona, 'The Judgment – Framing the Argument' in Conference Proceedings *50th Anniversary of the Judgment in Van Gen den Loos 1963–2013* (Luxembourg, Court of Justice of the European Union, 2013) 23, 26.

[29] G de Búrca, 'Giving Effect to European Community Directives' (1992) 55 *Modern Law Review* 215, 231.

[30] Senden (n 25) 242.

[31] In an attempt to mitigate this gap, the soft law literature offers several taxonomies of EU acts whose legal status is perceived to be uncertain by relying on diverse criteria, including, inter alia, their form, function, objective and effects. See O Ştefan et al, 'EU Soft Law in the EU Legal Order: A Literature Review' (2019) SoLaR Working Paper 17–20, www.ssrn.com/abstract=3346629. See also, inter alia, O Ştefan, *Soft Law in Court: Competition Law, State Aid and the Court of Justice of the European Union* (Deventer, Kluwer, 2013).

[32] Case C-521/06 P *Athinaïki Techniki v Commission* [2008] EU:C:2008:422, para 42; Case C-69/09 P *Makhteshim-Agan Holding and Others v Commission* [2010] EU:C:2010:37, para 38; Case C-362/08 P *Internationaler Hilfsfonds v Commission* [2010] EU:C:2010:40, para 52.

This seems to originate from the wording of Article 263(1) TFEU, which provides that only those EU acts that are 'intended to produce legal effects vis-à-vis third parties' can be the subject matter of judicial review in direct annulment actions. Neither in *ERTA* nor in *IBM* did the Court clarify what is meant by the statement in Article 263(1) TFEU that such '(binding) legal effects' must be 'intended' to be produced. The requirement of intention can be traced to all previous versions of Article 263(1) TFEU, even back to the original 1957 EEC Treaty. Its survival throughout all Treaty reforms, alongside the criterion of legal effects, cannot go unnoticed. So, what is an 'intended' legal effect, who must 'intend' to produce it and how can these issues be determined?

From one point of view, Article 263(1) TFEU can be read as referring to the subjective intentions of the author. According to this view, legal effects must not be produced accidentally or unwillingly, but, rather, be the conscious objective of the institution to which the act is attributed. The use of past tense ('was intended to') implies that the Treaty makers aimed at determining the subjective intention of the act's author at the moment of its adoption.[33] This argument cannot stand for a number of reasons. First, it comes into conflict with the nature of the Court's reviewability test, which entails a substantive assessment. If the task of the Court was to determine whether the author subjectively wished for a measure to produce certain legal effects, any further investigation into the substance of the measure would be redundant. One may even go so far as to suggest that if this argument were to be accepted, all instruments whose label suggests that the author had no intention to assign to them binding legal effects, such as recommendations and opinions, would in principle escape judicial review.[34] Second, the argument that Article 263(1) TFEU is concerned with the historical subjective intention of the author does not explain why the Court has found in some instances that a measure was indeed capable of producing legal effects, against the argument of its author that they had no intention to bring about such legal effects.[35]

So, does this mean that the author's subjective intentions are immaterial? Not necessarily. The general rule is that the criteria influencing the Court's reviewability assessment are objective.[36] Rather than investigating the author's actual intention, the Court emphasises the objective purpose of the contested instrument.[37] This means that whether a measure was intended to produce legal effects was approached from an 'objective point of view'.[38] By contrast,

[33] *Belgium v Commission* (n 6) Opinion of AG Bobek, para 77.
[34] ibid para 78.
[35] See, eg, the cases cited above in section II.A.
[36] Case C-301/03 *Italy v Commission* [2005] EU:C:2005:727, para 15; *European Commission v Council of the European Union* (n 23), Opinion of AG Kokott, para 53; *Hungary v Commission* (n 22) para 55.
[37] *UK v ECB* (n 12) para 52.
[38] *Italy v Commission* (n 36) para 15.

in other cases,[39] the Court expressly stated that a measure had to be interpreted 'on the basis of both the real intention of its author and the aim which the latter seeks to achieve'. In these cases, the Court looked into both the actual intention of the institution that drafted the measure as well as the objective pursued by that institution; this is particularly the case where the different-language versions of the measure may invite more than one interpretation.

In my view, there are convincing arguments in favour of the objective test. First, the Court's readiness to consider the actual intention of the author contradicts the rule of 'objectivity', which, according to the Court, characterises all the criteria influencing the reviewability test. Second, as I shall explain below, the Court applies an objective approach to discover the perceptions of concerned persons about an EU measure's capacity to bring about a change in their legal position. Third, an objective test enables an external observer to understand the exercise of executive power and its actual consequences. After all, it can be difficult, if not impossible, to prove the existence of real intentions. Fourth, a subjective standard would not suffice on its own. Even if the real beliefs were to be accepted as the appropriate standard for determining the issue of reviewability, an objective test would probably have to be construed to resolve conflicts between the viewpoints of the author of an act and the person(s) concerned.

One way to reconcile the inconsistencies between the two approaches in case law is to accept that the actual intention of the author is relevant, but only to the extent that this can be determined objectively.[40] In this sense, the Court would only examine objective evidence that may reveal the original intentions of the author. These findings about the objective purpose of the measure would then need to be assessed in the light of other criteria, such as the wording, content and context of the act, as well as the powers assigned to the author.

IV. PERCEPTION OF CONCERNED PARTIES

Habermas considered that speech acts entailed cooperative relationships of commitment and responsibility, in the sense that the success of the interaction relies on the cooperation of the participants.[41] If this is correct, then in order for

[39] Joined Cases C-659/13 and C-34/14 *C & J Clark International* [2016] EU:C:2016:74, para 122; Case C-486/12 *X* [2013] EU:C:2013:836, para 19; Case C-29/69 *Stauder v Stadt Ulm* [1969] EU:C:1969:57, para 3; Case C-445/09 *IMC Securities* [2011] EU:C:2011:459, para 25; Joined Cases C-261/08 and C-348/08 *Zurita García and Choque Cabrera* [2009] EU:C:2009:648, para 54; Case C-473/08 *Eulitz* [2010] EU:C:2010:47, para 22; Case 55/87 *Moksel Import und Export* [1988] EU:C:1988:377, para 15; Case C-268/99 *Jany and Others* [2001] EU:C:2001:616, para 47; Case C-188/03 *Junk* [2005] EU:C:2005:59, para 33.

[40] *European Commission v Council of the European Union* (n 23), Opinion of AG Kokott, para 53.

[41] M Cooke, 'Introduction' in M Cooke (ed), *On the Pragmatics of Communication* (Cambridge, MA, MIT Press, 1998) 2.

a duty or a commitment to exist, it must normally be communicated to someone and must have been understood by the latter as such.[42] The effects an author intended by issuing an act represent only one side of the story. The other side is how the act was perceived by the parties concerned about its effects. To illustrate this point, the claim that a measure is capable of having legal effects implies the existence of a legal relationship between two persons, consisting of rights and corresponding obligations which are subject to some change by the measure in question.[43] It is then necessary in each case to identify the person whose legal position is affected by a contested measure and to examine whether the message intended by the author was effectively communicated to the concerned person.

Who qualifies as a 'concerned person' depends on the normative scope of the contested act. The named addressees of an act are always concerned persons. Moreover, to the extent that such an act has influenced the adoption of a subsequent act with binding legal effects vis-a-vis third parties, the latter can also qualify as concerned persons (eg, a recommendation by institution A led to the adoption of a binding decision by institution B vis-a-vis person C). Finally, acts that are not addressed to specific persons but are of general application potentially affect the legal position of an innumerable number of people.

As we shall see below, case law has treated the perceptions of concerned parties as a distinct criterion in the context of the reviewability assessment with respect to two types of measures: acts that are capable of imposing obligations on others and acts entailing self-imposed commitments.

A. Perceptions about Measures That May Impose Obligations on Others

In *UK v ECB*,[44] the General Court (GC) assessed, inter alia, 'the way in which the parties concerned could reasonably have perceived' a European Central Bank (ECB) instrument entitled 'Eurosystem Oversight Policy Framework' to determine its capacity to bring about legal effects.[45] In particular, the question before the GC was whether the contested act could be perceived as proposing a course of conduct, similar to how recommendations are perceived, or whether it was an act that required compliance.[46] Since the ECB made the Policy Framework available on its website, it was uncontested that the act was publicised outside the internal structure of the ECB.[47] In its assessment, the GC relied on the wording and context of the contested act and considered that the perception of an

[42] J Austin, *How to Do Things with Words* (Oxford, Oxford University Press, 1962) 22.

[43] See Case T-671/15 *E-Control v ACER* (n 1) para 44; Case T-63/16 *E-Control v ACER* (n 1) para 47.

[44] See, inter alia, *UK v ECB* (n 12) paras 32–33, 36 and 40.

[45] ibid paras 32–33.

[46] ibid para 32.

[47] ibid paras 33–34.

act may vary depending on the 'nature of the parties concerned by that act'.[48] Furthermore, it took the view that the contested act concerned not only the central counterparties of payment, clearing and settlement systems, but also the national authorities who were responsible for regulating this policy area and 'liable, in the exercise of their powers, to impede clearing services activity carried out by CCPs situated outside the euro area'.[49]

Whilst the contested act did not produce any direct obligations vis-a-vis the former, according to the GC, it enabled the latter (ie, the national authorities) to reasonably perceive it as entailing legal requirements which demanded compliance. The GC concluded that the 'examination of the Policy Framework's wording and context, from the point of view of the regulatory authorities of the euro area Member States, tends to place that framework in the category of acts against which an action for annulment may be brought under Article 263 TFEU'.[50]

The GC's reasoning signifies that in assessing the capacity of an act to produce legal effects, one should interpret the act's wording and context not only in the light of the intention of its author but also from the point of view of the parties concerned. More importantly, once an act reaches the public sphere, the parties actually concerned and affected by that act may not be readily apparent in all instances or easily predicted by its author. The GC employed a reasonableness test to determine whether the perceptions of the applicants about the legal effects of the contested act were objectively justified. Similar versions of this 'reasonable reader' test have been applied elsewhere in case law, such as for determining the attributability of an act or the existence of legitimate expectations.[51] The process of identifying the parties that may be concerned by an act necessitates examining the regulatory scope of that act as well as taking into consideration the role of national authorities.

The approach in *UK v ECB* draws on the Court's reasoning in *Oleifici Italiani*.[52] In that case, the applicants – private companies responsible for storing and intervening in the Italian olive oil market – brought an annulment action against a Commission letter to the Italian authorities that blocked EU funding for the warehousing of olive oil on the basis of violation of applicable requirements. In assessing whether that letter was able to affect the legal position of the applicants, the GC emphasised its wording. It stated that the letter must be interpreted in the light of the factual and legal context in which it was drafted and communicated. The GC stated that it was 'important to establish the objective significance the letter could reasonably have had, at the time it was sent,

[48] ibid paras 32, 40.
[49] ibid para 42.
[50] ibid para 49.
[51] Case T-289/03 *BUPA and Others v Commission* [2008] EU:T:2008:29, para 260; Case T-216/05 *Mebrom v Commission* [2007] EU:T:2007:148, para 102; Case T-79/13 *Accorinti and Others v ECB* [2015] EU:T:2015:756, para 74 (no legitimate expectations were recognised).
[52] Case T-54/96 *Oleifici Italiani and Fratelli Rubino v Commission* [1998] EU:T:1998:204.

for a conscientious and prudent trader acting on behalf of a national intervention agency in the olive oil sector'.[53] The GC concluded that the contested letters merely expressed the Commission's opinions and proposals which had no binding force. This was also supported, in the GC's view, by the fact that the Commission did not have the power to issue decisions with binding force in that context. In the eyes of the GC, 'prudent and well-informed traders' such as the applicants 'would not be unaware of the legal nature of … the letter in issue'.[54] On that basis, the action was held to be inadmissible.

Another example that highlights the role of the perceptions of concerned persons in determining the capacity of a measure to produce binding legal effects is the Opinion of AG Jacobs in *Italy v Commission*.[55] In that case, Italy sought the annulment of several notes and letters of the Commission stating the latter's position regarding the management of Community structure funds. The Italian government argued that these acts imposed certain obligations on Italy, which were incompatible with the applicable EU legislation. In response, the Commission claimed that the contested acts neither have nor were intended to have any legal effects. AG Jacobs applied the substantive assessment to conclude that neither the factual nor the legal context or even the substance of the measure settled the matter. The persistent question was whether the contested measures entailed obligations or merely reflected the Commission's intention to follow a particular line of conduct.[56] AG Jacobs reached the conclusion that, on balance, the Commission's measures were inadmissible:

> Although an appearance of binding effect is clearly an element to be accorded importance, it should not be decisive in the instant case. Member States and national authorities involved in the management of Community structural funds are familiar with the procedures under the Structural Funds Regulation and are well equipped to carry out an initial legal assessment of the acts adopted by the Commission which goes beyond their mere appearance. The same analysis might however be less appropriate in the case of individuals who may be less legally aware.[57]

AG Jacobs' line of reasoning suggests that in determining whether a contested act can bring about legal effects, it is important to consider, amongst other relevant criteria, the perception of the addressee. This assessment entails an objective test, which AG Jacobs framed as follows: is the point of view of the applicants about the legal effects of the contested act equivalent to the view of a reasonable person under the relevant circumstances of the case at hand? AG Jacobs clarified that the standard of knowledge and expertise of this hypothetical reasonable person is dependent on the legal and factual background surrounding the contested act, including the identity of the persons affected by

[53] ibid para 49.
[54] ibid para 54.
[55] Case C-301/03 *Italy v Commission* [2005] EU:C:2005:550, Opinion of AG Jacobs.
[56] ibid para 55.
[57] ibid para 71.

that act. Based on the material facts in that case, AG Jacobs acknowledged that applying a different standard of knowledge between Member States and private companies might have been justified.

The Court in *Commission v Italy*[58] reached the same conclusion on the admissibility of the action; however, it used different criteria. It began by stating that a reviewable measure must be 'intended from an objective point of view to have legal effects in relation to third parties … [and thus] directly affect the latter's interests by bringing about a distinct change in their legal position'.[59] Applying this principle to the facts of the case, the Court focused on the wording of the contested measures and the context in which they were presented.[60] Moreover, it considered the nature and scope of the power that EU law had conferred on the Commission.[61] Although the Court's reasoning affirmed the proposition that the 'intended' legal effects must be determined by carrying out an objective test, it was silent as to whether the perceptions of the affected parties can inform this assessment.

B. Perceptions about Measures That May Entail Self-Imposed Commitments

The perception of concerned persons is relevant not only for determining the legal effects of measures that may impose obligations on others but also with regard to measures that may express self-commitments. A public authority expresses a self-commitment when it adopts a measure by which it limits the options of its future conduct. Such self-imposed rules of conduct are commonly employed to guide the actions of other persons by clarifying the scope of their rights and obligations.[62] Whilst public authorities are usually free to restrain their own discretion, in certain circumstances, the adoption of such a measure may give rise to a legally binding duty vis-a-vis its author.

In determining whether a measure of an EU institution relating to the exercise of its discretion classifies as a binding rule of conduct or not, the Court would normally assess whether it falls within one of the following two categories. If, on the one hand, the measure in question appears to reflect only the 'intention' of an EU body to follow a concrete line of conduct in a particular field, this would normally be regarded as a mere 'declaration of intent';[63] it would not amount to a self-binding commitment[64] and would be devoid of any

[58] *Italy v Commission* (n 36).

[59] ibid para 15.

[60] ibid paras 21–32.

[61] ibid para 28.

[62] H Hofmann, 'Administrative Governance in State Aid Policy' in H Hofmann and A Türk (eds), *EU Administrative Governance* (Cheltenham, Edward Elgar, 2006) 196–99.

[63] Case C-180/96 *United Kingdom v Commission* [1998] EU:C:1998:192, paras 28–29; Case T-245/11 *ClientEarth and International Chemical Secretariat v ECHA* [2015] EU:T:2015:675, para 103.

[64] Case C-114/86 *United Kingdom v Commission* [1988] EU:C:1988:449, para 13; Case T-185/05 *Italy v Commission* [2008] EU:T:2008:51, para 41.

legal value.[65] Where, on the other hand, the measure lays down the position of the EU body in a 'definite'[66] manner, it would be regarded as capable of giving rise to binding legal effects.

There are many examples of measures that can bring about legal duties vis-a-vis their authors in EU administrative practice, a prominent one being the Commission Guidelines in the field of State aid and competition law. The Commission has issued several such guidelines, which have been regarded by the courts to have generated a duty of the Commission to comply with the rules laid down by itself.[67] This means that concerned parties can bring an action for annulment on the basis that the Commission has failed to apply such guidelines. These guidelines can also be challenged indirectly, provided that the applicable requirements are met. The case law has identified similar self-imposed commitments of EU institutions in various types of instruments.[68]

As regards the nature and scope of the obligation triggered by these measures, EU institutions were not previously allowed to depart from self-imposed rules unless these were formally amended or repealed.[69] As the law now stands, the Court typically considers that the Commission can deviate from certain self-imposed Guidelines if it offers sufficient reasons for doing so.[70] Consequently, certain types of self-imposed commitments can be regarded to create a dual obligation: first, the author has a general duty to respect and follow its commitment; and, second, if it wishes to depart from this commitment, it must provide sufficient reasons to this effect.

The capacity of self-imposed commitments to legally bind their authors is premised on the idea that such measures can have a legally relevant impact on the fundamental rights of others. This is supported by the readiness of the courts to assess whether the reasons offered by EU institutions for deviating from certain

[65] Case T-680/13 *Chrysostomides and Others v Council and Others* [2018] EU:T:2018:486, para 420; Case T-786/14 *Bourdouvali and Others v Council and Others* [2018] EU:T:2018:487, para 419.

[66] *Italy v Commission* (n 21) paras 45–48.

[67] See, eg, Case T-7/89 *Hercules Chemicals v Commission* [1991] EU:T:1991:75, para 53; Case T-214/95 *Vlaams Gewest v Commission* [1998] EU:T:1998:77, para 89; Case T-27/02 *Kronofrance v Commission* [2004] EU:T:2004:348, para 79; Case T-44/00 *Mannesmannröhren-Werke v Commission* [2004] EU:T:2004:218, para 212; Case T-41/05 *Alliance One International v Commission* [2011] EU:T:2011:586, para 190.

[68] For a similar approach with respect to rules that affect the conduct of the Frontex, see Case T-653/13 P *Wahlström v Frontex* [2015] EU:T:2015:652, para 61; Case T-686/16 P *Possanzini v Frontex* [2017] EU:T:2017:734, para 43.

[69] Case C-68/86 *United Kingdom v Council* [1988] EU:C:1988:85, para 48; *Italy v Commission* (n 21) paras 43 and 46; Case T-113/05 *Angelidis v Parliament* [2007] EU:T:2007:386, para 75.

[70] Case C-429/11 P *Gosselin Group v Commission* [2013] EU:C:2013:463, para 64; Joined Cases C-189/02 P, C-202/02 P, C-205/02 P to C-208/02 P and C-213/02 P *Dansk Rørindustri and Others v Commission* [2005] EU:C:2005:408, paras 209–11; Case C-439/11 P *Ziegler v Commission* [2013] EU:C:2013:513, para 60; C-106/09 P *Commission v Government of Gibraltar and United Kingdom* [2011] EU:C:2011:732, para 128; Case T-127/04 *KME Germany and Others v Commission* [2009] EU:T:2009:142, para 33; Case C-397/03 P *Archer Daniels Midland and Archer Daniels Midland Ingredients v Commission* [2006] EU:C:2006:328, para 91; Case T-18/05 *IMI and Others v Commission* [2010] EU:T:2010:202, para 117; Case T-439/07 *Coats Holdings v Commission* [2012] EU:T:2012:320, paras 182–83; Case T-406/09 *Donau Chemie v Commission* [2014] EU:T:2014:254,

self-imposed commitments are compatible with certain general principles of EU law, specifically the right to non-discrimination and the principle of protection of legitimate expectations.[71] An EU institution would not be allowed to depart from its policy if that departure would be detrimental to others, that is, if the departure results in similar cases not being treated alike or where a person had the right to believe that the policy in question would be maintained.[72]

Where an EU measure is held to give rise to legitimate expectations, this translates into that measure being capable of producing a twofold binding legal effect: it generates a prima facie right to have the concerned person's legitimate expectations protected; and it imposes a corresponding duty on the author of that measure to either respect the expectations in question or show that it is justified in disappointing them. It is precisely this relationship between the right to protect legitimate expectations and the duties imposed on the authors of self-imposed commitments that enables the right-holders to enforce the obligations vis-a-vis the institutions. Establishing the existence of legitimate expectations does not necessarily lead to a successful claim. Even if an applicant is able to show that a measure prima facie created legitimate expectations, the issuing institution will always retain the right to show that some overriding public interest justifies not respecting these expectations.[73]

These principles are in line with the outcome in *Kotnik*,[74] where the Court was asked to rule, inter alia, on the binding effects of a Banking Communication by the Commission, which required a bail-in of shareholders and other bank creditors as a condition for the Commission to approve the provision of State aid to a bank. The main question in that case boiled down to whether the fact that these guidelines must be taken into account by the Commission, in order to approve the compatibility of the national measures, had the effect of those guidelines also producing binding legal effects on the Member States. The Court considered that the Banking Communication 'is not capable of imposing independent obligations on the Member State but does no more than establish conditions … which the Commission must take into account'[75] in the review of national aid measures under Article 107(3)(b) TFEU.

The Court's conclusion in *Kotnik* is correct. Given that, by default, the Banking Communication is to be taken into account by the Commission in assessing the national measures, it would indeed not be unreasonable if

paras 73–74; Case T-129/17 *RENV – DI v EASO* [2018] EU:T:2018:722, para 73; Case C-272/09 P *KME Germany and Others v Commission* [2011] EU:C:2011:810, para 100.

[71] For an economic approach under EU law, see, inter alia, E Sharpston, 'Legitimate Expectations and Economic Reality' (1990) 15 *European Law Review* 103. For a comparative perspective, see M Groves and G Weeks (eds), *Legitimate Expectations in the Common Law World* (Oxford, Hart Publishing, 2017).

[72] P Craig, *EU Administrative Law* (Oxford, Oxford University Press, 2012) 554.

[73] ibid 584.

[74] Case C-526/14 *Kotnik* [2016] EU:C:2016:570.

[75] ibid paras 44 and 70–71.

Member States took steps to comply with its provisions. However, this cannot be equal to the guidelines imposing obligations on Member States, where the Commission's own obligation to comply with the Banking Communication is restricted, in the sense that the Commission retains the discretion to depart from these rules if valid reasons for doing so are provided.[76] As a result, the Banking Communication can only impose obligations on the Commission. The source of these legal effects is not the guideline itself, but the right to the protection of legitimate expectations. A Member State's legal position can be affected by these guidelines to the extent that they trigger a right of that Member State to see that the Commission's limited duty is complied with.

It follows that where the exercise of discretion by a EU institution is governed by certain guidelines entailing self-imposed commitments and that institution adopts an act (eg, a decision) with binding legal effects vis-a-vis a person, that person can contest the final EU act via a direct annulment action on the basis that the EU institution has failed to comply with the (limited) duties imposed on it by the applicable guidelines. A successful claim would require that the applicant show that, in the exercise of its discretion, the EU institution has departed from the applicable guidelines without giving proper reasons.

What kind of judicial avenues may be available for challenging the validity of the guidelines per se? It seems that guidelines such as those issued by the Commission in *Kotnik* can produce certain legal effects vis-a-vis another person, to the extent that the EU institution has relied on these guidelines in exercising its conferred powers, leading to the adoption of another act with direct binding legal effects vis-a-vis that person. In such instances, a person can challenge the validity of the guidelines indirectly before the EU courts. Even where the guidelines are not the formal legal basis of the final decision (eg, in State aid cases), they may not escape scrutiny via indirect avenues of judicial review. So long as the EU institution has somewhat relied on the substance of the relevant guidelines, it can be argued that they formed a basis for the contested final act. Consequently, irrespective of whether they are explicitly mentioned in the contested decision, such guidelines can still have a 'direct legal connection with the contested decision' and thus be reviewed indirectly in the context of a direct action against the final decision.[77]

The above findings can apply by analogy to explore the legal effects of soft law instruments in diverse policy areas. For instance, under the Single Supervisory Mechanism, the ECB has developed an ecosystem of instruments entailing self-imposed commitments, which can also have legally binding force under the

[76] ibid paras 40–41.

[77] A Bouchagiar, 'The Binding Effects of Guidelines on the Compatibility of State Aid: How Hard is the Commission's Soft Law?' (2017) 8(3) *Journal of European Competition Law & Practice* 157, 159. See Joined Cases T-394/08, T-408/08, T-453/08, and T-454/08 *Regione autonoma della Sardegna and Others v Commission* [2008] EU:C:2008:482, paras 209–10. See also Case T-52/12 *Greece v Commission* [2014] EU:T:2014:677, paras 146–55.

aforementioned conditions.[78] The 'SSM Supervisory Manual',[79] which aims to provide internal operational guidance in the ECB's supervisory function, is an example of this category of measures.

V. INTENTIONS AND PERCEPTIONS IN TIMES OF CONFLICT

If it is accepted that the viewpoints of involved parties are to be determined objectively, the next logical step is to outline the methodology that the Court can follow to carry out this assessment in concrete cases. Here I only present some preliminary thoughts.

To the extent that there can be more than one viewpoint on whether certain conduct is capable of producing legal effects in a given case, the institution which drafted a measure and persons whose legal positions may be affected as a result of that measure may disagree. The disagreement may manifest in three forms. First, the subjective intention of the author of the act may differ from the subjective perception of concerned parties (Type 1). Second, a subjective view (whether of the author or a concerned person) may come into conflict with an objectively determined perception (of the author or concerned person) about the legal effects of an act (Type 2). Finally, there may be a conflict between opposite and mutually exclusive perceptions that have nevertheless been objectively determined (Type 3).

Based on the analysis of the case law above, it appears that Type 1 conflicts would not typically influence the courts' assessment on the reviewability of EU acts, unless these can be objectively verified. The courts would consider the actual intentions of the author to the extent that these can be discovered by looking at the institution's external behaviour and associated objective evidence. In Type 2 conflicts, the case law indicates that the objectively determined view would generally take precedent over the subjective view. Unlike the others, Type 3 conflicts require a more elaborate discussion.

A complex situation emerges when the divergence of views occurs between the author of an act and a concerned person, and when both views can be perceived to be objectively reasonable, for their own distinct reasons. This conflict is the only one that is legally relevant and should be the subject matter of judicial assessment. This conflict can only be resolved with reference to objective criteria. In taking an objective approach to consider this divergence of views, theoretically, the Court might ask, on the one hand, what the intention of a reasonable drafter under the relevant legal and factual circumstances would have been. On the other hand, it might ask how a reasonable concerned person

[78] For the opposite view, see R Bax and A Witte, 'The Taxonomy of ECB Instruments Available for Banking Supervision' (2019) 6 *ECB Economic Bulletin* 85, 93.

[79] ECB, 'SSM Supervisory Manual. European Banking Supervision: Functioning of the SSM and Supervisory Approach' (March 2018).

would, under the same circumstances, have interpreted the contested act. While both approaches aim to shed light on the objective meaning or purpose of a contested act, they might not always lead to identical conclusions. Indeed, it is possible to imagine a situation in which the Court found that an act did (or did not) produce certain legal effects and, at the same time, also recognised that a reasonable drafter of an EU act would not have been able to predict the capacity (or lack thereof) of that act to cause a change in the legal position of certain persons.

This is more likely to occur with respect to acts of general application such as the one contested in *UK v ECB*, because the identity of the persons who may be affected by these acts is largely undefined. In such a case, the author of an act may face objective difficulties in knowing a priori all the legal relations that may be affected. Can this be regarded as a good reason, on its own, for denying (or accepting) the capacity of that act to produce legal effects vis-a-vis those persons? I think not, if a concerned person can show that a reasonable person with equivalent knowledge and expertise would have perceived the effects of that act differently under the same legal and factual circumstances. An affirmative answer would arguably lead to a substantial interference with the rights of those affected persons to seek legal protection and the need of EU authorities to adhere to a general principle of good administration. Consequently, it seems justified, in my view, for the Court to always consider the perceptions of concerned parties as an integral component of its reviewability assessment.

What will be the impact of these principles with respect to soft law instruments of EU authorities, such as guidelines, policy frameworks and codes of conduct? The way in which national authorities and private parties perceive the legal significance of soft law instruments is relevant not only for assessing their practical effects but also for establishing whether they can be subject of judicial scrutiny at the EU level.

VI. CONCLUSION

After more than 60 years of litigation, the courts have yet to present a clear methodology for determining whether an EU act – be it hard or soft law – can be subject to judicial review in direct annulment actions under Article 263(1) TFEU. Despite the Court's attempt to define the notion of reviewable act in the *ERTA* and *IBM* cases, uncertainty about whether an act passes the judicial gates has persisted to date. To an external observer, this becomes apparent from the ambiguity in the manner through which the Court carries out its substantive assessment to determine whether a contested act is capable of producing legally binding effects. The catalogue of criteria that may influence this assessment is non-exhaustive and it is almost impossible to predict which criteria influence the courts' assessment in a given case and to what degree.

This chapter has aimed to shed light on the meaning, interplay and function of two important criteria used for determining the reviewability of acts: the so-called 'intention of author' and the 'perceptions of concerned parties'. Each of these represents the point of view of the participants in a communication. The role of the courts is to determine whether a piece of communication, expressed in the form of an act, entails legal effects. In that context, the messenger's intention and the receiver's perception about whether such legal effects have been produced by a contested act become relevant considerations.

The point of view of concerned persons can influence the Court's assessment relating to acts that may impose binding obligations on others, as well as acts entailing self-imposed commitments, typically described as soft law. Certain guidelines and other instruments aiming to limit institutional discretion fall within the scope of the latter type. The distinctiveness of these instruments lies in the duality of their legal effects: on the one hand, they impose an obligation on their author to comply with the requirements provided in that instrument (or alternatively to explain why departing from them is justified); on the other hand, the very existence of this duty gives rise to a corresponding right of the concerned persons – Member States or private persons – to see those commitments being met (or, alternatively, receive the reasons justifying a departure from them). In some cases, this right of concerned persons is protected with reference to legitimate expectations.

The intention of an author of an act and the perception of a concerned person about the capacity of that act to produce certain legal effects can differ. When this happens, I suggested that in the interest of coherent case law, the courts should only consider the objective viewpoints of the involved parties. In practice, this can be achieved by carrying out a balancing exercise between the objectively identified intention of the author and the reasonable perceptions of concerned parties.

The perceptions and conduct of Member States can have noticeable impact on whether EU soft law measures would be deemed to be legally significant and fall under judicial scrutiny. A concerned Member State's objectively determined perceptions can influence the Court's assessment on the capacity of an EU soft law measure to cause binding legal effects, particularly in the case of atypical measures where the legal effects assessment is less straightforward. The case law indicates that perceptions about legal effects are assessed in the light of the degree of knowledge, information and expertise held by a reasonable concerned person. EU courts would likely consider the perceptions of Member States bearing in mind their privileged status and involvement in the EU's decision-making processes; the corresponding viewpoints of private persons, whether businesses or individuals, may be taken into account with reference to a different and perhaps lower standard of reasonable knowledge and expertise.

Finally, the conduct of Member States can trigger new legal effects of existing EU soft law instruments. When a Member State relies on EU soft law, such as guidelines or recommendations, to adopt subsequent national acts with direct binding legal effects vis-a-vis private persons, it enables such EU measures to have an impact, albeit indirectly, on the legal positions of private persons in concrete cases, thus setting into motion the jurisdiction of EU courts to review the validity of EU soft law indirectly via the preliminary ruling procedure under Article 267 TFEU.

19

Soft Law and the Promise of Transparency in the Member States

OANA ŞTEFAN*

I. INTRODUCTION

THIS CHAPTER ASSESSES the informative function of EU soft law and its potential to increase transparency in a multi-level governance context. Tagged as interpretative/decisional instruments[1] or post-legislative guidance,[2] many communications, notices or guidelines are used to interpret laconic hard law instruments, such as the Treaties, directives or regulations, or to indicate the way in which EU institutions think it appropriate to exercise their discretion. In certain sectors, the Commission chose to regulate through soft law because of the advantages it represented: its speedy adoption process and its potential to increase the flexibility, transparency and legal certainty of decision-making.[3]

Ensuring transparency appears to be one of the main functions of such instruments and is often expressly stated in the text of EU soft law.[4] This is confirmed by interviews conducted within the European Network of Soft Law Research (SoLaR) project: in the words of one UK interviewee, soft law is 'not only a question of regulating, but a question of transparency, consistency, and certainty'.[5] In a post-Lisbon context, this function of soft law becomes even

* Thanks to Mariolina Eliantonio and Emilia Korkea-aho for their comments on earlier versions of this chapter and to Irene Agnolucci for her research assistance. All websites were accessed on 21 July 2020.

[1] L Senden, *Soft Law in European Community Law* (Oxford, Hart Publishing, 2004) 140.

[2] J Scott, 'In Legal Limbo: Post-legislative Guidance as a Challenge for European Administrative Law' (2011) 48 *Common Market Law Review* 329.

[3] F Rawlinson, 'The Role of Policy Frameworks, Codes and Guidelines in the Control of State Aid' in in I Harden (ed), *State Aid: Community Law and Policy* (Cologne, Bundesanzeiger, 1993) 56–58.

[4] Commission Notice on the notion of State aid as referred to in Article 107(1) of the Treaty on the Functioning of the EU [2016] OJ C262, 19 July.

[5] M Dobbs and O Ştefan, ch 15 in this volume.

more important, with Article 1 of the Treaty on European Union (TEU) stating that decisions should be taken as openly as possible to the citizen and Article 15 of the Treaty on the Functioning of the European Union (TFEU) calling for EU institutions to conduct their work as openly as possible.

Transparency is often seen as a relationship between an actor and a forum towards which it is transparent. Through its informative function, soft law is expected to enhance the links between institutions and individuals. This should be conducive to the creation of a climate of legal certainty, yet in the multi-governance framework of the EU, this is not always the case.[6] Transparency is also supposed to enhance the connections between European and national authorities, thus creating the premises for a uniform and consistent application of EU law.[7] Finally, transparency – in its wider sense of 'openness' – includes participation in decision-making, a point in relation to which many authors agree that soft law ranks fairly low.[8]

Even though widely proclaimed, the potential of soft law to increase transparency is relatively unexplored from an empirical point of view, with certain reports pointing to serious flaws.[9] Soft law exists in a myriad of different names, shapes and forms, and is issued according to variable procedures. Such instruments are often very long and technical, and understanding them requires considerable expertise. Furthermore, according to recent case law, soft law does not even have to be translated in all EU languages in order to be relied on against individuals.[10] Finally, the effects that such instruments can produce in the absence of legally binding force are arguably unclear, rendering soft law presumably unenforceable and unpredictable.[11] All these elements point to a mismatch: soft law, which is issued in order to enhance transparency in the activity of EU institutions, can also sometimes lack transparency or even confuse matters further.[12] In this context, this chapter analyses whether the statement

[6] O Ştefan, 'Helping Loose Ends Meet? The Judicial Acknowledgement of Soft Law as a Tool of Multi-level Governance' (2014) 21 *Maastricht Journal of European and Comparative Law* 359.

[7] S Prechal and M de Leeuw, 'Dimensions of Transparency: The Building Blocks for a New Legal Principle? (2007) 1 *Review of European Administrative Law* 51; M Cini, 'The Soft Law Approach: Commission Rule-Making in the EU's State Aid Regime' (2001) 8 *Journal of European Public Policy* 192, 194.

[8] S Vaughan, 'Differentiation and Dysfunction: An Exploration of Post-legislative Guidance Practices in 14 EU Agencies (2015) 17 *Cambridge Yearbook of European Legal Studies* 66; E Korkea-aho, 'Laws in Progress? Reconceptualizing Accountability Strategies in the Era of Framework Norms' (2013) 2 *Transnational Environmental Law* 36; Scott (n 2); S Smismans, 'New Modes of Governance and the Participatory Myth' (2008) 31 *West European Politics* 874.

[9] A van den Brink and L Senden, 'Checks and Balances of Soft EU Rule-Making' (2012) Policy Department C: Citizens' Rights and Constitutional Affairs 20, https://ssrn.com/abstract=2042480 or http://dx.doi.org/10.2139/ssrn.2042480.

[10] Case C-410/09 *Polska Telefonia Cyfrowa (PTC)* [2011] EU:C:2011:294.

[11] C Chinkin, 'The Challenge of Soft Law: Development and Change in International Law' (1989) 38 *International & Comparative Law Quarterly* 850.

[12] H Hofmann, 'Administrative Governance in State Aid Policy' in H Hofmann and A Türk, *EU Administrative Governance* (Cheltenham, Edward Elgar, 2006); Senden (n 1) 497.

that soft law increases transparency is a rhetoric strategy or is confirmed by practice.

This chapter relies on the data collected through the SoLaR project and on established case law of the Court of Justice of the European Union (CJEU). It first offers a conceptualisation of the principle of transparency in an EU soft law context. It then looks at issues relating to the access to soft law, before analysing the relational aspect of transparency, namely the capacity to enhance, through EU soft law, the links between individuals, national and EU authorities.

II. TRANSPARENCY IN A SOFT LAW CONTEXT

In its legal sense, transparency is a virtue[13] or a normative concept including standards by which the behaviour of public actors can be evaluated. It is a principle that was progressively integrated into EU law: first, through the work of the Court and, after the 1990s, through Treaty amendments and legislation. Alongside procedural rights and human rights, transparency is considered to be a 'trust-enhancing principle'[14] that strengthens 'the democratic character of the institutions and the trust of the public in the administration'.[15] Such accounts promote an understanding of transparency as a value of good governance, yet the notion has an inherent relational aspect that is also crucial. This aspect is materialised in links between transparency and other principles such as effectiveness, accountability, fairness and legitimacy, with academia warning against elevating transparency to the statute of an intrinsic value of policy formulation. In this vein, Heald emphasises the instrumental value of transparency as a means to achieve other principles.[16] There are important limitations attached to transparency, and its inappropriate use might sometimes undermine other objectives, such as effectiveness or privacy.[17] Seeing transparency as a value in and of itself fails to capture the complex set of institutional relationships between the actor and the forum towards which it is transparent, between the observer, the observed act and the method of observation.[18] Meijer defines transparency as 'the availability of information about an actor that allows other actors to monitor the workings or performance of the first actor',[19] emphasising

[13] A Etzioni, 'Is Transparency the Best Disinfectant?' (2010) 18 *Journal of Political Philosophy* 389, 389.

[14] K Lenaerts, '"In the Union We Trust": Trust-Enhancing Principles of Community Law' (2004) 41*Common Market Law Review* 317.

[15] Case T-14/98 *Hautala v Council* [1999] EU:T:1999:157, para 83; confirmed on appeal, Case C-353/99 *Hautala v Council* [2001] EU:C:2001:661, para 22.

[16] D Heald, 'Transparency as an Instrumental Value' in C Hood and D Heald (eds), *Transparency, a Key to Better Governance* (Oxford, Oxford University Press, 2006) 67–68.

[17] ibid 68–69.

[18] R Oliver, *What is Transparency?* (New York, McGraw-Hill, 2004) 2.

[19] A Meijer, 'Understanding the Complex Dynamics of Transparency' (2013) 73 *Public Administration Review* 429, 430.

the relational aspect of transparency. In a soft law context, this aspect is crucial for three reasons.

First, transparency is required by the law[20] and even more so in a post-Lisbon context. Article 15 TFEU makes it clear that, in the name of good governance, EU institutions need to conduct their work as openly as possible. By laying down rules simplifying how discretion will be exercised, the Commission increases the transparency of its actions. The Commission often states that it is driven by transparency goals when issuing soft law instruments. For instance, the guidelines on fines, which set out the criteria used when applying fines to undertakings that are in breach of competition rules, serve the declared purpose of enhancing transparency and impartiality/objectivity in the activity of the Commission.[21]

Second, soft law plays an important role in creating links between the institutions and individuals, natural or legal persons, thus enhancing the legal certainty and transparency of administrative activity. Through these instruments, the Commission explains the existing law in a specific sector, presents its own views on the law and clarifies those provisions of an open and indeterminate character.[22] In this context, Snyder talked about 'regulation by publication'[23] and Hoffmann about 'regulation by information'.[24] The mechanism is as follows: the Commission publishes guidance and regulates without recourse to binding rules. Individuals would adjust their behaviour in accordance to the guidelines issued by the Commission in order to pre-empt potential challenges to their practices. The interpretative communications of the Commission were found to provide a 'Magna Carta'[25] for individuals, clarifying matters relating to their rights and duties. Soft law is meant to help individuals to understand what the law is, what the boundaries of their actions should be and what they should expect in the case of infractions, increasing legal certainty.

Third, through its transparency function and 'regulation by information', EU soft law can strengthen the links between the EU institutions and the national authorities. In that regard, EU soft law constitutes a source of doctrine, guiding public administrations in their activities, and therefore has the potential to increase the consistency of EU action. This can be observed in financial regulation, with Article 16(1) of the European Supervisory Authorities' (ESAs) Regulations stating that guidelines and recommendations shall be issued with a

[20] Etzioni (n 13) 396 ff.

[21] Guidelines on the method of setting fines imposed pursuant to Article 23(2)(a) of Regulation No 1/2003 [2006] OJ C210/2, para 3.

[22] M Gardenes Santiago, 'Las comunicaciones interpretativas de la Comision: concepto y valor normativo' (1992) 19 *Revista de Instituciones Europeas* 933, 939–40.

[23] F Snyder, 'Soft Law and Institutional Practice in the European Community' in S Martin and E Noël (eds), *The Construction of Europe: Essays in Honour of Emile Noël* (Dordrecht, Kluwer, 1994) 199–201.

[24] H Hofmann, 'Negotiated and Non-negotiated Administrative Rule-Making' (2006) 43 *CML Rev* 153, 172.

[25] N Tornberg, 'The Commission's Communications on the General Good: Magna Carta or Law-Making?' (1999) 24 *European Business Law Review* 27.

view to establishing consistent, efficient and effective supervisory practices, and to ensuring the common, uniform and consistent application of EU law.[26]

Seeing transparency as a relationship brings to the fore the distinction between openness and transparency, which is not always very clear in the literature.[27] For some, openness mostly relates to the processes that allow us to see how organisations work, with Birkinshaw and Larsson arguing that transparency relates to the ability of the observer to understand and access the information delivered by the observed organisation.[28] Heald explains that openness should be understood as a characteristic of an organisation, while 'transparency also requires external receptors capable of processing the information made available'.[29] Transparency and openness are thus similar concepts that both entail more than simply access to information. Curtin et al enlarged the notion of openness even further. While transparency includes access and availability of information in a general sense (revealing 'the thinking behind a decision or the way in which a decision is made'),[30] openness is broader and entails the possibility for citizens to 'monitor and influence legislative and executive processes through access to information and access to decision-making arenas'.[31] The notions of 'vision' and 'voice' are relevant in this context, and they relate to two facets of openness: transparency qua access to comprehensible information and participation of citizens in the decision-making process.[32]

Far from settling the theoretical debate, this chapter employs the notions of openness and transparency interchangeably, and only deals cursorily with the participation aspect. Some authors find that preparatory and informative

[26] Regulation (EU) No 1093/2010 of the European Parliament and of the Council of 24 November 2010 establishing a European Supervisory Authority (European Banking Authority) [2010] OJ L331, 15 December, 12–47; Regulation (EU) No 1095/2010 of the European Parliament and of the Council of 24 November 2010 establishing a European Supervisory Authority (European Securities and Markets Authority) [2010] OJ L331, 15 December, 84–119; Regulation (EU) No 1094/2010 of the European Parliament and of the Council of 24 November 2010 establishing a European Supervisory Authority (European Insurance and Occupational Pensions Authority) [2010] OJ L331, 15 December, 48–83.

[27] Heald (n 16) 25; for an EU-specific literature review, see A Alemanno, 'Unpacking the Principle of Openness in EU Law: Transparency, Participation and Democracy' (2014) 39 *European Law Review* 72.

[28] P Birkinshaw, 'Freedom of Information and Openness: Fundamental Human Rights' (2006) 58 *Administrative Law Review* 189; T Larsson, 'How Open Can a Government Be? The Swedish Experience' in V Deckmyn and I Thomson (eds), *Openness and Transparency in the EU* (Maastricht, European Institute of Public Administration, 1998) 40–42.

[29] Heald (n 16) 26.

[30] D Curtin, et al, 'Constitutionalising EU Executive Rule-Making Procedures: A Research Agenda' (2013) 19 *European Law Journal* 1, 6.

[31] Etzioni (n 13); P Craig, *EU Administrative Law* (Oxford, Oxford University Press, 2012) 357; B Bugaric, 'Openness and Transparency in Public Administration: Challenges for Public Law' (2004) 22 *Wisconsin International Law Journal* 487.

[32] D Curtin and J Mendes, 'Transparence et Participation: des Principes Démocratiques pour l'Administration de l'Union Européenne' (2011) 137–38 *Revue Française d'Administration Publique* 101; A Meijer et al, 'Open Government: Connecting Vision and Voice' (2012) 78 *International Review of Administrative Sciences* 10.

soft law instruments fulfil an important function in the pre-legislative stage because it is through these means that the European Parliament is informed and consulted on future legislation.[33] Yet, the European Parliament is hardly involved in the soft law-making process.[34] Many soft law instruments are the result of consultation procedures. However, it has been argued that 'consultative procedures are less rigorously adopted and structured in relation to rules whose binding nature is uncertain',[35] with research showing that soft law is sometimes issued according to procedures that completely lack transparency.[36] Participation – and the lack thereof – is a key problem, challenging the argument that soft law enhances openness within the meaning of Article 15 TFEU if it is the result of opaque decision-making procedures. More empirical research is needed to determine whether the level of involvement of stakeholders and of the European Parliament is satisfactory or not.[37] This would involve a wider debate on the legitimacy of soft law instruments, as is addressed elsewhere in this volume.[38]

Concerned primarily with the relational aspect of transparency/openness, this chapter only briefly deals with some issues relating to public consultations. The focus is on assessing the first facet of transparency/openness: that of access to comprehensible information that can improve the relationship between EU institutions and the individuals on the one hand, and EU institutions and national authorities on the other. The chapter first considers issues of physical access and comprehensibility of EU soft law before looking at the specificities of the relational aspect of transparency.

III. ACCESS TO SOFT LAW

This section conceives the standard of openness/transparency in the EU to include public access to information, as well as the proactive institutional duty to ensure that information is provided in an accessible and understandable way.[39] There are several barriers to access considered here, relating to physical access and publication, as well as the sheer volume of soft law instruments. It is argued that translation issues, as well as issues relating to clarity, legality and quality of regulation, might be more acute in a soft law context.

[33] Senden (n 1) 483.

[34] Hofmann (n 24) 172.

[35] R Baldwin, *Rules and Government* (Oxford, Clarendon Press, 1997) 284.

[36] Scott (n 2) 336, O Ştefan, 'COVID-19 Soft Law: Voluminous, Effective, Legitimate? A Research Agenda', (2020) *European Forum*, http://www.europeanpapers.eu/en/europeanforum/covid-19-soft-law-voluminous-effective-legitimate.

[37] Van den Brink and Senden (n 9).

[38] U Mörth, ch 20 in this volume.

[39] A Alemanno and O Ştefan, 'Openness at the Court of Justice of the EU: Toppling a Taboo' (2014) 51 *Common Market Law Review* 109.

A. Barriers to Physical Access to Soft Law

Forms of soft law of general application abound, are extremely varied and are not always consistently published, thereby challenging transparency. It has been argued that international soft law comes in an 'infinite variety';[40] EU soft law is no exception. The list of European soft law instruments starts with the fifth paragraph of Article 288 TFEU: 'Recommendations and opinions shall have no binding force.'[41] However, a vast array of other instruments also come under the heading of European soft legislation. The most frequent designations are recommendations, opinions and resolutions,[42] but various other designations are employed too: declarations; Green and White Papers; conclusions; action papers; reports; programmes; communications; memoranda; statements of the representatives of the Member States meeting in the Council; inter-institutional agreements; codes of conduct; notices; guidelines; and practices. This variety is reflected in the sample selected by SoLaR, as a quick glance at Annex I will show. The different headings, as well as the sheer volume of instruments, might be confusing, as it might not be immediately obvious that various keywords do not indicate different degrees of legal effects.[43] Civil servants interviewed by SoLaR believe that EU guidance can *decrease* transparency, as too many instruments might obscure the interpretation of the law.[44]

Furthermore, Article 297 TFEU does not require soft law instruments to be published in the Official Journal. Nonetheless, as noted in a report on soft law commissioned by the European Parliament,[45] the Commission does publish soft law in the C series of the Official Journal, where the recommendations of the Commission and the Council are also published. However, some other instruments, published as COM documents, are available only online.[46] An important

[40] R Baxter, 'International Law in Her Infinite Variety' (1980) 29 *International and Comparative Law Quarterly* 549.

[41] Recommendations and opinions survived the initiative to better define the EU's instruments and to reduce their number, put forward in the Laeken Declaration on the Future of the EU (2001), https://www.cvce.eu/en/obj/laeken_declaration_on_the_future_of_the_european_union_15_december_2001-en-a76801d3-4bf0-4483-9000-e6df94b07a55.html. They were preserved by Convention Working Group IX on 'Simplification', http://european-convention.europa.eu/docs/wd9/4869.pdf, and figured in art I-33 of the Constitution. See K Lenaerts and M Desomer, 'Towards a Hierarchy of Legal Acts in the EU? Simplification of Legal Instruments and Procedures' (2005) 11 *European Law Journal* 744, 748–49.

[42] A von Bogdandy et al, 'Legal Instruments in EU Law and Their Reform: A Systematic Approach on an Empirical Basis' (2004) 23 *Yearbook of European Law* 91, 112.

[43] P Láncos, 'A Hard Core under the Soft Shell: How Binding is Union Soft Law for Member States?' (2018) 24 *European Public Law* 755.

[44] V Rošic Feguš, 'National Report of the Republic of Slovenia' in O Ştefan (ed), 'EU Competition and State Aid Soft Law in the Member States' (2020) SoLaR Working Paper, https://papers.ssrn.com/sol3/papers.cfm?abstract_id=2356227, 173.

[45] Van den Brink and Senden (n 9) 27.

[46] For statistics on the publication of soft law in the environmental field, see M Eliantonio, 'Soft Law in Environmental Matters and the Role of the European Courts: Too Much or Too Little of it?' (2018) 37 *Yearbook of European Law* 496.

number of the soft law instruments analysed by SoLaR are published in the C series of the Official Journal, yet some are published by the Publication Office under an ISBN and a DOI,[47] while others are published on the website of the issuing agency (the European Securities and Markets Authority (ESMA)), and some others are published as COM documents.[48] While the Commission now publishes annual reports in various areas, such reports might create confusion with regard to the applicable rules. Given the vast array of issues reported per annual volume, it might be a cumbersome task for individuals and national authorities to closely monitor these instruments in order to be up to date with the latest rules that the Commission might decide to publish therein. It is recommended that all these publication processes are better streamlined in order to facilitate access.

B. Lost in Translation and Transposition: Issues Stemming from the Multi-linguistic and Multi-level Nature of the EU

Translation issues are a classic problem in the multi-cultural and multi-linguistic EU.[49] To counteract such problems, the ESAs translate EU financial guidance in all official languages.[50] However, our research shows that the differences in translations might impair consistent application throughout Europe.[51]

Given the lack of binding force of soft law, there is no requirement to publish such instruments in all the official languages. Some of the instruments dealt with by SoLaR were available in most of the languages,[52] while others were only available in English.[53] Thus, individuals may encounter difficulties in understanding or accessing the text relevant to their case. This happened in *PTC*, where untranslated soft law was applied by the national authorities to a Polish

[47] DG for Employment, Social Affairs and Inclusion (European Commission), DG for the Internal Market and Services (European Commission), 'Buying Social: A Guide to Taking Account of Social Considerations in Public Procurement' (2011), https://op.europa.eu/en/publication-detail/-/publication/cb70c481-0e29-4040-9be2-c408cddf081f.

[48] Commission staff working document – Accompanying document to the Communication from the Commission Trans-European Network: Toward and integrated approach, COM (2007)135 final, https://eur-lex.europa.eu/legal-content/EN/TXT/HTML/?uri=CELEX:52007SC0374&from=EN.

[49] M Bobek, 'The Binding Force of Babel: The Enforcement of EC Law Unpublished in the Languages of the New Member States' (2007) 9 *Cambridge Yearbook of European Legal Studies* 43; E Paunio, *Legal Certainty in Multilingual EU Law: Language, Discourse and Reasoning at the European Court of Justice* (Abingdon, Routledge, 2016).

[50] F Demarigny et al, 'Review of the New European System of Financial Supervision (ESFS), Part 1: The Work of the European Supervisory Authorities (EBA, EIOPA and ESMA) – The ESFS's Micro-prudential Pillar' (2013) 56, https://www.europarl.europa.eu/RegData/etudes/etudes/join/2013/507446/IPOL-ECON_ET(2013)507446_EN.pdf.

[51] M Avbelj (ed), 'EU Financial Regulation Soft Law in the Member States' (2020) SoLaR Working Paper, https://papers.ssrn.com/sol3/papers.cfm?abstract_id=3668793, 14; O Ştefan and A Biondi, 'National Report on the UK' in Ştefan (n 44) 178.

[52] Most of the competition and State aid instruments.

[53] M Eliantonio and G Lisi (eds), 'EU Environmental Soft Law in the Member States' (2020) SoLaR Working Paper, https://papers.ssrn.com/sol3/papers.cfm?abstract_id=3656418, 11.

telecommunications company.[54] As mentioned by environmental officials interviewed by the Slovenian team, the language can also be an issue for the national authorities and not only the individuals.[55] Specific 'Brussels jargon' might be a problem too, with an interviewee in the UK noting that the State aid Manual published by the Department for Business, Energy, and Industrial Strategy (BEIS)[56] is a translation into common law terms of formal EU guidance originally written in English, such as the Commission Notice on the Notion of Aid.[57]

The multi-level governance structure of the EU and the need to nationally implement EU material might raise problems of transparency as well. While there is no obligation to transpose soft law, unsurprisingly, experiences are diverse and country- and field-dependent.[58] The Member States analysed by SoLaR chose between various options,[59] which, to paraphrase Abbott et al[60] and Terpan,[61] seem to reflect the continuum of 'legalisation'. The variations go from full engagement with soft law in the text of national hard law to brief website references and no engagement at all.[62] Following respective constitutional and administrative organisation rules, the transposition of EU soft law is done centrally, but also at the regional level, at the discretion of various authorities, such as in Italy, where certain EU guidance stemming from the Habitats Directive[63] was transposed into binding form only at the local level.[64]

First, in certain areas, the transposition might follow traditional routes and can be done through national soft law or even hard law. Examples of the former include the Bundesanstalt fur Finanzdienstleistungsaufsicht (BaFin) circulars (*Rundschreiben*) and information sheets (*Merkblatt*).[65] Similarly, a French *circulaire*[66] guides the action of the administration in relation to State aid and, together with Article 1511-1-1 of the Code general des collectivités territoriales,

[54] *Polska Telefonia Cyfrowa* (n 10) paras 31–34; see also O Ştefan, 'EU Soft Law' (2012) 75 *MLR* 879.

[55] K Vatovec, 'National Report on Slovenia' in Eliantonio and Lisi (n 53) 121.

[56] BEIS, 'Guidance. State Aid Manual' (2015), www.gov.uk/government/publications/state-aid-manual.

[57] Dobbs and Ştefan, ch 15 in this volume.

[58] Noted in relation to Germany by M Hartlapp and A Hofmann, 'The Use of EU Soft Law by National Courts and Bureaucrats: How Relation to Hard Law and Policy Maturity Matter' (2020) *West European Politics*, DOI: 10.1080/01402382.2020.1738095.

[59] Compiled by the author from the SoLaR Working Papers: Ştefan (n 44); Avbelj (n 51); Eliantonio and Lisi (n 53); M Hartlapp (ed), 'Studying EU Soft Law Effects in Social Policy' (2020) SoLaR Working Paper, https://papers.ssrn.com/sol3/papers.cfm?abstract_id=3668981.

[60] KW Abbott et al, 'The Concept of Legalization' (2000) 54 *International Organization* 401.

[61] F Terpan, 'Soft Law in the EU: The Changing Nature of EU Law' (2015) 21 *European Law Journal* 68.

[62] Hartlapp and Korkea-aho, ch 4 in this volume.

[63] Council Directive 92/43/EEC of 21 May 1992 on the conservation of natural habitats and of wild fauna and flora (Habitats Directive) [1992] OJ L206, 22 July, 7–50.

[64] G Lisi and M Eliantonio, 'National Report on Italy' in Eliantonio and Lisi (n 53) 70.

[65] M Hartlapp and A Schwerdtfeger, 'Studying EU Soft Law Effects in Financial Regulation: Insights from Germany' in Avbelj (n 51), 64; Hartlapp and Hofmann (n 58) 7.

[66] Circulaire du Premier Ministre, 'Application des règles européennes de concurrence relatives aux aides publiques aux activités économiques', 5 February 2019, no 6060/SG, http://circulaires.legifrance.gouv.fr/pdf/2019/02/cir_44368.pdf.

is meant to gather together all the relevant EU legislation. Soft law is sometimes transposed into hard law, such as the the Banking Communication,[67] which was transposed into the Slovenian legal order through an amendment to the Banking Act.[68] Second, the text of soft law can be reproduced without citing the source in the text of national acts, leading to hybrid combinations. For instance, the French Commercial Code[69] incorporates the thresholds of the *De Minimis* Notice.[70] Third, EU soft law is included in national acts by reference to the original source, such as the Aviation Act of Slovenia referring to the Aviation Guidelines of the Commission.[71] Fourth, EU soft law may simply be referred to on websites or in national guides. Examples in this regard include the Dutch practice to issue national guidance 'limited to a single phrase stating the Commission's guidelines on a certain issue also apply to the corresponding national provision',[72] with websites mentioning quick references to the EU text. Similarly, a reference to EU's Buying Social guide[73] is included in the list of further reading appended to the Finnish Handbook of Government Procurements.[74] Finally, the EU-inspired practice of questions and answers (Q&A) has been a valuable source of translating EU financial regulation soft law into the national legal orders, such as the Q&A included in the Perimeter Guidance Manual[75] by the UK's Financial Conduct Authority (FCA).[76] Fifth, soft law might not be included at all in the national legal order, but there would exist a certain faith in national authorities that they would know what rules to apply. Such a category was confirmed by the case law, for example, in the environmental sector in the UK,[77] as well as by interviews, such as with Slovenian officials feeling bound by EU State aid guidance to which Slovenia committed itself.[78]

[67] Communication from the Commission on the application, from 1 January 2011, of State aid rules to support measures in favour of banks in the context of the financial crisis [2010] OJ C329/7, 7 December, 7–10.

[68] Rošic Feguš (n 44) 152.

[69] Article L 464-6-1 and 2 of the French Trade Code (Code de commerce), which incorporates market share thresholds into French law.

[70] Communication from the Commission – Notice on agreements of minor importance which do not appreciably restrict competition under Article 101(1) of the Treaty on the Functioning of the EU (*De Minimis* Notice) [2014] OJ C291, 30 August, 1–4.

[71] Article 158(4) of the Slovenian Aviation Act: 'The operation of public airport may be financed from public resources as operating aid in accordance with the Guidelines on State aid to airports and airlines.' See Communication from the Commission – Guidelines on State aid to airports and airlines [2014] OJ C99, 4 April, 3).

[72] C Cauffman and N Philipsen, 'National Report on the Netherlands' in Ştefan (n 44) 117.

[73] DG for Employment, Social Affairs and Inclusion (European Commission), DG for the Internal Market and Services (European Commission) (n 47).

[74] E Korkea-aho, 'The Finnish Report on the Reception of Social Soft Law' in Hartlapp (n 59) 28.

[75] https://www.handbook.fca.org.uk/handbook/PERG.pdf.

[76] S Post, 'EU Soft Law Effects in Financial Regulation: Insights from the United Kingdom' in Avbelj (n 51) 136.

[77] eg, *Morge v Hampshire County Council* [2011] UKSC 2 [60]: 'it might be confidently expected that Natural England were aware of the terms of the Habitats Directive, the Commission Guidance and the Habitats Regulations, given that they were the authority responsible'.

[78] Rošic Feguš (n 44) 171.

The question is which of the above options would offer the maximum from the point of view of transparency and consistency. A traditional approach would be that the official reception through incorporation into soft or (even better) hard law would be preferred. Yet, this might just not correspond to the idea that flexibility is one of the most sought-after features of soft law: what happens if guidance is amended at the EU level? Would the national level always respond with a swift change in the corresponding instrument? Seen in this light, potentially the best solution would be the inclusion of soft law by dynamic reference, in either national hard or soft law, to the original source – including an expectation that this means a reference to the up-to-date version of the instrument at any given time. This is confirmed by public consultations in the area of financial regulation in the UK, where, to keep the volume of the rules at a manageable level, the FCA (non-binding) handbook only included references to corresponding ESAs guidance. This appears to have been done in agreement with most stakeholders' wishes, as summarised in a policy statement from the FCA, although a minority of respondents suggested additional signposts and a few suggested integrating the entirety of EU applicable provisions into the handbook.[79] Such an approach would resonate with wider conclusions that too much information might impair transparency.[80] Moreover, integrating soft law by way of reference might even increase the weight of EU soft law by showing that the rules are applicable internationally.

Another potential solution is the publication of Q&As referring to EU guidance. Such a practice, which is developed especially in EU financial regulation, has inspired national authorities to produce their own Q&As, potentially increasing transparency, especially for individuals, who can find relevant information faster. In Germany, for instance, all interviewees confirmed that this practice is on the rise,[81] while in the UK, the FCA has also integrated Q&As.[82] As mentioned by German interviewees, this might raise concerns of legitimacy, as well as of legal effects, as they are 'softer' than soft law. Similarly, the way in which ESAs Q&As are drafted is sometimes not transparent in itself, although they do involve national representatives.[83] Perspectives from Italy show a totally different picture: the Italian regulatory authority rarely considers them, as they are perceived to be directed mostly at the financial institutions within their day-to-day operation.[84]

[79] FCA, 'Markets in Financial Instruments Directive II Implementation – Policy Statement I' (PS17/5, 31 March 2017), https://www.fca.org.uk/publication/policy/ps17-05.pdf.

[80] G Michener, 'Gauging the Impact of Transparency Policies' (2019) 79 *Public Administration Review* 136.

[81] Hartlapp and Schwerdtfeger (n 65) 64.

[82] Post (n 76) 137.

[83] Hartlapp and Schwerdtfeger (n 65) 65.

[84] J Alberti and L d'Amico, 'The Implementation of ESMA's Guidelines at National Level – Italian Report' in Avbelj (n 51) 71.

C. Issues Relating to the Content of Soft Law

The literature discussed this point at length and it was argued that the duty to communicate the law in a clear and transparent fashion is part of the good administration requirement provided for in Article 41 of the Charter of Fundamental Rights,[85] and with legal certainty requiring that legal rules in force at a certain moment are clear and precise.[86] Yet, the content of soft law instruments is often ambiguous, as criticised in front of the CJEU itself by applicants[87] and Court members.[88]

Similarly, according to the SoLaR interviews, some soft law instruments lack in precision and clarity, which increases the potential for varying national interpretation.[89] German civil servants criticised the lack of clarity of EU social soft law.[90] Finnish respondents mentioned that environmental soft law is open to interpretation and hence is difficult to apply in practice,[91] and that the transparency of European Central Bank (ECB) guidance is even lower than that of the ESAs guidance.[92] Conversely, another Finnish respondent linked the lack of transparency with the high specialisation of the financial sector.[93] In the Netherlands, the perspective seems to be that in financial regulation, soft law may increase transparency because market participants appreciate the clarity that 'public documents' provide.[94] Similar positive perspectives on the transparency of financial regulation soft law were expressed by Slovenian officials.[95] French respondents were unanimous in maintaining that EU environmental guidance can clarify hard law.[96]

The views are mixed and it is difficult to draw patterns regarding which instruments or practices are likely to lead to maximum transparency. In competition, an area where soft law is something of an acquired taste, most interviewees agreed that soft law increases transparency and predictability.[97] However, as mentioned by the Italian report, there is a difference between these statements

[85] M Aziz, 'Mainstreaming the Duty of Clarity and Transparency as Part of Good Administrative Practice in the EU' (2004) 10 *European Law Journal* 282.

[86] Case C-63/93 *Duff and Others v Minister for Agriculture and Food* [1995] EU:C:1995:170, Opinion of AG Cosmas, para 25.

[87] Case C-310/99 *Italy v Commission* [2002] EU:C:2002:143, para 97.

[88] Case C-510/06 *Archer Daniels Midland v Commission* [2008] EU:C:2008:280, Opinion of AG Trstenjak, para 84; more recently, see Case C-295/12 *Telefonica* [2013] EU:C:2013:619, Opinion of AG Wathelet, para 144.

[89] Ştefan and Biondi (n 51) 189.

[90] M Hartlapp, 'Studying EU Soft Law Effects in Social Policy: Insights from Germany' in Hartlapp (n 59) 63.

[91] E Korkea-aho, 'National Report on Finland: The Use of EU Soft Law by National Courts and Administration in the Field of EU Environmental Law' in Eliantonio and Lisi (n 53) 31.

[92] P Leino-Sandberg and E Korkea-aho, 'Country Report on Finland' in Avbelj (n 51) 36.

[93] ibid.

[94] C Cauffman, 'Financial Soft Law in the Netherlands' in Avbelj (n 51) 95.

[95] M Avbelj, 'The Implementation of ESMA's Guidelines in Slovenia' in Avbelj (n 51) 102.

[96] G Lisi et al, 'National Report on France: The Use of EU Soft Law by National Courts and Administration in the Field of EU Environmental Law' in Eliantonio and Lisi (n 53) 46.

[97] Ştefan (n 44) 29 ff.

and what actually happens in practice, given that legal effects are not recognised for EU guidance at the national level.[98]

Transparency is also at a loss when soft law provisions conflict with hard law, partly because of the blurred line that divides the two categories of regulation. This is solved, in theory, by simply considering the hierarchy of norms: soft law would always be trumped by hard law. However, the overlap between hard and soft law is not always easy to grasp. Sometimes soft law interpreting hard law provisions creates new obligations and in such situations, soft law is generally considered ultra vires and is annulled by the courts.[99] As noted by Scott, in the case of vague, general hard law norms, it may 'frequently be impossible to make a clear determination of where the boundaries of the existing obligation begin and end'.[100] Even though a soft law instrument might not seem to introduce new legal obligations, it might promote a radical interpretation of an obligation provided in a regulation or a directive, thus having significant effects in practice on the legal situation of individuals or Member States. Indeed, one can envisage that in the absence of the soft law instrument, the national or European authorities might interpret the specific obligation provided in the hard law provision in a more lenient or indeed more stringent way. Interviewees on the SoLaR project confirmed the existence of a very thin line between interpretation of the law and clarification of the law.[101] Concerns regarding the legality of soft law have also been expressed, with Finnish interviewees raising matters regarding the competence of the ECB to adopt guidance.[102] The issue of competence was also mentioned by a Dutch official talking about competition law[103] and by a Slovenian official talking about environmental guidance,[104] who wondered why an authority should adopt non-binding tools instead of adopting hard law.

The extremely popular Notice on the Notion of Aid illustrates the importance of these concerns. Issued in 2016, the Notice is already amply relied upon at the national level, as shown by SoLaR research,[105] and features regularly in the case law of the ECJ.[106] It codifies the rather convoluted case law of the ECJ defining the notion of State aid. According to Article 107 (1) TFEU, support schemes granting a specific advantage to national industries and distorting EU competition and trade are prohibited unless they are approved by the Commission, which enjoys discretion under Article 107(2) and especially (3). The notice is controversial for two reasons. First, unlike other forms of State aid soft law, this is an instrument issued within the ambit of Article 107(1), which lays down the objective concept of State aid, an area where there is very little

[98] Alberti and Croci, 'National Report on Italy' in ibid 107.
[99] Case C-366/88 *France v Commission* [1990] EU:C:1990:348.
[100] Scott (n 2) 342.
[101] Lisi et al (n 96) 46.
[102] Leino-Sandberg and Korkea-aho (n 92) 36.
[103] Cauffman and Philipsen (n 72) 142.
[104] Vatovec (n 55) 121.
[105] Ştefan (n 44) 19.
[106] Thirteen State aid cases in the past three years, compiled by the author from curia.europa.eu.

discretion for the Commission to exert or to explain. Second, the Commission is limited in its interpretation of Article 107(1) by the case law of the Court, as is also acknowledged by the Preamble to the Notice. Yet, many paragraphs of the Notice refer solely to Commission practice. Thus, while the Notice must be commended for pooling a vast array of subtleties inherent within the notion of aid, its goal to promote transparency is undermined by the uneasy mix of codified case law, views of the Commission on issues not yet decided by the ECJ and views of the Commission on aspects pertaining to its limited discretion.[107]

While it can be argued that issues relating to the clarity, the legality and ultimately the quality of regulation are not soft law-specific, it is important to highlight that in a soft law context, such issues are difficult to correct. This is because of the very high justiciability thresholds[108] which often make judicial review of such instruments impossible,[109] as well as because of the lack of wider participation in the process of the adoption of soft law.

IV. THE RELATIONAL ASPECT OF TRANSPARENCY

The analysis now turns to limitations of transparency inherent in the relationship between the forum and its observers, as well as the relationship between transparency and other principles of law. As mentioned in section II above, soft law has the potential to enhance the links between individuals and institutions on the one hand, and between EU and national institutions on the other hand. The first aspect of this relationship is participation in EU soft law-making, which can concern private parties and national authorities alike. While legitimacy is not the primary focus of the analysis here,[110] public consultations will be briefly discussed as a specific soft law-making mechanism. The second aspect concerns the potential of 'regulation by publication' to increase legal certainty, equality and consistent application of EU law, yet this is rather limited by the limited effects that soft law can produce in a multi-level governance setting.

A. Consultations

The literature shows that even if it is true that the Commission undertakes lengthy public consultation before publishing soft law, such consultations are

[107] The discussion of the Notice on the Notion of State aid draws on A Biondi and O Ştefan, 'The Notice on the Notion of State Aid: Every Light Has its Shadow' in B Nascimbene (ed), *The Modernisation of EU State Aid Control Evolution and Perspectives of the EU Rules on State Aids and Services of General Economic Interest* (Dordrecht, Springer, 2018).

[108] M Eliantonio, ch 17 in this volume.

[109] Case C-16/16 P *Belgium v Commission* [2018] EU:C:2018:79.

[110] Mörth, ch 20 in this volume.

not always systematic and there is little information as to how they occur.[111] A study on the open method of coordination (OMC) showed the prevalence of technocratic and bureaucratic forms of representation, as opposed to substantive political or functional ones. This was connected to fairly limited levels of transparency at both the EU and the national levels, with OMC processes taking place behind closed doors.[112] As also revealed by Armstrong, in practice, the participation of various stakeholders' rights in OMC processes were limited,[113] resulting in uneven representation.

However, the lack of participation seems to be forum- and sector-dependent. Consultations on new soft law are frequently organised in competition and State aid law, as well as in other areas – such as energy, with consultation procedures sometimes required by hard law instruments.

In competition and State aid, the process is relatively streamlined.[114] This has also been observed by SoLaR interviewees, for instance, by Finnish officials who tagged competition soft law as 'democratic' as drafted following discussions with Member State representatives.[115] Only Italian respondents were marginally dissatisfied with the participatory aspect of EU soft law transparency (the view expressed was that the real problems in competition and State aid do not relate to soft law).[116] It was considered that the text of the proposal submitted to public consultation is already a compromise, with consultations becoming a simple formality that were not capable of influencing the content of the measure at issue. In relation to State aid, it was mentioned that it is impossible to check whether public consultations were taken into consideration by the Commission. While all documentation is available on the webpage of the Directorate-General for Competition (DG Comp), one would have to carry out extensive analysis to see how many of the arguments expressed by the participants made it into the final text.[117]

With regard to environmental EU guidance, French[118] and Slovenian[119] officials interviewed by the SoLaR team agreed that the Commission does not involve Member States enough in the process of drafting, which in turn may

[111] Scott (n 2) 336.

[112] S Kröger, 'The End of Democracy as We Know it? The Legitimacy Deficits of Bureaucratic Social Policy Governance' (2007) 29 *Journal of European Integration* 565.

[113] K Armstrong, 'How Open is the United Kingdom to the OMC Process on Social Inclusion?' in J Zeitlin and P Pochet (eds), *The Open Method of Co-ordination in Action* (Brussels, PIE-Peter Lang, 2005) 287.

[114] M Botta, 'Competition Policy: Safeguarding the Commission's Competences in State Aid Control' (2016) 38 *Journal of European Integration* 265, 271; Biondi and Ştefan (n 107).

[115] K Havu and L Tarkkila, 'National Report on Finland: The Use of EU Soft Law by National Courts and Administration in the Field of EU Competition and State Aid Law' in Ştefan (n 44) 47.

[116] Alberti and Croci (n 98) 111.

[117] ibid 110; see also Biondi and Ştefan (n 107).

[118] Lisi et al (n 96) 47.

[119] Vatovec (n 55) 121.

impair transparency and consistency. Paradoxically, this lack of consultation does not deter compliance at the national level.[120]

Consultations are required only not for soft law issued by the Commission, but also for soft law issued by EU agencies. For instance, consultations have to be organised, wherever appropriate, in order to issue guidance according to Article 16 of the ESAs Regulations. However, SoLaR interviews confirm participation concerns in relation to ESAs soft law. According to civil servants working in the area of financial regulation in Finland, it is unclear whether consultations have any actual effect and, moreover, negotiations points are sometimes re-opened in order to push for certain positions.[121]

More research is needed in order to assess the robustness of these consultations and their relevance for the legitimacy of soft law. With regard to the relational aspect of transparency, the views from national civil servants are very important, with a shared feeling emerging that national perspectives are not always taken into account when drafting EU soft law. This leads to the conclusion that EU soft law creates one-way relationships, with the Commission simply informing of its intentions, but not always listening to national voices.

B. Transparency and Other Principles of Law

Transparent 'regulation by publication' can, in principle, enhance legal certainty. This link is not always clear, with Birkinshaw finding that the notion of open government has been used in a pejorative sense, as provision of 'access to information under non-legally binding codes that do not create rights'.[122] Yet, this is not always the case, and the intensity of the link between transparency and legal certainty varies according to the sectors and levels of EU governance.

In some sectors, this link is particularly weak, given the judicial reluctance to recognise the legal effects of soft law. This was found in relation to the Lisbon Agenda and the OMC,[123] as well as for stand-alone soft law instruments issued in the social sphere, which do not necessarily accompany hard law.[124] However, in other sectors, soft law can be enforced through the traditional judicial route, hence creating rights and obligations.[125] In competition, soft law might be considered binding for the enacting institution. As laid down in cases such as

[120] Lisi et al (n 96) 46.

[121] Leino-Sandberg and Korkea-aho (n 92) 35.

[122] Birkinshaw (n 28) 190.

[123] S Smismans, 'From Harmonization to Co-ordination? EU Law in the Lisbon Governance Architecture' (2010) 18 *Journal of European Public Policy* 504.

[124] T Hervey, 'Adjudicating in the Shadow of the Informal Settlement?: The Court of Justice of the EU, "New Governance" and Social Welfare' (2010) 63 *Current Legal Problems* 92.

[125] O Ştefan, 'Soft Law and the Enforcement of EU Law' in A Jakab and D Kochenov (eds), *The Enforcement of EU Law and Values: Ensuring Member States' Compliance* (Oxford, Oxford University Press, 2017).

Dansk Rørindustri, by publishing soft law, the Commission imposes a limit on the exercise of its discretion and cannot depart from those rules on pain of being found to be in breach of the general principles of law such as equal treatment or the protection of legitimate expectations.[126] Thus, binding effects for soft law are not automatically acknowledged by the Court, but are mediated through the operation of general principles of law. In this respect, transparency is crucial. The case law discussing the legal effects of soft law cites together: transparency and legal certainty; transparency and objectivity; and transparency and the right to good administration as principles enhanced by the publication or amendment of soft law instruments.[127]

Yet, even in competition, the link between transparency and legal certainty in relation to EU soft law is weaker at the national level of governance. In *Expedia*, the Court held that the national authorities and courts were not bound by the provisions of EU guidance, namely the *De Minimis* Notice in competition law.[128] The French Competition Authority had complete discretion to take the thresholds mentioned therein into consideration and to judge that, despite a minimal coverage of the market, an agreement could still breach competition rules.[129] As noted by the Court, the notice was meant to make transparent the manner in which *the Commission* applies Article 101 TFEU,[130] while national authorities' disregard of the Notice could not interfere with principles such as legitimate expectations and legal certainty.[131] SoLaR research shows that, as a consequence, national authorities might have relaxed their approach towards EU guidance. If the UK competition authority has, for a long time, complied with EU guidance, it noted in *Mobility Scooters* that 'notwithstanding the potential application of the Commission's De minimis Notice, the [authority] will also consider a number of factors in determining whether the infringements are appreciable by reference to the actual circumstances of the agreement'.[132]

SoLaR has not undertaken any empirical research into the perceptions of individuals and whether they believe the information provided through EU soft law can help enhance legal certainty. SoLaR research does reveal a related aspect, namely the impact of 'regulation by publication' on the relationship between national institutions and EU institutions, shedding light on whether transparency through soft law is conducive to equal and consistent application of EU law at the national level.

[126] Joint Cases C-189/02, C-202/02, C-205/02, C-208/02 and C-213/02 *Dansk Rørindustri and Others v Commission* [2005]: EU:C:2005:408, para 211.

[127] O Ştefan, *Soft Law in Court: Competition Law, State Aid and the Court of Justice of the EU* (Alphen aan den Rijn, Wolters Kluwer, 2013) 218 and the case law cited therein.

[128] *De Minimis* Notice (n 70).

[129] Case C-226/11 *Expedia* [2012] EU:C:2012:795, para 31.

[130] ibid paras 28–29.

[131] ibid para 32.

[132] *Mobility Scooters*, CE/9578-12, at A.76.

With regard to certain sectors, such as competition law, the officials interviewed were more optimistic with regard to the transparency function of soft law and its potential to ensure uniform application of the law. Finnish interviewees noted, for instance, the value of soft law in increasing transparency and predictability.[133] Similar perspectives transpire from some of the judgments analysed. In *Wye Valley*, in relation to the Commission's guidance on environmental impact assessments, the UK Court of Appeal has stated that: 'The objective of the guidance is twofold: first, "the document aims to improve understanding of what can be reasonably considered to be covered by certain project categories that have proved particularly difficult to interpret in practice"; secondly, it is intended to provide an overview of existing useful sources of information at EU level.'[134] While some of the judges interviewed were rather sceptical about the benefits of using soft law in court, they did acknowledge that soft law can render administrative action more transparent.[135] Even though some courts, such as the French Conseil d'État, have never noted that guidelines can ensure the uniform application of EU law, French interviewees agreed that soft law can help with motivating both judicial and administrative decisions.[136] Such views are not always shared, with a Finnish interviewee finding it rather unclear how soft law should be used by national courts and whether it is preferable to rely on EU case law instead.[137]

Being transparent and engaging in 'regulation by publication' at the EU level cannot, in and of itself, guarantee that the relationships between EU institutions, national institutions and individuals are strengthened and that legitimate expectations, equality and consistency in the application of the law are improved. For this to happen, EU soft law also needs to gain recognition at the national level. This can be achieved, for instance, if national authorities issued their own guidance documents or expressly endorse Commission guidance (as also pleaded by Advocate General (AG) Kokott in *Expedia*).[138] Some authorities already do this – for instance, the French Competition Authority has established its own guidance on setting fines, which also aim at increasing transparency and explaining the different methodologies to the individuals,[139] and the public procurement guidelines are 'nationalised' in Finland.[140] Similarly, the Italian Competition Authority

[133] Leino-Sandberg and Korkea-aho (n 92) 36.

[134] *Wye Valley Action Association Ltd, R (on the Application of) v Herefordshire Council* [2011] EWCA Civ 20, 18.

[135] B Beijen, 'National Report on the Netherlands' in Eliantonio and Lisi (n 53) 107.

[136] Lisi (n 96) 46.

[137] Havu and Tarkkila (n 115) 47.

[138] *Expedia* (n 129) EU:C:2012:544, Opinion of AG Kokott, fn 40.

[139] Autorité de la concurrence, 'Communiqué du 16 mai 2011 relatif à la méthode de détermination des sanctions pécuniaires', www.autoritedelaconcurrence.fr.

[140] M Lamoureux and N Rubio, 'National Report for France' in Ştefan (n 44) 53–54; Korkea-aho (n 74) 28.

has also established its own guidance in competition and is committed to respect it, just as the Commission is itself bound by its soft law.[141]

Another way to enhance EU 'regulation by publication' is as a result of hard law provisions at the EU or the national level. For example, ESA guidance is subject to the 'comply-or-explain' mechanism provided for in the regulations, with researchers agreeing that ESMA is achieving convergence and consistency in European financial supervision.[142] Such success appears hard to attain for guidance issued by other agencies not following the 'comply-or-explain' framework, such as the Agency for the Cooperation of Energy Regulators.[143] National provisions can also act as an intermediary. In the UK, section 60(3) of the Competition Act 1998, which advises authorities to 'have regard to any relevant decision or statement of the [European] Commission'.[144] Georgieva[145] finds that the existence of such a consistency obligation in the national legal order might make the application of soft law in court more likely, as confirmed in very recent case law from the UK. In *MasterCard*, the Court of Appeal noted in relation to EU competition guidance that although not legally binding and allowing for flexibility, it facilitates a consistency of approaches across the Member States.[146]

Finally, by simply acting in the spirit of sincere cooperation, national authorities and courts might help EU soft law achieve its full potential for transparency. Interviews with judges confirmed that soft law is taken into account, even if not mentioned by the parties, because it is important 'to do the right thing' with regard to principles such as sincere cooperation and consistent interpretation.[147] Asking to act in the spirit of sincere cooperation with the EU is not a tall order, as such cooperation already happens to a certain extent at the national level. In a UK financial regulation case, the High Court also held that national soft law should be taken into account in order to 'ensure consistency between the [financial authority] and the court in the application of the market abuse regime'.[148]

Sincere cooperation can also be empowered by the EU institutional set-up – for instance, in financial regulation. As pointed out by Moloney, achieving consistency across the EU is the result of a compromise between, on the one hand, the soft character of ESMA guidance and, on the other hand, ESMA's

[141] Alberti and Croci (n 98) 95.

[142] J Schemmel, 'The ESA Guidelines: Soft Law and Subjectivity in the European Financial Market – Capturing the Administrative Influence' (2016) 23 *Indiana Journal of Global Legal Studies* 455, 464; M van Rijsbergen, 'EU Agencies Soft Rule-Making: Lessons Learnt from the European Securities and Markets Authority' (Dissertation, Utrecht University Repository, 2018) 195.

[143] O Ştefan and M Petri, 'Too Weak to Be Controlled: Judicial Review of ACER Soft Law' (2018) 37 *Yearbook of European Law* 525.

[144] *Independent Media Support Ltd v Office of Communications* [2008] CAT 13.

[145] *Expedia* (n 129) EU:C:2012:544, Opinion of AG Kokott, fn 40.

[146] *MasterCard and Others* [2018] EWCA 1536 (Civ) [106].

[147] Rošic Feguš (n 44) 170; Korkea-aho (n 91) 33.

[148] *FCA v Da Vinci Invest Ltd and Others* [2015] EWHC 2401 (Ch).

intergovernmental set-up.[149] National authorities thus have the freedom to decide on national supervision, but also have the possibility to impose common rules by cooperating within ESMA. This insight brings us back to the discussion on consultations dealt with above, and again highlights the importance of a two-way relationship and dialogue between, on the one hand, the forum issuing soft law and, on the other hand, its addressees. Hartlapp and Korkea-aho argue in this volume that diversity is key in terms of understanding the national reactions to soft law.[150] This chapter submits the modest proposal that, by relying on the duty of sincere cooperation, soft law could help achieve a certain degree of unity in this diversity, provided its transparency function is taken seriously.[151]

V. CONCLUSIONS

This chapter has explored the transparency enhancing function of soft law by looking at established case law of the CJEU and insights from the SoLaR project. While perspectives vary across the board, the picture emerging is that of a work in progress. The views from the case law and interviews show a certain trust in the potential of EU soft law to connect, through information, individuals, national and EU institutions. This is strikingly illustrated, among other things, by the warm welcome given to initiatives to codify and explain the case law of the Court through instruments such as the Notice on the notion of State aid. Yet, there is a certain reluctance to acknowledge that, in practice, such potential for transparency is achieved. This is for several reasons, which relate to the quantity and quality of instruments, the way in which they are published, but also for reasons pertaining to core drawbacks of soft law, such as their lack of legitimacy or uncertain legal effects in a multi-level governance context. For some of these problems, there are quick fixes, such as an improved accessibility to soft law or better translation and dissemination practices. For others, a deeper reform is needed, involving strengthening the links between the EU soft law issuing authorities and the national authorities and courts. A great first step in this direction would be for the EU to engage in a dialogue with its Member States regarding soft law.[152]

[149] N Moloney, *EU Securities and Financial Markets Regulation*, 3rd edn (Oxford, Oxford University Press, 2014) 950.
[150] M Hartlapp and E Korkea-aho, ch 4 in this volume.
[151] G Gentile, ch 5 in this volume.
[152] See the Recommendations of the SoLaR network in the Introduction to this volume.

20

The National Politics of EU Soft Law

Sweden and the Balancing Act between Output and Input Legitimacy

ULRIKA MÖRTH

I. INTRODUCTION

THIS CHAPTER ARGUES that soft law is part of the classic conflict in the EU between problem-solving/efficiency and democratic accountability, or what is often referred to as the tension between output and input legitimacy in political systems.[1] According to this argument, there is a complex interdependence between the capacity of a political system to deliver results to citizens (output legitimacy) and, at the same time, to be democratically legitimate (input legitimacy). The two sources of legitimacy are dependent on each other – a political system needs to be able to effectively make decisions *and* to be democratically legitimate. This chapter analyses these two sources of legitimacy when soft law is used in the EU. It asks whether soft law is considered to be a useful tool for resolving political stalemates in EU policy-making or whether it is a tool for a more inclusive democratic policy-making process. Alternatively, does soft law threaten and undermine the very idea of the democratic chain of command and control, since parliaments are less involved (if at all) in soft law-making?

The empirical analysis is based on how the Swedish government has argued for the use of soft law in the EU and in EU-related national policy-making, and how its position resonates with Sweden's traditional view of the relationship between law and politics, and with its intergovernmental view of the EU. The chapter has chosen Sweden as a case study because it is a Member State that has explicitly expressed an interest in using soft law (over hard law) in EU

[1] F Scharpf, *Governing in Europe: Effective and Democratic?* (Oxford, Oxford University Press, 1999).

policy-making. In addition, the Swedish corporatist tradition of self-regulation in the labour market makes it a good case for identifying the different sources of legitimacy for the use of soft law.

The case of Sweden illustrates how a government's position on EU decision-making – intergovernmental or supranational – is an important factor in explaining why some countries are keener to use soft law than others. This chapter argues that the more intergovernmental the position, the keener the interest for soft law and political rather than legal regulatory responses. The Swedish case illustrates how national societal and state structures are determinant factors behind this general position towards the EU. The Swedish decentralised and self-regulatory model on the labour market is important if we want to explain why voluntary agreements – intergovernmental and political responses – between participants in the EU-wide labour markets are strongly preferred by the Swedish government. This chapter reflects this finding with that of the SoLaR network with respect to France – a country with a tradition of state *dirigisme* and a more supranational position towards the EU than Sweden. The limited role of soft law in the French courts and administration in the case of EU social policy is striking.[2] In this field, in contrast to Sweden, there is traditionally extensive French state intervention and legislation, even though recent labour law reforms by President Macron could fundamentally challenge and redirect this tradition.[3]

The chapter is organised in the following way. Section II begins with an introduction of the history of the use of soft law in the EU, and on the general political context that it has emerged from, followed by a presentation of the conceptual framework on soft law and legitimacy. The focus of the chapter is on the open method of coordination (OMC) and other soft law instruments in social and employment issues. Social and employment policy-making represents a highly politicised policy area where the tension between output and input legitimacy is expected to be salient. The policy area offers insights into how Member States use soft law as they try to handle the tension between input and output legitimacy. The empirical focus of the chapter is on Sweden. The political and democratic consequences of and challenges to the use of soft law are discussed in the concluding section.

II. SOFT LAW AND LEGITIMACY

A. The Evolution of Soft Governance in the EU

The impetus to the use of soft law within the social and employment area goes back to the late 1990s and early 2000s, when new modes of governance emerged

[2] O André, 'National Report on France: The Use of the EU Soft Law by National Courts and Administration in the Field of EU Social Policy' in M Hartlapp (ed), 'Studying Soft Law Effects in Social Policy' (2020) SoLaR Working Paper, https://papers.ssrn.com/sol3/papers.cfm?abstract_id=3668981.

[3] ibid.

in the EU.[4] These new modes of governance were often characterised as voluntary non-coercive regulations or modes of soft law.[5] The concept of soft law was described by scholars of new modes of governance as an anomaly, because law is traditionally perceived as mandatory and not voluntary.[6] For that reason, some researchers argued that 'voluntary law' should be conceptualised as voluntary rules or soft governance and not as soft 'law'.[7]

The second path concerned other ways of making law and reaching decisions in an increasingly complex EU governance structure. An important answer to the call for overcoming stalemates, especially in sovereign-sensitive issues, was the White Paper on Governance that was adopted in 2001, nearly a decade after the European Council meeting in Edinburgh.[8]

Interestingly, the introduction of a new type of EU governance mode was nothing particularly new in the history of the EU. Soft law has always been the main regulatory tool in traditional intergovernmental policy areas such as foreign policy and defence. Similarly, guidelines and codes of conduct have long been important regulatory instruments in the EU, especially in policy areas in which the EU lacks or has a weak legal competence to pursue a legislative agenda.[9] But even within policy areas where the EU has strong competences, soft law has been present.[10] In cases where there are interlinks between intergovernmental policy areas and areas of (what used to be called) Community law, as is the case with defence equipment, the EU has created regulatory constructions – 'pillar one and a half' – to handle political deadlocks.[11] The dichotomy between hard and soft law can therefore be misleading, because the two regulatory instruments are often dependent on each other.

What was new in the early 2000s, at the time of the White Paper on European Governance, was a sense of political 'malaise' and deadlock in EU policy-making. The EU recognised there to be a need for new regulatory reforms to strengthen both the effectiveness of the EU (output legitimacy) and the democratic

[4] A Héritier, 'New Modes of Governance in Europe: Policy-Making without Legislating?' in A Héritier (ed), *Common Goods: Reinventing European and International Governance* (Lanham, MD, Rowman & Littlefield, 2001) 185–206; R Rhodes, 'What is New about Governance and Why Does it Matter?' in J Hayward and A Menon (eds), *Governing Europe* (Oxford, Oxford University Press, 2003) 61–73; NEWGOV, *Integrated Project 'New Modes of Governance' – Description of Work* (Florence, European University Institute, 2004); J Caporaso and J Wittenbrinck, 'The New Modes of Governance and Political Authority in Europe' (2006) 13 *Journal of European Public Policy* 471.

[5] U Mörth (ed), *Soft Law in Governance and Regulation: An Interdisciplinary Analysis* (Cheltenham, Edward Elgar, 2004).

[6] ibid.

[7] ibid.

[8] European Commission, 'European Governance – A White Paper' COM (2001) 428.

[9] F Terpan, 'Soft Law in the European Union: The Changing Nature of EU Law' (2014) 21 *European Law Journal* 68.

[10] M Aldestam, 'Soft Law and State Aid Policy Area' in Mörth (n 5) 11–36; L Senden, *Soft Law in European Community Law* (Oxford, Hart Publishing, 2004).

[11] U Mörth, *Organizing European Cooperation: The Case of Armaments* (Lanham, MD, Rowman & Littlefield, 2003).

legitimacy of the EU project (input legitimacy).[12] The launching of the OMC was therefore presented as a novel political and legal regulatory instrument that could assist the EU in both reaching decisions on social and employment issues and opening up the decision-making process for labour market participation.[13] In this context, soft law was introduced as transitional rather than as a static type of rule. The OMC process could lead to soft law rules that could eventually become the subject matter of national legislation, that is, hard law. An important part of the OMC policy-making was the creation of national action plans (NAPs). They were formally adopted by national parliaments, but substantively they reflected broad political goals agreed by the Council of Ministers and by various working groups.[14]

Besides the legalisation of soft law through its incorporation into hard law, there are other ways in which soft law can turn into hard law. The rulings of the European Court of Justice (ECJ) can, for instance, change the legal status of a soft law measure. Österdahl has argued that this process of hardening is what occurred with the EU's Charter of Fundamental Rights.[15] However, the role of the courts was never central in OMC policy-making; instead, there were other mechanisms in play that have served to enhance the national impact of OMC policy-making. One little-studied mechanism, which potentially makes soft law at least appear harder than its formal legal status, concerns the way in which national officials perceive legal rules. If they believe a rule to be hard and mandatory, they will act accordingly in the national implementation process.[16] This mechanism can be linked to the way in which administrative routines concerning the application of rules are institutionalised and taken for granted. In general, the institutionalisation of practices in public organisations can be an important factor behind how the status of rules changes.[17]

B. The Use of Soft Law in the EU

In the EU, soft law is regarded as a tool for making decisions in complex political processes. The EU is a multilateral and multi-layered organisation in which there

[12] U Mörth, *European Public-Private Collaboration: A Choice between Efficiency and Democracy?* (Cheltenham, Edward Elgar, 2007); U Mörth, 'The Market Turn in EU Governance: The Emergence of Public-Private Collaboration' (2009) 22 *Governance* 99.

[13] U Mörth, 'Sweden in a Multilevel Polity' in J Pierre (ed), *The Oxford Handbook of Swedish Politics* (Oxford, Oxford University Press, 2015).

[14] J Frykman and U Mörth, 'Soft Law and Three Notions of Democracy: The Case of the EU' in Mörth (n 5) 155.

[15] I Österdahl, 'The ECJ and Soft Law: Who's Afraid of the EU Fundamental Rights Charter?' in Mörth (n 5).

[16] Aldestam (n 10).

[17] U Mörth, 'Competing Frames in the European Commission: The Case of the Defence Industry/Equipment Issue' (2000) 7 *The European Journal of Public Policy* 173; KE Weick, *Making Sense of the Organization, Volume 2: The Impermanent Organization* (London, Wiley, 2009).

are constantly ongoing negotiations between political levels and actors with different and sometimes conflicting interests. The organisation of the political system, with a strong power-sharing constitutional set-up and elements from a parliamentarian political system (the *Spitzenkandidaten* initiative in particular), opens up a variety of ways to negotiate and reach decisions in order to avoid persistent political deadlocks.[18] That is probably why there are high political and legal expectations concerning the use of soft law.

The first explanation for the use of soft law in the EU is that soft law arguably increases efficiency of EU decision-making.[19] Whether this holds true in practice is an empirical question.[20] The second explanation for the use of soft law in the EU has to do with its potential democratic qualities. Whether these qualities are shown in practice is also a question that requires empirical research. There is a large amount of literature evaluating the EU through democratic standards, which points at different results and explanatory trajectories. The overall picture that emerges is that the EU suffers from a democratic deficit.[21] Whether the use of soft law has positive effects on the democratic qualities of the EU in terms of deliberative democracy is answered negatively by researchers such as Smismans,[22] but the effects may vary depending on how one measures deliberative democracy empirically, the specific policy area and the political context. Deliberative democracy has multiple definitions and interpretations – from a 'thin' interpretation that is similar to participatory democracy to a 'thicker' understanding of the power of arguments among citizens.[23]

The values linked to soft law may also conflict with one another, as is the case in the classic tension between efficiency and democracy.[24] This tension is often referred to as a struggle between output and input legitimacy.[25] However, in the EU, the use of soft law is legitimised with reference to both sources of legitimacy. When soft law was 'discovered' in the late 1990s, it was argued that it could enhance efficiency in EU decision-making. Soft law was perceived as an important way forward in the EU when the Member States wanted to retain national sovereignty on politically controversial issues.[26] These issues concern the functioning of welfare states such as taxes, pensions, social protection and,

[18] A Héritier, *Policy-Making and Diversity in Europe: Escape from Deadlocks* (Cambridge, Cambridge University Press, 1999).

[19] Senden (n 10).

[20] For a systematic analysis on this, see ibid.

[21] Mörth, *European Public-Private Collaboration* (n 12).

[22] S Smismans, 'New Modes of Governance and the Participatory Myth' (2008) 31 *West European Politics*, 874.

[23] For an overview, see A Bächtiger, J Dryzek, J Mansbridge and ME Warren (eds), *The Oxford Handbook of Deliberative Democracy* (Oxford, Oxford University Press, 2018).

[24] U Mörth, 'The Market Turn in EU Governance: The Emergence of Public-Private Collaboration' (2009) 22 *Governance* 99.

[25] Scharpf (n 1); F Scharpf, 'Legitimate Diversity: The New Challenge of European Integration' 01/2002 *Les Cahiers européens de Sciences Po* (Paris).

[26] Scharpf (n 1); Scharpf (n 25).

during recent years, migration and border control. In these situations, the alternative to soft law is not hard law, but an uncoordinated national action. This is because of the unwillingness of the Member States to delegate supranational decision-making powers to the EU within politically controversial policy areas. Here, soft law has to do with output legitimacy – making decisions at the EU level without losing national sovereignty.

In parallel to this political development, several concerns were raised in relation to the quality of hard legislation and 'the tide of rules coming from Brussels',[27] criticising both the content and the sheer number of legislative acts. The 1992 European Council Meeting in Edinburgh resulted in the formation of groups of Member States and industry representatives working on how to simplify and improve the legislation.[28] The work by the Commission and other EU institutions followed two distinct paths. The first aimed at improving the Community method or the traditional legislative process in the EU. A host of reforms known as 'Better Law-Making' and 'Better Regulation' were launched at the European Council Meeting in Edinburgh, followed by reforms on impact assessments of EU legislation.[29] Depending on the policy objective, it is critical that there be several options and complementary solutions to legislation.[30] In other words, authors of various Better Regulation agendas over the years have recommended soft law as a way to speed up the time-consuming legislative process and give the EU decision-makers more room for manoeuvre in an increasingly complex political landscape. However, the experience of Better Regulation agendas has led scholars to ask whether the new ways of reaching decisions and laws really deviate from the traditional Community method and the use of vague directives.[31] From these observations, one can identify an additional reason explaining why soft law is used for the purpose of moving forward in EU decision-making. Soft law paradoxically fulfils the need for unclarity and ambiguity in a complex decision-making environment. It is an important component in a complex political system that needs to balance between political clarity and national interests. The trick is to be sufficiently clear so that the decision-makers can agree on a decision, but also to be to some extent unclear and open to multiple interpretations in order to facilitate agreement on sensitive

[27] C Radaelli, 'Whither Better Regulation for the Lisbon Agenda?' (2007) 14 *Journal of European Public Policy* 190, 192.

[28] European Commission, 'Report of the Group of Independent Experts on Legislative and Administrative Simplification' COM (1995) 288 final; Unice, *Releasing Europe's Potential through Targeted Regulatory Reform: The Unice Regulatory Report* (Brussels, Unice, 1995).

[29] A Renda, *Impact Assessment in the EU: The State of the Art and the Art of the State* (Brussels, CEPS, 2006).

[30] European Commission (n 8); European Commission, 'Action plan: simplifying and improving the regulatory environment' COM (2002) 726 final; European Commission, 'Communication from the Commission on Impact Assessment' COM (2002) 276 final; 'Better Lawmaking' COM (2002) 278 final.

[31] J Scott and DM Trubek, 'Mind the Gap: Law and New Approaches to Governance and the European Union' (2002) 8 *European Law Journal* 1.

political issues. The observers have suggested that 'policy instruments thus offer a means of structuring space for short time exchanges, for negotiations and agreements, setting aside the most problematic issues, and thereby allow for ambiguous consensus'.[32]

The overall picture is that the Better Regulation reforms have more to do with the effectiveness of the traditional legislative method and less with the need to introduce a more democratic and deliberative process. Consequently, the role of soft law is in practice about escaping deadlocks,[33] and little attention has been given to how the use of soft law created problems of democratic accountability. The improvement of the regulatory environment with the overall aim of becoming the most efficient economy in the world – as decided in Lisbon 2000 – was placed high on the political agenda.[34] The case of the better regulation agenda suggests that a general political malaise in the European project triggered reform activities that initially had social ambitions. These ambitions were taken over by performance goals and economic competitiveness. Nonetheless, the main goal of the reform was to inject some activism and positive thinking into European integration. Whether this 'politics by labelling' entails profound changes in terms of how the institutions and organisations work is another question. Performance and economic competitiveness always have been important to the European political project. Indeed, the very core of the European project is the creation of the internal market. Hence, the shift to new modes of governance in the EU is perhaps not a shift in any profound way, but merely a way of making things happen in a political project which recurrently faces political deadlocks and legitimacy crises.

What is interesting for this chapter and its analysis is how the use of soft law is legitimised on account of its deliberative democratic values. Although decision-making on soft law often excludes the European Parliament and national parliaments, especially if the soft law does not precede or evolve into hard legislation, it is part of the societal turn in EU governance.[35] In fact, in the early days of the societal turn of EU governance, the Commission argued that the use of soft law was important for the purposes of alleviating the democratic deficit in the EU.[36] The emphasis on consultation with various stakeholders in the White Paper on Governance is an example of how the Commission wanted to improve

[32] H Kassim and P Le Galès, 'Exploring Governance in Multi-level Polity: A Policy Instruments Approach' (2010) 33 *West European Politics* 1, 8; see also B Palier, 'Ambiguous Argument, Cumulative Changes: Social Policies in France in the 1990s' in K Thelen and W Streek (eds), *Beyond Continuity* (Oxford, Oxford University Press, 2005) 127.

[33] See, eg, A Héritier, *Policy-Making and Diversity in Europe: Escape from Deadlocks* (Cambridge, Cambridge University Press, 1999).

[34] Mörth, *European Public-Private Collaboration* (n 12).

[35] Mörth (n 13); C de la Porte and P Nanz, 'The OMC: A Deliberative Democratic Mode of Governance? The Cases of Employment and Pensions' (2004) 11 *Journal of European Public Politics*, 267.

[36] European Commission (n 8).

the traditional legislative process. The role of civil society and various interest organisations was considered crucial to the establishment of consultative collaborations between the Commission and societal actors.[37] These types of collaboration were not supposed to have any formal legislative power, but were nonetheless considered to be an essential part of the Commission's consultation phase within the Community method. The Commission emphasised the need for 'a reinforced culture of consultation and dialogue'.[38] By involving business and civil society actors in the legislative process, legislation would, according to the White Paper, be of better quality and easier to implement. Of the individual regulatory instruments, the OMC was interpreted as being oriented towards deliberative democracy, although not in the deepest and most radical form.[39] Even the comitology process was considered as the beginning of a deliberative democratic phase in the EU.[40]

In this conception, soft law is linked to input legitimacy, involving the broadening of the scope of decision-makers in line with more deliberative and participatory democratic ideals.[41] In practice, these ambitious democratic ideals are difficult to realise. However, the evolution of the OMC and new modes of governance in general show how the debate on the EU's democratic deficit played an important role in launching these reforms.

Figure 20.1 summarises the main sources of legitimacy on the politics of soft law.

Figure 20.1 The politics of soft law

Aim	Retaining national sovereignty	Societal inclusion
Source of legitimacy	Output	Input
Values	Efficiency	Deliberation/participation

The first aim concerns the capability of soft law to allow Member States to retain national sovereignty. No formal delegation of power takes place when soft law is used in EU policy-making. The source of legitimacy in the left column is output, and the emphasis is on how political systems need to perform if they are to be seen as legitimate. The main political value is efficiency.

The second aim relates instead to the capacity of soft law to open up a broad range of societal actors that otherwise would not have been included in the traditional hard law legislative processes. The source of legitimacy in the right column is input, and the main political values are deliberation and participation.

[37] ibid.

[38] ibid 16.

[39] J Habermas, *Between Facts and Norms* (London, Polity Press, 1997).

[40] EO Eriksen and J Fossum, 'Europe in Search of its Legitimacy' (NOPSA Triennial Conference, Aalborg, 15–17 August 2002).

[41] J Habermas (n 39); J Dryzek, *Deliberative Democracy and Beyond: Liberals, Critics, Contestations* (Oxford, Oxford University Press, 2000).

It is assumed that a more active and participatory society legitimates the decisions that the EU makes.

In the next section, we take a closer look at how the Swedish government and the EU institutions have argued for the use of soft law in the EU with a special focus on the two above-mentioned sources of legitimacy.

III. THE SWEDISH POLITICS OF SOFT LAW

A. Sweden in the EU Integration Process

Swedish governments, irrespective of party-political ideologies, have all been in favour of intergovernmental decision-making as a preferred mode of governance in the EU.[42] The sympathy for intergovernmentalism does not mean that the government always argues for soft law over hard law; rather, Swedish governments have interpreted intergovernmentalism as a preference for a political process over a coercive process with strong legal and judicial actors, especially in areas that are sensitive from a domestic perspective. Soft law fits the intergovernmental policy mode, as courts and other legal actors only play a small role in soft law-making. This emphasis on the political process can be traced back to a Swedish tradition concerning the relationship between politics and law.

When Sweden became a member of the EU in 1995, there was hardly any domestic discussion on the role of EU law as part of the Swedish legal system, and whether and, if so, how the rules of the internal market have an impact on policy areas that were defined as national political issues. To the political establishment, it therefore came as a shock when the ECJ ruled on the compatibility of the Swedish retail monopoly on alcoholic beverages with the free-market principles in the *Franzén* case.[43] Although the court concluded that the sales monopoly was not in violation of the then EC Treaty, the fact that a core national issue such as public health could be questioned by the Court based on the rules of the internal market was an eye-opener for the Swedish government and the political elite. Ten years later, the Court ruled that Sweden could no longer ban private imports of alcohol because the 'monopoly has a discretionary power to refuse to import alcohol beverages requested by clients'.[44] Swedish law was amended in order to comply with the ruling, to the effect that under the current law, a retail monopoly is not the same thing as an import monopoly. Thus, it can

[42] U Mörth, 'Europeanization as Interpretation, Translation and Editing of Public Policies' in K Featherstone and C Radaelli (eds), *The Politics of Europeanization* (Oxford, Oxford University Press, 2003).

[43] Case C-189/95 *Criminal Proceedings against Harry Franzén* [1997] EU:C:1997:504. See also J Örnberg Cisneros, 'The Europeanization of Swedish Alcohol Policy' (PhD dissertation, Stockholm University, Department of Political Science, 2009).

[44] Case C-170/04 *Klas Rosengren and Others v Riksåklagaren* [2007] EU:C:2007:313.

be argued that EU membership brought about a distinct change in the Swedish political mindset.

Against this background, it comes as no surprise that the Swedish government welcomed the OMC when it was discussed at the European Council's meeting in Lisbon in 2000. Göran Persson, the then Swedish Prime Minister, argued that:

> The process is political, not judicial. If some country fails it does not wind up in front of the EU Court … The road chosen in Lisbon surely means more cooperation, but it does not mean more supranationalism.[45]

As the Prime Minister referred to 'more cooperation', the main source of legitimacy for the use of soft law appears to be output legitimacy, but it is also quite evident that the positive view of a less legal and judicial decision-making process in social and employment issues resonated with the Swedish model of the labour market.[46]

The literature on Europeanisation often argues that EU decisions need to have national resonance in order to be implemented. The OMC indeed fits the Swedish idea of societal governance. Input legitimacy is important for the Swedish government and the Swedish corporatist tradition and its ambition to include a broad range of societal actors in policy-making processes.[47] In the OMC processes, the national resonance was created along iterated policy dialogues that followed, to some extent at least, a Swedish corporatist tradition.[48] Thus, there were democratic values linked to the use of soft law (input legitimacy). Both in the EU and in the Member States, the OMC was legitimised by a conception of deliberative democracy and as a way of moving beyond hierarchy and the role of parliaments.[49] It can be argued that the OMC empowered social non-governmental organisations (NGOs) in the sense that the production of so-called national action plans (NAPs) created arenas for dialogue between NGOs and government officials, sidestepping national parliaments.[50] In policy terms, the OMC did not bring many new changes when it was introduced into the policy field of social inclusion in Sweden.[51] This could be explained by the fact that this model was already being used in Sweden. It can also be argued that little learning and other deliberative processes took place. From a Swedish perspective, the societal turn in the form of a broadening of societal actors in the

[45] Swedish Parliament, Protocol 1999/2000:92. Translation from Swedish to English by the author.
[46] Mörth (n 13).
[47] Mörth (n 42).
[48] Mörth (n 13).
[49] De la Porte and Nanz (n 35).
[50] K Jacobsson and H Johansson, 'The Micro-politics of the OMC: NGOs and the Social Inclusion Process in Sweden' (International Meetings on Law and Society in the 21st Century, Humboldt University, Berlin, 25–28 July 2007).
[51] ibid.

policy-making process also challenges the corporatist tradition. Societal actors are no longer limited to organised interests in the labour market, which has been the hallmark of the corporatist model in Sweden. NGOs and other actors of civil society become part of transnational civil society movements and can put pressure on state actors.[52]

But it was not only the corporatist tradition that was put under pressure by the OMC. The development towards more informal political processes is problematic from the viewpoint of the Swedish Parliament, because it makes decision-making less transparent and weakens the possibility for democratic accountability.[53] The increased speed of EU decision-making and the growth of informal negotiations between the Swedish government and EU institutions are often criticised by the Swedish Parliament.[54] This means that both the aim of enhancing decision-making and that of including more societal actors in the decision-making process challenge the role of parliaments. The national parliament will indeed only be able to control EU actions *ex post* and not *ex ante*. This concern will probably increase because of the recent regulatory 'innovation' by the European Council, as will be discussed in the next section.

B. The Use of Decision Notes as a Preferred Means of 'Soft Governance'

During recent years, with the increased importance of the role of the European Council in the EU, the European Council has developed a new type of working method – decision notes – within sensitive and complex political issues such as migration and economic and social developments.[55] An informal European Council meeting on economic and social development in the labour market was held in the Swedish city of Gothenburg in November 2017. The decision notes were written down by the Chair of the European Council and were meant to be used in the informal dialogue between the heads of state and government in the context of the European Pillar of Social Rights.

This Pillar is aimed at strengthening the EU's social and employment policies, and it can potentially have significant consequences for how these policy areas will be regulated in the future.[56] The Pillar sets out 20 key principles and rights to support fair and well-functioning labour markets around three chapters: 'equal opportunities and access to the labour market', 'fair working

[52] M Bexell and U Mörth (eds), *Democracy and Public-Private Partnerships in Global Governance* (Basingstoke, Palgrave Macmillan, 2010).

[53] Swedish Parliament, *EU-arbetet i riksdagen* (The EU Work in the Swedish Parliament) 2017/18: URF1.

[54] ibid.

[55] Mörth (n 13).

[56] Z Rasnaca, 'Who is in Charge of the European Pillar of Social Rights?' (March 2019) *Green European Journal*, www.greeneuropeanjournal.eu/who-is-in-charge-of-the-european-pillar-of-social-rights/.

conditions' and 'social protection and inclusion'.[57] The Pillar is described as an agenda (just like the Better Regulation reform agenda) and it lacks any formal legal force, even though the recommendations are expected to give rise to hard legislation, especially at the national level.[58]

The use of non-binding recommendations fits into the Swedish government view on the importance of retaining national sovereignty, but at the same time engaging with the European-level discussions on social and labour-related issues.[59] The political opposition has argued that the Swedish labour market model – the corporatist tradition emphasising sector-wide negotiations – will be put under pressure if there is hard legislation at the EU level.[60] To counter suspicions domestically, the Swedish Prime Minister has argued that there will be 'no legislation that will jeopardise the Swedish and Nordic model' used in negotiating wages and other labour issues.[61] This statement is probably aimed at reassuring the actors in the Swedish labour market that the Swedish labour market model will be kept in its current form.

The critics of soft law, such as the decision notes, sometimes argue that it functions as a 'back door' into a deeper EU and shifts competences from Member States to the EU without any formal decision by the former to delegate powers to the EU. There is indeed a risk that democratic control and influence from the European Parliament and national parliaments will be undermined if politically sensitive issues are dealt with using informal processes by the European Council. A case in point for Sweden is the future development of the eurozone. Sweden is outside the common currency due to the 'No' in the national referendum in 2003, but follows the economic criteria for the eurozone. Sweden views the current efforts to strengthen the political and regulative dimension of the eurozone with concern. The evolution of the banking union in which Nordea (the largest bank in Sweden) participates may limit the room for manoeuvre for Swedish politicians and put them in a state of fait accompli. In other words, Sweden may de facto be softly forced into the eurozone while it is at the same trying to be outside in accordance with the result of the national referendum.

IV. CONCLUSION

This chapter started out with the following questions: is soft law considered to be a tool for settling controversies within EU policy-making or should it be a tool for a more inclusive democratic policy-making process? Or does soft law

[57] European Commission, 'Delivering on the European Pillar of Social Rights' (2019), ec.europa.eu/social/main.jsp?langId=en&catId=1226.

[58] See Rasnaca (n 56).

[59] See Swedish Prime Minister Ştefan Löfven in *Europaportalen* (2019), www.europaportalen.se/2019/11/lofven-sverige-ska-delta-fullt-ut-i-eu.

[60] Conservative Party leader Ulf Kristersson in ibid.

[61] Löfven (n 59).

threaten and undermine the very idea of the democratic chain of command and control, as parliaments are less involved (if at all) in soft law-making? In this concluding section, I will start with the first question and will then move on to the more general discussion on soft law and democratic legitimacy.

The answer to the first question is that both the EU and the Swedish government argue that soft law is good, as it enhances the EU's problem-solving capacity (output legitimacy) and legitimises its activities (input legitimacy). The role of soft law for the EU's problem-solving capacity seems rather straightforward. The use of non-binding regulatory tools has long been an important strategy for the EU to handle sovereignty-sensitive issues, as argued by Scharpf. Whether the same also holds true for the role of soft law with respect to input legitimacy is more difficult to settle, as the answer requires empirical research. Much also depends on what the democratic values are that the decision-making process should fulfil in order to be democratically legitimate. The democratic values that are linked to the OMC and other types of soft law instruments are deliberation and participation. The question of the added value of soft law from a democratic perspective – in other words, the extent to which soft law contributes to more deliberation and more participation – is difficult to answer. We may observe, for instance, that the decision-making process is more open to new types of actors, but little deliberation takes place. Or we may observe that there is a lot of deliberation within the working groups on employment issues, but this has very little to do with *democratic* deliberation, at least in the Habermasian interpretation of deliberative democracy with the requirement of will formation by the people, for instance.

The Swedish government's generally positive view of the use of soft law in the EU resonates with the intergovernmental position of Sweden as a Member State. It also resonates with the Swedish traditional corporatist structures of decision-making processes, which entail the inclusion of labour organisations and other representatives of civil society. Thus, according to many Swedish governments, the use of soft law is good for resolving problems at the EU level, but it also reflects a participatory democratic value that is an intrinsic feature of the Swedish labour market model. In addition, the positive view of soft law, interpreted as a political process than a coercive legal process with strong judicial actors, resonates with the Swedish view of the importance of political decision-making in the EU, as the *Franzén* case illustrates. This intergovernmental position towards the EU and the argument of how soft law help retains national sovereignty could of course be interpreted as illusory in a political system characterised by multi-level governance and a degree of embeddedness between different political levels and actors. However, the Swedish government claims that certain important decisions at the EU level will not challenge or threaten formal sovereignty, even though the decisions stem from the EU as a system of multi-level governance. Hence, the decision-making through soft law may not challenge formal sovereignty, but it will probably limit the autonomy of national decision-making.

In the Swedish political debate, how voluntary agreements can be turned into hard law by the European Court of Justice is seldom discussed. That could be the case with parts of the European Pillar of Social Rights. This potential scenario could entail a strong argument for being in favour of hard legislation on social rights, with possible legal exceptions for a country that wishes to preserve national sovereignty and autonomy on certain issues. Paradoxically, the soft law option could be a dangerous regulatory strategy for those who advocate national autonomy and voluntary rules. Furthermore, the recent development in the European Council to make decision notes and use other types of intergovernmental regulations could result in legislative proposals in national parliaments. These legislative proposals will then become part of the traditional chain of command and control in the political system, and could strengthen the role of national parliaments in EU decision-making. This is another example of the complex interdependence between different kinds of rules and actors, and how this relationship may change over time.

This brings us to the broader question of whether soft law threatens and undermines the very idea of the democratic chain of command and control, since parliaments are less involved (if at all) in soft law-making.

The challenges for democratic legitimacy (input legitimacy) and how it can be combined with the political ability to make decisions (output legitimacy) are huge. A possible way of looking at the use of soft law is that whilst soft law may bring with it a broadening of actors and regulatory mechanisms, the democratic legitimisation of the decision-making process has not changed. It is still dependent on democratic accountability mechanisms according to the hierarchical system of command and control. Another possible perspective concerns the executive. The use of soft law can strengthen the executive power, with the consequence of having the governments acting as legislators and weakening the European and national parliaments. The role of the parliaments will change into controlling governments *ex post* and not influencing the decisions of governments *ex ante*. This is not the only concern for national parliaments with respect to the role of soft law in the EU. There is also a general concern about how the increased use of informal negotiations between governments, the Commission and the European Parliament creates an unclear responsibility structure. How can the principle of accountability be upheld in the sense of being answerable for one's actions or inactions in times of complex and non-transparent decision-making? Unclear accountability structures may resemble the development that Habermas described as a kind of 'executive federalism of a self-authorizing European Council' in a 'post-democratic exercise of political authority'.[62]

Moreover, in an era of new political dimensions of conflicts – between traditional/authoritarian/national and global/alternative/liberal values – the political

[62] J Habermas, *The Crisis of the European Union: A Response* (London, Polity Press, 2014) viii.

role of soft law in the EU may increase. The increase in the use of soft law could be a result of sheer necessity. There may not be another option to deal with, for instance, issues of migration and the distribution of refugees among the Member States. Soft law may be the only way forward in situations of political deadlock, when the Member States emphasise the importance of national sovereignty and national border control. Coercive decisions may be hard to enforce, as is shown by the implementation of the decision in 2015 by the Council on the distribution of refugee quotas.[63]

This development has also changed the Swedish position to call for more hard law, such as legislation that links the distribution of funding from the EU budget to the respect for the rule of law. Sweden belongs to the group of countries called the 'Democracy Promoters' that strongly advocate that the EU suspends funding in cases of rule-of-law concerns.[64] Stefan Löfven, the Swedish Prime Minister, also advocates abolishing the veto power in foreign policy decisions concerning issues of human rights and international conflicts.[65] One preliminary conclusion is therefore that the generally positive view by Swedish governments on the use of soft law in the EU has changed or will change. This is due to the emergence of national identity-driven politics in several Member States and the importance of the rule of law. The dual role of soft law as a way of reaching decisions at the EU level and retaining national sovereignty will not be of interest only to the Swedish government, but others as well in this new European political landscape. For instance, France, a political system characterised by state *dirigisme* and a supranational position towards the EU, will also have to consider this complex balancing act between the aim of reaching EU decisions and retaining national sovereignty in a political context of national populism. The recent labour law reforms in France, as mentioned in section I above, might open up the possibility for a more societal and inclusive regulatory process that could have ramifications for the French EU regulatory policy.

The national politics of soft law will continue to be an intrinsic part of the political power struggle over an intergovernmental or a more supranational EU. In practice, the struggle for power in the EU is much more complex. The tension between output and input legitimacy deserves more attention among politicians and other decision-makers in order to understand what is at stake in the EU and national politics of soft law. The problem is that reforms in the EU are double-edged and there is seldom any serious reasoning on how the EU can be effective and performance-oriented, on the one hand, and more participatory and deliberative, on the other hand. This double-edged nature of EU policy reforms undermines the democratic legitimacy of the EU. The traditional mode

[63] Council Decision (EU) 2015/1601 of 22 September 2015 establishing provisional measures in the area of international protection for the benefit of Italy and Greece [2015] OJ L248/80.

[64] The Swedish Prime Minister introduced the debate in the Swedish Riksdag in November 2019: https://www.riksdagen.se/sv/aktuellt/2019/nov/11/eu-politisk-partiledardebatt-i-riksdagen.

[65] Löfven (n 59).

of governance in the EU, which avoids political deadlocks by making political issues non-political issues, is a strong part of a decision-making culture in the EU. The realm of the political sphere expands with the use of soft law, but the democratic realm remains within the parliamentarian chain of command and control. This could lead to a situation in which those who have power are not democratically accountable for the decisions they make and those who can be democratically accountable have no power.

21

Final Thoughts

NIILO JÄÄSKINEN

A GOOD PIECE of academic work contributes to the advancement of scholarship by increasing our knowledge and providing new insights. The work at hand, representing the results of the European Network of Soft Law Research (SoLaR), fulfils these requirements impeccably.

The nine thematic chapters, and the 10 EU Member State chapters which follow a standard structure of questions discussed, contain an interesting compilation of findings and discussion on the functioning of soft law at the EU and national levels. In addition, a fresh comparative view is provided by Francis Snyder's chapter on soft law in China. The SoLaR participants have raised our understanding of soft law to a new level, especially from an empirical point of view. In the following, I engage with some of the findings that I found particularly interesting.

First, despite the academic and policy interest that EU soft law has received during the last three decades, according to SoLaR research, it appears *quantitatively* less important than hard law. Andreas Hofmann demonstrates in Chapter 3 that EUR-Lex currently lists 37,175 legal acts as legislation in force, of which only 614 are recommendations and 417 are opinions, these acts being the forms of EU soft law recognised in the Treaties. Even if outside these categories there exists an important and increasingly growing number of other informal and non-treaty-based forms of soft law instruments with different titles such as frameworks, communications, guidelines, letters, codes and notices, it seems obvious that in quantitative terms, hard law prevails as the preferred form of regulation in the EU. In contrast, Mariolina Eliantonio, Emilia Korkea-aho and Oana Ştefan point out in Chapter 1 how at a time of crisis like the COVID-19 pandemic in 2020, recourse has widely been taken to soft law instruments because EU soft law is cheap, fast, flexible and easy to issue. It may be concluded that EU soft law has not replaced hard law in any significant measure, but rather has supplemented it or, to a lesser extent, acted as an ersatz because of the limited timeframe available for issuing the measures or due to a lack of EU legislative competences in the field in question.

Second, both at the EU level and the Member State level, soft law does not seem to act as an independent form of regulation, but rather as a complementary way to disseminate information concerning policy objectives or to clarify the intended interpretations of hard law instruments. The national chapters describe how interpretative or decisional soft law – taking their cue from Linda Senden's well-known typology of soft law instruments – with a close connection to hard law prevails over steering instruments with no or weak links to hard law. If legislation is understood as communication between the norm-giving authorities and the addressees of the norms, as it should in my opinion, then soft law instruments could also be characterised as supplementary channels of information reinforcing the original message, either by providing additional information with an identical content or by amending it with more precise and up-to-date information, or even both. Hence, we are rarely dealing with purified forms of soft law or hard law, but rather some sort of a hybrid of both.

Third, most of the national chapters seem to indicate that soft law is not a new phenomenon, but more of a modern 'New Public Administration' take on traditional sublegislative non-binding administrative regulation which, in the form of *circulaires*, instructions, guidelines and so on, has served the objectives of enhancing the uniformity of interpretation and application of hard law acts, and the coherence of administrative decision-making in many jurisdictions. This finding, depending on the perspective adopted, can be understood either as a centralising element of public administration or as a means to enhance legal certainty and to protect the legitimate expectations of the norm addressees. Juxtaposing the modern concept of soft law with traditional non-binding administrative acts of general application connects the concept of soft law to classic public law problems concerning its internal and external legal effects towards its addressees such as officials within the administration, other public authorities or subjects, and private law subjects. The chapters illustrate how even in its modern form, soft law cannot escape classic issues such as the notion of reviewable acts and standing in administrative law litigation, often based on somewhat circular criteria establishing conceptual links between the capacity of an act to modify the rights of a subject outside the internal sphere of public administration to its legally binding nature or vice versa. Moreover, national differences regarding the powers of the courts to control administrative action become highlighted in this context, for example, when the powers of the Cypriot courts that are limited to formal procedural control of administrative decision-making are compared to the wide reformatory powers of the German administrative courts.

Different public law traditions seem to lead to different outcomes, but only to some extent. With the notable exception of France and the UK, EU Member State courts and the Court of Justice of the European Union have not so far accepted soft law instruments as legal acts reviewable by courts. Here we can see a tension between the normative and factual purpose of governmental measures such as soft law instruments. Does the objective of a measure, such as intended economic benefits, equate to its normative significance? In other words, are important actual effects of a measure judicially relevant legal effects? In most legal systems, the scope of judicial review has, on the one hand, in one way or the other been linked to the normative sphere of rights and duties of persons, and, on the other hand, to the idea of the discretion of public authorities not subject to judicial control. These limits are being tested in debates on the justiciability and reviewability of soft law instruments, as shown in the chapters of this volume.

Fourth, the reviewability and, to a lesser extent, justiciability of EU soft law acts receive an in-depth discussion in Mariolina Eliantonio's and Napoleon Xanthoulis's thematic chapters. Both authors are unsatisfied with the existing case law and argue for a widening of the scope of judicial review of EU soft law measures, pinpointing the evolution of the case law of the French Conseil d'État as an example worth following. While not contesting much of the argumentation presented in these two chapters, I nevertheless feel that the authors do not pay sufficient attention to the reasons why there are limitations applicable to judicial reviewability of legislative, regulatory and administrative decisions in all legal systems and to how they are justified.

One could mention here the existence of alternative ways of constitutionally legitimised control structures of the use of public powers such as parliamentary accountability, various ombudsperson-type authorities, and criminal and civil liability of authorities and state administration. The role of courts in general, and that of the administrative courts in particular, is also different in different jurisdictions. For example, in a system where judicial review serves as a means of controlling the objective legality of the administration and where the rules on standing are traditionally generous, it may be easier to adopt a more lenient approach towards the reviewability of soft law acts than in systems where judicial review seeks to protect subjective rights of private applicants and rules on standing are strict. Typical concerns justifying the limited reviewability of soft law acts often refer to the need of securing an internal sphere of discretionary autonomy for authorities and to the need to limit the remit of courts to situations where their decisions can incur *a normative change* in the legal positions of the parties concerned.

Moreover, judicial protection is a societally and economically scarce resource which cannot be lightheartedly allocated to cases that are better dealt with other types of remedies or that do not deserve the attention of courts. In fact, the adoption of more lenient criteria of reviewability would, of course, not only be limited to soft law acts, many other forms of administrative action without clear normative effects would also be captured by such lenient criteria. This might lead to the burdening of court systems with an unforeseeable amount of litigation. It must be emphasised that a satisfactory level of quality and efficacy of judicial protection is difficult to maintain if the caseload of the courts becomes too great.

Fifth, the country chapters hint at the finding that soft law in general, and EU soft law in particular, is used by administrations and courts as an intellectual device in the *context of discovery* of the decisions to be made and interpretations to be applied. It seems to be a handy and efficient tool in situations where the decision-maker needs to orient themselves in an unfamiliar territory. In contrast, in the *context of justification* of administrative and judicial decisions, there seems to be considerable national variation. In some countries and courts, it is more usual or acceptable to refer to EU soft law as belonging to the normative *major* premise of the judicial conclusion than in others. That said, it seems that soft law cannot act as a stand-alone justification of an administrative or judicial decision, but always needs some hard law backing. Hence, soft law can be considered as justiciable in the sense that it is permissible to invoke it in courts as supporting a certain interpretation or outcome, but it is not considered a necessary and sufficient justification in the same sense as the so-called binding sources of law.

Sixth, with the notable exceptions of Imelda Maher's and Ulrika Mörth's chapters, this work is very much a treatise by lawyers for lawyers. The paradigm around the debates is not governance in the political science or sociological senses, but *Law* with a capital letter. From this may stem the certain dissatisfaction with soft law that a reader senses from most of the chapters. In contrast, Maher and Mörth seem to be at ease with the horrendous fact that soft law is *not binding* and regard soft law as an alternative among others in the governance toolbox. For many other authors, the 'softness' of soft law seems to be an ontological and methodological problem that could and should be fixed by making it more akin to hard law – for example, rendering soft law acts reviewable in courts and making its typologies, effects and methods of adoption and publication uniform so as to fulfil the requirements of good law-making. Many of these requirements, of course, overlap with those of *good administration*, a principle that is protected as a fundamental right in the EU Charter of Fundamental Rights and some national constitutions, and no reasonable person could, for example, oppose the proposals for enhancing the quality of soft law that Eliantonio, Korkea-aho and Ştefan present at the end of their introductory chapter. This said, to my mind, soft law is not a soft belly of the legal system, but an indispensable element of modern public law.

Seventh, the necessity of soft law leads me to my last observation of a more legal-philosophical nature. In my opinion, our conceptual uneasiness with soft law and the inevitable normative and judicial consequences that it entails are due to the fact that we do not have a uniform and uncontested concept of law, but rather many diverging conceptions of law. In this respect, it is useful to recall legal philosopher JW Harris' distinction between law as a momentary normative order (the 'legal order') and as a historical intellectual tradition (the 'legal system').

JW Harris places the difference between a momentary and a non-momentary understanding of law in a central position in his legal theory.[1] As a momentary regime, law includes legal norms concerning a particular human activity in a particular area at any given time, the norms which indicate what is legally commanded, forbidden or permitted. The practice of jurisprudence or legal science presumes the existence of such momentary legal order, ie, 'valid law'. On the other hand, according to Harris, law as a non-momentary, historical legal system concerns a *tradition* shared by the officials of a given legal community or jurisdiction. Legal principles and other 'weight-bearing' devices of legal thinking belong to this non-momentary system, and their normative function is to guide or justify decision-making. Their criteria of 'validity' relate to the *efficiency and political-moral acceptability in the community of officials* sharing the same legal system.

If we make this distinction between the legal order as a momentary system and the legal system as a historical non-momentary system, it becomes obvious that soft law does not belong to the first one. It is 'soft' – in other words, not valid or binding, or an expression of legal norms. However, soft law certainly belongs to the legal system if the latter is understood as a historical tradition governing the decision-making of officials. The chapters in the present work clearly demonstrate that soft law is capable of guiding and justifying administrative and judicial decision-making, yet without providing a self-sufficient complete normative justification of these decisions in the ways in which fully interpreted legal norms can. Thus, in conclusion, soft law is and is not law, depending on which perspective of law one applies: that of the legal system or of the legal order. In this respect, it bears some resemblance, for example, to unincorporated international agreements in dualist systems.

Perhaps the most significant aspect of the modern scientific worldview is that we have learnt to accept indeterminacy as a necessary ingredient of the universe because otherwise we may not ever come to understand many of its laws and phenomena. In the same vein, perhaps modern law is also intelligible only when soft law is taken into account as a particular form of law and when its uncertainty and elusiveness are cause for appreciation, not for dissatisfaction and despair. It is the great merit of the SoLaR project and this work that our understanding of soft law now lies on a more solid empirical and theoretical fundament.

[1] JW Harris, *Law and Legal Science: An Inquiry into the Concepts Legal Rule and Legal System* (Oxford, Clarendon Press, 1979).

Index

www.ingramcontent.com/pod-product-compliance
Ingram Content Group UK Ltd.
Pitfield, Milton Keynes, MK11 3LW, UK
UKHW020232290926
15470UKWH00002B/490

9 781509 932030